Black Powder Hobby Gunsmithing

By
Sam Fadala
and
Dale Storey

DBI BOOKS, INC.

Editorial Staff

Senior Staff Editor
Harold A. Murtz

Production Manager
John Duoba

Production Assistant
Jamie L. Puffpaff

Electronic Publishing Manager
Nancy J. Mellem

Electronic Publishing Associate
Robert M. Fuentes

Editorial Assistant
Holly J. Porter

Cover Photography
John Hanusin

Managing Editor
Pamela J. Johnson

Publisher
Sheldon L. Factor

Arms and Armour Press, London, G.B., exclusive licensees and distributor in Britain and Europe; Nigeria; So. Africa and Zimbabwe; India and Pakistan. Lothian Books, Takapuna, N.Z., exclusive distributor in New Zealand.

ISBN 0-87349-153-X
Library of Congress Catalog Card #94-70142

Contents

Preface 5

Chapter 1: The Frontier Gunsmith 6

Chapter 2: Tooling Up 13

Chapter 3: Gunsmithing Safety 23
- *How-To Tip:*
  - Unloading the Muzzleloader

Chapter 4: Muzzleloader Locks 29

Chapter 5: Building Lock Kits 39
- *Step-by-Step Projects:*
  - Assembling the Siler Lock Kit 40
  - Assembling the Pennsylvania Style Mule Ear Lock 49

Chapter 6: Lock Tuning 54
- *Step-by-Step Project:*
  - Tuning a Lock 56

Chapter 7: Muzzleloader Triggers 62

Chapter 8: Gunstock Materials 67

Chapter 9: Stock Finishes and Finishing 72
- *Step-by-Step Projects:*
  - Finishing a Stock 76
  - Refinishing a Stock 79

Chapter 10: Wood Repairs 80
- *How-To Tips:*
  - Fixing Large Dents
  - Epoxy/Fiberglass Repair
  - Reinforcing with Pins
  - Replacing Missing Wood
  - Repairing Broken Stocks
  - Extending the Forearm
  - Repairing Cracked Stocks
  - Stripped Wood Screws

Chapter 11: Wood Embellishment 86
- *How-To Tips:*
  - Incise Carving
  - Decorative Inlays
- *Step-by-Step Projects:*
  - Fitting Wire Inlays 90
  - Checkering a Stock 92
  - Relief Carving 94

Chapter 12: Stock Styles 97

Chapter 13: Muzzleloader Metals 102
- *How-To Tip:*
  - Heat-Treating Metal Parts

Chapter 14: Bluing and Browning Metals 108
- *How-To Tips:*
  - Metal Polishing
  - Browning and Bluing Methods
- *Step-by-Step Project:*
  - Rust-Browning a Barrel 113

Contents

Chapter 15: Metal Embellishment 115
  How-To Tip:
    ● Engraving

Chapter 16: Muzzleloader Barrels 120

Chapter 17: Barrel Ribs 130
  How-To Tips:
    ● Attaching Ribs with Screws   ● Attaching Ramrod Guides   ● Attaching Ribs with Solder

Chapter 18: Metal Castings 135

Chapter 19: Muzzleloader Ramrods 139
  How-To Tips:
    ● Making a Wooden Ramrod   ● Fitting a Ramrod Base Tip   ● Candy-Striping a Ramrod

Chapter 20: Muzzleloader Sights 147

Chapter 21: Professional Muzzleloader Maintenance 157
  Step-by-Step Projects:
    Cleaning with Water 160
    Cleaning with Solvent 162
    Cleaning the Revolver 163
    Advanced Cleaning 165

Chapter 22: Understanding the Modern Muzzleloader 167
  How-To Tips:
    ● Fitting a Scope   ● Adjusting the Stiker   ● Fitting a Sling
  Step-by-Step Projects:
    Glass-Bedding a Rifle 171
    Fitting a Recoil Pad 173

Chapter 23: The Muzzleloading Shotgun 175
  How-To Tips:
    ● Fixing Barrel Dents   ● Threading Choke Tubes   ● Repairing Ribs and Guides
    ● Patterning a Shotgun

Chapter 24: Tuning the Caplock Revolver 183
  Step-by-Step Projects:
    Correcting Revolver Timing 184
    Improving Trigger Function 189

Chapter 25: Building the Blackpowder Gun Kit 191
  Step-by-Step Projects:
    Building Navy Arms' Brown Bess Rifle Kit 195
    Building Thompson/Center's Hawken Rifle Kit 199
    Building Mountain State's Mountaineer Rifle Kit 204
    Building Traditions' Deerhunter Rifle Kit 207
    Building Lyman's Plains Pistol Kit 209
    Building CVA's Hawken Pistol Kit 213
    Building Navy Arms' 1860 Army/Reb '60 Revolver Kit 218
    Building Traditions' Trapper Pistol Kit 220
    Building Traditions' Derringer Kit 223

Chapter 26: The Custom Gun 226
  Step-by-Step Project:
    Building a Custom Rifle 227

Manufacturers' Directory for Blackpowder Gunsmithing 256

Preface

THIS BOOK ENTERTAINS four levels of blackpowder hobby gunsmithing: Kitchen Table, Home Workshop, Hobby Plus Help, and Academic.

Kitchen Table home hobby gunsmithing is so-named because this level of work can be accomplished on a kitchen table, ideally with a sturdy, portable board as a working surface to safeguard the tabletop. The tools required are absolutely basic: screwdriver, small hammer, pliers—tools readily found and reasonably priced. In the interest in getting off on the right foot, we strongly recommend the use of good gunsmithing tools and *not* the types found at the local hardware store. The typical screwdriver found in the garage will probably not fit the heads of most screws found on firearms. The screwdriver blade should exactly fit the slot in the screw head, both in thickness and in width, to prevent burring. Countless firearms, old and new, bear marks, burrs and gouges that are the result of using the wrong tools for simple disassembly or even minor adjustments. A good source of gunsmithing tools is Brownells, Inc., a company that is mentioned often in this book because of its large inventory and wide selection of tools. Some of the kits discussed in this book are candidates for Kitchen Table smithing. Others are not. Also possible at this level are minor repairs and alterations to muzzle-loading firearms, plus basic adjustments, modest embellishments and refinishing projects.

The Home Workshop level is done in a reasonably well-equipped workplace. Thousands of hobbyists own and work in home shops containing tools that range from basic to semi-sophisticated. Some home workshops even rival professional gunshops, up to and including lathes and high-quality power tools. All of the blackpowder kits included in this text can be built in a home workshop. Relatively high-level repairs, as well as embellishments, adjustments and refinements to muzzleloaders, are readily accomplished in the home workshop. Furthermore, full-blown custom muzzleloaders can be built in the well-equipped home workshop.

Hobby Plus Help builds upon the Home Workshop level. Gun repair, embellishment, customizing, personalizing and, in fact, all aspects of muzzleloader smithing—even custom gun building—can be successfully accomplished by the hobbyist who hires a little professional help. The hobbyist tackles all aspects of the project that he and his tools can handle. Then, he calls upon the professional gunsmith to drill that precise hole, heat-treat that important part or blue that barrel. It's a beautiful working relationship. The hobbyist has the pleasure of being in charge of his project, but also the assurance that he can get a little help on those phases of the project that call for specialized professional attention with high-level tools not always found in the home workshop.

The fourth level of blackpowder hobby gunsmithing is the Academic approach. Not all smithing can be done by the hobbyist, or even by the local pro, but this does not excuse the hobby smith from understanding the problem or adjustment. All dedicated shooters should try to learn as much as they can about firearms and gunsmithing. This book serves as a depository of information for the muzzleloader fan who may not want to build his own kit, let alone a custom firearm, but who at the same time desires an understanding of the mechanics and working parts of the frontloader. Possible repair options, embellishments, drop-in barrels, bluing, browning, sight options, parts nomenclature, wood variations, stock styles, lock designs and functions—these are only a few of the topics discussed in this book, all of interest to any enthusiastic frontloader devotee.

These are the four levels embodied in *Black Powder Hobby Gunsmithing*, a book for everyone who loves the smoke 'n' boom game.

The Frontier Gunsmith

THE GUILD SYSTEM was alive and well in America long before the first white man set foot on the continent. Native Americans divided their work among the most capable of the tribe in any given endeavor. There were specialists in string-making, bow-manufacture, arrow-crafting and other aspects of archery. The medicine man handled sickness and spirits, both evil and good. All labors were divided according to individual ability and talent. The frontier gunmaker was also party to a sort of guild system. Oftentimes, he did not make his own locks, or his own barrels. However, there were gunsmiths on the early frontier, as well as the Eastern seaboard, who were multi-talented. They were blacksmiths, woodworkers, metalsmiths, repairmen and gunmakers—all in one person. These men were capable of building a gun lock, stock and barrel, as well as fixing a cracked wrist or making a new "tube" (nipple) for a percussion frontloader.

Not all early gunmaking was art. Not by a long shot. There are modern gunmakers far more talented, as well as blessed with better working conditions, tools, knowledge and materials, than those who draw-filed a barrel in the good old days. But there were also master craftsmen of the past who built muzzleloaders that rival anything turned out today, sometimes from scratch, and more often with some parts made by others. Division of labor—a guild system, if you will—remains powerful to this day. Barrels are made by barrelmakers. Locks are made by locksmiths. Most modern day blackpowder gunsmiths and gunmakers rely heavily on ready-made parts. But there are also modern gunsmiths who can do it all. Even among these do-everything craftsmen, however, locks and barrels are normally purchased in finished form. Nonetheless, these talented workers generally can repair a broken lock or build an entire rifle, with special concentration on the stock, which is often created from a plank of wood.

In a very real sense, the frontier gunsmith and the home hobby gunsmith have a lot in common. The obvious is a high interest in firearms, as well as a penchant for doing things for themselves. Ned Roberts, author of *The Muzzle-Loading Cap Lock Rifle*, praised the early American gunsmith who could repair a broken lock or build a complete rifle, all with minimal implements. Roberts noted that these men worked with tools we consider crude by modern standards, making beautiful rifles of high accuracy without sophisticated machinery or measuring devices such as a micrometer caliper, which was not invented until about 1850. Roberts noted that "German, Swiss and Pennsylvania Dutch riflesmiths back in the early 1700s did not have a lathe on which they could turn a piece of iron, cut a thread or drill a hole, or do any of the hundred-and-one operations that are done with the lathe by rifle-makers today. Yet in spite of these handicaps, they managed to make every part of a rifle—barrel, lock, sights, stock—assemble them and thus turn out the completed rifle."

Tools were often handmade by gunsmiths. Norman Brockway, who was known for rifles of superlative accuracy, built most of his own tools with which he crafted his fine front-loading rifles, and these tools are a study in their own right. Roberts discusses many interesting vintage tools in his famous book. He also praised the mountain gunsmiths who passed on their skills to younger craftsmen, keeping alive the tradition of riflemaking and smithing at the grass-roots level. The tradition never died. Today's high interest in building blackpowder rifle, pistol and revolver kits, as well as home hobby gunsmithing at many levels, is proof that shooters continue to enjoy a hands-on relationship with firearms.

William Knight, student of history and blackpowder shooting, made a thorough search of Colonial gunstock finishing.

This is the Henry rifle factory in Boulton, Pennsylvania. The type of gun building that went on here was more hands-on than assembly line in nature.

His studies revealed a great deal about gun building and gun builders, as well as early finishers. Knight noted that many modern muzzleloader custom riflemakers are more talented than their predecessors of Colonial times, at least as evidenced by products from both groups. Many old-time gunmakers were only part-timers, requiring incomes from other areas to make a living. In the early 1800s, handmade rifles (there were no other kind) ran from $6 to about $20 each. Knight points out that the Colonial gunsmith did not have the luxury of working on a specific piece at leisure, because he had to produce in order to survive or perish. While on the other hand, a century earlier, gunsmiths of the early 1700s were entirely products of the European guild system, which specialized in gun part making and guarded their trade secrets jealously.

Materials

John G.W. Dillin reported in 1924 that the number of parts necessary to construct a "Kentucky rifle" were between 44 and 50, including the barrel and lock, as well as stock, pins, screws, springs and other elements. The rifle barrel was made of soft but metallurgically tough steel. Considering blackpowder pressures, this steel was more than sufficient for the job.

Stocks were made of curly maple when possible. Dillin says this wood was a product of both sugar and red maple trees. It was common for a ratio of one in fifteen trees to offer suitable stock wood with proper color and grain structure. Cherry wood was also employed as a stock material, as was black walnut and red maple in the South.

The ramrod was most often made of split hickory, usually embellished with a barber-pole effect (striped). The stripes were wide and of a brown tint, possibly stained with aquafortis (strong water), which was commercial nitric acid.

Brass was the most common metal used for patch box, trigger guard, sideplate, ramrod pipes, front sight, buttplate and other furniture appointments. Sometimes German silver (electrum or nickel-silver) was used in place of brass. Less often, iron was used for these parts. Silver was not uncommon for making certain ornamental parts. Dillin reports, incidentally, that the flintlocks found on early American longrifles were often handmade by the smith, although in time, many locks were imported from England and Germany.

Workmanship

Already touched on, the early American gunsmith's work was not always top-notch, but could generally be counted on for its soundness. Some rifles and pistols were clearly utilitarian. Others were both functional and beautiful, showpieces of their era and any other time in firearms history, including the present.

Springs were expertly tempered, which Dillin considers

proof of early artisan ability and understanding. Stocks were sometimes stained, with soot and oil rubbed thoroughly into the wood, and sometimes an early type of varnish was used, not unlike the finish employed by Italian violin makers. This type of finish was known as Cremonese varnish, an oil-based product. Interestingly, certain plain wood stocks were artificially treated to give them the appearance of having good wood grain when they did not. The plain maple stock was wrapped with string, very tightly, the string first impregnated with tar. Then the tarred string was burned off, which, in turn, left a grainy pattern in the plain wood stock.

Rifling

Arguments concerning who rifled barrels in days of yore continue. Some say the riflesmith did the job. Others feel that bores were rifled primarily by specialists. The truth lies in both camps. It's obvious from the remains of rifling benches in old-time, one- or two-man gunshops that some gunsmiths did rifle their own barrels. At the same time, it's also true that other smiths counted on barrelmakers to do the job. Dillin cites evidence for both conclusions. L.K. Siner, a Philadelphia gunsmith, remembers his father having barrels sent to the Nippes factory on Mill Creek, 8 miles west of the city, for rifling. The records of John Henry, famous riflesmith of Lancaster, Pennsylvania, show clearly that he rifled barrels for other gunmakers, as well as himself. The invaluable testimony of Milton Warren, presented in a long quote at the end of this chapter, indicates that many gunsmiths of early America did indeed rifle their own barrels.

A photograph of a rifling bench appears in Dillin's 1924 book, *The Kentucky Rifle*. The picture was taken outside of the Henry rifle plant at Boulton, Pennsylvania. Charles Henry, the last member of the great Henry riflemaking family, is giving a demonstration of the rifling bench in the photograph. The rifling bench was designed to control each cut so that grooves and lands were properly assigned in the bore. Rate of twist was also determined by the specific rifling bench used. Rifling styles changed over the years, but it's

"I built it myself." Bill Storey, 15, assembled this Thompson/Center 50-caliber hunting rifle by himself, using the instructions that came with the kit, plus additional information supplied by the text of this book.

The modern kit represents a middle ground for blackpowder gunsmiths. Much of the work is already accomplished, but it takes a personal touch to perfect the finished product.

interesting to note that barrels of high accuracy were made in the days of the seemingly crude (by modern standards) rifling bench.

The Forge

Traditional riflemaking was greatly advanced through the use of a forge. A forge is essentially an apparatus which produces intense and sustained heat, so that metals can be worked by first softening them. Metals were often shaped through heating followed by specific hammer blows. A type of forge used by early gunsmiths consisted of a flat surface (forge table), perhaps made of brick or stone, containing charcoal or soft coal. A bellows was attached so that blasts of air could be directed to the coal bed. Sufficient heat was generated to work metals into many gun parts, including sights, trigger guards, all lock parts, and so forth.

An interesting first-hand account of early-day gun building comes from Mr. Milton Warren, who witnessed the practices of gunsmithing methods at the Whitesides factory in Abingdon, Virginia. Mr. Warren was apprenticed to John Whitesides of Abingdon (then known as Wolf Hills). Whitesides was a gunmaker from the old school, noted as an artisan of his day who used Colonial methods in crafting his fine rifles. Whitesides was known for his fancy wire scroll stock inlays, as well as barrel and lock embellishments. His story is preserved in Dillin's aforementioned book. It goes like this:

The modern blackpowder gunsmith is not so unlike the frontier smith. He still enjoys doing much of the work "by hand," although electrically operated tools are used by most professionals and hobbyists. This is the shop of Dennis Mulford, who specializes in longrifle replicas.

Excerpts From "The Kentucky Rifle"

(Photos and text from John G.W. Dillin's *The Kentucky Rifle*, George Shumway Publisher)

You would probably call Abingdon an old-fashioned community; the people were very much alike and had never changed their methods of living very much. It was considered extravagant to buy anything that could be raised at home. The men chopped down the timber, cleared the ground and raised little patches of corn, tobacco and vegetables. There were enough sheep to supply wool for clothing, which was home made. The women carded, spun and wove the wool into cloth and handy cutters and sewers made it into wearing apparel for all of us. There were rifles in every home—the man who was too poor to own one was considered destitute. We all hunted, shooting matches were regular functions and hunting and shooting stories were standard fireside diversions. I am afraid that many of us took more pride in hitting what we shot at than in turning out a full day's work. Mr. Whitesides had been an axe-maker, capable of forging his dozen every day, and he was famous for the quality of his axes, but there seemed to have been something in him which he could not hammer into an axe; and being a very fine shot with a rifle and not finding one to suit his fancy, he made one, which was so good that his neighbors wanted duplicates of it and he began making them on orders.

It took about a week to make a good, plain rifle, of which time two days would be spent on the stock. Besides rifles, we made a great many under-hammer boot-lag pistols. They are simple things and one could be made in a day.

This is how we made our guns:

Mr. Whitesides owned, on Smith's Creek, a little water-power sash sawmill (a straight saw set in a rectangular frame or sash, working up and down on an eccentric, through a log). The same power was also used to run a crude lathe and a large grindstone on which rifle barrels were finished.

At "Old Shady," over the mountains about fifteen miles, there was an iron mine and smelter worked by three or four men. The ore was smelted in a charcoal furnace, run into chunks of suitable size for ready handling and drawn out on a big anvil with a trip hammer into rods, bars and such shapes as local smiths demanded, and then peddled around and sold to them. It was good iron and it worked fine.

While we carried a few guns in stock, they were usually made to specifications as to length of barrel, weight, ornamentation, etc. Not infrequently the order would be to "make a gun just like" the one used by some famous marksman in the vicinity.

For the barrel a bar of iron of the right length, width and thickness would be selected, and half of its length, at welding heat, turned around a core rod somewhat larger then the ultimate bore desired. The core was then withdrawn and the other half treated in the same way, the whole being worked into rough octagonal form. Next a rod slightly smaller than the final calibre was used and the barrel finished as nearly perfect as possible.

During the welding process the smith used a hammer while his helper wielded a sledge. If the whole barrel had been welded at one heating the rod could not have been removed; as it was, sometimes it welded fast and had to be

Outside the Henry Rifle Works at Boulton, Pennsylvania, a demonstration is given showing the methods used to rifle a barrel.

cut out with a cold chisel and the blemish worked over.

We did not bother much with flatters or shaping devices of any kind—just trusted to hand and eye—yet when the barrel left the anvil they were very straight and regular, requiring but little grinding.

Charcoal was used exclusively for forge fire; in fact, we did not know that stone coal could be used for such welding as we did.

The bore of the barrel was sized with a cutting bit or reamer, on a hand brace—just began at one end and worked through to the other with the same motion that a carpenter uses in boring holes in wood. The lathe could not be used for this purpose because it was only belt-geared and did not run steady enough—it would have broken the reamer. Anyway the hole in the barrel was so true that it only required a little work to smooth it out. Of course, now and then, a barrel showed flaws and sometimes these did not develop until it was rifled. We just threw it away, made some remarks to the mountains, took a drink of spring water and welded another barrel.

In straightening a barrel a fine thread was passed through it and attached to a light hickory bow to hold it taut. There was no difficulty in seeing the shadow where the thread did not touch. The crook was located by touching the place with a little saliva, placed on the anvil and tapped lightly until the thread touched and the process repeated until barrel and thread were in contact from end to end.

Straightening always began in the middle of the barrel, just as in welding, the old man saying that he would "chase the d____d rascals out at the ends," and it was about as easy for him to take the kinks out of a rifle barrel as it is for a boy to make shavings with a sharp knife and a pine stick.

The barrel was now centered by inserting a plug in each end, taken to the grindstone and fastened into a frame so adjusted that it allowed the center of the barrel to come within one-half of its desired diameter to the stone. It was worked back and forth until the stone no longer cut when it was shifted to the next octagon and so on until all were ground and the whole was bound to be evenly finished and all the octagons alike. Inequalities were removed by draw filing and hand polishing.

The barrel, now ready for rifling, was taken to the rifling machine, or bench, as we called it, a contrivance simple enough in its working but not easy to describe.

It consisted of a hard wooden bar of cherry, three inches in diameter by four and one-half feet long, with four deep radial grooves, each making one turn in four feet, extending from end to end. To the proximal end of this bar was fastened a loosely revolving handle and to its far end a chuck for holding a steel rifling rod. The wooden bar passed through a ten-inch dialed headpiece whose circumference was divided by deep rectangular notches into eight equal parts, while from its round central opening there passed into each of the four grooves on the bar an iron lug to hold it in place. This arrangement was set on a frame in smoothly working longitudinal guides.

The barrel was clamped into the frame with it axis in direct line with that of the spiral wooden bar. Into a piece of tough hickory wood, rounded to closely fit the bore of the barrel, a piece of thin, very hard, sharply toothed steel was set to act as a saw or cutter. This section of wood was now connected with a rigid steel rod the length of the barrel and fastened in the chuck.

The cutter, kept well oiled, was pushed back and forth, the guides on the central bar carrying it around spirally, until it no longer bit, when the dial was turned one notch and then anoth-

This is an example of an old barrel boring machine with a barrel clamped in place, ready for use.

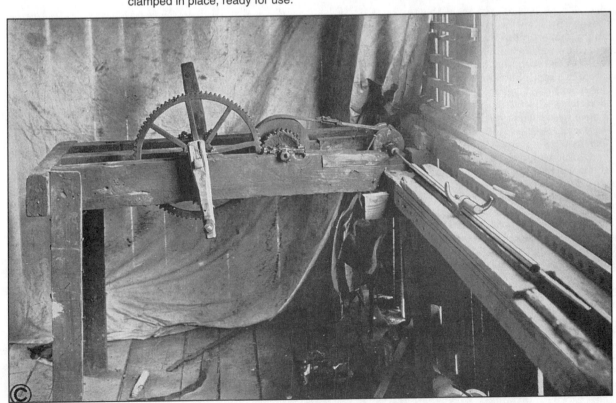

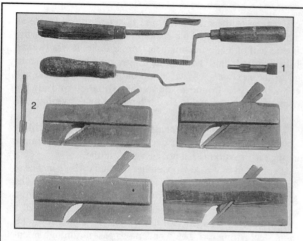

These are some of the tools used by the frontier rifle-smith. Tool #1 threads the barrel for the breech plug. Tool #2 prepares the breech for the threading tool. The remaining seven pieces are all stocking tools made of persimmon wood.

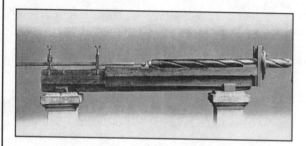

This is an example of a rifling bench that was used in Virginia during the early 1800s.

er until all of the right rifle grooves had been well started.

The saw was now taken out of its bed and elevated by having a shim of paper placed under it and the work done over and over until the rifles were as deep as desired. With sharp saws and good working iron, a neat job could be done in about two hours. Burrs were smoothed off and the calibre polished with lead plugs and fine emery powder.

Sometimes a lug was brazed on to the barrel for the tube, but more frequently a cylindrical drum was used, this being the cheaper way.

Barrels were browned with a mixture of aqua fortis, blue vitriol, tincture of iron and water. Almost anything that will rust iron will brown a barrel, but to get a good job it must be rubbed down smooth between coats.

Tubes were made by drawing them out on an anvil, filing them to shape and drilling with different-sized drills, finally finishing with a very fine tapered reamer. During the earlier years of my apprenticeship we made all tubes by hand, but later bought them and could fit one for fifty cents, whereas for the others we charged six bits.

All of our locks were made by hand—mostly the back action kind—possibly because they are a trifle easier to make, but probably they just happened to be the style on the Holston.

The lock plate was hammered out on the anvil, filed into accurate shape; the springs—which were made from old whip saws, swords and bayonets mostly—laid on, the hole marked and drilled and screwed in place with hand-made screws and with the tumbler and hammer all made on the anvil and filing vise, the lock was ready for the gun.

Small holes were made with the lathe, all larger ones with a bow drill.

For stocking material we went to the mountains and got close-grained rock maple—the trees that grow on thin rocky soil are always closer rained and curlier than those that grow in open ground on heavy soil. Sometimes we used walnut, now and then cherry, and occasionally a customer would bring his own stock blank of apple wood. A cherry crotch makes a beautiful stock and apple finishes up very smooth and stays where you put it; it also takes inlaying well, but both apple and cherry depend upon their grain for beauty, while curly maple can be finished with various stains and is just about the prettiest wood in the world. We always mentioned a gun as her and name them Betsy, Samanthy and Jane.

Lumber was sawn into two-inch planks on the sash mill and a pile of it was always stacked up in the corner of the shop seasoning. It was entirely air-dried and it took about four years to properly ripen a gun stock blank.

Yes, I guess we could have split out the lumber and hewed it down to dimension; I know we could, for there were men in the mountains who could take a broadaxe and scutch out puncheons for floors and school seats so smooth that there would not be a mark showing.

The wynde was taken out of the stock blank with a plane, centered all round with a marking gauge and the butt plate put on, after which barrel and trimmings were let into the wood—all with gouges, chisels and rifflers of our own making—and the stock worked down to form with drawer knife and rasp and sandpaper until it was ready for staining. This was accomplished by freely brushing the wood with strong aqua fortis, then holding it over a fire until it was pretty deeply scorched, after which it was rubbed down to a smooth surface, the hard ridges of the wood barely showing, and finally treated with a light coat of alkanet root in oil, after which it was varnished with shellac in alcohol or rubbed with oil—the more coats of the latter the better.

When first turned out the wood was just a trifle glary, but after the gun had been used a while and rubbed down many, many times it became as smooth as satin and as richly blended as tortoise shell.

My boss was something of an artist in making designs for the scroll wire inlaying he delighted in. He simply drew a pattern of anything he fancied on the stock and sunk very finely tapered chisels and specially shaped gouges into it and into these marks drove sharp-edged strips of silver or brass and filed it down flush with the surface and when finished this method of ornamentation gave beautiful results.

For the common run of guns everything was of iron, butt plate, trigger guards, trigger plate, thimbles, escutcheons and all, but for the fancy ones we worked out from sheets of German silver, brass and silver various designs for inlays and bought guards and butt plates (I think from Pittsburgh). Buckhorn sights were standard equipment on all rifles with a silver bead in front.

After the gun was finished the old man would say, "Well, Milt, she's finished, but she ain't wuth a d___ if she won't shoot straight; let's try her." He was by all odds the best rifle shot I have ever known and no gun ever suited him unless it was capable of driving a tack three times out of five at fifty yards.

Our guns were all nicely finished; they were symmetrical and pleasing to the eye; they felt good in the hand and at the shoulder, and they shot where they were held. The men who bought them could hold them right. It is too bad that progress and civilization have eliminated both man and gun.

Tooling Up

OLD-TIME GUNSMITHS USED many different tools, up to and including power tools, usually water-operated. That's why many gunshops were situated near running water, where energy was free for the taking. An entire study of old tools is not in the scope of the present work. There are collectors and collections of such tools, along with entire books on the subject. Suffice it to say that yesteryear's gunsmith made many of his own implements and bought others as needed, from jackknives to wood planes. Some historians speculate that old-time smiths preferred drawknives, spokeshaves and wood planes because these tools did not gouge wood out, as a rasp did. Rather, they cut with a sharp edge, resulting in a smoother surface that did not demand filing in degrees, from coarse to fine.

William Knight, a researcher mentioned in Chapter 1, discovered accounts of sandpaper purchases by Colonial gunsmiths, but not in great quantity. Knight believes sandpaper was used only in special cases, when scrapers did not create a perfectly smooth surface. Knight further speculates the use of sandpaper was not acceptable to the frugal, economy-minded Colonial smith, who did not like throwing things away. Buying sandpaper to use and discard was not to the smith's liking. Scraper blades were quite another matter. They worked well, and still do. Those who have used broken glass to remove an old finish have learned, with care and practice, a surprisingly smooth surface can be obtained with a sharp edge. Of course, sandpaper is no luxury today.

Knight learned about many different kinds of scrapers used during Colonial times. These blades were long lasting, and they could be made by the gunsmith in various shapes for different tasks. Many were built from sawblade stock with a thickness of about 1/16- to 1/8-inch. One mode of scraper manufacture may be of interest to the reader. A strip of iron similar to a barrel skelp was heated in a forge, then reduced in thickness through hammering. The hammered metal was then placed in a kiln, packed in charred bone and heated with a

charcoal fire for one to three days, depending upon the thickness of the metal to be cured. This process added carbon to the metal to make steel. The steel, in turn, could be further shaped, then hardened through heating and quenching. Thus, a scraper was manufactured. The blade removed wood with a very fine shaving, especially if its edge was kept very sharp.

Today's home hobby blackpowder gunsmith builds few to none of his own tools. Instead, he relies upon factory tools readily supplied by manufacturers the world over. The sophistication of today's tools runs high. The hobby smith may start with the most basic tools, escalating the list as needs and personal interest demand. Kitchen table repairs and basic starter kits require few tools, whereas more involved work calls for more sophisticated equipment. The sky's the limit with high-class home workshops. And don't forget that amateur work can be enhanced by hiring out a few of the more complicated procedures best handled by a professional gunsmith.

Getting started in muzzleloader home gunsmithing requires, first of all, an interest in wanting to build, repair, enhance or otherwise work on a blackpowder firearm. The initial interest can remain at the Kitchen Table Level, with basic kit-making and minor repairs, and then proceed all the way to handmaking a custom firearm. The amount of monetary input is, of course, based on the desire of the hobbyist. "Working on my muzzleloaders is therapy for me," one hobbyist said. "There is nothing more relaxing or more rewarding than building and repairing my own guns. I like to work with my hands after working with my mind all day at my job," he continued.

There is satisfaction in doing it yourself, too, especially for those perfectionists who are willing to keep at a job until it's done right. But there's more to home hobby muzzleloader gunsmithing than its hand-on enjoyment. There is study as well. The body of knowledge encompassed within the boundaries of the hobby are astounding—from assembly of the simplest kit, to embellishment of metal and wood,

A full set of twist drill bits in fractions, numbers and letters.

(Below) Perhaps no other tool on the gunsmith's bench is required for more jobs than the pliers—everything from getting inside a small action and inserting a spring or pin, to holding red-hot rods during the forming process. These German-made pliers from Brownells are strong, quality instruments that are indispensable even for the neophyte gunsmith.

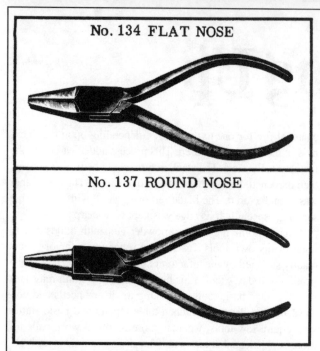

No. 134 FLAT NOSE

No. 137 ROUND NOSE

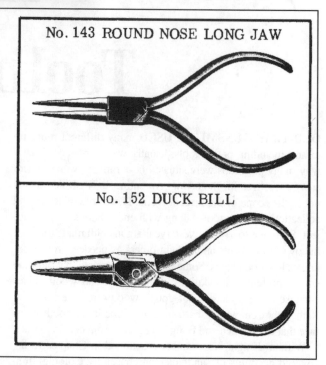

No. 143 ROUND NOSE LONG JAW

No. 152 DUCK BILL

heat-treating of metals, understanding the properties of various woods and the nature of numerous chemicals, the use of countless tools, not to mention the safety attitude involved at all levels. Therefore, tooling up is more than acquiring tools. It's acquiring knowledge as well. Oftentimes, it's not the materials used as much as how they are treated that defines the outcome of a project.

Kitchen Table Gunsmithing Tools and Supplies

A flat surface is required for a work space. A table, desk or small bench are all workable. Naturally, a large sturdy bench is even better, if available. Whatever is used, it should be able to support modest weight, certainly a vise of some type. Many excellent vises in numerous sizes and weights are available today. Lighting must be adequate. Remember, working on guns may produce a little wood dust, so be certain the area will not be damaged by such dust. Ventilation is also required. Whereas a work mask will keep out objectionable dust particles, it is wise to vent any chemical product, as well as dust, to

the outside. Do not forget to protect a good table with a piece of $3/4$-inch plywood, as well as cloth to capture shavings and other debris. Also, never clamp a vise directly to a good table.

Buy a **vise** as large as your work surface will support. Add light brass or copper jaw covers so the steel vise jaws will not damage metal surfaces. Wood can sometimes be lightly held in unprotected jaws without much damage, but different pads such as hard rubber or nylon are available for vise jaws. Brownells' catalog includes several types, but also check your local hardware or home improvement store. The vise is a third hand for the gunsmith, and its use is constant and unavoidable.

Drills, both hand and electric power, are useful in home hobby muzzleloader gunsmithing. The drills used in this text are all metal drills because they will work on wood or metal. Specific brands are not important because all drills are good; however, the more expensive ones may offer special qualities, such as variable speeds.

A complete set of fractional **drill bits** starting at $1/16$- and going up to $1/2$-inch is recommended. Although it is impos-

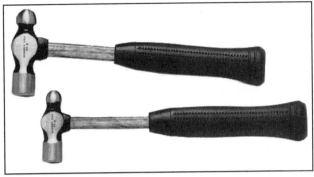

One of the handiest tools in the shop is a hammer, and Brownells has two that qualify for Gold Medal status. The 1-inch nylon/brass combination (above) is perfect for many jobs in the shop or at the range. The nylon face offers a non-marring surface and resists breaking. The brass face is the "basic" tool for use with punches, etc. The 3/4-inch Plastic/Brass hammer (below) is for light, precise tapping of punches with either hammer face.

Ballpeen hammers come in handy for heavier jobs requiring a soild rap, and these from Brownells have a cushioned grip and unbreakable fiberglass handles. They're available in weights from 2 to 12 ounces.

(Below) The Cadillac of screwdrivers is this Magna-Tip Super-Set from Brownells. With 44 custom, interchangeable bits that will fit virtually any gun screw, this kit has it all. There are nine different blade widths, each with four to six blade thicknesses, each with it's own place in the bench tray. The Super-Set comes with both the regular and short driver handles that allow a firm grip.

(Above) Special screwdrivers for guns are an absolute must! This set of fixed-blade drivers from Brownells has specially precision-ground tips to fit the screw slot properly through the full width and depth of the slot. The handles are sized and shaped perfectly for a good grip.

sible to suggest only one set of sizes, because of the different sizes of holes that are required for various applications. Brand names are not important, and bits can be purchased from almost any supply house. But whatever you buy, be sure they are of the best quality. Many foreign-made sets are not sharp and won't bore through even soft metal. You get what you pay for!

Buy a good set of **gunsmith screwdrivers**. It's more economical than buying a cheap set and replacing it later. Brownells' Special Starter Magna-Tip Super Set offers

many different sizes of regular slot drivers from small to large. Special sizes can be added as required for different projects by purchasing Brownells' Magna-Tip Super-Set Add-On Pak. Also, keep your screwdrivers sharp and straight, because a rounded screwdriver bit can burr a screw head. Screwdrivers can be ground to make them fit a special screw head slot (see your local gunsmith if you do not have a grinder). Keep these screwdrivers separate from other tools sets or tool boxes, and use them only for gunsmithing, never as pry bars or chisels.

Various types of **pliers** will be used: Standard jaw pliers, needle-nose pliers (small and medium sizes), Vise Grips and diagonal cutters are recommended. The specific applications of various pliers are common knowledge for anyone who has done any amount of hobby work. Standard jaw pliers are used wherever applicable, with the more specialized types suited to various tasks.

Useful **hammers** include a small ballpeen, 2- to 4-ounce head; brass hammer, 2-ounce; and rubber or plastic mallet, or combination rubber/plastic mallet (rubber one side, plastic other side). The 2- to 4-ounce head is the workhorse of the shop. It is used for drifting sights, center-punching, drifting pins and similar duties. The brass hammer is used where a steel hammer may mar or deform a surface, and it can be used in lieu of the 4-ounce head for many tasks. Plastic or rubber mallets are used for inletting barrels (tapping a barrel into its stock channel) and also for tapping other metalwork into place without deforming or marring the surface as a metal hammer would.

An assortment of **punches** are needed: a steel drift punch set running from $1/16$- to $5/16$-inch diameter; a brass punch, $1/4$-inch preferred; a nylon punch, $5/16$-inch; and a center punch. (Note: Brownells' nylon/brass drift punch set is recommended.) Drift punches are used to drive pins. Brass and nylon punches are used to drive sights and other parts that fit into dovetails (slots). A full set of punches is desirable. Remember, a broken punch can be turned into a slave punch, or ground down for a center punch or turned into a marking chisel. A slave punch is one that is very strong. It's basically a short, stout punch for stubborn tasks, where a long punch may snap.

The following **saws** are useful: hacksaw, jeweler's saw, coping saw and hand wood saw. Hacksaws are for use on steel. The jeweler's saw is for cutting out inlays, patch boxes, toe plates, and other parts made of thin metal stock (brass and silver). Oftentimes, a coping saw is used in place of a jeweler's saw, and for making intricate cuts in thin wood stock. A hand wood saw is used for sawing other wood stock.

These **files** are recommended: mill files, 6-, 8- and 12-inch; bastard cut files, 6-, 8- and 12-inch; bastard cut round file, 10-inch; rasp, 10-inch cabinet maker's fine tooth; two three-square files, 8- and 10-inch sizes; jeweler's or needle file set; and file handles for some of the files, but not all of them. Remember that file handles are important, not only for worker comfort, but especially with regard to safety. A file handle protects the smith's hand from the sharp tang where the handle is fitted. Some files come with handles, others do not. It's a buyer's choice. In spite of the advantages of a handle, files are sometimes used without them to perform specific functions, such as shaping around cheekpieces and lock panels. The smith must be extremely careful when working without a handle.

Ideally, have one set of files for woodworking, another for metalworking. The file types are not broken down into wood and metal files because it is obvious a coarse-cut file is not used for smooth finish file work. Also, files for wood are the same as those used for metal, but in appropriate types—such as a wood rasp for "hogging" wood (removing a lot in short order), or a bastard cut, which is not as fast as a rasp but still too rough for final work, or a smooth mill file for final filing.

The reason for two sets of files is to keep one set sharp for working with wood, as metal files dull quickly.

Some **chisels** are needed: $1/8$-, $1/4$- and $1/2$-inch. Also, an assortment of **gouges** will be used: $1/4$-, $3/8$- and $1/2$-inch. Chisels are flat and used to work on flat surfaces. Gouges are rounded and used to work contoured areas, such as rounding barrel channels and rough-shaping any surface. This should provide a useful starting point. Regular gunsmith chisels and gouges should be purchased. They have longer blades that promote entry into hard-to-reach spots.

Also useful is a **tap and die set**. Taps are used to cut threads in metal holes and are available as individual purchase or in sets. The die cuts threads on the outside of a metal shaft, such as a screw. Sizes required for most hobby gunsmithing are 6x32, 8x32, 10x32, $1/4$x28 and $1/4$x20. Metric sizes may be required for certain foreign-made firearms.

The following **stones** are recommended: soft and hard Arkansas bench stones or diamond lap stones. Bench-size stones 2x6 inches are excellent. These are long lasting with

Brownell's Nylon/Brass Drift Punch is a great combination for the gunsmith. Interchangeable heads on a knurled steel body offer the versatility that's needed for many jobs. The nylon head has steel reinforcement to prevent bending or breakage while giving completely mar-free punching action. The brass head is used for harder-than-nylon but softer-than-steel impact where slight discoloration is acceptable.

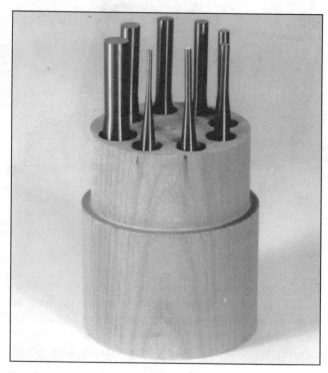

The Starrett #565 Pin Punch Set comes in a handy wooden holder to keep the punches organized. Precision-ground from tool steel, hardened and highly polished, these punches are well proportioned and have knurled bodies for a sure grip. The set of eight is available from Brownells.

proper use, which excludes sharpening a pocketknife or other functions that create a dip or groove in the stone, rendering it useless for sharpening a wide chisel or planer blade. Also useful are 1/4- and 3/8-inch round stones for sharping a gouge. The addition of other sharpening stones is never a mistake, in different sizes and grits for different metal hardnesses.

Other tools include: **adjustable wrenches**, 4- and 8-inch; **knives** such as an X-Acto knife set and an ordinary pocketknife; a 6-inch **adjustable square** will suffice, although a 12-inch adjustable square is more common and may be the builder's choice; **wood planes**, one 6-inch block plane and one small block plane, which may prove invaluable when shaping a stock or working an area such as a cheekpiece; a small **propane torch** should be acquired; as well as one electric **soldering iron**. Any small piece of steel with a flat surface can work as an **anvil** at this level of home gunsmithing. Some hobbyists will want to consider a **Dremel tool**, which is ideal for many applications and is often a perfect light power tool for specific jobs, such as grinding, cutting, inletting, polishing and cleaning with wire brush attachment; however, this is an optional tool. **Scribes** for marking on steel are generic and available through Brownells.

Other supplies include: **sandpaper** (preferably with **sanding block**), in 80-, 120- and 220-grit; **wet/dry sandpaper** in 320-, 400- and 600-grit; **linseed oil** and **turpentine** for wood finish-

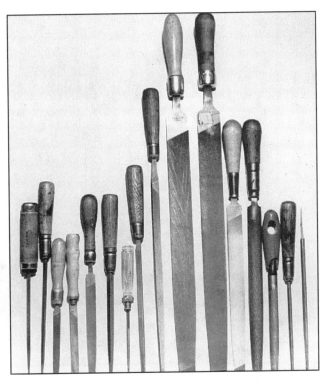

A large selection of files in the home workshop is ideal because the more sizes and cuts, the better.

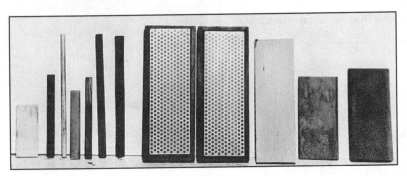

From left: three ceramic stones, four natural stones, two diamond laps, one ceramic stone and two more natural stones.

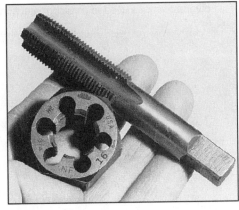

A tap and die set for threading holes and rods.

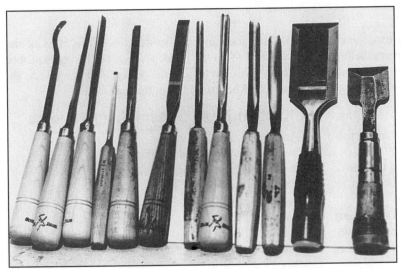

A good selection of chisels and gouges is necessary for higher level smithing.

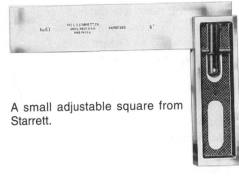

A small adjustable square from Starrett.

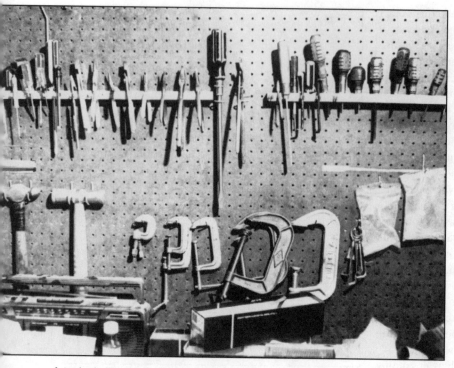

A typical shop wall with an array of tools easy to get at.

Two different scribes used to scratch metal and make lines for future reference and layout.

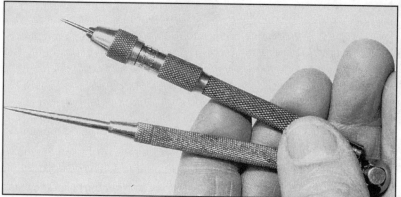

A small propane torch finds many uses in blackpowder hobby gunsmithing.

ing; **fiberglass repair kit**; **soft solder** such as low temperature, Hi-Force 44 and **solder flux** for metalworking; **emery cloth**; a 6-inch flexible **ruler**; soft- and hard-lead **pencils**, useful for various marking applications, as well as **Magic Markers**, which can be substituted for **Dykem** (a liquid blue that coats metal to create a surface that can be marked with a scribe).

Also useful is **inletting black with container and brush**. This is a paste applied upon the surfaces of metal parts that will be inletted into wood. The black color is then transferred to the wood, showing high spots that must be reworked for proper metal-to-wood fit.

It is difficult to make a truly complete list of tools for any operation, because specific tools are needed for specific tasks. However, those listed here will more than suffice for the work accomplished by the hobby gunsmith at this level.

The nearby list includes the projects found in this book which use the tools and supplies mentioned. This list is incomplete in terms of all the projects which can be accomplished with these tools, but shows the reader what can be accomplished at the Kitchen Table Gunsmithing Level.

Kitchen Table Gunsmithing Projects

Tuning a Lock
Overall Rifle Tuning with Adjustments
Overall Handgun Tuning with Adjustments
Changing or Modifying Sights
Refinishing Stocks
Finishing Stocks
Building Lock Kits
Refinishing Metal Parts
Wood Repairs
Minor Firearm Repairs (not requiring larger equipment)

Home Workshop Gunsmithing Tools and Supplies

This level represents a move up from the standard flat surface provided by a table or a bench to a larger and better-equipped work area. It also suggests a higher level of workmanship, as well as tool supply, meaning a home workshop, garage area, basement, spare room or other location devoted solely to hobby work. Safety becomes an even greater concern due to the addition of larger power tools. Now the bench is more than a table. It's a stout wooden unit, ideally, framed out of 2x4s and covered with 3/4-inch plywood. It should be firmly attached to a wall (bolt it into the studs) to forestall motion. This bench should be wired with electrical outlets on each corner, as well as an outlet in the center. Multiple outlets allow facile use of power tools.

Although Home Workshop Gunsmithing demands greater knowledge of both tools and functions, it does not preclude taking a project to a professional gunsmith for help. Oftentimes, this is more a matter of lacking a specific implement, such as a drill press or lathe, rather than lacking knowledge of the work to be accomplished. Also, a task that may require many hours of handwork may be completed in moments with the proper power tool.

All of the Kitchen Table tools and supplies are included in the Home Workshop, along with the following:

The **vise** used here is as large as the hobbyist can afford. A strong vise with 4-inch jaws opening to 6 inches is about right. Some smaller vises can do incredible work, but a larger vise has the strength to handle larger projects. For added versatility, the vise should have a swivel base.

An assortment of **wrenches** with open ends up to 1/2-inch, plus 2-, 4- and 12-inch crescent wrenches, are useful. So is a **breech plug wrench**.

A small **acetylene torch**, such as a plumber's torch, that has its own refillable bottle provides good heat for various projects. This torch is not sufficient for welding, but will perform all soft soldering tasks, and even some light work with low-temperature silver-solder. This torch has a regulator attached to the fuel bottle, but has no additional oxygen source.

A 6-inch **bench grinder**, preferably top-grade, is ideal, but a small grinder is workable, and far better than no grinder at all. Tool distributors boast a large assortment of grinders, and remember these tools can last a lifetime. A grinder makes short work of tool-sharpening, shortening screws and bolts, rough-shaping metal parts, and many other gunsmithing chores. A good grinder for the workshop is a Baldor 6-inch with a 6x3/4x1/2 wheel size, 1/3-horsepower motor, 3600 rpm, wheel centers 12 1/4 inches apart and a weight of 29 pounds. This is a top-of-the-line model. The home workshop hobbyist can usually get by with a less expensive model. An additional silicone carbide wheel should be added if carbide tools are used, because these are very hard and require a special sharpening wheel.

Sophisticated drilling operations call for a **drill press** for both wood and metal. Accuracy of hole placement is greatly enhanced with one. It's also used for tapping, as well as starting a frozen screw or bolt that resists other loosening efforts, and for polishing and jewelling.

This CVA decapper/takedown tool is handy to have in the shop for assembly/disassembly jobs.

A grinder is useful for tool sharpening and a near-must piece of equipment for the advanced home workshop.

Assorted hand planes shown with a modern electric plane.

A power hacksaw makes quick and easy work of sawing steel—this is Hobby Plus Help equipment.

For initial cutting of stocks from planks, a **band saw** makes quick work of an otherwise time-consuming task. It's also useful for general wood cutting in the home shop. An 18-inch **block plane** is useful for squaring a plank prior to layout. It is also workable for initial stock shaping. Moreover, a **power hand planer** is highly useful in squaring badly warped planks where a large quantity of wood must be removed. It's a time-saving tool, but not essential. The one pictured is a Bosch. Also, useful in rough-inletting a stock barrel channel, a **router** can make the job go easier.

Note, the larger tools previously mentioned are high-ticket items that can be purchased at Sears, MSC Industrial Supply Company, Woodworker's Supply or most any industrial tool supply house.

A wooden **sweat box** is used for browning barrels and other metalwork. This is a shop-made item, not for sale commercially as this is written. The size depends upon the barrel to be browned. It is wise to make the box long enough for any barrel. The box used in this work had inside dimensions of 48x24 inches with a depth of 18 inches and a hinged lid.

The **Murray Sanding Drum** is a wheel that attaches to an electric motor for all levels of sanding—from rough shaping through final polishing. It is a metal-flanged wheel with an outer rubber drum that expands under rotation to tightly hold the sanding belts. Maximum speed is 1725 rpm.

Other supplies include: Accurate measurements are important at all levels of hobby gunsmithing, and a **compass** and **dividers** further this cause. A compass has one sharp point with a lead pencil held in the other leg, while a divider has two sharp metal points and is used for layout on steel—where a point can scratch a line into a metal surface coated with Dykem. A good **dial caliper** can come in handy at this level.

The nearby list includes the projects found in this book for this more advanced level of home hobby gunsmithing.

Home Workshop Gunsmithing Projects

Building Lock Kits and Rifle, Pistol and Revolver Kits
Building Rifles and Sidearms from Parts
Finishing Semi-Inletted Stocks

Hobby Plus Help Gunsmithing Tools and Supplies

These operations take the home hobby gunsmith into the realm of semi-professionalism, including building rifles and sidearms from basic parts, making certain parts from unshaped materials, creating specialized tools to expand the workshop's range of functions, and in effect leading to the creation of custom blackpowder firearms, not to include barrelmaking or lockmaking from scratch. However, with the tools presented in Hobby Plus Help, a gunsmith with the interest and desire could reach further into the realm of making an entire blackpowder firearm from raw materials.

All Kitchen Table and Home Workshop tools and supplies are included in Hobby Plus Help, along with the following:

The **metal lathe** is used for all major functions requiring threading, crowning and parts manufacture. It is the heart of the advanced shop. Those who own a lathe are well aware of its function, and its accessories, and this is not the forum for discussing lathe operation *per se*. Plus, the person planning to buy his first lathe will find full instructions with the implement, as well as help in the form of school classes. Many community colleges offer machine shop courses.

Some basic tooling is needed for the metal lathe: **tool holders**, left, right and straight; **three- and four-jaw chucks**; **face plate**; **dead centers**; **live centers**; and a **steady rest**. Also useful are a **mill vise** and **tool post grinder**. With these tools and attachments, nearly all metal parts of the blackpowder firearm can be made. Regular **high-speed tool bits** are also important, plus a small selection of **carbide tool bits**.

An air compressor will not be found in many lay shops, but it is definitely a high-use piece of equipment in some home workshops.

Dale Storey makes a special gun part on a lathe.

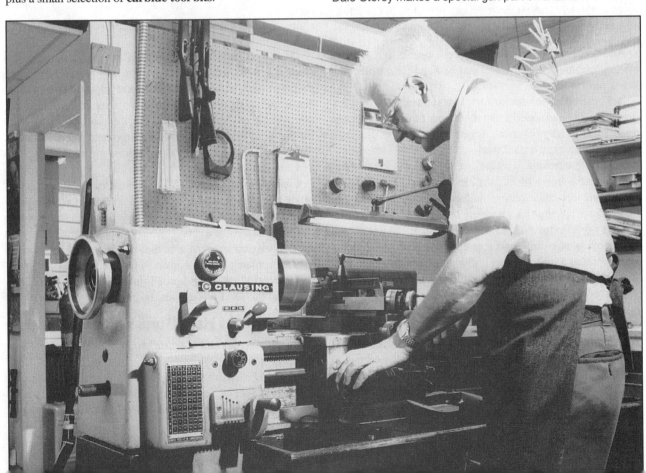

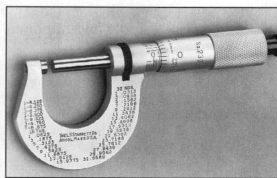

A 1-inch micrometer from Starrett.

Starrett dial indicator is used mainly on a lathe or milling machine.

A small milling machine makes a big difference in the advanced shop.

Additional **bench grinders** may be desirable so a separate silicone-carbide grinding wheel can be fitted for the sharpening of carbide tools.

A 12-inch **disk sander** and/or a **belt sander**, or a combination disk and belt sander, make short work of tedious projects. The disk is usually not much more than 6 inches in diameter, but it will do a great deal of work.

A **milling machine** is useful, but not essential to this level of operation—many of its uses can be accomplished with a metal lathe that has a milling vise and tool post grinders. The mill is a machine that uses a variety of cutters to remove metal in a very precise manner. As with the lathe, this tool is owned by hobbyists who fully understand its operation. First-timers who purchase a mill will find instructions with this high-level machine, and machine shop classes are usually offered by some schools. Mills can be purchased through Brownells and other tool outlets.

A multiple-use power source, the **air compressor** serves to drive many implements, such as air drills, bead blast cabinets and other air-driven tools. If it is used with the bead blast cabinet, it should have a minimum of a 3-horsepower motor. Also used to air-clean parts or dust surfaces, air compressors are sold by many industrial tool outlets, including Sears and similar stores.

Other tools include: **Polishing buffers** are handy because a fixed wheel with quick-change polishing mandrels add to a shop's versatility; **oxygen-acetylene or electric welders** will prove useful, though acetylene is most versatile in the shop, and a Victor oxygen-acetylene torch was used most frequently for the work in this text; **thread gauges** and **micrometers** of various types are useful in taking precise measurements down to a thousandth of an inch.

Optional tools include: A **bead blast cabinet** can accomplish that special effect on metal and is available from Grangers; usually found only in the professional shop, **bluing tanks** are expensive to build or buy, and they require frequent use to justify their inclusion in the shop. The hobbyist is urged to take his bluing jobs to a professional shop.

The nearby list shows special projects that can be accomplished at this semi-professional level.

Hobby Plus Help Gunsmithing Projects

Building Rifles and Sidearms from Scratch
Making Parts
Making Extensive General Repairs, Wood and Metal
Making Special Tools for the Shop
Advanced Projects Considered Professional Work

Gunsmithing Safety

IF YOU WANT to see a crowd of people yawn uncontrollably, talk about safety. For example, when a flight attendant explains the airplane's safety features, most of the passengers lean back with closed eyes. Nonetheless, safety is the most important aspect of any endeavor. Fire hazard, health endangerment and bodily harm are possible through the misuse of tools and chemicals. Don't let any of these things happen to you. Be safe.

Beware the loaded firearm. Too obvious to mention? Unfortunately not. The hobbyist may come in contact with a firearm he has no knowledge of. "I hear you do a little gunsmithing. Would you take a look at this old rifle? It belonged to Uncle Harold back in Missouri." Here is a brief story of an Uncle Harold rifle: The muzzleloader was located in an attic. The kids who found it decided to play with the rifle, which

included pouring sand down the bore and packing the sand hard with the ramrod. To tell if a blackpowder rifle or pistol is loaded, a ramrod is inserted downbore. If the ramrod stops short of the breech, there's obviously something down there—most likely powder and ball. But in the case of the sand-packed frontloader, the ramrod trick was useless.

Using a cleaning rod, sand and dirt was laboriously coaxed from the bore. When no more showed up, a ramrod with a screw was run home. The screw did not engage, but it came out with lead strips attached. Not only was the old rifle packed with sand and dirt, it was also loaded. Debreeching proved the powder charge was dry and ignitable. The rifle could have gone off. Plus, the sand-packed bore obstruction may have resulted in a burst barrel. The warning about loaded firearms can never be sounded too often. Furthermore, the

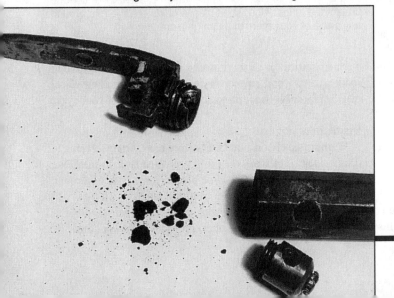

Here is a load that had been left downbore for years. The cardinal rule before working on any firearm: Make sure the gun is unloaded.

Unloading the Loaded Muzzleloader

First, try removing the nipple with a conventional nipple wrench. Soak the powder charge by running oil through the nipple seat, cleanout screw hole or down the nipple vent if the nipple will not come off. Withdraw the projectile with a stout cleaning/loading rod with a screw attached, if possible. If the projectile will not come out, then remove the breech plug. With the breech plug removed, a hammer-driven brass or steel rod is used to force the round or conical bullet free. Do not damage the rifling with the rod. The use of a muzzle protector centers the rod in the bore, rather than allowing it to scrape the lands of the rifling. If any doubt exists as to the safety of unloading a loaded firearm, seek the help of a professional.

old cliché, about familiarity breeding contempt is true. A hobbyist who handles guns on a daily basis has to be watchful of the most basic rules of the game, and rule number one is to check any firearm before working on it to make certain it is not loaded.

Another brief story of a loaded firearm centers on a percussion pistol left loaded about sixty years ago, as best the present owner could determine. Grandpa kept the piece ready to go. When he passed on, nobody bothered to check the condition of the pistol. The breech plug defied removal, and using a torch to free the breech plug was, of course, out of the question. Drilling it out was also impossible, since drilling creates heat, too. In this case, the pistol barrel was carefully but firmly clamped in a vise and a large wrench was used to remove the breech plug.

Firearm Safety

Blackpowder

Remember, blackpowder has a low ignition temperature. It goes off readily, so it must be stored away from all heat or spark sources. Blackpowder is also percussion-sensitive, a fact worth noting when trying to remove a stuck projectile. Sufficient manhandling of blackpowder may cause the propellant to detonate.

Percussion Caps

As the name implies, percussion caps are percussion-sensitive. A blow can set them off. So can heat. Caps have been known to fly like tiny rockets when set off. Store them safely away from all heat/percussion sources.

Wooden Ramrods

When restoring an older firearm, or working on any blackpowder gun, be certain the wooden ramrod is not cracked. A cracked ramrod can break, possibly jamming in the barrel. Check ramrod tips for security. A tip left downbore and shot over the rifling may cause damage. Also, make ramrods long enough for a good grip.

Work Area Safety

Clothing

Aprons keep clothing clean, but they should fit snugly to prevent being grabbed by any machine. Wear short-sleeve shirts, or keep shirt sleeves rolled up firmly. I know of an accident that occurred when a long-sleeved shirt was caught up at the tail stock end of a lathe, resulting in lifelong scars. Luckily, the operator was able to reach the shut-off button before his arm was broken. Rings and watches have no place at the workbench either for the same reasons. In a large shop, hard-toed boots are a plus should a heavy object drop on a foot. Even though proper clothing is worn, remember to allow a machine to come to rest before getting hands near moving parts.

Eye Protection

Even at the Kitchen Table level of home hobby gunsmithing, foreign materials can fly into your eye. Let this

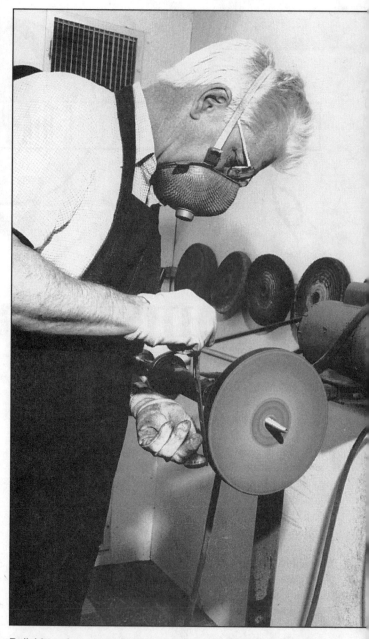

Polishing gloves are fine, but should fit snugly, not loosely. Note the eye protection. Extremely short-term polishing on this particular machine does not require hearing protection, but for long-term polishing, ear plugs are wise. A respirator is used to protect the lungs. Also, short-sleeve shirts are the rule around any piece of equipment that can grab clothing.

warning suffice for all work where anything from chemical to spark, chard, wood chip or piece of a broken grinding wheel may be possible—wear protective lenses in front of your eyes.

Ventilation

Warning labels on hundreds of products, from solvents to finishes, tell us to work only in a ventilated area. In the home workshop, ventilators should be placed at the ends of a room, rather than overhead, because overhead fans direct fumes right up into the face. Use air cleaners with filters where possible. If in doubt of air safety, have an expert check your work area.

Contrary to some opinions, blackpowder is a powerful propellant capable of destroying a firearm, as was the case here with a test breech. The hobby gunsmith needs to know blackpowder can develop high pressure.

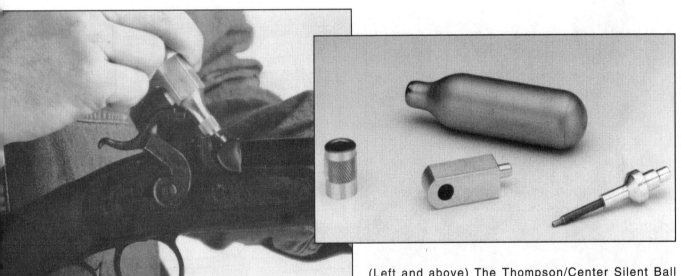

(Left and above) The Thompson/Center Silent Ball Discharger Kit, with accessories and adapters, uses CO_2 power to force a load out of the barrel.

Safety Masks

Also, save your lungs with a face mask. While a mask cannot filter out certain chemical elements, it can greatly reduce dust and particle inhalation.

Hearing Protection

Today's sophisticated shooter or hobbyist knows that hearing loss is connected with loud noises, high-pitched whines and other problems associated with how ears react to sound. As noted in the Safetymaster publication, *Hearing Protection Training Manual,* "Noise, or unwanted sound, is encountered during every facet of our lives, both at work and off the job. The effects of chronic exposure to excessive noise on hearing are insidious and slow-developing, although well-documented." Ear muffs and ear plugs of many types are available, but these high-grade instruments do no good on the shelf. They must be worn by the hobbyist to do their job.

Chemicals

Solvent toxicity is an important consideration. Read all

labels and follow all directions. Solvents are important in hobby home gunsmithing, but as with all chemicals, they must be respected and used wisely. Many thinners, paint removers and other chemicals are flammable. They must be kept away from any flame source, including pilot lights. Never use gasoline as a solvent—use commercial solvent instead. Remember, stains can stain more than wood. Every chemical sold over the counter today carries specific warnings and suggestions on the container for safety. Most chemicals also have safety guides available, with written instructions for the proper use of the product.

Keep oily rags or solvent-soaked rags in a closed container. Get rid of these rags in a safe manner. If in doubt, call your local fire department for instructions concerning proper disposal of any chemical or rag permeated with any chemical.

Another chemical, browning solution, demands the same respect due all other chemicals. Remember, these solutions contain acid, so read and obey all label warnings.

Although hobbyists seldom find themselves around bluing tanks, remember that both heat and chemicals are involved. Wear proper protection for eyes and skin.

Chemical disposal is not only a matter of safety, it is the law. Call your local fire or sanitation department for instructions. Check your telephone directory for firms specializing in approved methods of disposal.

Epoxy and Glue

These, too, are chemically based products. Some people are especially sensitive to these products and may have to wear rubber gloves to safeguard their skin. Mix epoxies correctly, following all directions, including safety precautions.

Electrical Outlets

At all levels, from Kitchen Table to Home Workshop, electricity must be respected. Avoid working next to outlets with liquids that could spill into the outlet itself. Check electrical cords for breaks and repair them as necessary. Avoid using electrical cords around machinery that may grab them.

Flooring

What lies beneath the work area, be that location a kitchen or large home shop, is highly important. Molten solder, welding slag, metal debris, sawdust and other products of labor should

Checking the tanks before operation, Dale Storey (right) and Dan Anderson prepare for a bluing session. When the tanks are in operation, gloves and eye protection will be worn. A pre-bluing checkup is a wise safety precaution to determine if the tanks are in sound operating order.

These are typical safety data sheets commonly used for solvents.

be captured on a safe surface, not one that is combustible in nature.

Work where you won't be interrupted, especially if machinery is in use. Interruptions break concentration, and a loss of concentration can lead to an accident.

Tool Safety

File Handles

The file handle protects the hand from the tang section of the file, which can penetrate into the palm. Be especially watchful when filing a rotating piece of stock held in the jaws of the lathe. A file handle is absolutely essential here.

Sharpening Chisels

When sharpening a chisel, use the proper stone resting upon a non-slip surface. Keep both hands on the chisel handle, thereby preventing damage from a slip off the stone.

Cutting Implements

An uncle of mine used to say, "Always cut toward yourself with a knife. That way, when the knife slips, you'll get yourself instead of me." Obviously, this was a reverse warning: The right way to use a cutting instrument is with the force directed away from any part of the body, so if it does slip, you will slice only air, not yourself. Use only the amount of pressure necessary for cutting. Pushing as hard as you can with any cutting tool can cause a loss of control.

Hacksaws

Cutting hard materials with a hacksaw means possibly heavy pressure. When the blade finally cuts through the material, the hacksaw can drive forward. Be watchful and slow down toward the end of a cutting cycle. Hold materials to be cut in a vise, not by hand.

Drilling

Be certain of what lies beneath the stock you are drilling. A hole through the kitchen table is always hard to explain. A hole in your knee is even more embarrassing. Maintain a proper grip on any drill because, otherwise, it can torque right out of your hand. When using a hand drill, never lean your weight upon it. The drill bit can break, and your face may make sudden contact with the topmost handle of the drill.

Even in the home workshop, a fire extinguisher is nice to have handy.

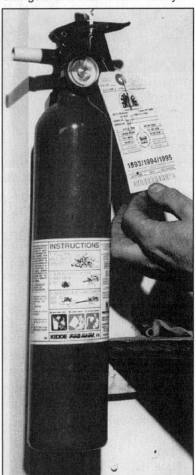

Working around any sort of equipment demands your attention. A lapse of concentration could cause injury.

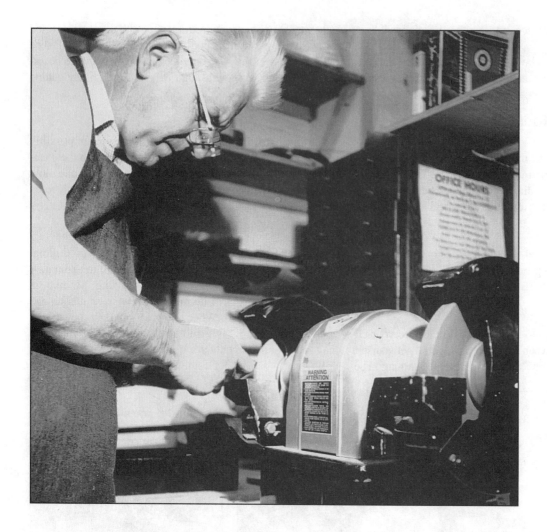

Safety is paramount in using any tool, from screwdriver to lathe. Machines often have warning labels permanently attached. Heed what they say.

Proper Bases

Grinders, sanders, polishers—any larger implement—should be controlled via a base of adequate size and stability, preferably attached to the floor in the more advanced shop.

Welding

The obvious high heat factor associated with welding demands great respect. Proper eye protection in the form of welding goggles, as well as clothing to safeguard the body, are essential. Do not weld on wooden surfaces; watch out where hot pieces of welding rod are placed; use proper tips on the torch; be careful about materials that give off toxic fumes when heated; have a fire extinguisher handy when welding; consider a course in welding to gain proficiency in the art, as well as enhancement of safety practices. Electric welders also demand proper eye protection. These should not be used on wooden benches either, nor for welding materials that can give off noxious gases.

Soldering

Heat, once again, is involved in the soldering process, demanding the usual precautions of a safe work surface, plus protection for eye and body. Flux is normally of acid base, and hands should be washed immediately after coming in contact with it. Silver solder can get too hot, burning instead of flowing, which may yield toxic fumes. Ventilation is essential, and fumes should never be inhaled. As always, read all label warnings with these products and follow directions.

Power Tools

Safety shields on various power implements are there for a reason. Leave them in place. Power sanders must be used with the safety shield, plus hands well out of harm's way. Do not wear gloves. Watch out for long sleeves that can be grabbed by a disk or belt. Protect your eyes from flying debris. These rules apply to all machinery with overt moving parts, including polishers. Polishing gloves can be worn to prevent hand burns, but they should fit snugly. Remember, any rotating wheel can put debris out at high speed, so eye protection is vital. Protect your lungs with a dust, fume and mist respirator. Ventilation is vital.

Conclusion

Safety is more than a matter of common sense, it's also a matter of knowledge. You have to know what can harm you, and how to avoid the hazards.

Muzzleloader Locks

THE BLACKPOWDER HOBBY gunsmith needs a basic working knowledge of lock types in order to understand the operation of these various mechanisms. This chapter is not a full treatise on locks, but rather an introduction to various types and styles.

Firestick

Essentially a hand-held cannon, the firestick (*baston-a-feu*), as it was fondly known, was simply a metal tube. The tube held powder and projectile rammed home into a breech section. Firesticks were common in the Netherlands in the 15th and 16th centuries. Some firesticks were designed to serve as clubs or battle axes as well as guns. One example was 2 feet long with a touchhole at the topmost part of the breech section. The implement could be used after firing to strike an enemy. Another firestick had a hatchet attached to one end.

Ignition for the firestick was simple—a slow match was held in one hand, the firestick was aimed, and the slow match was presented to the touchhole. Very little fire escaped from the touchhole due to the Venturi principle, the theory that far more gas is emitted from a larger orifice than a smaller orifice. Thus, flame exited with much greater force from the larger hole (the muzzle) in the firestick instead of through the smaller touchhole.

Matchlock

Firearms history is cloudy at best, but the matchlock seems to be a natural progression from the firestick design. One problem is invention overlap. It's impossible to say a specific lock type went out of service at a given date, while another took over at the same time. A 15th-century German manuscript describes matchlock designs. A serpentine or cock was used to hold the slow match or fuse. This is the only important functional difference between the matchlock and the firestick, aside from the development of different overall firearm styles when the matchlock came along.

The serpentine pivoted on an axis and was designed in a backwards S-shape so the lower portion of the S protruded below the firearm, representing a trigger. The upper portion of the reverse S was situated above the firearm. When the lower "trigger" stem of the serpentine was activated, the top stem pivoted toward a touchhole on the top of the gun. The slow match, held in the upper end of the cock, then came in contact with the touchhole. This system was altered numerous times. Sometimes the match was held atop the barrel, with a type of flash pan used to hold powder and to direct flame from the powder into the touchhole.

Wheellock

The matchlock progressed into many sub-styles, and eventually it was superseded by the wheellock design. Some historians credit the Germans of the 16th century with devising the wheellock. An attempt was made to attach a flint and steel to the side of the gun; after all, the flint-and-steel principle of creating sparks dated back to caveman days. If a flint-and-steel mechanism could send sparks into a pan, igniting the powder, the flash from the pan could, in turn, enter a touchhole for ignition of the powder charge in the breech. The latter setup was already in operation in matchlock days anyway. So furthering the principle was not entirely difficult.

An example known as the Monk's Gun, supposedly built around 1510-1515, is an early example of a spark-fired gun, although it is not a true wheellock. It has a serpentine, but instead of holding a slow match, it grasps a hunk of flint or pyrite. A sort of plunger is used in concert with the serpentine. By withdrawing the plunger, via a thumb or finger ring, a roughened steel bar is scraped against the pyrite held in the jaws of the serpentine (cock). This action produces sparks

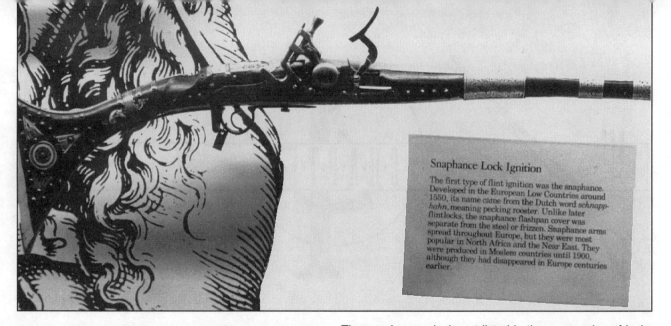

The snaphaunce lock, not listed in the progression of locks in the text, was somewhat a forerunner of the flintlock.

Flintlock

In a way, the flintlock was inferior to the wheellock in operation; however, wheellocks were intricate, difficult to produce in quantity and expensive. Something simpler was needed to serve the average shooter, and the flintlock came along to fulfill that need. It existed in dozens, if not hundreds, of variations. No single flintlock design can be singled out as definitive. However, the standard flintlock seen most frequently today is comprised of a lockplate with various functional pieces attached. A hammer or cock pivots on the lockplate. The cock has a tang or comb section on the backside and a set of jaws. A jaw screw goes through a top jaw, then into a lower jaw to serve as a very small vise.

A piece of carefully shaped flint is tightly clamped between the jaws, along with a bit of tanned leather (usually), which is wrapped around the flint. The leather is called a flint pad. While tanned leather is common today, as well as on the lock jaws of sporting rifles of the past, thin sheets of lead were often used as flint pads for old-time muskets. The jaws bite down on the tanned leather, thereby securing the flint. Tightening can be done using a screwdriver to turn the top jaw screw. The object of the hammer, or cock, is to present the flint squarely against the face of a frizzen. Incidentally, the frizzen was also known as a frizzle. Over time, the frizzen has carried other names, as well, including battery, hen or steel.

The frizzen is powered by the frizzen spring mounted on the outside of the lockplate. The frizzen spring also has an old-fashioned name which is "feather spring." The frizzen spring's purpose is to direct the frizzen out of the way when the hammer-driven flint strikes down against its face. This action diverts the frizzen toward the muzzle, thereby exposing another important feature of the flintlock, the pan, also known as the flash pan. The pan contains FFFFg powder, the finest granulation of blackpowder currently available to sportsmen. The object of the flintlock is to shower sparks into the pan as the flint scrapes curls of hot metal from the face of the frizzen.

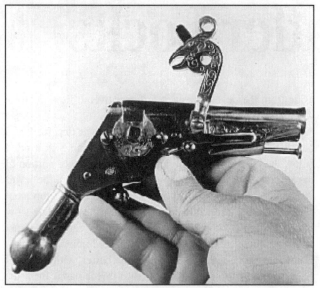

An Italian dag showing a wheellock design. It is one of the hundreds of different lock interpretations designed over the years. Note the serpentine with jaws.

which fly into a touchhole placed immediately in front of the serpentine's jaw.

The true wheellock is given a 1515 invention date, in Nuremburg. As noted by the name, this model incorporates a wheel, rather than a sliding steel bar. The wheel is an integral part of the lock system and functions much like a clock mechanism. The wheel is wound up with a key or spanner, as one might wind a clock, which puts spring power to work. To shoot the wheellock, the flash pan lid is opened; the cock is placed in contact with the wheel; pressure on the trigger releases the spring-powered wheel, which flies into action. The rotation of the wheel against the pyrite held in the jaw of the cock creates a shower of sparks. Numerous improvements turned the wheellock into an ignition system of high merit and reliability. Instead of a slow match, or even a few sparks, coming in contact with the pan powder, a shower of sparks was created. The more sparks, the more chance for ignition of the powder charge in the breech.

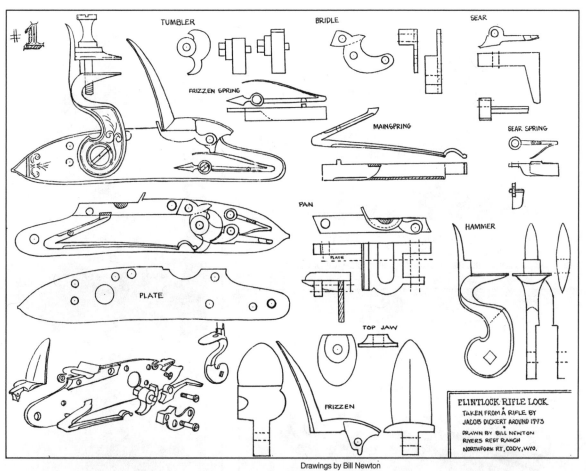

#1

TUMBLER

BRIDLE

SEAR

FRIZZEN SPRING

MAINSPRING

SEAR SPRING

PAN

HAMMER

PLATE

PLATE

TOP JAW

FRIZZEN

FLINTLOCK RIFLE LOCK
TAKEN FROM A RIFLE BY
JACOB DICKERT AROUND 1793
*
DRAWN BY BILL NEWTON
RIVERS REST RANCH
NORTHFORK RT, CODY, WYO.

Drawings by Bill Newton

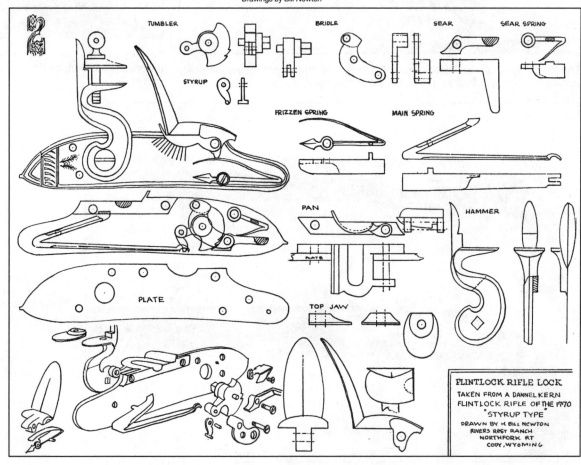

TUMBLER

BRIDLE

SEAR

SEAR SPRING

STYRUP

FRIZZEN SPRING

MAIN SPRING

PAN

HAMMER

PLATE

PLATE

TOP JAW

FLINTLOCK RIFLE LOCK
TAKEN FROM A DANNEL KERN
FLINTLOCK RIFLE OF THE 1770
"STYRUP TYPE"
DRAWN BY H. BILL NEWTON
RIVERS REST RANCH
NORTHFORK RT
CODY, WYOMING

Flintlock from this point of view shows exterior, with frizzen spring, as well as hammer (cock) with flint in jaws aimed directly into pan. Frizzen is forward because the hammer is in the fired position. Also, see the touchhole in side flat of barrel.

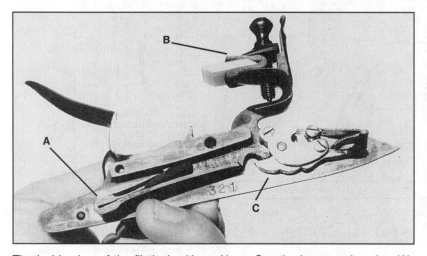

The inside view of the flintlock with workings. See the larger mainspring (A), as well as jaws with leather pads (B), and tumbler with bridle (C).

Top view of the flintlock pan, with frizzen in forward position, as it would be with the pan open.

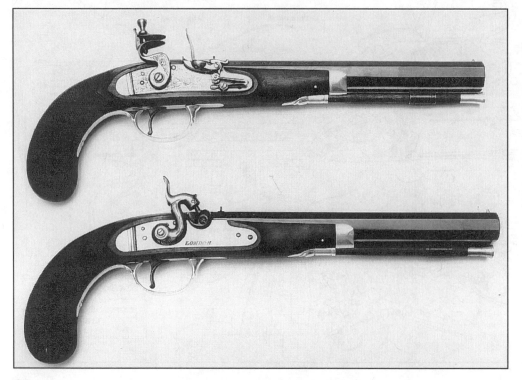

The flintlock and percussion types are seen here in two Navy Arms William Moore replicas.

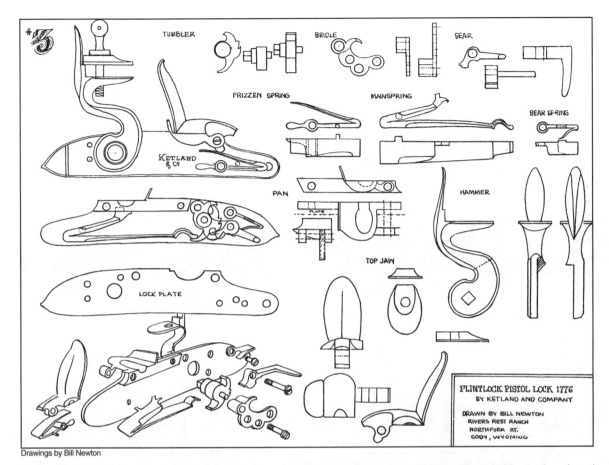

FLINTLOCK PISTOL LOCK 1776
BY KETLAND AND COMPANY

DRAWN BY BILL NEWTON
RIVERS REST RANCH
NORTHFORK RT.
CODY, WYOMING

Drawings by Bill Newton

Eventually, the frizzen can become worn to the point where sparks no longer are generated from flint/frizzen contact. However, with a good, well-positioned flint and a properly hardened frizzen face, the flintlock works quite well.

Looking at the inside of the flintlock, which faces inward into the stock's lock mortise and cannot be seen when the lock is in place on the firearm, we find a tumbler. It rotates with the hammer or cock. Half-cock and full-cock notches are integral to the tumbler. These notches are engaged by the sear, which operates via a sear spring. The sear spring must be depressed in order for the nose of the sear to disengage from the notches in the tumbler. Also seen on the inside of the lock is the mainspring, which powers the hammer by forcing the forward side of the tumbler downward. The lock may have a bridle, a piece of metal that spans over both tumbler and sear, providing solid pivot points for both tumbler and sear. The sear releases the tumbler when the trigger is activated, thereby allowing the hammer to fall forward.

There may be a fly in the tumbler, which can also be called a detent. The fly serves an important function with double-set triggers. It prevents the sear from falling into the half-cock notch and is, in effect, an override device that does not interfere with the activation of the full-cock notch. The fly allows the firearm to be brought into firing position without the sear hanging up in the half-cock notch. In other words, the function of the fly is to serve as a half-cock override. A stirrup may also be present in some locks. The stirrup rests between the tumbler and spring tip, reducing friction in the system at this location.

The rest of the flintlock story is rather self-evident. The flint scrapes the frizzen, and as the frizzen rotates toward the muzzle, the pan cover is lifted, uncovering the pan powder, which is ignited by the sparks. A flame or flash results, and it is this fire that dashes through a hole in the side of the barrel flat (the touchhole) and to the main charge in the breech. If the flintlock were as hit-and-miss as many modern writers propose, the Eastern settler never would have survived, nor would the pioneer have been able to settle the land west of the Mississippi River. Of course, flintlocks failed to ignite with 100-percent reliability. That's where the term "flash in the pan" comes from, a flash that does not result in ignition. There is also a hangfire, which is a time lag between pulling the trigger and the gun going off, and a misfire, which is pulling the trigger without ignition following.

Percussion Lock

The caplock or percussion lock is the most popular black-powder ignition system in use today. The invention of a workable percussion cap in the 1800s precluded the necessity for pan powder. Ignition is produced by a blow upon the cap, which contains a percussion-sensitive mixture. The mixture gives off a spark, and the spark, in turn, finds its way to the powder charge in the breech. How it finds its way varies considerably with different percussion lock designs. It was no

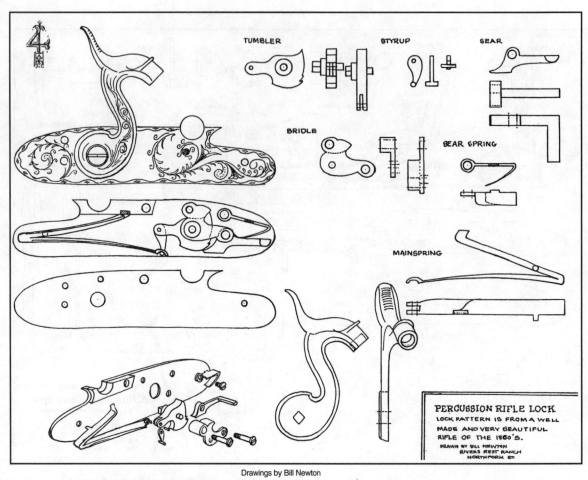

TUMBLER STYRUP SEAR

BRIDLE

SEAR SPRING

MAINSPRING

PERCUSSION RIFLE LOCK
LOCK PATTERN IS FROM A WELL
MADE AND VERY BEAUTIFUL
RIFLE OF THE 1860'S.
DRAWN BY BILL NEWTON
RIVERS REST RANCH
NORTH FORK RT.

Drawings by Bill Newton

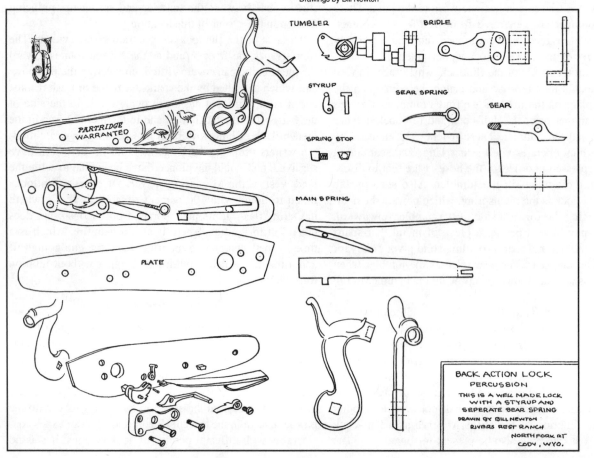

TUMBLER BRIDLE

STYRUP SEAR SPRING SEAR

SPRING STOP

MAIN SPRING

PARTRIDGE WARRANTED

PLATE

BACK ACTION LOCK
PERCUSSION
THIS IS A WELL MADE LOCK
WITH A STYRUP AND
SEPERATE SEAR SPRING
DRAWN BY BILL NEWTON
RIVERS REST RANCH
NORTH FORK RT
CODY, WYO.

A back-action lock with mainspring, as well as tumbler and other internal lock parts, behind the hammer.

(Below) Back-action lock with nipple and drum. Note the flash cup around the nipple to contain and divert cap debris.

A front-action lock with mainspring in front of the hammer.

great trick to convert flintlock rifles to percussion ignition because the locks were truly quite similar in nature. That is why we do not go into a detailed explanation of the exterior or interior workings of the caplock here. When converting, the flintlock was replaced with a percussion lock, plus a drum and nipple arrangement.

The drum is simply a metal tube that screws into the side flat of the barrel where the touchhole used to reside. The end of the drum is secured with a cleanout screw. The side of the drum is fitted with a nipple, also screwed into place. The hammer of the percussion lock whacks a cap that's placed upon the cone of the nipple, thereby setting it off. Fire from the cap darts through the hole in the nipple, into the drum, and then finally into the main charge in the breech. The drum and nipple arrangement worked so well that we still have rifles using the system, including new factory models. But many new ways have come along to mount a nipple on a blackpowder firearm, including a bolster arrangement where a lump of metal integral to the barrel held the nipple. In time, dozens of new caplock styles came along. Here are a few:

Front-Action Lock

This is the workhorse lock of the percussion ignition system today—a standard of the hour. The mainspring is in front of the hammer as opposed to behind it, hence front-action lock. This type of percussion lock functions well on single-barrel pistols and rifles. It is also entirely workable for side-by-side double guns, because the locks can be fitted down under the side of the barrel, as on the double-barrel shotgun, for exam-

ple. The front-action percussion lock is entirely acceptable, and that's why it remains so popular today.

Back-Action Lock

As opposed to the front-action lock, this type has the mainspring in back of the hammer. The back-action lock allows the wrist area of a rifle to be slimmer than the front-action lock allows. There is no panel or moulding around the lock in the stock, which promotes more trim firearm design. The back-action lock also adapts well to swivel-breech firearms and to certain over/under double-barrel configurations. It is excellent for takedown breech systems, too, because the lockplate is located on the wrist of the rifle, rather than up front by the barrel. The back-action percussion lock has been used on slug guns, which are target muzzleloaders with huge barrels.

Front-Action Sidehammer or Mule Ear Lock

A short-lived style because it appeared toward the end of the blackpowder era, the sidehammer remains a superb percussion lock design due to its simplicity and reliability. The main feature of the sidehammer is its direct ignition quality. The nipple is fitted directly to the barrel. Thus, fire from the nipple darts into the main charge in the breech without the spark having to route through a drum and nipple, bolster or other arrangement. Also, simplicity of design means fewer working parts. Certain sidehammer designs use complicated trigger systems, because of older lock styles with sears activated by lateral instead of vertical movement. Another good feature is that cap debris is directed away from the shooter. Also,

35

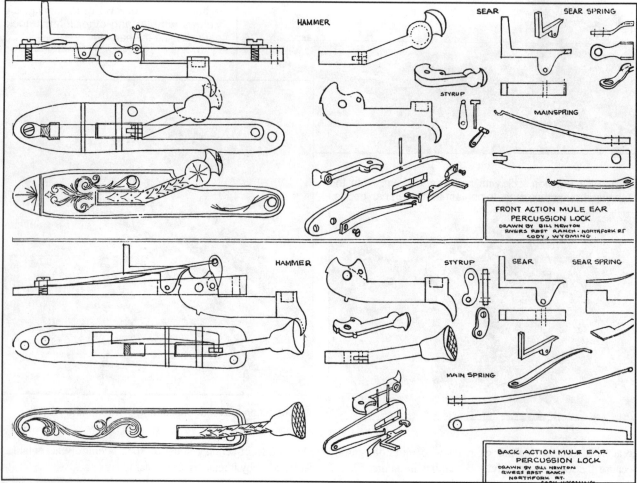

Drawing by Bill Newton

many sidehammers have deep hammer noses that tend to contain the cap debris. A detriment of older sidehammers is a rather long hammer fall. This feature is corrected on the patented Storey sidehammer lock, which employs a strong coil mainspring and a shorter hammer throw. The Storey version of the sidehammer lock also has a sear that moves vertically, allowing the use of a regular trigger.

Back-Action Sidehammer Lock

Possibly the most versatile percussion lock system, it could be used on almost any gun. The design works well on single-barrel rifles and pistols, especially for takedown rifles or switch-barrel sets. It functions on a double gun, too, albeit somewhat awkwardly, due to protrusion of cocked hammers on either side of the firearm. This type of lock is built with two hammers on one lockplate and is possibly the best lock for

over/under guns. Quick positive ignition is a high point of this lock type, excellent especially for target guns requiring shorter lock time. On the debit side of the ledger, these locks are somewhat difficult to build. Furthermore, incorporating a half-cock notch is difficult, although it can be done at higher cost in labor.

Underhammer Lock

This is another simple design. The nipple is screwed directly into the bottom of the barrel of the pistol or rifle. Cap debris is directed downward and away from the shooter. There were many different styles of underhammer locks over the years, most employing the trigger guard as a mainspring, a simple but intelligent idea. Double-set triggers are not entirely compatible with the underhammer lock, although they can be used. The underhammer lock allows the building of an economical

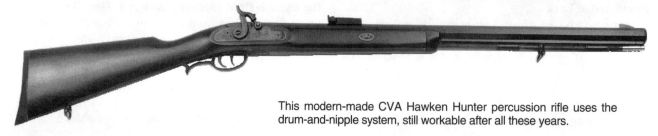

This modern-made CVA Hawken Hunter percussion rifle uses the drum-and-nipple system, still workable after all these years.

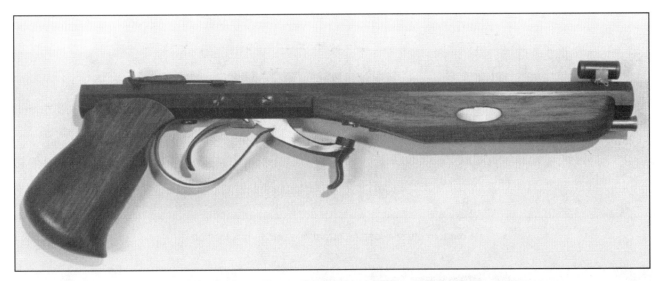

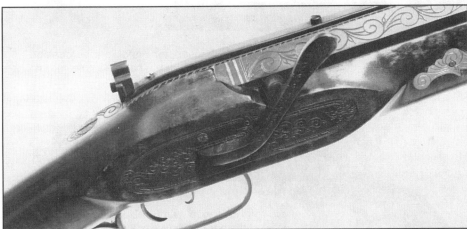

(Above) An underhammer lock with the trigger guard serving as the mainspring to power the hammer. Fire from the cap goes directly into the breech.

(Left) Storey sidehammer lock cocks to the side. Fire from the percussion cap darts straight into the powder charge in the breech.

muzzleloader. Good on a hunting rifle, it is even better on a target rifle due to positive ignition qualities. Underhammer locks have been satisfactorily employed on heavy bench target rifles, as well as competition shotguns.

In-Line Ignition Locks

The heart of the modern muzzleloader firearm, this lock works on the principle of a plunger system, although in recent years the in-line system has undergone several modifications, including a hammer gun with nipple threaded into a solid breech—no plunger. While popular on modern blackpowder guns, the idea is nothing new at all. The Friendship Special over/under shotgun used the in-line system for years. This is an over/under shotgun with two spring-loaded plungers, developed by shooters who frequented the famous Friendship, Indiana, annual blackpowder match. Also, the in-line ignition system was found on converted Enfield and Japanese Arisaka bolt-action rifles turned into muzzleloaders.

The in-line lock, if it can be called a lock, is ideal for the modern muzzleloader (see Chapter 22 on the subject). When the trigger is pulled, the cocked spring-loaded plunger runs forward, the nose of the plunger striking a percussion cap seated on a nipple mounted directly into the rear of the barrel. In-line ignition is the result, the fire from the cap flying directly into the powder charge in the breech. The in-line ignition sys-

The modern muzzleloader with in-line ignition looks, at first glance, like a cartridge-shooting big game rifle.

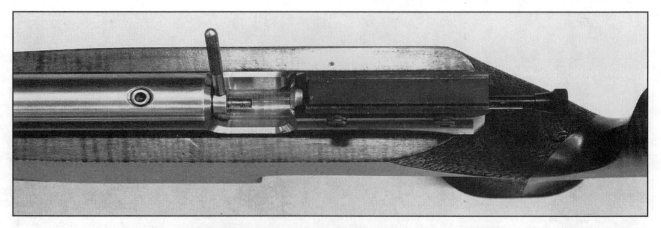

A modern muzzle-loading target rifle with in-line ignition.

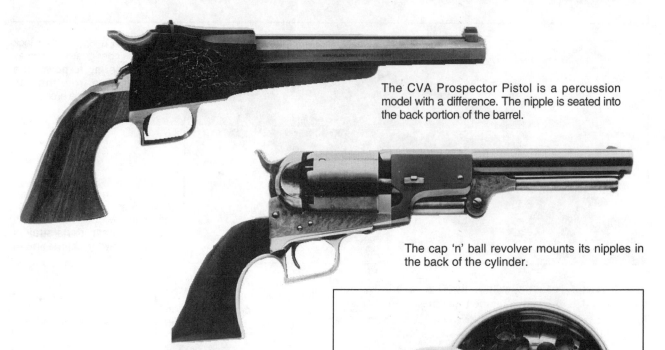

The CVA Prospector Pistol is a percussion model with a difference. The nipple is seated into the back portion of the barrel.

The cap 'n' ball revolver mounts its nipples in the back of the cylinder.

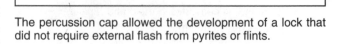

The percussion cap allowed the development of a lock that did not require external flash from pyrites or flints.

tem allows the use of modern-style stocks, modern triggers and safeties, and many other features associated with cartridge firearms.

Cap 'n' Ball Revolver

The cap 'n' ball revolver uses a rotating cylinder with chambers, just as found on a modern revolver. But the front end of the chamber accepts a round or conical lead projectile. The middle of the chamber holds powder. And the back end of the chamber is closed to contain a seated nipple. A cap is placed on the cone of each nipple, and when the hammer drops, it strikes the cap, detonating it. A jet of a flame is then directed into the powder charge in the cylinder chamber for ignition.

These are some of the lock types the modern blackpowder home hobby gunsmith should be familiar with. It is not at all a complete collection of locks, for that would demand a book of its own. However, understanding the different ignition systems is important for anyone who intends to work on locks, either tuning them, refining them or building them.

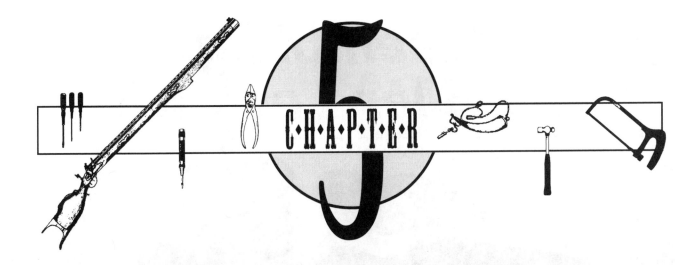

Building Lock Kits

SOMEWHAT MORE demanding than most rifle, pistol or revolver kits, the lock kit is a highly useful undertaking, especially for the hobbyist whose goal is to create as much of his own blackpowder shooting gear as possible. Quality control is in the hands of the builder, and a demanding person can construct a superb lock. Amateur locksmiths may even wish to modify the package—altering spring locations, going the extra mile on tuning and polishing, adding the personal touch. Building a lock is a great teaching experience. There is no better way to understand the workings of a muzzleloader lock than making one yourself. The hobby gunsmith who constructs his own lock really knows what makes it tick. Also, lockmaking involves heat-treating various parts, which is an interesting and useful sideline of its own.

The lock is the heart of the blackpowder shooting system. Hand making a lock shows the hobbyist where wear generally occurs, so he knows what to look for later with a lock that fails to function properly. The builder also gains expertise at assembly and disassembly, since the lock must be taken apart and put together numerous times while assembling it from a kit. Future repair knowledge is greatly enhanced through lockmaking. The internal parts of the lock forever become a part of the hobby gunsmith's reservoir of know-how, such as how the fly fits into the tumbler and its relationship with the half-cock notch, fit between bridle and tumbler, sear action and so forth. Flintlock building includes learning about frizzen spring tension and how to install the frizzen for best results. A great deal of satisfaction can be derived from building the lock kit. Although the task is challenging, it is also rewarding.

Furthermore, while the goal of hobby home blackpowder gunsmithing is not profit-oriented, a few do-it-yourself builders end up quite expert in lockmaking and have been known to build kits for profit.

Important: The hobbyist taking on the construction of a lock kit may have to call upon some professional help. For example, access to a drill press is important and is a major tool in lockmaking. While it is not impossible to make a lock without a drill press, drilling holes perfectly straight without one is exceedingly difficult. Help may also be required in heat-treating, especially since a high-level heat source is required to do the job correctly. An oxygen-acetylene torch provides the level of heat demanded to raise parts to a working temperature.

On the other side of the coin, polishing can be done by hand, keeping all lines and surfaces of the lock flat and true. Hand polishing is time-consuming, and it requires persistence; however, the job can be done perfectly. An electric polisher makes the work go faster, but fine hand polishing makes the finished product more perfect.

This chapter concerns the building of two fine locks. The first is the excellent Siler flintlock unit, containing twenty-one parts made of first-class castings. The second is the equally good Pioneer Arms Company Mule Ear Lock Kit. These kits differ not only in design and application—the first a flinter, the second a percussion model—but they also differ in construction. The interested reader should study the building of both kits carefully, for there is something different to learn in each one.

In making any kit, instructions are extremely vital. Never embark on kit making without reading all of the instructions at least once before picking up a single tool. In other words, know your destination before beginning your journey. Also, be certain you understand every phase of the lock-making process before beginning work. If you do not, get help either from a professional blackpowder gunsmith or the maker of your lock kit. Remember that mistakes can be costly, not only in lost time, but in parts replacement. The wrong maneuver may ruin a part, and a new part will have to be purchased in order to complete the project.

Assembling The Siler Lock Kit

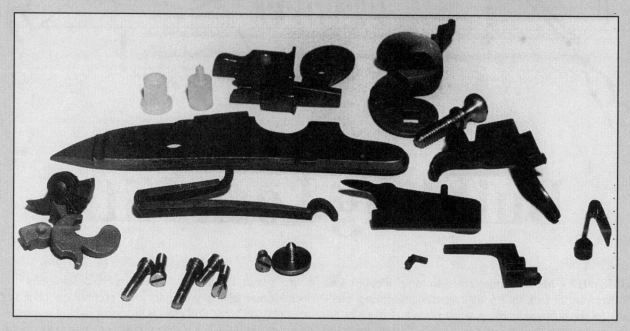

All parts for the Siler flintlock kit.

Tools

C-clamps or Parallel Clamps
Center Punch
Drill Press
Drill Press Vise
Drill Bits: $9/64$, $11/64$, $13/64$, $5/16$ and No. 33
Bottom Drill Bit: $13/64$
Chucking Reamer: $5/16$
Taps: 12-24 and 6-40
Hacksaw
Oxygen-Acetylene Torch
Screwdrivers
Smooth Mill Cut Files
Wire Brush

Supplies

Arkansas Stone
Block of Scrap Wood
Candle
Dykem, Layout Blue or Black Magic Marker
Kasenit
Light Motor Oil
Rapid Tap Fluid
Sand with Metal Container
Short Lengths of Wire

Setting Up

Remove all parts from the package and lay them out neatly on the bench, ensuring that you understand not only the function and purpose of each one, but also where each piece fits to make a completed lock. Also, make certain the proper tools are available before starting the job. Be careful with the small fly., because once dropped it may be gone forever.

Removing Flashing and Gates

Strike the flashing and gates from each part. These are excess materials resulting from the casting process in the moulds. All must be removed before construction proceeds. Flashing and gates are readily apparent, resembling the excess overlap often seen on plastic parts for children's toys and model kits. The material exists on all parts, including the fly. A hacksaw is useful in removing the majority of the gate, followed by hand filing. A variety of files, all smooth mill cut, do a perfect job, each file shape applied where it best serves. The goal in removing gates and flashing is to keep all surfaces flat, true and straight, rather than rounded, off-line and crooked. A little extra time here is worth spending.

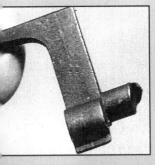

(Above left) This is the sear for the Siler lock. Note the gate, which is the protrusion visible on the far right. The gate must be filed off before the part can be fitted. (Above right) This is the sear after filing. It is ready to be drilled for the sear screw.

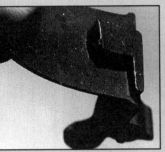

(Left) This is the frizzen for the Siler lock, with the gate still intact. The gate must be filed off before the part can be fitted to the lock. (Right) The frizzen with gate filed off, ready to be fitted to the lock.

Drilling Lockplate Holes

Drill holes in the lockplate. Use a No. 33 drill bit for all the holes that are punch-marked in the plate, *except for the spring screw and frizzen spring holes*. These are drilled later. Holes to drill now: mainspring, bridle screw, sear spring screw and sear screw. Place the lockplate on a solid piece of wood and hold firmly. The wood platform under the lockplate prevents the drill from catching as it passes through the metal, spinning the plate or breaking the drill bit. Run the drill press on its lowest speed. Drill slowly, using a cutting fluid, such as Rapid Tap, to promote a clean, true hole.

Tapping Lockplate HFoles

After drilling, each hole is tapped with a 6-40 tap. Use the drill press *by hand only* to start the tap. Clamp the tap in the chuck of the drill press, and rotate by hand with the tap aligned with the drilled hole. Keep tension on the quill handle, and carefully start each hole. Do not tap completely through, only start it. Final tapping can be completed all the way through by hand. Tap these holes: bridle, sear spring and sear screw—not the mainspring hole.

Drilling the lockplate.

Starting a tap in the drill press *by hand.* The drill press is not running, but is used as a vertical guide for accuracy.

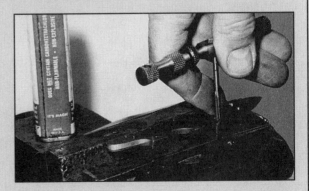

Finishing a tap with a tap handle. The tap was started by hand in a drill press.

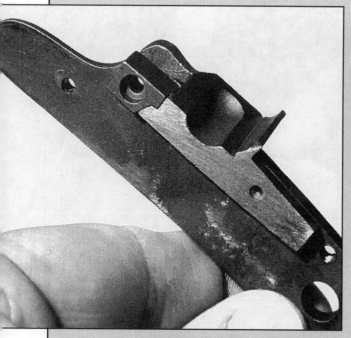

Siler pan fitted and ready for drilling and tapping.

Siler lockplate and pan, ready for fitting.

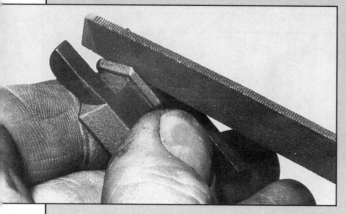

Final filing on the pan to make it correctly fit the lock-plate.

Fitting Pan and Lockplate

Very closely fit the pan to the plate. If you have trouble finding where to file, use a candle flame to blacken the two surfaces that will be mated together. Then, rub the two pieces together. The high places between the two will now show up as bright, shiny spots where carbon has been disturbed. Repeat the candle routine until the two pieces fit together without high spots.

Drilling the Pan

With the pan clamped firmly in place, carefully drill a No. 33 hole through both the pan and lockplate, as illustrated. With all parts still firmly clamped in place, use a $13/64$-inch drill bit and drill the pan portion to the depth of the screw head that will be used. Use the stop feature on the drill press to prevent drilling this hole too deeply. *Do not drill all the way through the pan.* After drilling the $13/64$-inch hole, use a $13/64$-inch bottom drill bit to finish the countersink hole for the screw head. Once again, the stop on the drill press is used to prevent drilling the hole too deeply. This affords a flush fit for the head of the screw holding the pan to the lockplate.

Remove the pan from the lockplate and drill a $9/64$-inch hole in the pan where the No. 33 hole was previously drilled.

Tapping Pan and Lockplate

The lockplate is now tapped to 6-40. Place the pan back on the lockplate and thread the screw tightly in place. If the screw head rises above the surface of the pan plate, it can be filed to fit flush.

Fitting Frizzen and Pan

The frizzen is fitted next. At this point, carefully mate the bottom of the frizzen with the top of the pan. This step requires minor filing for a perfect fit.

Drilling the Frizzen Pivot Screw Hole

Place the frizzen on the pan with the frizzen in its closed position, all the way back against the fence, which is the raised portion at the rear of the pan. What follows is one of the more difficult aspects of the lock assembly, not because of construction problems, but due to difficulty in securing the frizzen in the drill press vise. The goal is to maintain accuracy while drilling the frizzen pivot screw hole. This is one of the deeper holes to be drilled. A clamp, plus the drill press vise, was used in this step to hold the frizzen to the lock as securely and accurately as possible. The entire unit must be held immobile during this operation or the frizzen will not be fitted properly.

Using a No. 33 drill bit, start at the pre-marked location on the lockplate and drill one hole completely through the plate, the frizzen and the pan bridle. The pre-mark is established on the Siler kit by the factory and aids in accurate hole location. Leave everything still clamped together. Now use a 9/64-inch bit in the drill press. This is inserted into the same hole already established with the No. 33 bit, but this time the hole will *not* be drilled all the way through. This hole is drilled through the lockplate and the frizzen, *but not through the pan bridle.* Use the stop on the drill press to prevent the hole from going all the way through the pan bridle.

Loosen the clamp and remove the frizzen, still leaving the lockplate held in the drill press vise. Using a 6-40 tap, thread the pan bridle for the frizzen pivot screw. Now, check to see if the frizzen was drilled all the way through, as it should have been. Sometimes, in an attempt to ensure the 9/64-inch hole is not drilled too deeply and into the pan bridle, the frizzen hole is short-drilled. Check this out. If the frizzen hole is not complete, finish the job before going any further.

If the head of the frizzen pivot screw is not countersunk into the lockplate, follow the same procedure as outlined for the screw that held the pan to the lockplate.

Drilling and Tapping the Frizzen Spring Hole

Next, using the No. 33 bit, drill the frizzen spring hole where it is marked on the outside of the lockplate. The spring screw punch mark may not allow proper tension of this spring,

Showing the bottom of the Siler frizzen, where it covers the pan. It has been carefully filed smooth for proper fit.

Drilling and fitting the frizzen to the lockplate.

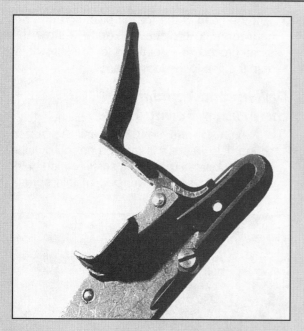

Siler frizzen spring installed on the lockplate.

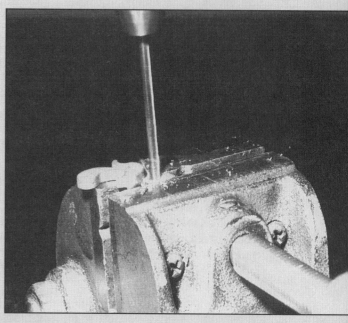

Drilling the bridle where it attaches to the lockplate.

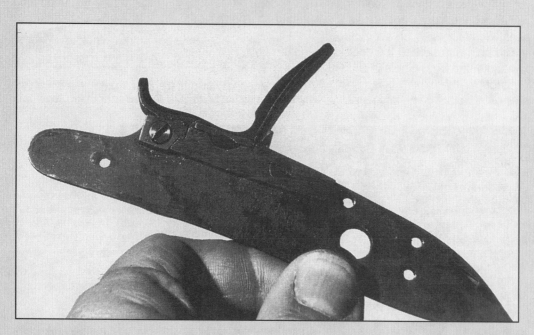

Frizzen installed on the lockplate.

but there is one sure way to gain proper tension. The frizzen must be in the *open* position for this to work. Compress the sharp-pointed end of the frizzen spring 1/8-inch upward and clamp it tightly to the lockplate. Once done, take a 9/64-inch drill bit and insert it through the frizzen spring hole. This is to spot the hole to be drilled through the lockplate. Once spotted, complete the drilling with a No. 33 bit through the lockplate and thread the hole with a 6-40 tap while the frizzen spring remains clamped to the lockplate.

Checking Fit of Frizzen and Pan

Hold the lock up to the light and check how the frizzen fits to the pan. If it fits flush, no light will shine between the frizzen and the pan. If light shows, judicious filing is used to bring these two parts together with a flush fit. Once again, the candle trick can be used—blackening the metal parts with candle smoke, and then placing the parts together to see where the carbon rubs off, showing a place that needs to be filed. The pan should open and close easily, but firmly.

This shows the plastic guide which is used to locate the correct position of the bridle.

Locating the tumbler hole in the bridle using the plastic guide and preparing to drill this hole. The plastic guide is used for guidance.

Drilling the Bridle

The bridle is the next step. At the punch mark on the the thickest portion of the bridle, drill a $9/64$-inch hole through the bridle. Now screw the bridle to the lockplate using that hole.

Screw the plastic locator into the sear spring hole and pivot the rear of the bridle against the plastic locator. Put Dykem or layout blue on the inside of the bridle (black Magic Marker will also work). Thread a 6-40 tap into the sear hole from the outside of the lockplate. Thread it all the way down to the point where it touches the bridle. The point of the tap will leave a bright mark. Remove the bridle, center-punch the mark, and drill with a $9/64$-inch bit. If no drill press vise is available, at the least, use a piece of wood as a drilling platform. *Caution:* Watch out for your fingers should the drill bit catch and spin the bridle around. Drill slowly!

Drilling the Tumbler Holes

The goal of this step is to establish a $5/16$-inch hole through the lockplate for the hammer shank of the tumbler. Clamp the lockplate into the drill press vise, being careful not to damage the edges of the lockplate with unnecessary force. Using a $5/16$-inch chucking reamer in the drill press, ream the hole through the lockplate. If a chucking reamer is not available, a $5/16$-inch straight-shank core bit can be used for this operation, or as a last choice, a $5/16$-inch twist drill bit.

Replace the bridle on the lockplate with its two screws. Insert the plastic drill guide in the tumbler hole of the lockplate and drill an $11/64$-inch hole through the bridle.

Fitting the Tumbler Shank

The goal of this step is to make the tumbler shank fit through the $5/16$-inch hole in the lockplate and the $11/64$-inch hole in the bridle. To do this, chuck the large shank of the tumbler in a drill press or lathe and, using a file, true up the opposite, smaller end of the tumbler shank to $11/64$-inch, or until it just fits the hole in the bridle. Now reverse the operation. Chuck the small end of the tumbler shank and true this end to $5/16$-inch, or until it fits into the lockplate. Both tumbler shanks must be closely fitted to allow the tumbler to turn smoothly. Both sides of the tumbler should be smooth-faced during these operations. In other words, true these surfaces with a fine file.

Drilling the Fly Hole

Now the tumbler is drilled to accept the fly. Using a 5/16-inch bit, drill the fly hole in the fly recess, approximately three-fourths of the way through to the opposite side of the tumbler. Place the fly in the tumbler. Check for fit—the fly should swing freely in the tumbler.

Tapping the Tumbler

Center-punch the squared face of the larger shaft of the tumbler and tap it using a No. 33 drill bit and a 6-40 tap. Go slowly when tapping. Use plenty of cutting fluid and frequently back out the tap to clear away the debris or the tap may break off in the tumbler. This is the most difficult tapping operation of the lock. A mistake here may mean ordering a new tumbler.

Drilling the Sear Pivot Screw Hole

This step includes drilling the pivot screw hole in the sear. Secure the sear in a drill press vise and drill it with a 9/64-inch bit at the punch mark (provided as a pre-located point). The sear is now ready to install.

Fitting Hammer and Tumbler

Using a small flat or three-square file, fit the hammer to the tumbler. Place the hammer on the tumbler and tap it lightly into place. See where the high spots are and file them down to fit. Remove an absolute minimum of metal in this operation. Repeat the procedure of tapping the hammer into place, followed by careful filing, as many times as necessary. The goal is a tight-fitting hammer. A loose

Locating the sear pivot screw hole in the bridle.

hammer shows sloppy workmanship and does not wear well.

Tapping the Jaw Screw

Tap the lower hammer jaw for the jaw screw using a 12-24 tap. This hole is pre-drilled, and only tapping is required. Point the tap directly at the center of the square hole in the hammer to line it up correctly. This properly aligns the jaw screw when tapping is completed.

Assembling the Lock

Assemble the lock with all springs in place. It should operate perfectly, if you've properly performed all the steps.

Take a few moments to decide on the final finishing you wish to do on the parts to be hardened: sear, tumbler, frizzen and fly. After hardening, it is more difficult to work these pieces. The springs are properly tempered as they come from the kit, so spring tempering is not a problem.

Hardening Lock Parts

The sear, tumbler, frizzen and fly must now be hardened. The heat-treating methods used here come with the Siler lock instructions and are recommended. They were followed to the letter and the results were perfect.

The term heat-treat refers to two operations: first, to harden (heat and quench), and second, to temper (soften) to a useful hardness. The tool steels used in Siler locks will harden clear through when quenched (immersed) in oil alone, therefore water should not be used to quench since it can cause cracks to occur.

Hardening: The most successful hardening equipment is some sort of open flame such as oxygen-acetylene torch, forge or propane torch (MAPP gas sold at Sears produces more heat than propane). Using propane or MAPP gas, two or more torches are needed for parts as large as the frizzen.

An electric furnace is not suitable for hardening since it has no flame and too little oxygen. It can remove carbon leaving a soft surface, but it is excellent for tempering since it does not adversely affect carbon at these lower temperatures.

Twist each part on the end of short lengths of wire (so it can be hand-held and quenched easily) and heat it uniformly to a bright red (1500 degrees), then quickly immerse it in a quart or two of light motor oil. Move it around in the oil for about 30 seconds, then leave it in the oil to cool. It should harden on the first try, but if not successful the same procedure can be used again. Success means too hard to file.

Tempering: Hardened parts have to be softened to a useful hardness by heating to specified temperatures. This can best be done with a furnace that has a temperature indicator, or next best with a kitchen stove.

Another tempering method that requires a lit-

Hardening the frizzen by heating.

Quenching the heated frizzen in oil as part of the hardening process.

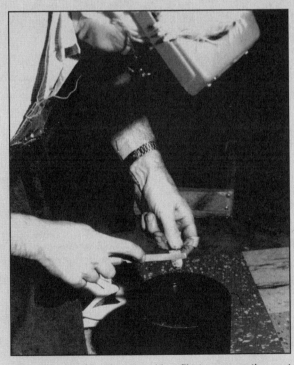

Checking the Siler frizzen with a file to ensure the part is hard after the heat-treating process is complete.

Drawing the sear back after hardening. A bed of sand is used to distribute heat evenly to the part. This brings the part to correct hardness.

tle more skill is by color. The part must be polished and then placed on a half-inch of sand in a container such as a large jar lid. When heated slowly on the burner of a kitchen stove, in good light, colors can be seen in stages from straw, then tan, brown, purple, blue and gray. Parts should be removed from the heat when the following appear, in order of their appearance: Frizzen—pale yellow (375 degrees, RC 62-64); sear, tumbler and fly—full blue with some fading into gray (600 degrees, RC 54-56).

The Way Out of a Bad Hardening Attempt: Overheating during hardening, or use of an electric furnace, can decarbonize the surface metal .002- to .003-inch deep. If grinding that amount off does not expose hard metal, Kasenit (case-harden compound) will restore the surface. After so treating, do not quench but let the part air cool, then wire brush the compound off, reheat and quench in oil, then temper.

This steel will not decarbonize when properly done, but case hardening can be used to salvage an improper job.

Final Fitting and Assembly

After the hardening process is completed, stone the engaging surfaces with a hard Arkansas stone to get a smooth and crisp trigger. Now, your lock is ready to install on a fine rifle or pistol.

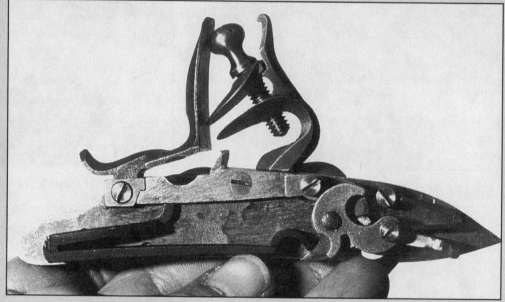

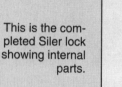

This is the completed Siler lock showing internal parts.

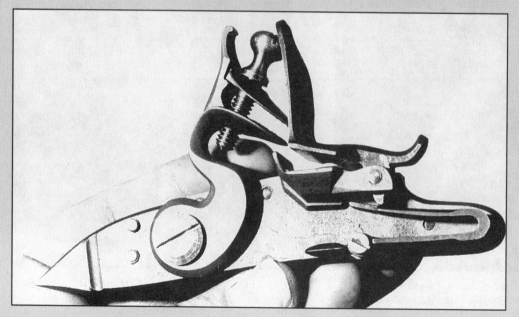

The completed Siler lock from the external side.

Assembling The Pennsylvania Style Mule Ear Lock

Here is the Mule Ear lock kit, showing parts, ready for assembly.

Tools

C-clamps or Parallel Clamps
Drill Press
Drill Press Vise
Drill Bits: $1/8$, $1/16$, $3/32$, $1/8$, $9/64$, No. 5, No. 30, No. 31, No. 33, No. 42
Chucking Reamer: $3/32$
Tap: 6-40
Hacksaw
Oxygen-Acetylene Torch
Pliers
Screwdriver
Smooth Mill Cut Files
Vise with Padded Jaws
Wire Brush

Supplies

Block of Scrap Wood
Glue or Fingernail Polish
Kasenit
Light Motor Oil
Rapid Tap Fluid
Sand with Metal Container
Short Lengths of Wire

Setting Up

Lay out all parts and check them against the parts list to be sure everything is included. There should be a lockplate, hammer, hammer pivot pin, strut, mainspring, strut pivot pin, sear, sear pivot screw, sear spring and sear engagement screw.

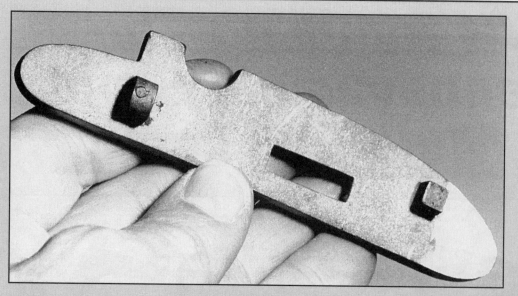

Mule Ear lock-plate, cleaned and ready for assembly. Gates and flashing have been removed.

Drilling the hammer pivot pin hole on the Mule Ear lock.

Removing Flashing and Gates

Remove flashing and gates from all parts using a hacksaw and file. This is the excess material resulting from the casting process. Keep all surfaces flat and straight, rather than rounded off or crooked.

Drilling the Lockplate

With a No. 5 bit, drill through the pre-marked hole in the large bolster on the front portion of the lockplate. This is where the strut will ride through.

Using a No. 30 bit, drill the pre-marked hole in the small bolster approximately three-fourths of the way through. This hole will house the sear spring.

On the pre-marked hole for the sear pivot screw, drill completely through with a No. 33 bit. Then take a 9/64-inch drill bit and counterbore

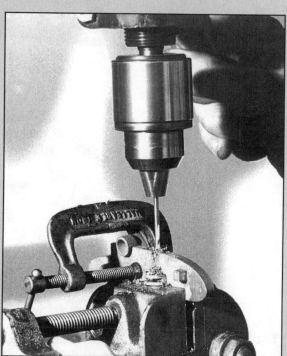

The sear spring hole drilled in sear spring stud.

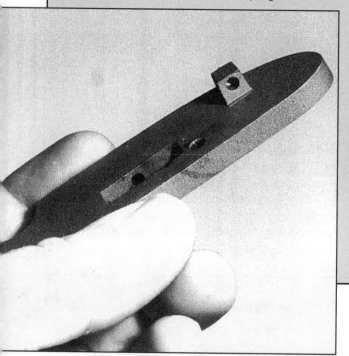

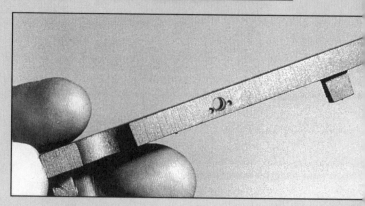

The hammer pivot pin hole in the lockplate. Center punch staking retains the pin.

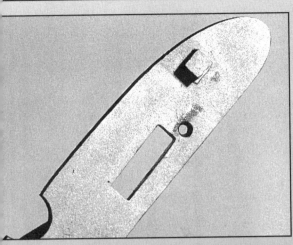

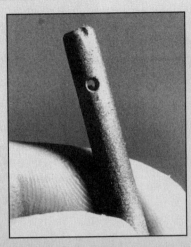

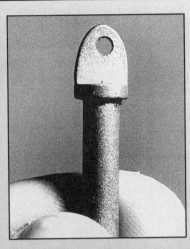

Sear pivot screw hole drilled and tapped on the Mule Ear lock.

Takedown hole drilled in the strut and marked for proper assembly.

Strut drilled for strut pin.

the hole from the *inside* of the lockplate to a depth of about 1/16-inch. This will improve the sear pin screw fit and make the hole easier to tap. Tap the No. 33 hole with a 6-40 tap completely through from the inside of the lockplate.

Drilling the Strut

The strut is worked on next. Drill a 3/32-inch hole through the cast hole in the large end of the strut. This is the end that fits into the hammer slot. Drill a 1/16-inch hole where it is spotted on the small end of the strut. This is the takedown hole. Make a note of this spotted hole and place a small file mark on the end next it to show this is the top part of the strut. When installed on the finished lock, the mark will face the top of the lockplate.

Drilling the Sear Set-Screw Hole

The sear pivot screw hole comes drilled and countersunk in this kit. Clamp the sear bottom-side up in a drill press vise. Using a No. 33 bit, drill the sear set-screw hole at the pre-spotted location, but do not tap the hole at this time.

Drilling the Strut Pivot Pin Hole

Drill and ream the strut pivot pin hole, where pre-spotted on the lockplate, with a No. 42 bit and a 3/32-inch chucking reamer. If the reamer is not available, drill it with a 3/32-inch bit.

Drilling the Hammer Pivot Pin Hole

File the rectangular hole in the lockplate so the hammer will fit inside.

Counterbored hole in the sear for sear pivot screw.

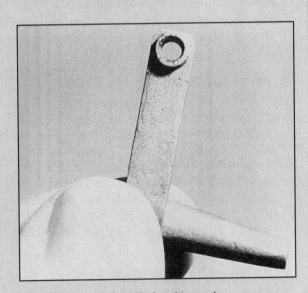

Sear set-screw hole drilled and tapped.

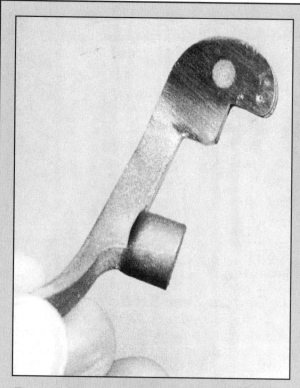

The Mule Ear hammer ready for drilling and fitting.

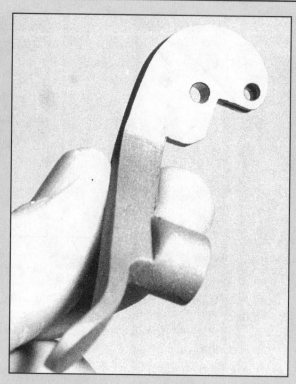

The hammer drilled for pivot pin and strut.

Place the hammer in the lock and clamp securely with a small C-clamp. Then secure the lockplate in a drill press vise and, with a No. 31 bit, drill the hammer pivot pin at the pre-marked spot. Use a sharp, new drill for this operation and plenty of cutting fluid. Back out and clean the bit frequently. This is a deep hole, so go slowly. Once the hole is completely drilled through the lockplate and hammer, replace the bit with a 1/8-inch bit and clean up the No. 31 hole. This makes a more perfect fit for the 1/8-inch hammer pivot pin.

Drilling the Sear Notch Hole

Assemble the hammer and strut without springs. Engage the sear into the lockplate. Pull the hammer to full-cock position, or as far as it will travel in that direction, and keep it in that position. In a drill press vise, tighten the sear down so it will not move. With hammer at full-cock, run a No. 33 drill bit into the bottom of the hammer .060- to .070-inch deep. This must be a clean cut, as this is the sear notch hole.

Installing the Sear Set-Screw

Now disassemble the lock and thread the sear nose with a 6-40 tap and install the sear set-screw. This screw is very hard, so be careful not to break the head slot. The sear head set-screw will stick up about .050-inch above the sear. Use glue or fingernail polish on top of the sear set-screw to hold it in place.

Hardening the Hammer

Now harden the hammer at the sear notch hole following the kit directions to the letter. The hammer is constructed of 1095 steel and should only be hardened around the sear hole. Do not harden the ears of the hammer, as they may crack when driving in the strut pin. Make certain the ears can be filed easily, which indicates they are not overly hard.

Heat the hammer sear hole with the torch flame applied to opposite side of the hammer, to prevent burning the sear hole. Heat to a cherry red color (1500 degrees Farenheit) and quench only the sear hole in lightweight oil. Air cool the rest of the hammer.

At this time, if you cannot easily make a file mark in the ears, then they are too hard. Draw the ears to a yellow color with a torch. Then allow the hammer to air cool. You should now be able to file the ears. If not, reheat the ears again. Do not draw the area around the sear engagement hole, as this may cause it to get too soft.

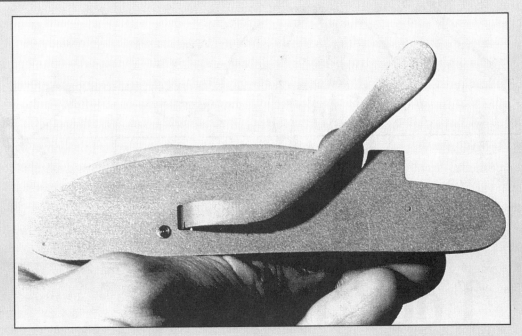

This is the completed Mule Ear lock.

A view of the completed Mule Ear lock from the internal side.

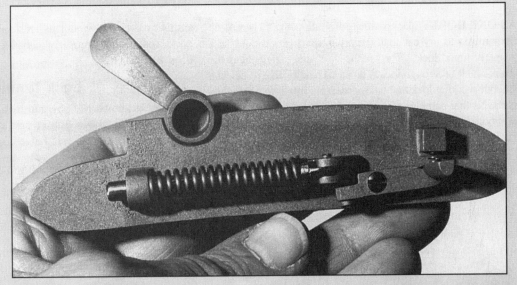

Assembling the Lock

After the hammer is hardened, reassemble the lock as follows: Clamp the lockplate into a vise with padded jaws. Position the lock with the inside facing upward.

Use a pair of pliers to grip the large end of the strut, place the mainspring on the strut, and with the body squarely behind the pliers and strut, force the strut through the bolster until the disassembly hole appears and slide a small pin through it. Now relieve all pressure and the strut is captured in place.

Insert the hammer in its respective hole and pin it in place with the hammer pivot pin.

Pull the hammer rearward until the strut and the strut pivot hole in the hammer align, then drive in the roll pin.

Grasp the lock with the hammer spur held by the first two fingers and with the back of the lock cradled by thumb and forefinger; pull the hammer back, removing tension on the takedown pin. Remove the pin and let the hammer slowly ride forward. Be careful not to pinch your fingers with the hammer.

Place the sear spring in its hole in the sear spring bolster. Press the sear into place. Insert the pivot screw and thread it into place. The sear should fit snugly against the lockplate without binding. It should also work freely on the pivot screw.

Lock Tuning

AS ONE HOBBY blackpowder gunsmith put it, "There is no finer music to my ear than the crisp, sharp snick-snick of a properly tuned lock." The antithesis of that statement is the clunk-clunk of a rough lock. The ear is readily able to detect a smooth-working lock that enjoys properly fitted, well-polished parts. Neither hammer nor sear bind or make contact on metal or wood. Internal parts of the lock function with precision. The hammer feels like it is pivoting on a roller bearing, with silky smooth travel throughout its arc from nose-forward to full-cock. That's what a properly tuned lock is all about. *Polishing is the key.*

Lock Tuning

As a blackpowder hobby gunsmith, it's wise to remember that the well-tuned lock is more than a joy to the ear. It's a joy to the eye, too, at the target range. Lock time, the interval or

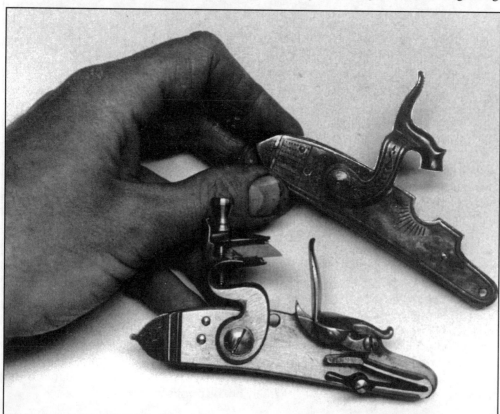

Here is a flintlock and a percussion lock, ready for tuning.

Flintlock Hints

Here are a few special pointers associated with tuning the flintlock:

- Polish the engagement point where the frizzen spring puts tension on the frizzen. This gives smoother frizzen movement as the frizzen falls from the battery position.
- Be certain to match the leading edge of the flint to the face of the frizzen. This is easily accomplished by loosening the jaw screw and allowing the hammer to ease forward until the edge of the flint is matched against the face of the frizzen. The flint is held in place (with fingers) while the jaw screw is retightened. Now the edge of the flint will be mated against the face of the frizzen, which is best for creating sparks. This is a minor point, but worth attending to. Also, be certain the flint is of high quality and sharpness. A high-quality flint, properly knapped, is probably of greatest importance in the creation of adequate sparks.
- Be certain the flint is held firmly in the jaws of the hammer. Replace worn leather.
- Check the location of the touchhole. Sometimes a slow-firing lock is the product of a poorly placed touchhole, whereby the spark from the pan does not have a chance to fly directly into the touchhole. When this condition is

A good visual test for a properly aligned flint—lower the hammer carefully until the flint rests against the face of the frizzen and check for contact. Note that the edge of this flint makes full contact with the face of the frizzen. This can be adjusted by loosening the jaw screw, allowing the flint to make contact, and then tightening the jaw screw.

serious, the original touchhole may have to be plugged, and a new touchhole liner installed.

- The frizzen face must be properly hardened in order to create sparks. So you may have to case-harden the frizzen if it is improperly hardened. If this does not work, a new frizzen may be in order.

lapse between trigger pull and powder charge detonation, is not terribly fast on a muzzleloader to begin with, and even slower on a poorly tuned lock, affecting overall accuracy. Furthermore, trigger pull is an important part of lock tuning. The trigger mechanism is an integral part of the lock, and a heavy trigger pull with creep does nothing to aid accuracy, whereas a light (but safe), crisp pull aids the shooter in getting that shot off with the least disturbance of aim.

Here is a commercial mainspring cramp—this one offered by Dixie Gun Works.

Lock Tuning Tools

A few simple, inexpensive tools—combined with a couple hours of patient work at a smooth, flat surface—can result in a tuned lock. Tools include: a small box to hold loose parts; screwdrivers that fit the various screw heads associated with the lock to be tuned; a commercial mainspring cramp or small crescent wrench or Vise Grips; a 1/8-inch drift pin punch; small ballpeen hammer, 2- to 4-ounce head; a selection of metal files; light machine oil; three sheets of wet/dry sandpaper, 320-, 400- and 600-grit; small stones of medium and fine cut are also useful for this project, however, the above-mentioned sandpaper will suffice for polishing when placed on a flat block of steel; gun oil for smooth reassembly; and an abrasive jewelling tool used with valve grinding compound is an option.

Lock Tuning Done Easily

Since the internal workings of either a percussion lock or a flintlock are, for the purposes of lock tuning, the same, this chapter does not differentiate between the two types, except for a few important remarks on the flinter above. Certain percussion locks of later design may have a stirrup on the tumbler, a device which engages the mainspring. And on the flintlock, of course, the frizzen spring along with the frizzen are located on the exterior of the unit. Otherwise, lock structure is sufficiently similar to allow a single discussion on both types.

Tuning a Lock

Tools

Ballpeen Hammer, 2- or 4-oz. Head
Drift Pin Punch, 1/8-inch
Files
Jewelling Tool
Mainspring Cramp, Small Crescent Wrench
    or Vise Grips
Screwdrivers
Vise

Supplies

Flat Block of Steel
Gun Oil
Light Machine Oil
Polishing Stones of Medium and Fine Cut
Sandpaper, Wet/Dry 320-, 400- and 600-grit
Small Box
Valve Grinding Compound

Setting Up

Study the lock first. This means investigating it not only for the obvious purpose of determining its structure, but also for quality. Run it through its cycle of operation several times to determine all points of contact between parts. Locate all bearing surfaces and make mental, if not written, notes concerning probable points of contact that can use polishing. (Be sure to retain all lock parts in a box for safekeeping. Parts tend to get lost easily.)

Removing the Mainspring

Bring the mainspring under control. A mainspring cramp serves this purpose. The hammer is brought to full-cock first, then the cramp is placed on the mainspring to keep it

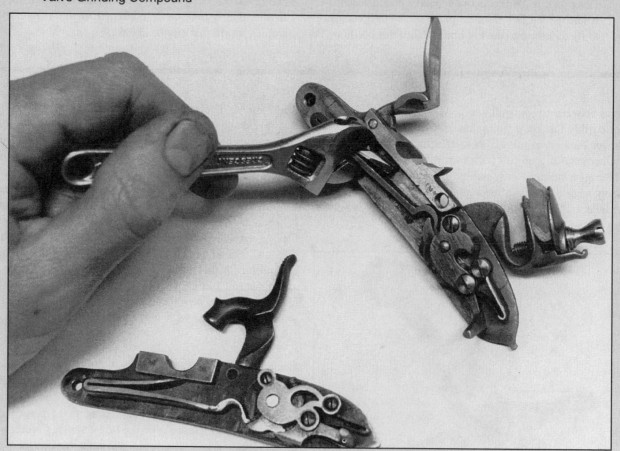

This is the hammer in the cocked position (top) with a crescent wrench used as a mainspring cramp. The bottom lock shows the mainspring in the fired, relaxed, position. Note: Although the crescent wrench is employed here as a spring cramp, there is such a specialized tool. It may be purchased from Dixie Gun Works, Mountain State Muzzleloading or Log Cabin Sport Shop.

compressed, just as if the lock were permanently in the battery or cocked position. We do not want to compress the spring any further—we only want to control it while in the full-cock position. Grasp the hammer and release the sear. The spring cramp now has the mainspring under control, and the spring can be removed from the lockplate. A pair of Vise Grips or a small crescent wrench can be substituted for a spring cramp, but only with care.

Tip: If tension on the mainspring is released by loosening the Vise Grips or wrench, be certain to note the location of the jaws on the spring, so when it is recompressed for installation on the lock, the Vise Grips or wrench are placed on the same spot of the spring. The cramp can be left in place on the spring while work is done on the lock, but it must not be left in place over a long period of time because the spring may take a permanent set.

Important: If the lock has a stirrup connecting the mainspring and tumbler, it must be returned to the same position when the lock is reassembled. If this isn't done, the lock may fail to function properly. Undue stress will be placed on the stirrup or connecting point on the mainspring or tumbler. Take note of that position before disassembly.

Removing the Sear Spring

The goal of this step is to remove the sear spring. Loosen the screw holding the sear spring and gently pry the spring away from

Removing the sear spring with a screwdriver.

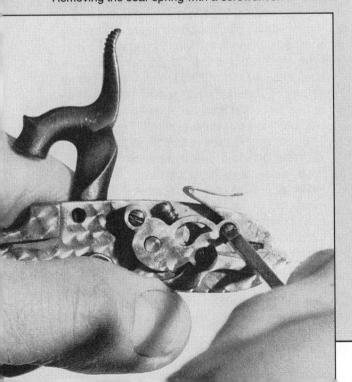

the recess that holds it in the lockplate. Hold your thumb on the spring to control it. Once the tension is eased, remove it completely from the lock and place it in the box with the rest of the parts. Leave the screw in the sear spring so it will not get mixed in with other screws in the box.

Removing Sear and Bridle

Remove the sear and place it in the box with the rest of the parts. Next, remove the bridle. This exposes the tumbler. Be careful! If

Removing the sear screw with a screwdriver.

Removing the bridle from the lock. The bridle is between the thumb and forefinger.

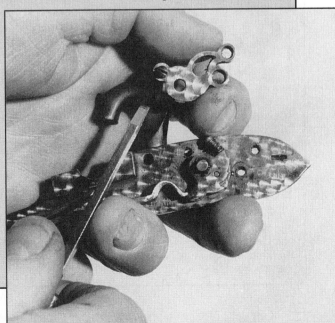

Removing the hammer from the tumbler using a drift punch inserted into the hammer screw hole.

there is a fly in the tumbler, it can be on either side. If it is on the left-hand side of the tumbler, it will be readily visible. Remove it immediately and put it in the parts box for safekeeping. If the fly is on the right-hand or lockplate side of the tumbler, care must be exercised when the hammer and tumbler are separated so the fly does not escape and become lost.

Removing Hammer from Tumbler

The next step is removing the hammer from the tumbler. Hammer screws often have a very thin head slot, plus the screw may be extremely tight. It is imperative under these conditions to have a screwdriver that fits the hammer screw head slot *perfectly* or damage may occur, either to the slot or the lockplate should the screwdriver slip. Once the hammer is removed, the tumbler must be moved away from the hammer. The best way to accomplish this is to place the lockplate on top of a vise or similar hard surface, place a drift punch down inside the threaded portion of the tumbler and firmly, but gently, tap the punch until the tumbler slides out of its fit with the hammer. If there is a fly in the tumbler, make provisions to catch the tumbler as it falls away from the hammer and lockplate. Do not use a screwdriver to pry the hammer off the tumbler from the outside of the lockplate. This could score the lockplate and/or the hammer, and it does not work very well anyway.

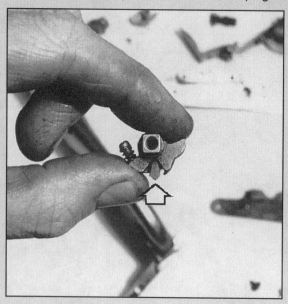

Held between the smith's fingers is a tumbler, with a fly, which is seen at the lowermost position on the tumbler (arrow). Notice the pointed portion of the fly. Remember, the fly engages the sear to override the half-cock notch.

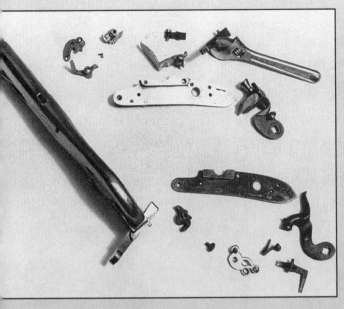

Two locks completely disassembled—one using a crescent wrench as a mainspring cramp, the other using Vise Grips as a cramp.

Examining Lock Parts

The lock is now disassembled. Study all parts. If any of them show deep pits or machine marks, they will require careful, light filing before polishing commences. *Note:* If the sear and tumbler are soft enough to be filed, they eventually will have to be case-hardened because they are too soft. However, to save time later, go ahead and file, as well as polish, before having them case-hardened. After all rough parts are filed smooth, polishing is in order. The sequence of parts polishing is not important, as long as every piece receives attention. Polishing with a nice selection of stones is ideal, but wet/dry sandpaper combined with a smooth, hard surface works well. It's a good idea to lay the sandpaper on a small block of steel to keep the surfaces flat during the polishing process.

Polishing Lock Parts

With a piece of 320 wet/dry sandpaper on a flat surface, plus a few drops of light oil on the sandpaper, start with the lockplate. It has the most area to polish, and the new sandpaper is best for this work. The part is literally scrubbed back and forth across the oiled sandpaper to polish it. Keep your strokes even and straight for best results. After using 320 paper, a piece of 400-grit paper is substituted and the part is repolished. If a high polish is desired, further finishing may be accomplished with 600-grit paper. The use of 600-

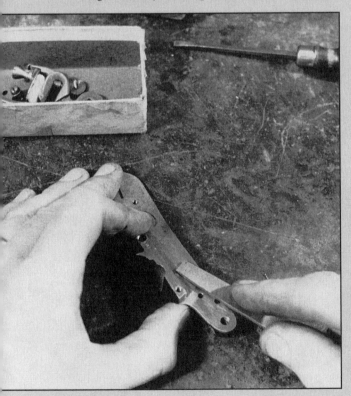

Carefully filing machine marks from the inside of the lockplate. Note the parts box (top) to retain all lock parts during the entire tuning operation.

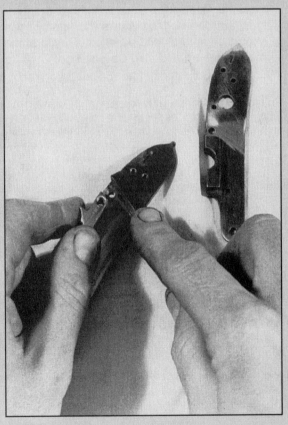

Hand polishing the inside of a lockplate with a stone.

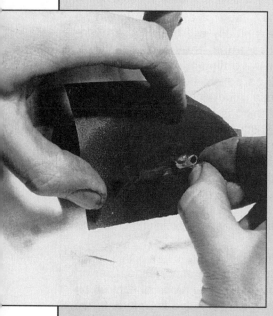
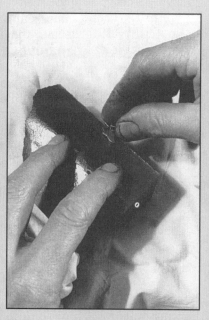

Polishing the inside portion of a sear using 320 wet/dry sandpaper on a steel block.

Polishing a tumbler using 320 wet/dry sandpaper on a steel block.

Polishing the portion of the tumbler where the mainspring contacts the tumbler.

grit requires time and patience, but it's worth the effort in terms of results. After the plate is adequately polished, move on to the bridle, tumbler and sear.

Note: On flintlocks, including percussion locks of the flintlock style such as the Siler lock, the mainspring rides directly on the tumbler, and the surface where the spring rides should be smooth and polished. The tip of the mainspring should also be polished to make

the two engaging surfaces between the tumbler and mainspring work smoothly.

Every *working* surface must be polished, but only to the point of removing tool marks. In most cases, it is unwise to remove more metal than necessary to obtain a smooth surface.

Warning: The sear engagement can be set at this time, but this is a job for a professional gunsmith, because a bad job may cause accidental discharge of the firearm.

Polishing the inside of a lockplate using 320 wet/dry sandpaper on a steel block.

Polishing the inside of a bridle using 320 wet/dry sandpaper on a steel block.

Polishing the front portion of the mainspring with a small stone. This is the portion of the mainspring that contacts the tumbler.

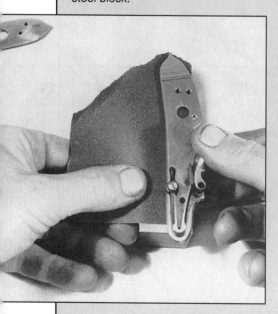

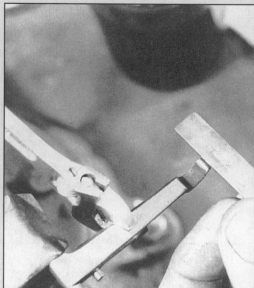

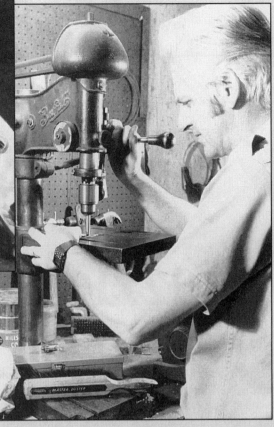
Jewelling a lockplate with a drill press and jewelling tool.

A properly tuned, polished and jewelled lock. Note the stirrup between the tumbler and mainspring.

Jewelling Lock Parts

The internal parts may be jewelled at this time, and Brownells offers a special tool for this task. Jewelling creates a swirling effect on the metal. A little valve grinding compound smeared on the parts promotes a more pronounced jewelling pattern. Jewelling helps retain oil and looks sexy, but is not necessary.

Assembling the Lock

After polishing and/or jewelling, all parts must be thoroughly cleaned to remove any grit left behind. Don't forget to clean the screw holes and threads, too. Apply a light coat of gun oil on all parts before reassembly.

Note: Be careful when tightening the screws that hold the bridle and sear on the lockplate. On some locks, when these screws are completely snug, the sear or tumbler may bind. If this occurs, slightly back out the screws to release tension so the tumbler and sear work smoothly and freely.

Test the function of the lock. There should be a silky smoothness not enjoyed before. The sear should snap into half-cock and full-cock notches with a positive snick! snick! sound. If the lock drags when cocked, this indicates that there are high spots on certain parts. To locate these problem areas, look for scratches left from high spots on the guilty parts. The lock must then be disassembled and the problem parts repolished.

Lock tuning is important. One lock I worked

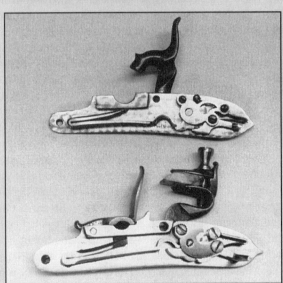
A pair of tuned locks, percussion (top) and flintlock—the top jewelled, the bottom polished, but not jewelled.

on was so rough that I could actually watch the hammer fall. After tuning (polishing), the lock functioned perfectly. Before tuning, the rifle performed poorly at the range, but afterward became a joy to handle and fire, shooting tight groups.

Muzzleloader Triggers

FROM THE DAYS of crossbow to the present, numerous trigger designs have gone from drawing board to reality. Some are extremely complicated, while others are simple by comparison. The blackpowder hobbyist does not need to understand extremely complex triggers. He must, however, have a grasp of the basic trigger types associated with front-loaders. The following is an overview of the more common muzzleloader triggers encountered today. Remember that with muzzleloaders, most triggers serve the function of tripping the sear. An exception is the modern in-line ignition muzzleloader with a trigger which is a release-type instead of a trip-type mechanism.

Single Trigger

The simplest trigger for muzzleloaders is the single trigger style, pinned directly into the stock. There is no trigger plate. Also, there is no adjustment in this trigger design. It is a basic system, almost crude in function, yet effective. The single trigger is usually found on inexpensive firearms. Old-time smoothbore fowling pieces often wore single triggers, as did yesteryear's trade muskets. Unless the hobbyist is restoring an old firearm that originally had a single trigger, and he is interested in duplication for authenticity, there is no place in modern times for the simple single trigger.

Single Trigger with Metal Trigger Plate

The next step up in trigger design is the single trigger mounted on a metal trigger plate, rather than pinned directly to the stock. Although this system remains basic, it is better than the first style described. The trigger plate acts as an anchor for a tang screw, and it also serves as a solid base for the trigger to pivot upon. The single trigger suffers from the problem of travel before engaging the sear. This superfluous travel can be corrected by installing a small, weak mouse-trap-type spring on the trigger plate. The spring holds the trigger against the sear, precluding unwanted travel. The trick is to use a spring with the correct tension. The spring must be strong enough to support the trigger, but not so strong that it interferes with the proper function of the lock.

Another means of eliminating trigger travel before sear engagement is to drill and tap a small screw directly under the trigger. The screw is threaded to engage the trigger and lift it up until it nearly touches the sear, eliminating unwanted travel in the trigger. Any adjustment to make a lighter trigger pull with this system is accomplished within the lock itself, dealing with sear and hammer engagement, and not with the trigger directly.

The single trigger on a metal trigger plate is found on many rifles and pistols—a popular design that is both simple and effective. In fact, these triggers can be found in many different treatments, from dead basic to fancy scroll-bottomed units with open filigree work in the web behind the trigger.

Single-Set Trigger

This is a significant step up from the two more basic types already mentioned. Single sets may take a number of forms, but the simplest entails a split spring with a roller on one end that engages the front, top corner of the single trigger blade. The trigger blade must have a radius cut to allow the roller to set and fire. The trigger is pivoted on a trigger plate. The spring and roller are positioned so, when the trigger is *pushed forward*, the roller travels along the trigger blade until it reaches the top corner or "spike" of the blade. At this point, the trigger is set. A stop or adjustment screw is positioned in the trigger plate to limit trigger travel.

By adjusting this screw up or down, the engagement between the roller and trigger is controlled. This, in turn, reg-

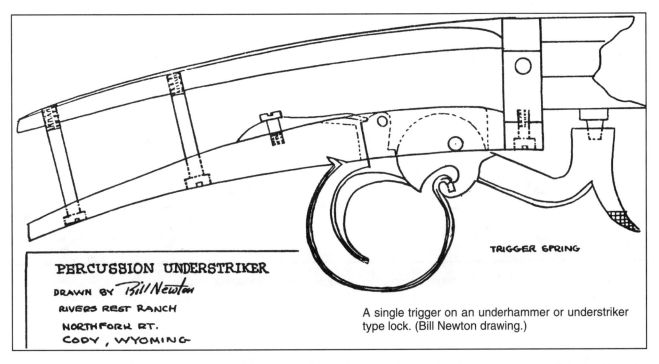

PERCUSSION UNDERSTRIKER
DRAWN BY *Bill Newton*
RIVERS REST RANCH
NORTHFORK RT.
CODY, WYOMING

TRIGGER SPRING

A single trigger on an underhammer or understriker type lock. (Bill Newton drawing.)

ulates the pressure required on the trigger before the roller pops over the spike of the trigger blade to slam the trigger against the sear, setting off the lock. The single-set trigger requires careful manufacture. Furthermore, precise adjustment is demanded to get the most from this type of trigger. When correctly built and adjusted, the single-set system performs well. The advantage of this design is a beautifully light trigger pull, but the trigger must be set before the lock can be cocked.

Single-Set (Multiple Function) Trigger

This single-set design differs from the more basic single-set trigger because the gun can be fired in two ways. The trigger can be set, thereby creating a very light letoff, or the trigger can by pulled without setting, which will also fire the gun. There is still only one trigger in this setup, but the mechanism is quite sophisticated. The trigger is set with a push forward. Click! The firearm is ready to be shot. Trigger pull in the set mode is measured in mere ounces, not pounds, of pull, which makes this form of the single-set trigger ideal for target work. Single-set triggers were found on some dueling pistols, target pistols and high-grade pistols. In reality, the blackpowder hobby gunsmith will rarely encounter this particular trigger type, but knowledge of its existence is useful. An easy way to spot this type of trigger is to look for the small set-screw located directly behind the trigger. This

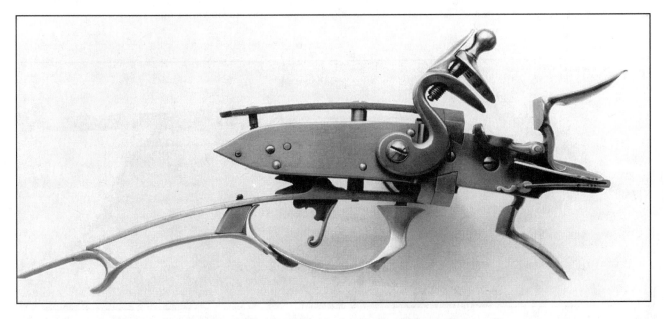

This is a single trigger pivoted in the trigger plate on a high-quality swivel breech flintlock rifle.

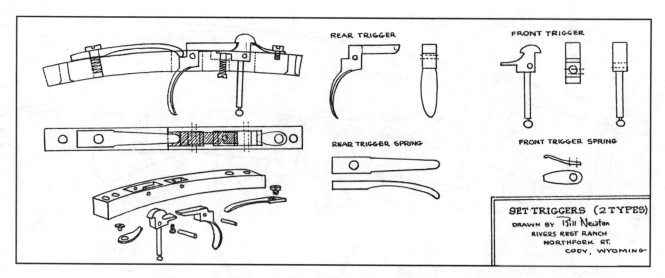

This is a single-lever double-set trigger system. (Bill Newton drawing.)

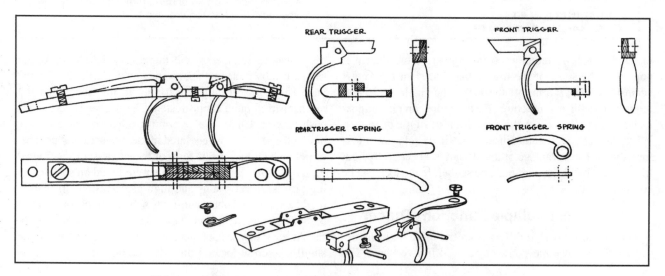

This is a double-lever double-set trigger system. (Bill Newton drawing.)

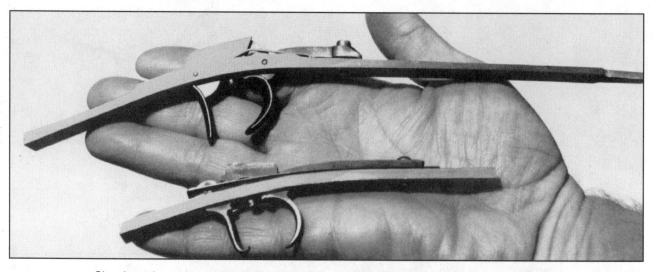

Showing a long trigger plate on a double-lever double-set trigger (above) and a short trigger plate on a single-lever double-set trigger.

The rear trigger has been pulled back to set the front trigger. The rifle will be fired with the front trigger.

screw adjusts the engagement of the trigger and controls trigger pull letoff (weight) when the trigger is in the set mode.

Single-Lever Double-Set Trigger

There are two types of double-set triggers—the single-lever and double-lever, both with two triggers. On the single-lever, the rear trigger must be pulled in order to set the front or "hair" trigger. As with the single-set trigger, an audible click announces the trigger is in the set mode. The object of setting the rear trigger is to promote a very light letoff for the front trigger. In the set position, a few ounces of pressure activates the lock and shoots the firearm. This particular system is simple and excellent. Double-set triggers of this type are found on original percussion guns of medium to high quality and numerous old-time target firearms.

In certain double-set trigger designs, the trigger must be set or the gun cannot be fired because the lock will not cock with the trigger unset. In this particular design, the lock need

not have a fly in the tumbler to override the half-cock notch because the trigger maintains tension on the sear upon striking, thereby causing the sear to miss (not engage) the half-cock notch automatically.

There is an adjustment screw between the triggers on this setup. The screw is threaded through the trigger plate and engages the front trigger, which controls the set trigger engagement. The deeper the screw is threaded upward, the less engagement there is between the front and rear trigger, hence the lighter the trigger pull becomes. Remember, the trigger can be set too light for the experience of the shooter, and therefore the set-screw must be adjusted with safety in mind.

Double-Lever Double-Set Trigger

This is the most common type of trigger found on today's muzzleloaders, as well as many originals. The gun can be fired in either the set or unset mode with this type of trigger.

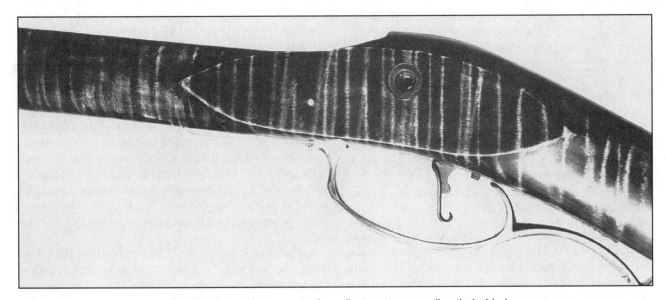

On the single trigger, note the adjustment screw directly behind the trigger used to take up overtravel.

This is a modern trigger on a modern muzzleloader.

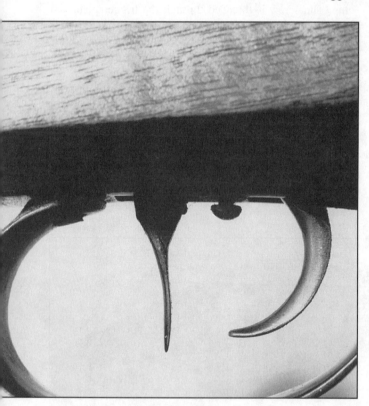

On the double-set trigger, note the adjustment screw directly between the set and hair triggers.

Therefore, the double-lever double-set trigger is versatile. There must be a fly in the tumbler when this trigger is used, in order for the sear to override the half-cock notch. There may be a short trigger plate as found on earlier rifles, or the long trigger plate as found on the Hawken Brothers' rifles. The long trigger plate readily accommodates an anchor point for a tang screw.

This extra steel in the wrist also adds a measure of strength. The double-lever trigger is so effective that most marksmen set the rear trigger as a matter of practice, even though the gun can be fired without setting it.

Once again, there is an adjustment screw between the triggers on this system, as described for the single-lever double-set trigger.

Trigger Variations

There have been numerous trigger system variations over the years. In recent times, Thompson/Center's Patriot single-shot target pistol used a double-lever double-set trigger that worked in reverse of the norm. The front trigger was the set, while the rear trigger was the hair. This was done, in part, to afford better reach of the finger to the firing trigger, whereas if the front trigger were the firing trigger, it would nearly be out of reach due to the design of the pistol stock.

Among the different trigger systems, the triggers themselves may be of various designs. Some are curved; others are straight. A thin front trigger is often found on the single-lever double-set system because there is minimal pressure demand on this trigger. Artistic carving may be found in the guard web directly behind the trigger. These touches are products of the gunmaker's imagination and taste. That is why there have been so many hundreds of artistic variations throughout the history of muzzleloader craftsmanship.

Varied trigger knowledge is important to the blackpowder hobby gunsmith because it adds to his understanding of firearms. In reality, the hobbyist will work mainly with the triggers that are provided with the kit he builds, or the triggers that exist on blackpowder firearms he purchases.

Gunstock Materials

TODAY'S SMITH, PROFESSIONAL or amateur, works with more gunstock materials than his predecessors, by far. Over the years, hundreds of different woods, as well as synthetics, have been used to create gunstocks. Most woods were found unsatisfactory, for one reason or another, and synthetics have come to the fore only in the comparatively recent past. English gunmakers of the 19th century, according to W.W. Greener, worked with a great variety of woods for stocks, including beech, which was well-known and apparently favored for its heaviness, although it had, according to Greener, "no figure." Birch was considered inferior to beech, Greener pointed out, but ash was "pretty." Birdseye maple was not appreciated by smiths of the time, he wrote.

In America, numerous woods were employed in gunmaking. Cherry found favor with some. Tulip wood was tried, as was Honduras walnut, among dozens of other walnuts. The English decided walnut is probably the best gunstock wood and, of course, all gunmakers everywhere agree that walnut is hard to beat. Fine wood has always been limited in supply, and that goes for walnut as well as other types, but it has been possible over the years to find enough walnut to go around. And it still is. In spite of walnut's excellent properties, however, Captain John G.W. Dillin, author of *The Kentucky Rifle*, pointed out that maple was king of stock materials during the golden age of gunmaking in early America.

"The stock, invariably running to the end of the muzzle, in flintlock days was made, wherever possible, of curly maple, cut from both the sugar and red maple tree, one tree in about fifteen being of sufficient curl to answer the demand of the smith, whose taste demanded fine wood," wrote Dillin. No wonder curly maple was chosen. It was then, and remains, a beautiful wood. A good piece, properly finished, serves well as a gunstock and, with personal preference considered, remains as handsome a stockmaking material as anyone could ask for.

But that was then. This is now. Today, muzzleloader stocks are made from numerous woods, as well as synthetics. Fine custom rifles demand great wood, and today's handmade smokepole often carries a stock of curly maple. But more commercial blackpowder rifle stocks are built of walnut than maple. Thompson/Center, for example, uses American walnut on its firearms, having access to a supply of excellent wood for the purpose. Of course, the same company will sell you a rifle with a synthetic stock. It's a mark of the times—the old-fashioned gunstock remains built of curly maple, cherry and other woods, but synthetics are popular, too.

The modern gunmaker, when choosing stock material, needs to specially consider the wood used for stocks. It should be relatively light in weight. Ironwood, for example, has ample strength to make a gunstock for any rifle. However, ironwood is so dense that it is too heavy for practical gunstock making. So gunstock wood should be strong, but on the lightweight side. The grain of the wood must be close, not porous. Open-grain wood is not ideal for embellishment, whereas closed grain is capable of accepting inlays and carving, while at the same time thwarting moisture. Tight-grain wood is also less likely to warp than open-grain wood.

For strength, the grain pattern should be relatively straight through the wrist and grip area of the stock. Straight grain is also acceptable in the forestock region. In the buttstock, wavy grain patterns can be beautiful, and this wood is sought after. The blank must be cut precisely so the best features of the wood are present where they belong—straight grain where this is desirable, curly grain where appearance is paramount. Good gunstock wood has an absolute minimum of sapwood which is pithy and soft. So a blank with no sapwood is best.

A light discussion of various woods includes many that are not popular in the world of muzzle-loading, but deserve mention because they can be used. For example, a few takedown Storey Custom Buggy Rifles were built using French walnut because the person who ordered them wanted that wood for his stocks. There are several kinds of walnut, all suitable for blackpowder gunstocks, even though some are seldom used for the purpose.

Walnut

This is the most used wood for gunstocks because it has the properties best suited to building a stock. American walnut, also known as black walnut, is native to this country. It is hard and dense. Some pieces exhibit a beautiful burl figure. English walnut is the same genus and species as French walnut, and the terms are interchangeable. There may be argument about this, but botanists say these two woods are the same. Sometimes there is confusion in naming woods because of geography. Walnut grown in France is, by fact, French walnut, but scientifically it does not differ from English walnut. The same wood may also be grown in Germany, in which case it is German walnut, but that does not change its genus and species.

Claro walnut is a hybrid taken from trees that show both English and American walnut traits. Claro is often grown in California, so the wood is also known as California walnut. Circassian walnut is an Asian strain that gets its name from the Caucasus Mountains. This wood is all but unavailable today, yet the hobby gunsmith should at least know about it for the purpose of reference. Turkish walnut resembles Circassian in beauty and grain structure. The best pieces of Turkish walnut have contrasting close-grain coloration. There are numerous other walnuts, far too many for worthwhile inclusion here. But in the main, the modern smith will work with American, Claro and French/English walnut when, indeed, he uses walnut at all for muzzleloader gunstocks.

American walnut is the least expensive of the three. It is a good wood and somewhat underrated. American walnut of high quality is rising steadily in price. Because of the cost, some factory rifles are now made with cheaper woods, such as birch stained to resemble walnut, rather than true American walnut. Also, thousands of American military rifles were once stocked with black walnut. Today, a synthetic stock is used on the M-16 service rifle because of expense, weight and durability factors. American walnut can have a beautiful grain pattern, and sometimes the color is also exceptional. Black walnut takes embellishment well, and it is sufficiently tight-grained to thwart warpage.

Claro walnut costs more than American walnut. It often car-

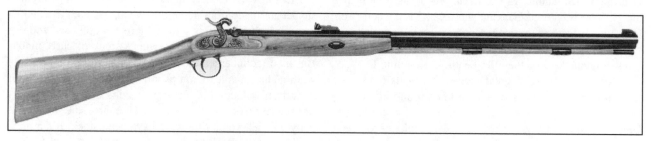

This particular piece of American walnut shows the straight grain pattern that makes for strength in a stock.

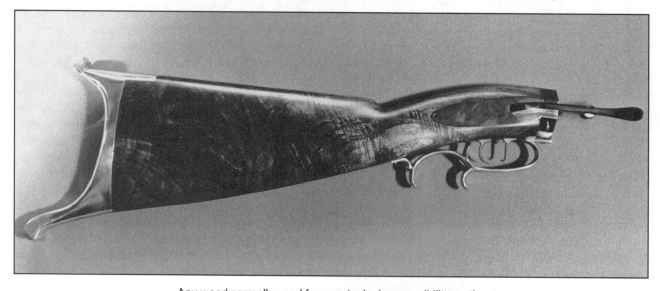

Any wood normally used for gunstocks is a possibility on the muzzleloader. This Storey custom rifle shows off its beautiful stock of American walnut.

ries a beautifully contrasting color pattern with grain tending to orange streaks. These streaks, along with yellows and golds, stand out markedly against the darker portions of the wood. Claro is not quite as dense as American walnut, and therefore may warp more easily, plus black walnut is stronger. Claro costs more because of fine figure. It can be used on muzzleloaders, of course, although Claro is not the popular choice.

English or French walnut has been used on fine muzzleloaders in the past and will continue to be used, but not to any great degree. It costs too much and is not historically correct where the "Kentucky" rifle is concerned. But cost is the biggest problem for English walnut, with some blanks running $1000 or more. That's a heap of greenbacks for a chunk of wood. English walnut carries all of the good traits of a gunstock wood, including color and density.

This brief rundown on walnut only scratches the surface. There are even sub-types within the species. For example, American walnut can be distinguished by its grain structure such as fiddleback, flame grain, crotch and burl. These names are not scientifically distinct, but they help to distinguish one American walnut blank from another.

Other Woods

Birch, as noted earlier, has been used extensively for stocks, often stained to resemble walnut. Birch is a good, strong

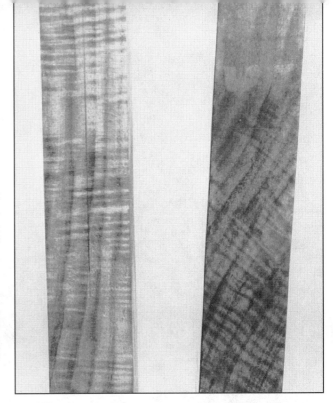

Good wood is not cheap, nor easy to find. High-grade blanks can run as high as $1000, with exceptional pieces of wood costing even more.

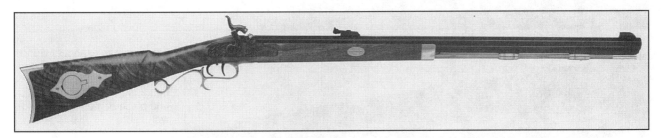

American black walnut can show good figure, as on this Thompson/Center Hawken rifle.

Don't forget that stocks are not confined to rifles alone. The grips on this CVA cap 'n' ball revolver are made of walnut.

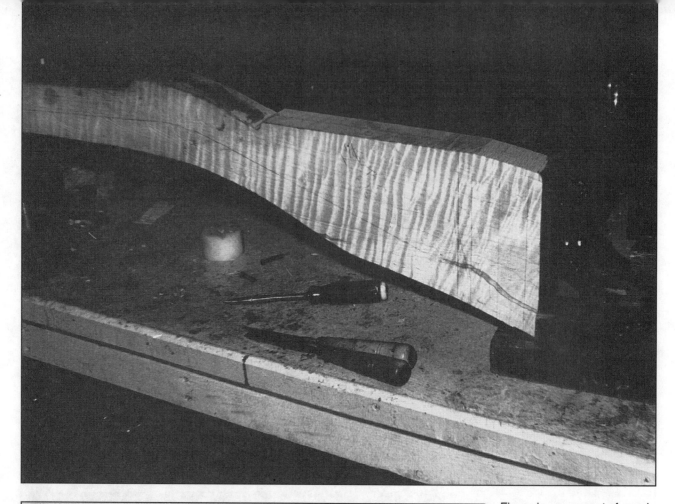

Figure is one aspect of wood that is never overlooked by the professional or hobbyist making a custom stock. This fine piece of maple is loaded with figure.

A contrasting grain pattern makes the dark stripes on this maple stock stand out.

wood. It's not necessarily pretty, but it serves well and is also a good wood for laminates. Birch is not a good choice for a custom frontloader, however. High-grade mahogany is a fine wood for furniture and is, of course, another example of a hardwood employed in gunstocks. It's less dense and softer than walnut. The cheaper grades of mahogany are useless, even for furniture. High-grade mahogany can be turned into a gunstock, but few blackpowder rifle stocks were made from this wood because of cost.

Maple, on the other hand, is the king of blackpowder gunstock wood for the Pennsylvania/Kentucky replica. Curly maple, also known as tiger tail maple, is especially handsome. Maple can be very hard because it is a close-grained wood. Fiddleback maple and ribbed figure maple are ideal for the custom blackpowder long rifle.

Fruit woods are occasionally used for gunstocks. Strong yet light, apple wood is difficult to work, but can be turned into a stock. It takes carving well, due to close grain and

Curly maple, also called tiger stripe, tiger tail and fiddleback maple, makes a handsome muzzleloader stock, as on this Mowrey Plains rifle.

The synthetic stock followed on the heels of the modern muzzleloader design. Since the modern muzleloader is not historical in nature to begin with, there is no reason the stock must be made of wood.

The laminated stock is now at home on the modern muzzleloader. This Knight MK-85 Grand American rifle is proof that laminates have arrived in the world of the blackpowder rifle.

hardness. Pear wood is similar to apple. It is an attractive wood, but has not gained great favor with American gunmakers. Wild cherry is not often used today in stockmaking. However, cherry was employed by early American stockmakers, and examples of antique muzzle-loading rifles with cherry wood stocks are not rare at all. Cherry wood does not have the personality of other stockwoods, and that is probably one reason for its lack of use here. It can turn a dull reddish-brown in color with little grain showing.

Many other lesser-known wood types can and have been used. Myrtle wood is absolutely beautiful with high-contrast grain in the better examples. It is used along the coast of Oregon in many decorative household items, including clocks and coffee tables. Myrtle is on the heavy side, and it can have soft spots. It's used very little for making blackpowder rifle gunstocks. While not historically correct, Mesquite riflestocks are strong and handsome, albeit on the heavy side. One hobby gunsmith in the Southwest built an entire series of matching muzzleloaders, all with mesquite. It can have terrific grain structure, including knots, whorls and sometimes wild patterns. But it's not always easy to find a mesquite blank, and, of course, this hardwood is difficult to work. Beechwood was known not only to the British, but also to American gunmakers. It is a strong, tough wood, but has very little figure and is low on the list of muzzleloader stock woods. Exotic woods are not included here because they are seldom used to make gunstocks and are more suited to pistol grips and forend caps for modern rifles. Of course, the hobby gunsmith can use whatever he likes for his own stock wood.

Laminated Stocks

Before the dawning of the written word, bowmakers discovered that putting two materials together in a bonded fashion increased performance and durability. So laminates are nothing new, dating to prehistoric times. While old-time frontloaders did not have laminated stocks, today's modern muzzleloader may very well have one. Laminated stocks are tough and long-lasting, although not waterproof, as sometimes believed, and should be finished just like any other wood stock. Laminated stocks can be heavy, but on big bore muzzleloaders the weight is welcomed. These stocks can be made from contrasting woods for color. Birch is often used for laminates because it is strong and can be cut into sheets. The tree is roto-milled into these sheets, then vat-dyed. Laminations are bonded together with phenolic resins. Delamination, where individual slats of wood part from each other, is all but unknown. Common laminate combinations, aside from birchwood, are walnut to walnut, walnut to cherry, walnut to maple.

Synthetics

There are at least two basic types of synthetic stocks now in use: laminated fiberglass and injection moulded. Impregnated, high-pressure laminated fiberglass cloths are coupled with chopped glass strands. Also, a grained effect can be moulded into the synthetic stock, giving the stock a wood-like appearance. The attributes of the synthetic stock are strength, durability and stability. Laminated fiberglass stocks can be lightweight, although not all are. Synthetic stocks are common today on modern muzzleloaders, although not traditional.

Stock Finishes and Finishing

THERE HAVE BEEN more gunstock finishes over the years than pages in this book. The purpose of this chapter is to familiarize the hobbyist with various finishes, as well as stains, plus outline the methods for finishing his own gunstocks.

Finishes and stains have quite a history. Bill Knight's study of Colonial stock finishes touches on a dozen types from that time period alone. Staining, for example, was done very early in arms history, and the Colonials had plenty of ways to stain wood in order to bring out the grain pattern. Curly maple demanded staining and was quite popular with old-time gunmakers. Among the stain types were plant extracts, iron oxide pigments, nitric acid with iron, potassium permanganate, chromium trioxide, and many others. Plant extracts were represented by natural dyes, often extracted by boiling wood in water to form a concentrate. Walnut husk extract, Knight notes, is just one natural dye used by early gunmakers in this country. Add all of the chemical dyes to the list, and we have a long line of stains that can be used to treat gunstocks prior to final finishing.

Finishes were probably invented to safeguard the wood, or so we think. But modern gunmakers suspect that visual improvement was soon just as important as weatherproofing when it came to applying finish to a gunstock. Most expert gunmakers have a personal preference in finishes, and many have their own unique formulas. The Colonial gunsmith, to choose a time period, made his own finish, mainly a choice between "boiled oil" or varnish, the latter costing more, according to Knight. Linseed oil was popular at the time. It was also known to the Romans and, before them, the Greeks. There is no definite history of linseed oil, but this oil does remain a viable choice today, although it has both fans and foes.

Finish Types

Linseed Oil

The fans of linseed oil argue that it is historically correct, as well as perfectly suitable as a finish. Even those who like linseed oil, however, admit that its proper application takes time, as well as hand-rubbed effort. Those who don't like it insist that a linseed oil finish never dries, and that it offers little protection against the elements, allowing moisture to pass through the finish and into the pores of the wood. This ancient finish, obtained from seeds of the flax plant, can give a beautiful finish, in time, but there is strong evidence against its ability to weatherproof a stock all by itself. It is known as "boiled linseed oil" to most of us. This does not mean that linseed oil is refined through boiling, nor should it be boiled.

The literature shows that linseed oil is refrigerated, which helps to separate out non-drying products (waxes). The oil is treated with caustic soda to further remove non-drying elements. Only then is the oil heated, not by itself, but along with petroleum products that promote drying. Now the boiled linseed oil is ready to go to work. And work it takes. Mixed about 50/50 with turpentine to penetrate the wood better, it is applied by hand and rubbed into the wood—hence, hand-rubbed finish. More on finishing methods later.

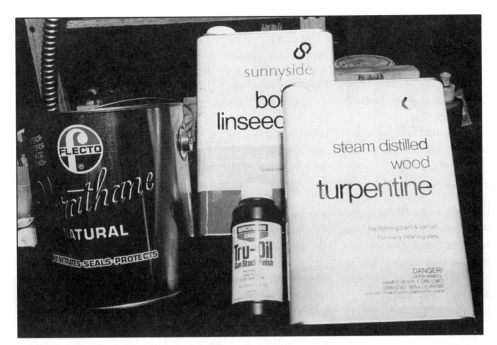

These are the four important liquids used for stock refinishing: Flecto Varathane Natural 66 Clear oil, boiled linseed oil, Tru-Oil and turpentine.

Treated Linseed Oil

While linseed oil, by itself, may not offer the kind of waterproofing a stock finish should afford, linseed oil can be mixed with other products so it does dry harder, offering a much more durable finish. Birchwood Casey Tru-Oil is a perfect example of boiled linseed oil plus varnishes and dryers. It is not a rub-in type of finish, but rather one that is applied evenly, then allowed to dry. Tru-Oil dries hard and has considerable sheen which hobby smiths may wish to reduce. (See the refinishing project in this chapter for details.) Some gunsmiths report excellent results with another mixture: linseed oil plus Flecto Varathane Plastic Oil. Proportions of this mixture seem to vary with the individual gunsmith. One mixture was 90 percent linseed and only 10 percent Varathane. The idea is to employ the values of both finishes: linseed for penetration and beauty, Varathane for hardness and waterproofing.

Consider the time investment alone. A few years ago, a stock finished with the boiled linseed oil method was the pet project of a hobby gunsmith I know. The finish was not truly completed for about a year, and this meant hand-rubbing oil into the wood at least once a week for that time period. Finally, the hobbyist added a little Varathane to his linseed oil, and within a few applications the stock began to take on a hard finish.

Varnishes

Early American gunmakers used numerous types of stains and finishes. In the old days, gunstock finishes were natural, not synthesized. They were born of vegetable, animal and mineral products. Literature from the 19th and even 18th centuries strongly suggests the cabinetmaking industry of the times preferred varnish over linseed oil as a finish. Moreover, a study of gunstocks from these periods also proves varnish was the preferred finish. It only makes sense. Did gunmakers have time to do a hand-rubbed finish on a stock? Gunsmiths were busy people, and they were also in business to make a living. Chances are terribly slim that many of them used the boiled linseed oil method of finishing a gunstock.

Varnish is a resinous solution used to provide a hard lustrous and generally transparent protective surface. Although linseed oil still has good properties, such as refinishing a rubbed out section on a stock without reworking the entire stock, it does not waterproof the wood. Varnish does offer, if not waterproof, certainly a water-resistant finish. That's why Tru-Oil, which is a linseed oil product, adds varnish. Once again, books have been written on the subject of finishes, and our forum is not the platform to discuss every type of varnish from the Egyptians' use of this finish to the modern gunsmith.

Stains

Before going into a good finish and finishing method for the modern blackpowder hobby gunsmith, here is a brief look at stains. Just imagine—before you lies a fine piece of wood, with plenty of character embodied in excellent figure for the full length of the wood. As pretty as the wood may look, especially when wetted lightly with a damp cloth to further bring out the figure, that stock could end up relatively plain looking if it is not properly stained before final finish is applied. Proper staining not only accentuates the grain pattern, it can also bring out the best possible colors in the wood. The hobbyist may wish to experiment with different stains before committing to one specific stain for a particular piece of wood. Ideally, there will be scraps from a plank with which to work. Treat these small scraps with various stains to see which one best enhances the grain pattern, as well as promoting the best color.

Some commercial stains come with built-in sealers. These are not right for gunstock staining because they can be difficult to work with. Stains that do not contain sealers are much better because they allow experimentation, such as staining one piece of wood several times with the stain going well into the wood, which may not happen if the stain contains sealers that close the grain of the wood. Wood sealer is applied later, in a separate step of the finishing process, followed by an application of commercial paste wood filler. These two steps fill the wood, providing a surface ready for the final finish.

Commercial Stains

This catch-all heading includes all of those stains available at the paint store, as well as the gunshop. There are far too many of these to list here. It's wise for the hobbyist to experiment on scrap wood with most commercial stains to ensure the result is what he wants. One good commercial stain worthy of note is Birchwood Casey's Colonial Red, which heightens the color of wood in the direction of red, as the label promises. It's best to dilute this stain about 50/50 with water before applying, as well as dampening the stock before application. Ask the salesman in the paint store what he recommends in a commercial stain for the specific wood you wish to treat. Unlike salesmen of many other products, the paint store person often knows quite a bit about his product.

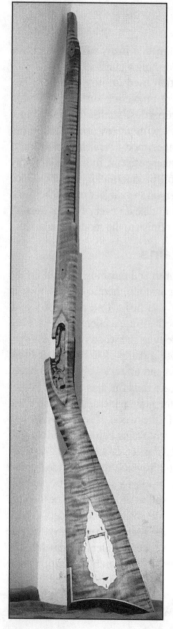

This is a natural oil finish. No stain whatsoever was used on the wood. Color and figure were well accented without stain.

Chromium Trioxide

Sound familiar? It should. Chromium trioxide was mentioned in the beginning of this chapter as a stain used by the Colonial gunsmiths of early America. It's available at pharmacies these days. What you get is a bottle with a few red crystals in it. You make stain by adding water to the bottle. Chromium trioxide is best applied to a damp wood surface, so take a clean cloth, wet it, squeeze it out well, then rub the stock all over to dampen the wood. Then, apply the chromium trioxide stain rapidly, but evenly, using a soft, clean cloth. Chromium trioxide is not the last word in stock stains, but it is mentioned because of its authenticity. In fact, wood stained with chromium trioxide may tend to a greenish hue as the years pass. Chromic oxide is a compound, CrO_2, used for pigments, incidentally, and it is green in color.

Potassium Permanganate

Here is another old-time stain, as mentioned by Bill Knight in his study of Colonial gunstock finishing. $KMnO_4$ is a purple-colored crystal. Its use as an oxidizing agent in antiseptics and in various deodorizers is well known. It also is available at pharmacies in the form of tablets to be dissolved in water. Although the tablets are purple in color, they do not turn stock wood purple. It is important to neutralize the acid in the wood before applying this stain because the acid will counteract the potassium permanganate, bleaching it out, as it were, returning the stock to its original color after a period of time. Use ordinary baking soda to treat the wood. Make a solution by mixing a couple tablespoons of baking soda in 8 ounces of water, and apply this mixture to the stock before staining. Potassium permanganate heightens the brown colors in the wood and may also bring out a mild yellow color.

Nitric Acid

One more old-time stain is worth noting, and that is aquafortis, mentioned often in old-time gunsmithing books. The name means "strong water," which is appropriate because aquafortis is simply commercial nitric acid diluted in water, as sold for hundreds of years. The initial application of aquafortis brings out yellow to green hues. The stock looks awful. However, heat changes the color of the wood. A portable electric plate is ideal for this work because it has no flame to burn the wood. Simply hold the aquafortis-treated stock above the electric element of the plate and move the stock constantly to

Pistol grips, as on this caplock revolver, make excellent projects for the hobbyist.

ensure even heat. The wood will change from yellows and greens to a burnt umber (dark red) hue.

Kitchen Stains

Many wood stains come straight out of the kitchen. Once again, it is wise for the blackpowder gunsmithing hobbyist to try unfamiliar (unproved) stains on scrap wood before using them on stocks. However, some kitchen stains are worthwhile. Strong tea can stain wood, for example. The effect is mild and can be pleasing on a stock that requires very little enhancement. Strong coffee works the same way. Red or purple berries, raspberries or blueberries, boiled in water to make an "ink" will stain wood. So will grape juice concentrate, as well as a multitude of different food colorings. Shoe and clothing dyes also work, as does iodine, just to mention a few.

Preparing the Wood

Fixing Small Dents

Minor dents can be removed by applying water to the surface of the stock. This raises the wood and, in many instances, uplifts the interior pocket of a dent more than the wood surrounding it. Sanding brings the pocket of the dent and the surface of the stock closer together. Repeating the process can

Under harsh field conditions, a good finish is imperative. This well-sealed and oil-finished stock will not absorb moisture—if it's finished with the process described in this chapter.

eliminate minor dents. Larger dents demand more attention. One way to lift larger dents is with a clothes iron and damp cloth. Use an old iron, because the bottom of the iron will be stained in the process. A small piece of wet terry cloth, large enough to cover the dent and a bit more, is placed directly over the dent. Then the hot iron is laid down on the cloth. Sssss! The steam produced by the hot iron heating the water in the cloth brings up the pocket of the dent. Naturally, a huge cleft in the wood will not respond to this treatment. However, the hot iron/wet cloth method has raised some fairly bad dents for me. Sanding between applications of the wet cloth/hot iron brings the surface of the stock and the pocket of the dent to the same level.

Repairing Major Dents

See Chapter 10 on wood repairs. A large dent must be considered a repair, not a fill-in or steam-job. Ideally, the smith will have on hand the same wood the stock is made of, or very similar wood. He creates, in effect, an inlay. A mortice is prepared that takes the place of the damaged section of the stock. The inlay will, of course, take the same shape as the mortice. Rarely does a large stock repair go so well that it is impossible to detect. However, in some instances the inlay can be made to appear decorative, so the repair turns into a stock embellishment instead of an eyesore. In such instances, the inlay may be of material other than wood, such as silver or brass. It all depends on the location of the stock damage. If the damaged section lies in an area that would normally accept a decorative inlay, all the better. It's up to the imagination of the woodworker to make the inlay appear as a planned project, rather than a repair job.

Stock Finishing/Refinishing Projects

The stock finishing project in this chapter is one, and only one, way to finish a gunstock. It is hardly the only way. However, it is a time-tested method, plus it's within the scope of any interested hobbyist. As an option, a drying box is helpful in areas of high humidity. This covered wooden box provides a dust-free, dry environment for the curing of a freshly coated piece of wood. The homemade box often has ventilation holes on opposite sides, covered by a furnace filter material to stop dust.

Finishing is one thing; refinishing is another. The project on refinishing gives you some tips for renewing the finish on a firearm that has seen service in the field. *Note:* If a stock is highly ornate, with intricate and extensive carving, engraved inlays and other fancy embellishments, refinishing is a job for the pro. This is especially true for collectible and fine original muzzleloaders.

Composite Stocks

Many modern muzzleloaders have stocks made of synthetic materials. These stocks can eventually become bruised and scratched, requiring refinishing. The way to do this is with paint. These stocks are often painted with a flat-black spray paint or a crinkle paint that when dry provides a non-glare surface.

Finishing a Stock

Supplies

- Baby Oil
- Clean Rags
- Commercial Paste Wood Filler
- Drying Box (optional)
- Flecto Varathane or Tung Oil
- Linseed Oil with Turpentine
  or Mineral Spirits
- Rottenstone or Powdered Pumice
- Sandpaper, 80-, 120- and 220-Grit
- Sandpaper, Wet/Dry 320-, 400-, 600-,
  and 1200- or 1500-Grit
- Stain
- Tru-Oil
- Wide-Mouth Container with Tight Lid

Sanding the Stock

Handsanding with coarse, medium and fine sandpaper is required before the stock can be worked any further. Thorough sanding produces the kind of smooth, scratch-free surface on the wood demanded as a base for a good finish. Starting with 80-grit paper, the stock is sanded, removing all file marks and small dents that usually occur during the wood-shaping process. Do not oversand around the buttplate. This may leave a gap between the edge of the stock wood and the buttplate that could be difficult to correct later. Be sure to preserve all lines. Do not sand away any definitive stock lines, and be very careful around cheekpieces. They have tight corners that must be sanded carefully so that edges are not destroyed.

Now switch to 120 sandpaper to remove all scratches left from sanding with the 80-grit paper, following the same careful handsanding procedure. Next, switch to 220 and repeat the process, this time removing scratches left from the 120. This concludes all prepatory sanding.

Whiskering (Raising the Grain)

Thoroughly dampen, but do not soak, the stock with water applied by your hands. Now let the stock dry. This raises the grain, bringing "whiskers" to the surface of the wood.

After the stock has dried, continue the sanding process with the same piece of 220-grit paper used earlier. Do not use new paper to remove the whiskers of grain that have risen to the surface of the wood. The used paper

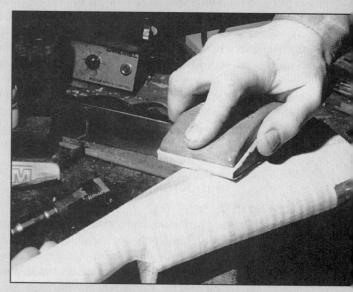

Sanding with progressively finer grits produces the smooth surface necessary for finishing.

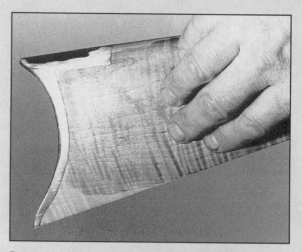

Dampening the wood with water to raise the grain.

makes a smoother surface. Repeat this step at least twice—dampening the stock and sanding with used 220 paper—to make an even smoother surface. There is a point where no more whiskers will rise to the surface, however.

Staining the Stock

Stain may now be applied; follow any instructions included with the stain. Several types were discussed earlier, but remember not all stocks require staining. In fact, some stocks do very nicely with no stain at all. Staining really says the figure of the wood needs help. At its best, stain is applied to

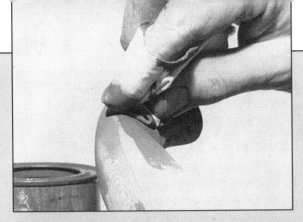

Stain is applied to the stock.

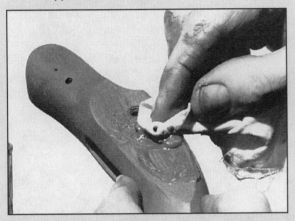

Paste wood filler is applied to the stock.

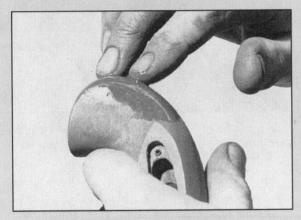

Oil finish is applied to the stock with just your fingers.

excellent seal of the wood, and is compatible with linseed oil. Tung oil is another workable sealer. Apply it generously and allow it to work its way into the wood. Seal inside the inletted regions, as well as the entire outside of the stock. For 100-percent sealing, apply under the buttplate and/or pistol grip cap. The first application of sealer gives the stockmaker a chance to see what the finished product will look like when the stock is completed. Penetrating sealers bring the wood to life, highlighting otherwise hidden colors.

Succeeding applications of sealer are applied as the stock requires, watching the wood for dry spots that indicate the sealer has penetrated and more is required. Apply it until the wood builds up a sheen. Eventually, the smith will notice the wood seems incapable of absorbing any more sealer. In other words, the wood seems saturated. Set the stock aside to dry for 24 hours. A drying box is helpful in areas of high humidity to speed up curing time.

Applying Stock Filler

After the sealer has dried, a stock filler is applied. A natural-color commercial paste filler from the hardware store is acceptable. Follow the directions. Apply only to the surface of the stock, not to inletted portions. The wood may fill with oils alone, but a paste filler saves time and the end product looks the same.

Finishing the Stock

Next, the time has come to apply the first light coating of oil finish. Tru-Oil from Birchwood Casey is a time-tested product trusted by thousands of stockmakers. Light coatings applied with the fingers alone are necessary for best results. Numerous light applications of oil are better than fewer heavy applications.

Allow ample drying time between oil applications. *Tip:* After closing the bottle of oil, place it upside down on the bench. This helps to keep the contents from drying out and getting thick. Also, standard baby oil applied to the hands each time after contact with the oil helps to remove finish later when washing hands with soap and water.

Cutting Back the Finish

After the stock has dried, the oil, sealer and filler must be cut back so the stockmaker

highlight features already inherent in the wood. Incidentally, although several stains were already named, it should be mentioned that Brownells has a good selection of water-soluble stains in powder form. These are mixed according to instructions. Also, to bring color out, pure boiled linseed oil may be applied in a 50/50 mixture with turpentine or mineral spirits. This is not a sealer, but rather accentuates grain and color.

Sealing the Stock

Next, apply Flecto Varathane (No. 66 Clear), which penetrates well, provides an can see how much wood filling has been accomplished. Use wet/dry 320-grit sandpaper *and a vehicle* made of linseed oil and turpentine (or mineral spirits) mixed 50/50 in a wide-mouth container with a good lid to prevent drying. Wet/dry paper about 3½ to 4 inches long and 2 inches wide is folded once and dipped in the vehicle. Make sure the sandpaper does not dry out; the vehicle promotes smooth sandings. It also enhances oil absorption into the wood and helps remove minute scratches left from the initial sandings. Finally, the vehicle prevents scratches that dry sandpaper may cause. A rag is used from time to time to wipe the surface of the stock for inspection of the wood surface. Keep the sandpaper wet with the vehicle and replace it as required.

After the surface of the wood has been

Final rubout on a highly figured piece of curly maple.

made scratch-free, wipe the stock off with a cloth and set it aside to dry for a while. Inspect the stock in a couple of hours to see how the grain has filled. Apply two or three additional light coats of Tru-Oil by hand. Let the stock dry thoroughly in a dust-free environment between applications. After drying, sand the stock again with 320 wet/dry paper and vehicle. Repeat this process until the grain of the wood has been filled. Keep using 320 paper because it cuts faster than finer grit paper.

At this point, apply two coats of finishing oil, allowing it to dry between coats. Now cut back with 400-grit sandpaper and vehicle. Work lightly, being careful not to cut too deeply through the finish that has already been applied to the stock wood. After sanding with 400-grit and vehicle, let dry and then

apply two light coats of finishing oil. After thoroughly drying, sand with wet 600-grit and vehicle. At this point, a decision is made: high-gloss finish or dull lustre?

Applying a High-Gloss Finish

For high gloss, apply two additional thin coats of finishing oil and allow to dry to a hard surface in a dust-free location. Do not sand any further. *Tip:* The Tru-Oil finish should be fresh and thin, not old and congealed. Even when mixed with turpentine or mineral spirits, using fresh Tru-Oil is necessary.

Applying a Dull Lustre

For a subdued finish, at the end of the finishing procedure, a final sanding with 1200- or 1500-grit wet/dry paper and vehicle will cut

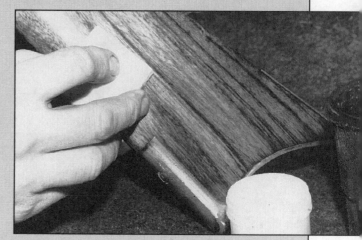

Using a felt pad with turpentine/linseed oil vehicle, plus rottenstone (in white container), for final rubdown of the stock finish.

the shine on the surface of the stock. Carefully accomplished, this final touch provides a dull and even sheen. Fine sandpapers are not always easy to locate, but try auto body paint shop supply houses. Another means of cutting a shiny finish is an application of rottenstone or powdered pumice. These mildly cut the outer layer of the finish.

As pointed out earlier, professional stockmakers usually have their own unique methods of stock finishing, as well as their own pet finishes. With experience and experimentation, however, a hobby stock finisher will come upon finishing methods and a finish that he can call his own, just like the pros. Remember to test all aspects of finishing on pieces of scrap wood before trying them on stocks. It's the smart way to see how things are going to work out.

Refinishing a Stock

Supplies

- Baby Oil
- Clean Rags
- Commercial Paste Wood Filler
- Drying Box (optional)
- Flecto Varathane or Tung Oil
- Linseed Oil with Turpentine or
     Mineral Spirits
- Rottenstone or Powdered Pumice
- Sandpaper, 80-, 120- and 220-Grit
- Sandpaper, Wet/Dry 320-, 400-, 600-,
     and 1200- or 1500-Grit
- Small Stainless Steel Brush
- Stain
- Stripping Agent
- Tru-Oil
- Wide-Mouth Container with Tight Lid

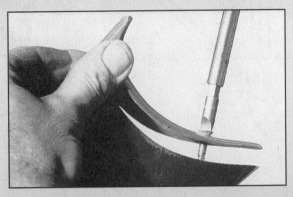

All metal parts, like this buttplate, must be removed before stock refinishing.

The old finish must be stripped off before a new finish can be applied.

Preparing the Stock

In order to refinish a stock, remove from the stock as many metal parts as possible, including inlays, buttplate, nose cap, trigger guard and escutcheons. Often, some parts cannot be removed without damage. These include glued-in inlays, nose caps cast on the stock, and so forth. The parts that cannot be removed should not come in contact with harsh strippers.

Stripping the Old Finish

When buying a paint stripping agent from the hardware or paint store, tell the salesperson what finish you intend to remove so that you'll end up with the best product for the job. Read all instructions and safety precautions before attempting to use any of them.

Apply stripper to the stock. After it has removed as much of the old finish as possible, there still may be a few areas that have retained the stubborn finish. A small stainless steel brush is handy for those hard-to-get areas of the stock. If the firearm has checkering, be especially careful in that area. Checkering can be cut back—the sharp edges of the diamonds dulled or even obliterated. Do not gouge the wood. Sanding is a good way to remove old finish, although it requires time and patience.

Making Repairs

Once the old finish is removed, attend to the stock repairs. Raise the dents as previously detailed in this chapter. Cracks can be glued or epoxied, and chipped-out areas can be replaced with inlays. Large chunks of missing wood may have to be repaired with a special inlay. See Chapter 10 on making repairs.

Replacing Stock Parts

The removal of old finish and the steaming of dents may have altered the dimensions of the stock to a minor degree, which means stock parts may have to be refitted. The buttplate, for example, may extend beyond the surface of the wood, in which case it will have to be filed down flush.

Finishing the Stock

At this time, follow the procedures outlined in the project on stock finishing.

Wood Repairs

THE BLACKPOWDER HOBBY gunsmith will encounter stock damage at some point, because gunstocks are vulnerable to many forms of injury. Cracks, breaks, oil soaking, dents, dings, scratches, pieces broken away from the stock, stripped screw holes and loss of finish are specific forms of stock damage. Hard use, abuse and neglect, as well as ordinary wear, take a toll on any stock. At the same time, wood is enduring, as proven by the countless old muzzleloaders that remain intact. Therefore, while stocks fall prey to many different types of injuries, wood damage is repairable, and repairing a stock to safe working condition is a rewarding experience for anyone interested in gunsmithing.

Repairing stock damage on original muzzleloaders requires an important decision: How much alteration should transpire on this firearm? It is entirely possible to destroy the value of an old-time gun by refinishing that piece to simulate new condition. On the other hand, since certain muzzleloaders from the past are essentially sound and have little collector value, they should have their wooden stocks restored to peak status. Incidentally, basic gunstock repair and full restoration of a gun are two entirely different undertakings. The hobby gunsmith can often do the former to full satisfaction. The repaired stock will look presentable, and it can be counted on to withstand normal use without breaking. Two important criteria are met by such repair: appearance and function.

Full restoration is quite another matter. There are experts who work solely in this field, restoring antique firearms to as near original status as possible. These gunsmiths are at the top of their trade. They are specialists in restoring not only wood, but also the metalworking of a firearm. The job may take many hours of intense labor, with strict attention paid to every detail. Through this painstaking work, the blackpowder firearm is returned to the form it enjoyed when it left the gun shop as a new piece—or nearly so. Some restoration artists even go to the extent of studying a specific finish and duplicating it by mixing the proper ingredients themselves.

The wood repairs discussed in this chapter deal mainly with firearms that have fallen on bad times and are in need of stock rejuvenation. Most of these guns are of current manufacture: replicas, non-replicas, modern muzzleloaders and other rifles, pistols, revolvers and shotguns that use wood for stocks. Stock damage can often occur while building a kit gun. For example, it's an easy matter to ding a stock while in the process of building a kit. I know of one muzzleloader that suffered a cracked wrist before the rifle ever saw the field or range. Many old-style long rifles have fragile wrist areas susceptible to cracking, or even snapping in two. Also problematical are the thin forend sections of full-stock long rifles. The forepart of the stock on these firearms is fragile. *Tip:* When taking a full-stock rifle apart, be extremely cautious with the stock once it is separated from the barrel. Even a rap or tap on the buttstock can cause a vibration that can crack the barrel channel.

Fixing a Large Dent

In order to raise a large dent or a bruised section of the stock, the wood must be swelled out. Essentially, dents and bruises are compacted regions where a blow has forced the wood to compress. Even hardwoods are compressible. This is readily provable by taking a small piece of hardwood and rapping it with a hammer.

A wet cloth and hot clothes iron are used to raise a dent or bruise on a wooden gunstock. Saturate the cloth with water. Then place the wet cloth directly upon the dent and press the hot iron upon the wet cloth. This causes steam, swelling the dent to the surface of the stock. The number of steamings

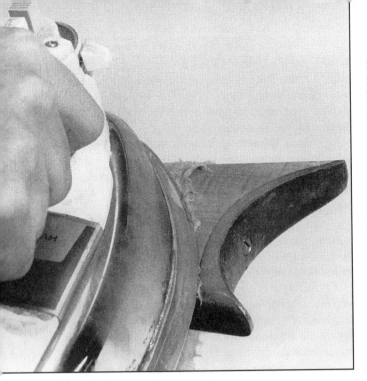

Applying a hot clothes iron and damp cloth to a stock dent, forming steam which penetrates the wood and raises the dent.

depends upon the depth of the dent. Sometimes the results are remarkable. Dents that appeared hopeless have been completely raised to the level of the wood.

Once the dent is raised, the area is sanded smooth to match the rest of the stock, resulting in a region without finish. Careful selection of wood stains, plus the proper finish, can often blend this unfinished area to match the rest of the stock. Oil-finished stocks are easier to touch up than varnished stocks. The smaller the repair area, the easier to refinish, of course.

Finally, be sure to remove the old finish before making a dent repair if the stock is going to be completely refinished anyway. Removing the old finish allows steam to penetrate the dented area much better, rather than trying to force steam through a hard finish. But if you're not completely refinishing, do not remove any finish if a small dented area is to be repaired—that only enlarges the area that will require refinishing later.

Cracked Stocks

Cracks in gunstocks are common, not only in vintage firearms, but also as a result of unintentional slips in kit making or through field damage. Remember, the fresher the crack, the easier it is to repair successfully, so don't wait any longer than you have to before getting started on the job. High-quality epoxy is ideal for repairing stock cracks. While five-minute epoxy is excellent for many applications, the thirty-minute variety is better for repairing stock cracks. Also excellent is the epoxy used for glass-bedding, such as Acraglas from Brownells.

Plan ahead. Study the cracked area carefully before getting out the epoxy. Know exactly how the stock must be held together or banded once the adhesive is applied. Ideally, try a dry run using large 1/2-inch rubber bands made from a tire

inner tube to hold the wood securely in place. Be observant of metal parts. Sometimes these, such as a trigger guard, may have to be left on the stock during gluing to help properly position a crack. When the part is removed, it may be difficult to correctly mate and close the pieces of wood together. The cracked area may tend to warp apart. If the inner tube rubber bands won't serve the purpose for a particular crack repair, C-clamps may do the trick. Be creative. Use whatever device is necessary to hold the stock solidly during gluing. The damaged area must be under full control during the gluing process or the job will never be right. Be careful to pad any clamps so you don't dent the wood, or even crack other areas. Try to distribute the clamping force over an area wider than the immediate crack.

Wood and metal parts that are not directly involved in the repair job must be protected from epoxy by coating them with a release agent. Wood parts can be coated with heavy-duty wax, the paste type used for hardwood floors. If the wood is properly finished and sealed, the wax can easily be removed later. The release agent provided with fiberglass kits does a good job on metals, but is not ideal for wood. The problem with this particular type of release agent is its tendency to flow into the wooden area under repair, making a bond impossible. So wax all wood in the area of the repair that may come in contact with epoxy, except, of course, the crack area itself. Then use the standard release agent on metal parts near the repair area so they are not inadvertently bonded. Now wax-coat the inner tube rubber bands, because if they're not treated, they may bond to the repair job when excess epoxy oozes out of the repair zone.

All preliminary planning is now out of the way. A test has been run by mating and closing the crack with C-clamps or rubber bands to ensure the crack closes properly. Don't be sur-

After repair, the crack is still visible, although the rifle is now in serviceable condition and ready to go into the field again.

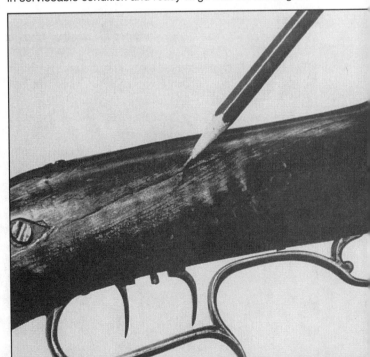

prised if an old oil-soaked crack remains visible after repairs. This is common. The use of acetone, described more fully later, may bleach out an oily area to some extent. Mount the stock in a vise with padded jaws. Prepare the epoxy as directed in the instructions. Use only the resin and hardener. Do not add stains or fillers to the mix. Carefully spread open the crack by hand, but do not apply too much force or the crack will turn into a break. Work the epoxy down into the cracked region with a small stick or any other tool that suits the job, such as a dental probe.

Epoxy has a tendency to "wet out" well, working deeply into the pores of the wood. Unfortunately, this is not always the case when epoxy has been incorrectly mixed. In fact, the crack repair may blossom into a full-blown headache under these circumstances, so be certain to mix the epoxy strictly as directed.

Now that the epoxy has penetrated the cracked area, it is time to fix the rubber bands in place. Earlier rehearsal of the repair, as suggested, makes this operation go quickly and smoothly. Remember, time is important when working with epoxy. Even thirty-minute formulas begin to set up rather quickly. Be sure to wipe away any excess epoxy that squeezes out of the crack. This is easier to do when wet.

The cracked region should be retained under pressure for a full twenty-four hours. Then, just as the plastic surgeon removes bandages from his patient, the gunsmith carefully removes the rubber bands or C-clamps. If release agent was properly applied, the rubber bands should slide right off. If they stick a little, pull them gently until they part company with the stock. Normally, a little clean-up of the immediate repair area is sufficient, and the project is completed. Sometimes a bit of refinishing is necessary. If the repair has been done correctly, the crack will be nearly invisible and, in some cases, actually impossible to see without magnification.

As alluded to earlier, an old crack is much harder to mend than a fresh one. Oil-soaked cracks present the special problem of color difference because the area of the crack is darker than the rest of the stock. Fading the darker area back to match the rest of the stock may be impossible. However, treatment with acetone sometimes works well in cleaning and lightening an oil-soaked region. Open the crack carefully. Work acetone down into the crack, then allow the area to dry completely before continuing with the project. Rinsing the cracked area several times with acetone may clear out enough oil to make a significant difference in final coloration and bonding of the repair.

Broken Stocks

Here, we have a stock actually broken into two or more parts, rather than simply cracked. The repair job is obviously somewhat more involved, but is quite similar to fixing a crack. Ideally, all parts of the stock need to be present. So the first step is to determine if parts are missing. Place the stock down on a clean, flat surface. Gently put the stock back together as you would the pieces of a puzzle, but do not force any pieces into place. This may cause the parts to splinter out.

Once again, the idea is to rehearse the coming repair as a dry run, rather than diving directly into the project and ending up with missing or ill-fitted parts. Determine the strategy for using rubber bands or C-clamps. Sometimes a long wood clamp can be used hold a broken stock. It is also possible to combine various clamps to hold a broken stock in an extremely secure posture. For example, the long wood clamp, a C-clamp and rubber bands have been used in concert to perform small miracles in broken stock repair.

As before, release agents are applied to all parts not involved in actual bonding. Don't forget to protect the clamps and rubber bands with the release agent, too, or these may bond to the stock.

Once the clamping strategy has been devised, it is time to disassemble the stock so epoxy can be applied to the broken parts. Do this job very carefully, or broken parts may be further damaged. Make certain no release agent has found its way onto the parts to be repaired.

An original muzzle-loading riflestock that has been epoxied and banded together. Note the long rubber bands formed from tire inner tubing that hold the repair in place until it is cured.

Once again, mix the epoxy precisely as described in the instructions, using the exact proportions of hardener and resins. Do not add anything to the mixture—no fillers, no stains. Apply epoxy to those parts to be bonded together. Coat the broken sections carefully. There is no reason to slop epoxy over areas of the wood that will not be bonded.

The pieces are now put back together just as the job was rehearsed earlier, and the clamps and rubber bands are also applied as they were in the dry run. The stock should be left for a twenty-four-hour curing period.

After the epoxy has fully polymerized (chemical reaction of parts A and B), remove all clamps and enjoy looking at your handiwork. Only minor cleanup is necessary when the project has been done correctly. In some instances, the broken parts will not mend perfectly, and it may be necessary to use a file to match surfaces of some seams and cracks. After filing seams and cracks that required surface matching, refinishing is in order. Sometimes, this means a total stock refinishing job—sanding, staining, filling and applying finish. However, it is always gratifying to watch a stock go from "She'll never be the same" to "She looks like new!"

A good repair not only looks great, it is also strong. Often, the repaired area is stronger than the wood around it. An example of this I know of is a Plains rifle broken in two at the wrist. A repair was made as described above. The same rifle suffered the same accident a year later. The stock was again broken in two at the wrist, but the previously repaired section remained intact, even though the full impact was directly upon the repair.

Reinforcing Pins

Sometimes pins are required to reinforce a joint. A pin, which is simply a small metal rod, can often be hidden underneath the trigger guard or the tang. Now and then, a pin must be used in a region where it will show. This is cosmetically unfortunate; however, the major goal is to return a broken stock to full, safe function.

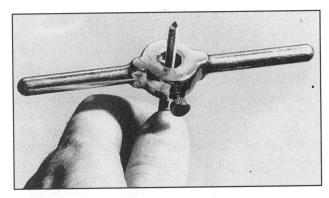

Threading a brass rod for use as a reinforcing pin to repair a cracked stock.

An excellent pin can be cut from a section of brazing rod using sidecutters or a hacksaw. Pieces of various lengths or different diameters can be used depending on need. A threading die can be used to thread the rod. For those who do not wish to thread a section of brazing rod, Brownells offers ready-made threaded brass rods that serve the same reinforcement purpose.

To install a pin, a pilot hole is drilled directly into the stock, but of slightly smaller diameter than the reinforcement pin. Then the pin is installed into the pilot hole via hand drill, not electric drill, as the former is easier to control under these circumstances. The pin is chucked in the drill and literally screwed into the pilot hole. *Caution:* Be careful not to run the pin all the way through the stock and out the other side, which will often chip out a piece of wood. Pins are an excellent means of reinforcing a break that demands extra strength, and with a little care, they don't have to be visually offensive.

Replacing Missing Wood

On occasion, a piece of wood may be missing from a stock break, which requires replacement. The job is time-consuming and exacting. Often, it's difficult to locate a replacement piece of wood that perfectly matches the stock. When this happens,

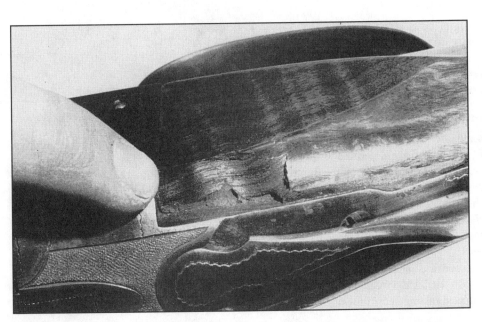

This type of wood damage, with a piece broken away from the stock, can be repaired by cutting and fitting a new piece of wood. This requires minor inletting.

the repair always remains visible because stock figure, grain and color never match up. Under these circumstances, the patch job will never be perfect, but the muzzleloader hobbyist should know how to do the project anyway.

The stock must be analyzed carefully concerning the exact configuration of the missing piece of wood. The piece may be a small chip from the toe line of the stock or a section behind the breech plug between the tang and the lockplate. Each specific area requires somewhat different attention; however, with a file and/or chisels, the section must be cleaned up. The idea is to alter an irregular divot in the wood into a mortice that has flat surfaces, so a piece of wood can be neatly fitted into place.

A piece of wood, hopefully well-matched in grain pattern and color, is prepared to fit the mortice in the stock. However, the wood is not patterned to make an exact fit like a puzzle part. The repair piece is shaped to fit the flat part of the mortice, but is left oversized with plenty of excess above the surface of the stock. The replacement wood is shaped and reshaped in a trial-and-error method until it fits the mortice in the stock as closely as possible, with the exception of the excess left above the surface of the mortice. This excess wood is later reduced so it matches the original surface of the stock.

As always in repairs of this nature, a release agent is necessary. Wax is applied around the area of the stock which will not be glued. The new piece of wood is glued in place, either with wood glue or epoxy, then held by rubber bands. The job is allowed to cure with bands in place. Then the new piece is shaped to the contour of the stock with files and sandpaper. If the new piece protrudes into the stock mortice, then inletting must be performed in order to ensure the refitting of barrel or other metal parts. Of course, finishing must follow because we have essentially a brand new piece of wood. Staining is especially important because, done properly, it may result in a color match-up between the new and old. Ideally, trial pieces taken from the replacement wood can be stained before final staining of the newly fitted piece.

Essentially the same as a missing piece of wood, a section of stock may be rotted, usually due to oil saturation. This section must be removed and replaced. Therefore, a mortice is cut into the stock to remove the bad wood, and a new piece is fitted as previously described.

Epoxy/Fiberglass Repair

Another alternative to filling a missing section of wood is the use of epoxy/fiberglass as a filler. The purist will not find this method to his liking; however, there are many blackpowder firearms, both old and new, that are essentially "shooters" and have no collector value. Making repairs with epoxy/fiberglass on these rifles is sensible. Especially around the breech plug region where recoil may have caused damage, this type of filler can make an excellent repair.

What kind of epoxy? In this instance, a commercial kit is ideal. A kit like Brownells' Acraglas contains the following: resin, hardener, mixing sticks, graduated mixing cups, brown

In this repair, a piece of new wood was fitted between the tang and the lockplate. The result of this patch job is a minute line barely visible to the naked eye after staining and refinishing the wood.

This is an epoxy/fiberglass fill that does not obviously show up because it has been added to a very dark piece of wood, and because dye was used to darken the epoxy/fiberglass mixture.

dye, release agent and powdered fiberglass material that creates a true filler.

The process of working with epoxy in wood repairs begins by taking out the bad wood, just as rotten wood was removed, using chisels and other appropriate tools, until good wood is encountered. These areas may be refreshed with acetone in order to clean them up, incidentally, especially if they are discolored. Acetone does more than cleaning; it also prepares the wood for the epoxy by removing oil. After cleaning with ace-

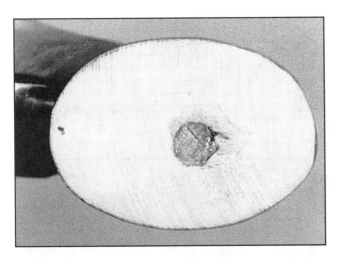

The original wood screw hole in the butt of this pistol stock was drilled in the wrong location. It has consequently been filled with a wooden dowel. The hardwood dowel has made a permanent repair, and a new wood screw hole can now be drilled in the correct location.

This is a wood repair in which the forearm of the stock is being extended via a 45-degree angle joint. Note the two pieces of wood are held in place with two C-clamps, and there is a piece of flat iron as well. By placing a thin shim between the piece of flat iron and the new piece of wood, the new wood will end up slightly higher than the original forearm. Then it can be trimmed down to meet the lines of the original forearm in a perfect fit.

tone, allow the wood to dry completely before epoxy is applied.

All metal parts are treated with a commercial release agent, and all wood parts are coated with wax. In using epoxy/fiberglass as a filler, a thick paste is formed about the consistency of heavy grease. This mixture is settled into the mortice. If the mortice is to make contact with a metal part, such as a tang, trigger guard or barrel, a little extra epoxy/fiberglass mixture is ladled into the mortice, so when the metal part is fitted, some

of the mixture oozes out. This creates a hand-in-glove fit. Of course, excess epoxy/fiberglass must be removed with a file after the job has cured.

Stripped Wood Screw Holes

These are a common problem in gunmaking and repairing. A firearm that has been disassembled numerous times may exhibit this malady, and there are several ways to correct this situation. One is with the use of steel wool. Fine steel wool is forced into the hole and serves as packing when the screw is replaced in the hole. If the stripped wood screw hole is too large for this method, then a couple of toothpicks with super glue are placed in the hole as filler.

Sometimes a screw hole is extremely chewed out, or perhaps it is located incorrectly, which occurred in one instance in building a kit for this book. In these cases, the screw hole must be completely filled with a wooden dowel. A twist drill bit is used to drill out the original misplaced (or severely enlarged) screw hole, creating a larger channel for the wood dowel. A section of wood dowel is then cut off longer than the hole is deep and glued inside, forming a plug. After the plug is securely in place, the exposed tip of the dowel is trimmed back to meet the surface of the wood. Then a new screw hole is drilled. Hickory dowels are excellent due to their hardness; however, softer dowels may also be used.

Extending a Forend

Now and then, a riflestock will be shortened in the forend area for one reason or another. Later, the owner of the rifle may wish to return it to its original length. A piece of wood needs to be added to the existing, but shortened, forearm. Ideally, the wood will be a near-perfect match for obvious cosmetic reasons. The key to success in this repair is the creation of a 45-degree angle joint. Forearm tips are generally small, so the angle will supply more surface area for the bonding of epoxy or glue between the new and original wood. The small size of the forend also precludes the use of reinforcing dowels. Therefore, the burden of bonding the two pieces together rests solely on the adhesive. Maximizing mating surfaces adds significantly to the bonded area, making for a more secure mating.

Fit the angled pieces together with C-clamps, plus a piece of 1/4x2-inch steel flat stock to protect the wood. The added piece of forend wood can be made to rise slightly above the parent forearm section by using a thin shim between the parent wood and protective steel plate. This places the new wood slightly higher than the original wood, so the added piece can be trimmed down to match the plane of the original forend for a perfect match. Naturally, the newly fitted piece of wood must be inletted to match the barrel channel of the original forend. Be careful. The new piece of forearm can be broken off rather easily and is essentially on its own until the bedding job is completed.

These are a few simple, but extremely worthwhile, wood repairs the hobby blackpowder gunsmith can perform with total satisfaction. Such repairs often turn an almost retired firearm into a refreshed working piece.

Wood Embellishment

THE HOBBY BLACKPOWDER gunsmith is perfectly capable of embellishing riflestocks, pistol stocks, revolver grips or any other wooden part of a muzzleloader. The major forms of wood embellishment include carving, inlaying, checkering and pin-ons—for lack of a better term. Much of the work can be done with minimal tools. Of course, as the hobbyist's skills advance, he will want to purchase special tools for wood embellishment, but to start out with, the modest tools discussed below are sufficient. Practice on scrap wood before attacking a gunstock or other piece that will be expensive to replace.

Relief Carving

Relief carving is also known as raised carving. The plan is to remove the background of a given pattern so the pattern itself stands out. There are many ways to carve wood, with many different tools. This discussion centers on the instruction of Ken Gross and Charles Richardson, two gunmakers who have excellent ideas concerning relief carving and who both feel the amateur can do a good job with modest tools. We tend to think of relief carving as an intricate art demanding years of experience before an acceptable piece is turned out. But that's not the case. Anyone who likes to work with hand tools can do a reasonable job of relief carving, if he takes his time.

Relief Carving Tools

The standard workplace discussed earlier is perfect for carving, but very good light is essential. Without plenty of light, it's difficult to define lines.

A modified jackknife makes an excellent carving tool. A blade about 1³/₄ inches long and about ⁵/₁₈-inch wide is about ideal. The object then is to grind a special hookpoint

out of the jackknife's blade. The hook is ground at the front of the point, on top, leaving the original contour of the blade intact. This tiny hook should sweep slightly upward. For personal safety, it is important to dull most of the knife blade using an oilstone. The blade edge becomes a handle of sorts, and if left sharp, the worker will be cut. The forward ³/₈-inch of the blade is left sharp; this is the portion directly below the hook.

An X-Acto handle with four blades is also useful for carving. There are dozens of different X-Acto blades available at the hobby shop. Four good ones for wood carving are the following:

- X-Acto sharp-pointed knife blade—any size will do. Try the medium sizes first. This blade is used only to outline the pattern on the wood.
- X-Acto flat chisel blade—this blade should be one of the larger sizes, and it can also be ground to different widths for special cuts.
- X-Acto gouge blade—large in size. It is a U-shaped blade that can virtually scoop wood out and is important in removing a lot of wood from the background of the carving.
- X-Acto veiner blade—V-shaped. It is best for carving in its smaller sizes.

Although X-Acto blades come sharp from the factory, it's wise to further sharpen them. Sharpening is accomplished with 600-grit wet/dry sandpaper on a flat surface. The blade is drawn lightly across the sandpaper, using the paper as a sharpening stone. Do not press hard. A few light passes will improve the X-Acto blade from sharp to very sharp.

A small, flat carving chisel about ³/₁₆-inch wide, plus a

A very complete set of carving tools: general carving tool set, X-Acto knives, gouges and chisels, and a Moto tool.

shallow gouge chisel about 1/8-inch wide, facilitate wood removal. These tools easily remove a lot of background wood, making the relief carving stand out, as it must to create a raised pattern.

Beautiful sets of carving chisels are available and are highly recommended for the advanced hobbyist who intends to do a great deal of relief carving. Brownells offers different sets.

Cut "O" needle files, for wood, in three different shapes are ideal for wood carving. These are half-round, knife-edge and crossing shapes, which is half-round on two sides.

Ken Gross considers the emery board useful in relief carving. The common emery board, for fingernail care, has a fine-grit side and a medium-grit side. The emery board can be cut with scissors into many different shapes. Pointed or rounded, these bits of emery board fit into tight places and remove wood slowly, which is ideal for the finishing stages of relief carving.

Already mentioned for sharpening X-Acto blades, sandpaper is also useful for careful removal of wood during the later finishing stages of relief carving. An assortment of finer grits is most useful.

Pumice powder in medium and fine grits is ideal as a polish for the latter stages of carving. Apply with an old toothbrush for good results. Do not wet the powder.

One small bottle of rubber cement is needed. It is ideal for attaching patterns to the wood because this type of glue is readily removable by rubbing it off with a finger when dry.

Relief Carving Patterns

Simple designs are recommended until proficiency is achieved. Scroll patterns can be intricate, but some can also be basic. So can leaf designs. One means of transferring a pattern to wood is by placing the pattern directly upon the area to be carved with carbon paper in between. Using a No. 2 pencil, trace over the lines of the pattern until they are transferred to the wood via the carbon paper. Then use a No. 3 or harder pencil to trace over the carbon lines on the wood. Press hard enough to leave an impression all along the lines. These impressions act as guides for the cutting tools.

An alternate method of transferring a pattern is to glue it in place directly on the wood area to be carved using rubber cement, which easily rubs off when dry.

A third method is to draw the pattern free-hand directly on the stock, using a soft lead pencil. Naturally, this requires some artistic skill, but it's surprising to see how well many hobbyists do.

Relief carvings are not as "tall" as they appear. In attempting to remove background wood, if a gouge is used, it must be used carefully. Take wood away only around the pattern. Do not cut too deeply, but only to the depth already established, about 1/32-inch. Don't forget to practice first on scrap wood. It's amazing how rapidly a hobbyist's ability in wood carving grows with a little bit of practice. Also, never hurry. Oftentimes, patience is the carver's best ally.

Incise Carving

Along with relief carving, incise carving is a useful art to know. Incise carving can be used to accentuate relief carving, especially around finials on moulding. As the name implies, carving is "incised" into the wood—the term means, accord-

The point of the pencil is directed at an example of incise carving.

William Kennedy, well-known blackpowder gunsmith, working on relief carving.

ing to the dictionary, "to cut into, or cut marks upon, with a sharp instrument." A sharp, small blade is needed—an X-Acto tool is ideal. Incise carving is nothing more than a line cut into the wood, a relatively simple way to add finishing touches to an interesting carving pattern.

Inlaying

This is a process of fitting embellishments, called inlays, into the wood. They may be made of many materials, including wood, silver, gold, plastic or numerous other things.

Wire Inlays

This is an exceedingly old process, predating firearms. As master gunmaker William Kennedy notes, wire inlay goes back to the days of the crossbow and edged weapons.

Ironically, it is not done with wire. It is accomplished with a ribbon of metal—usually silver, sometimes brass. Essentially, a narrow trough is cut into the wood in the form of a pattern and the ribbon is forced into this trough, roughly speaking. The inlay is called wire because, when embedded in the wood, it appears as wire. Ideally, the hobbyist should practice making cuts in scrap wood before attempting to install wire inlay on a gunstock.

Decorative Inlays

Bear in mind, first, what an inlay is. It is a small, usually (but not always) flat piece of decorative material made of wood, plastic, metal, ivory—just about any relatively hard substance with a decorative shape. The idea is to install this bit of material into the wood. Normally, the surface of the inlay and the surface of the stock are flush when the job is

done, but in certain cases the inlay could sit higher. An inlay could also lie beneath the surface of the stock, probably beneath a layer of clear plastic. It does not matter what the inlay looks like or is made of. What does matter is the concept: An inlay is installed into the stock and becomes an integral part of it.

Metal inlays should closely match the surface of the stock when set into the mortice because it is more difficult to reduce the height of a metal inlay through sanding. Note: Escutcheons and barrel wedges for keys are inlays, too. See Chapter 26 on the custom rifle for fitting these types of inlays.

Inlaying Tools

Gather four to six chisels, needle files, fine files, garnet paper, small mallet or hammer, and also white glue. Inlay chisels can be made from hacksaw blades broken into segments approximately 2 inches long, forming various "blades." These are ground to different thicknesses, such as $1/16$-inch, $1/8$-inch, and so forth. They are driven downward into the wood, and therefore must be straight. If crooked, the trough made by the chisel will also be crooked.

Checkering

Although checkering was not as popular on old-time muzzleloaders as it is today on modern firearms, quite a number of the old-timers were checkered, particularly shotguns, as well as some high-quality pistols and rifles. Modern gunmakers may wish to embellish their stocks this way, especially when attempting to replicate or restore an original old-time firearm. As far as function is concerned, the idea that checkering is necessary for grip, and that a rifle will certainly fall from our

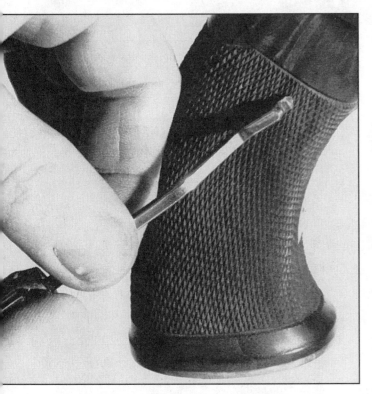

Final deepening of checkering using a single-line cutter.

hands if not checkered, is unfounded. Checkering is mainly for show.

There were many variations of checkering patterns on old-time firearms. The hobbyist attempting to duplicate original checkering must carefully study pictures or samples to familiarize himself with these styles.

The process involves cutting V-shaped grooves into the wood of the stock. Of course, the grooves must be evenly spaced in order to create a raised diamond. It's a criss-cross process. Lines are cut evenly spaced going one way, then lines are cut with the same spacing at an angle, creating what appears to be a raised diamond. Fine-line checkering results in very small diamonds, whereas lines cut farther apart make larger ones. While it is a mark of expertise to do fine-line checkering, as fine as 32 lines per inch, the beginner is wise to work with a much coarser pattern, more like 18 lines per inch, and simple designs. The level of work established for this particular project does not demand fine-line checkering or sophisticated patterns, although advanced checkering patterns are pictured for the purpose of illustration.

Before starting, here are a few hints: Practice first on scrap wood before attempting to checker a stock. Use a flat piece of wood, such as walnut. Also, practice on contoured surfaces before attempting wrap-around checkering patterns, as on pistol grips. Wrap-around checkering is difficult to master. Use good lighting and, if necessary, modest magnification. Checkering is precise work. Have a comfortable place to work. Checkering patterns require time and concentration.

Checkering Tools

The tools for checkering are few and not terribly expensive, although carbide cutters cost more than standard types. Of course, carbide cutters last longer and stay sharper longer. Brownells sells a number of checkering tool sets. In the past, gunsmiths often made their own tools, but the blackpowder hobby gunsmith can readily buy his.

A checkering cradle is useful to maintain control over the gunstock. This is a somewhat high-level tool for the hobbyist, but once a do-it-yourselfer gets started in checkering, there is no stopping him, so the cradle ends up being a good purchase after all.

Also needed: Two single-line cutters, one set up as a push tool, the other a pull tool; spacing tools, one right-hand and one left-hand, both 18 lpi (lines per inch); a Dem-bart S01 tool; a compass and/or set of dividers, as well as a ruler or straightedge; No. 3 or 4 pencils; and cellophane tape.

Pin-Ons

Numerous decorative objects with pins behind them can be installed in the gunstock, pistol grip or revolver grip rather easily. Drill a tiny hole in the wood to accommodate the pin, and then glue the decoration into the stock wood. A similar process is used for small objects without pins after a pin is attached to these objects. A small hole is drilled into the object, and a pin is glued into that hole. Now, the object can be glued onto the stock wood as described above.

Fitting Wire Inlays

Tools

Chisels, four to six different sizes, or special Inlay Chisels made from Hacksaw Blades (see chapter text)
Fine Files
Mallet or Hammer
Needle Files

Supplies

Clean Rag
Soft Lead Pencil
White Glue

Designing the Inlay

Using a soft lead pencil, a design is applied to the gunstock. A little wire inlay is beautiful; an excess is gaudy.

Tapering the Metal Ribbon

The thin metal ribbon used in wire inlay is about .010- to .020-inch thick and about $1/32$- to $1/16$-inch wide. The leading edge of the strip can be carefully filed down to create a bevel. This tapered edge is more easily inserted into the trough cut into the wood.

Creating the Trough

Using a small hammer, drive the homemade inlay chisel down into the wood following established pattern lines. The chisel is gently tapped, driving it to a depth slightly

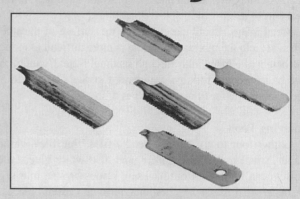

These wire inlay tools, which are miniature chisels, are made on a grinder from pieces of hacksaw blade. The two on the bottom-left have a slight radius in the cutting tip.

A wire inlay pattern is drawn directly on the wood with a lead pencil.

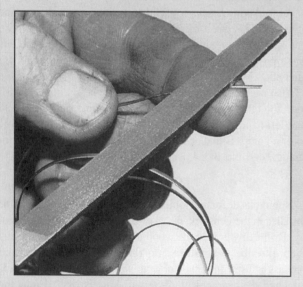

Filing a sharp edge on the inlay wire. This edge sinks into wood.

Using a small hammer and special inlay chisel to cut the trough into which the wire inlay will fit. The pattern is followed religiously.

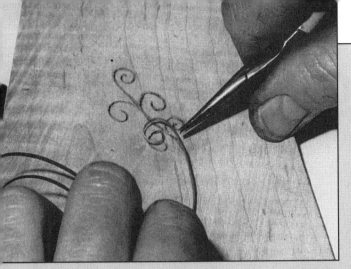

The trough has already been cut with the chisels, following the pattern. Now, the inlay is bent to match the trough.

Tapping a piece of wire inlay into the trough which has already been filled with white glue.

deeper than the width of the wire inlay. Since the chisel blades are thin, preferably with tapered edges, they go in easily and need not be forced. Leave no spaces between each chisel cut. The idea here is to produce a continuous line with the chisels, a smooth trough into which the wire ribbon can be pressed in place.

Contouring the Metal Ribbon

A strip of metal ribbon is shaped and bent to match the trough created by the chisel cuts. The ribbon must be one continuous piece placed into the trough, then tapped gently using the light hammer or mallet. Intricate designs have crossover, but the hobbyist is encouraged to stay with simple designs that do not demand special fitting. Where lines cross, the ribbon is bevelled to match, but such work demands expert ability.

Setting the Metal Ribbon

A tiny trickle of white glue is laced onto the wood around the wire ribbon, and while the glue is still wet, all excess is wiped away with a clean, damp cloth. This leaves a clean line of white glue around the ribbon, and the wetness of the glue, as well as the damp cloth, swell the wood out to create an even better fit between trough and wire inlay.

Filing the Inlay.

At this point, the inlay will be higher than the trough. Once the glue is totally dry, the ribbon can be carefully filed down to match the surface of the stock.

Putting white glue into the trough using a toothpick. See the piece of wire inlay ready for placement.

Filing the wire inlay with a smooth mill file to bring it down to the stock's surface.

Checkering a Stock

Tools

- Checkering Cradle (optional)
- Single-Line Cutters, Push and Pull Types
- Spacing Tools, Left- and Right-Hand (18 lpi)

Supplies

- Cellophane Tape
- Compass or Dividers
- Medium Cardboard
- Oil Finish
- Pencils, No. 3 or 4, or Grease Pencil
- Paintbrush
- Ruler or Straightedge
- Toothbrush

Drawing the Pattern

There are truly no established checkering patterns for muzzleloaders. Therefore, patterns must be drawn freehand, directly on the stock with a special pencil that will mark any surface. These can be purchased from Brownells. The lines define the border of the checkering pattern. Before drawing, be certain the pattern really fits the stock, whether on the wrist of a rifle or the grip of a handgun. Because once cutting begins, there is no going back.

Cutting the Border

With a single-line cutter, carefully cut in the borders, following the lines drawn on the stock.

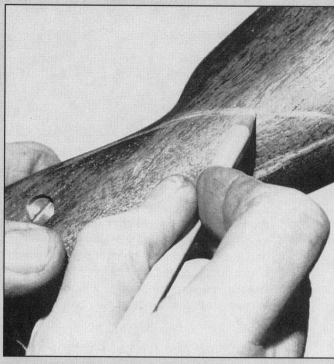

Drawing the pattern directly on the stock using a grease pencil.

Cutting Master Lines

In this step, establish the master lines from which all of the checkering will be done. A three-to-one ratio diamond cut from a piece of file folder (medium cardboard) will be used to establish the master lines. The cardboard diamond serves as a template.

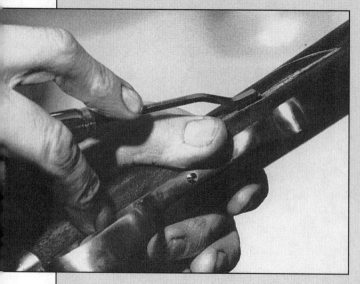

Cutting the border with a single-line cutting tool.

A portion of the border is cut into the stock.

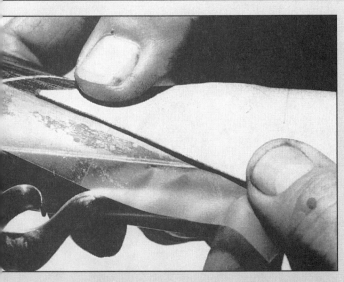

Using a paper diamond tamplate and cellophane tape to establish one of the master lines (left-hand).

Lay the diamond on the stock in the direction that you wish the pattern to run. Take a piece of cellophane tape and lay it along one edge of the diamond. With a single-line cutting tool, cut the lines from border to border. Remove the tape, then lay the diamond back on the stock, aligning the diamond template with the line just cut. Lay a fresh piece of tape along the other angle of the diamond from border to border. Using the tape as a guide, cut the second master line of the diamond.

Cutting the Lines

Now, the spacing tools are put to use. Starting with either the left- or right-hand tools, place the guide portion of the cutter in the master line and carefully cut a new line

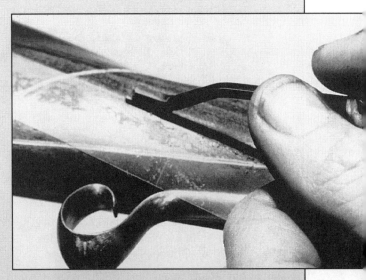

Using a single-line cutter following the cellophane tape as a guide, the master line is cut into the stock (left side).

from border to border. Place the guide tool in the line just cut and repeat the process, making line after line in the wood until the pattern's parameters are filled with lines. Then switch to the other master line and follow the same procedure, until the pattern is completely filled with cut lines.

With the single-line cutters, push and pull types, deepen each cut line in the pattern until the diamonds form sharp points. Use an old toothbrush periodically to clean out the rows.

Finishing the Pattern

The checkering pattern is completed. Now, brush two light coats of finish into the checkering, being careful to seal, but not fill, the pattern.

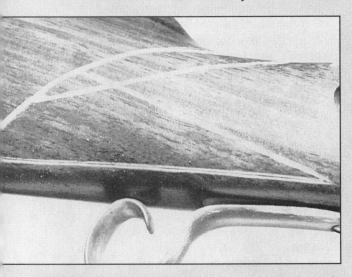

Borders and master lines are cut on the stock, ready for checkering layout.

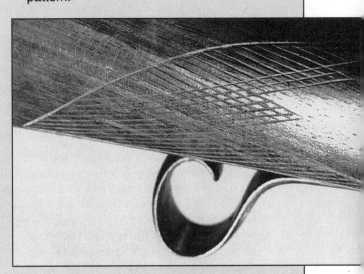

A checkering layout in progress. By following the master lines with equidistant cuts, the diamond effect is created.

Relief Carving

Tools

Carving Chisel, 3/16-Inch
Dremel Tool (optional)
Files, Bullsfoot Rasp and Smooth Mill
Gouge Chisel, 1/8-Inch
Hacksaw Blade Scrapers (see text)
Modified Jackknife (see text)
Needle Files with Half-Round,
   Knife-Edge and Crossing Shapes
X-Acto Knife with Sharp-Pointed, Flat-
   Chisel, Gouge and Veiner Blades

Supplies

Emery Board
Garnet Paper
Pencils, No. 2 and 3
Pumice Powder, Medium and Fine Grit
Rubber Cement
Sandpaper, Wet/Dry 600-Grit
Stain
Toothbrush

Fitting the Pattern

After drawing a pattern with pencil and paper, place the pattern on the area to be carved. Move it around a bit to see that it truly fits the area you wish to carve. If the pattern is too large, reduce it for a nice balance.

Checking Carving Depth

Remember that wood will be removed in the process of relief carving. On a custom stock, about 1/16-inch of wood contour must be above the edge of the buttplate to accommodate the relief carving. If a higher carving is desired, more wood height allowance is required. The same consideration of additional wood is necessary for any object to be carved, including wood revolver grips.

Preparing the Wood

Sand the wood to a smooth finish before beginning relief carving. Then, using a paintbrush apply a light coat of stain to the carving area. Use the same stain that will be applied in final finishing. As wood is removed during carving, so is stain. This leaves a sharp contrast between stained and unstained areas, showing the smith where wood has been, or has not been, removed. The use of stain in relief carving is, as Gross puts it, a visual aid.

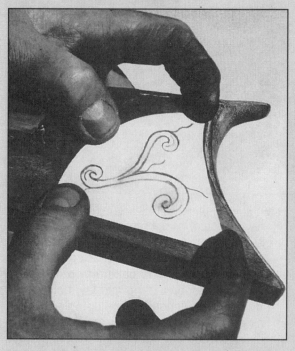

The carving pattern is positioned on the buttstock.

Placing the Pattern

The pattern must now be transferred to the stock. In the sequence we are showing, the pattern is glued in place with rubber cement. A light, even coat of cement is ideal. The pattern is pressed into place with care, all air pockets worked out, as well as excess deposits of glue caught in between the wood and the pattern. Fingers do this job well.

When satisfied that the pattern is placed correctly, allow the glue to dry, then rub off all excess dry glue with your fingers. Dry rubber cement rolls off in little balls.

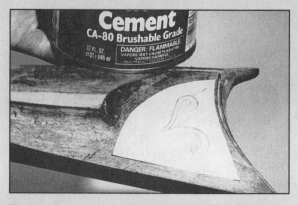

The pattern is glued to the stock with rubber cement.

Removing background wood in the pattern using a $3/16$-inch chisel blade.

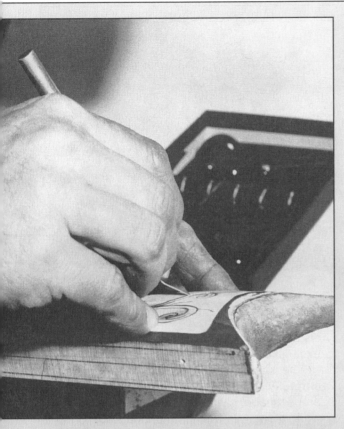

Tracing with an X-Acto knife or special pocketknife to cut the pattern into the wood.

Carving the Pattern

The cutting begins. Using the special pocketknife described earlier or an X-Acto knife, the entire perimeter of the pattern is cut to a depth of about $1/32$-inch. This cut is made just outside of the exterior pattern line. This is called outlining.

Remove all of the pattern paper covering the background of the design, but not the actual design pattern itself, which remains glued to the wood.

Since the relief carving is raised carving, the next step is to remove the wood that constitutes the background of the design, leaving the design itself in a raised posture. The $3/16$-inch chisel blade is used in this step. The goal is to cut away the background to a uniform depth. The height of the finished carving in our example is about $1/32$-inch, the depth of the first outline cut. Bullsfoot rasps and smooth mill files can also be used to good advantage here and can be purchased in different shapes and sizes. They are small and flat-bottomed, making background leveling much easier.

Moulding the Pattern

The moulding of the carving is an important step in gaining a truly finished appearance to

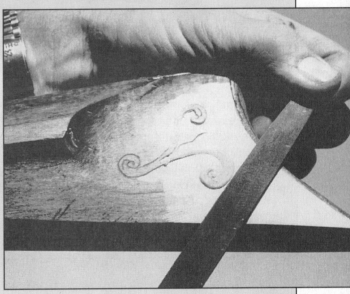

The background wood surface is filed with 6-inch smooth mill file.

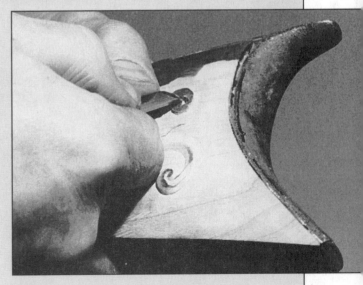

A carving chisel is used to sculpture the inner portion of one part of the pattern.

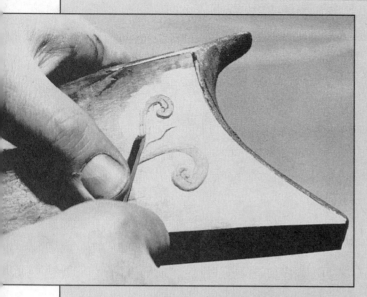

Using a ⅛-inch chisel to mould the scroll.

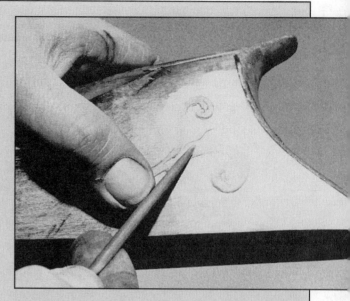

A half-round needle file is used to smooth the scroll.

the work. Moulding is accomplished quite well with gouges, sandpaper and, in some cases, a Dremel tool with small wood bits attached. Naturally, the use of any power tool in carving demands special care. The Dremel tool, for example, works beautifully; however, a slip can cause significant wood removal, making a mistake that could be impossible to rectify. Hand tools are slower, but are controlled easier than power tools. The beginner should consider confining himself to X-Acto knives, chis-

els and needle files until he has gained some experience in the art.

The sharp edges of the pattern are now carefully rounded, literally moulded to the proper shape, giving definition and form to the work, along with a smooth appearance to the scroll or leaf carving. A sense of depth is added by altering a flat surface into one that actually has low and high spots. There are entire books devoted to wood carving, and it is advisable for the beginner to study these texts in order to further his knowledge of this fascinating and attainable (by the average hobbyist) activity.

Sanding the Pattern

After moulding, the final task is smoothing the work with sandpaper. Open areas in the pattern are easily smoothed with small pieces of garnet paper, but tighter regions, especially with lines close together, require specialized abrasives, such as specially cut pieces of emery board. These should be shaped according to demand—custom fit, as it were, to reach those tight places in the pattern. Excellent scraper blades can be made from sections of hacksaw blade. These petite scrapers are ideal for removing minute amounts of wood. They do a nice job, leaving a relatively smooth surface when properly used (a light touch). Hacksaw blade scrapers reach into crevices in the pattern that few other tools can get to.

Also, dry pumice powder applied with a toothbrush will leave a smooth, polished surface on the wood pattern.

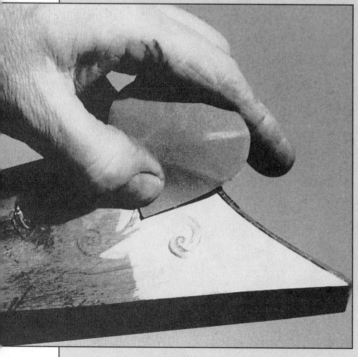

This specially cut piece of sandpaper is used to reach the hard-to-get-at places in the carving pattern.

Stock Styles

THE BLACKPOWDER HOBBY gunsmith needs a working knowledge of stock styles. Muzzleloaders exhibit numerous stock designs, many of which can be traced back to the dawn of gun building—from the crude firestick that was no more than a barrel and a chunk of wood, to the golden age of the Pennsylvania/Kentucky long rifle, a pinnacle of grace and design. Before a hobbyist can intelligently work on a stock, be his goal embellishment, restoration or repair, he should know why the stock is shaped as it is, and how to either retain or improve upon that particular configuration.

During the golden age of the American long rifle, many different schools of stock design arose, each significant and distinctive in its own right. Dedicated students can recognize differences in patch boxes and inlays, for example, from one school to the next. There was the famous Lancaster school, which noted gunmakers Henry Albright and Melchoir Fordney championed. Both are indicative of a region—Lancaster County, Pennsylvania. While their styles were of the same tradition, each incorporated personal touches on their rifles. Another regional style emanated from the York school, with fine craftsmen like Samuel Grove and the Gobrecht Family practicing their individual, yet similar, arts.

Mixing Stock Styles

"I made it myself" can be a statement of deserved pride, or an admission that may lead to embarrassment. Knowing stock styles is important for the hobbyist interested in making a custom rifle, or even customizing an existing piece. For example, one hobbyist I know created a long rifle that emulated the Pennsylvania/Kentucky era. However, he had mixed stock styles, and his rifle bore few of the redeeming traits of the originals. It's all right to alter a design intelligently; however, mixing stock styles haphazardly may result in a firearm that neither looks good nor handles properly.

Another newcomer to gunmaking displayed a riflestock he felt had beauty, style and grace, which perhaps it did. But the rifle also handled poorly, especially in the recoil department. The comb was slightly Roman nose in form, with a great deal of drop at the butt and very little drop at the comb. With heavy powder charges, the rifle whacked its owner smartly on the cheekbone every time he touched it off. Ultimately, the handsome rifle was not sold, but neither was it fired with heavy loads ever again. This example of a stock that looked good, but failed to handle recoil well, illustrates why the hobbyist must be properly informed about the ramifications of stock design.

Rifle Stock Styles

Full-stock, half-stock and three-quarter length are three basic muzzleloader stock styles, but it is also important for the hobby gunsmith to understand stock designs in terms of strength as well as style. When working on a stock, remember there are weaker areas that can break. Moreover, it is good to know stock styles in terms of appropriateness. For example, lavish embellishment of a basic poor boy stock style is unfitting.

Three-Quarter Stock

This is associated with military rifles that wore bayonets, because this design allowed attachment without interference from forend wood. The three-quarter stock was heavy in construction, especially in the wrist and buttstock, to withstand the rigors of the battlefield in hand-to-hand combat when bayonet thrusts and swift buttstock strokes were used to disable or dispatch the enemy.

Full-Stock

Identifying the full-stock rifle begins with the forend and its

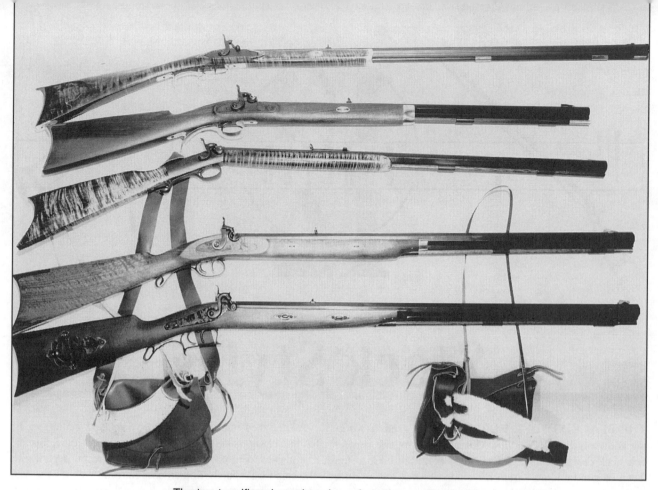

The two top rifles shown here have forend caps. The center rifle wears no forend cap at all. The two bottom rifles have not only forend caps, but also entry thimbles.

nose cap, which is generally constructed of silver, brass or cast pewter-type material. Sometimes a copper sheet is used. The less expensive long rifle design, known fondly as the poor boy, generally eliminates the nose cap. Incidentally, poor boy is not a derogatory title. It simply means a working rifle without much embellishment. The nose cap serves to protect the vulnerable forend of the full-stock rifle. Behind the nose cap, the forestock continues in a long, slender form, following the barrel that rests in its mortice. This section can be entirely plain, or it may be carved or inlayed.

The next feature of the full-stock rifle is where the ramrod enters, called an entry thimble. Normally made from brass, silver or steel, it protects the thin section of the stock that covers the ramrod. Once again, the full-stock poor boy design may be devoid of an entry thimble. The lock is positioned at the rearmost portion of the forend section of the stock. Behind the lock is a transition zone where the stock slims down, known as the wrist. It is the weakest point of the full-stock design, with thin wood and no support from the barrel. The attachment of a trigger guard also offers little support to the wrist, unless a long trigger plate is used, which may strengthen the area. Early flintlocks often used very thin wrists. It is not uncommon to find these with wrist repairs. Later Plains rifles went to heavier wrists, plus long upper and lower tangs that gave metal support to this area.

Going to the top of the stock, right behind the wrist, is a sec-

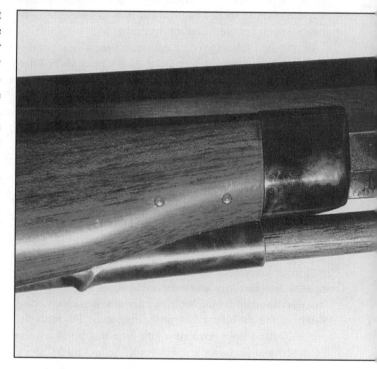

This rifle stock exhibits both a forend cap and an entry thimble. The forend cap protects the fore-part of the riflestock, while the entry thimble provides an accurate and stable recess for the ramrod.

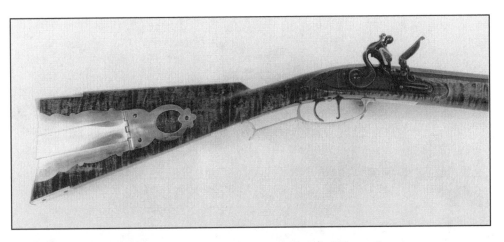

Many of the early flintlocks had very small wrists, as replicated here on this fine custom rifle. Cracks and breaks are possible in this region, and the blackpowder hobby gunsmith should be on the lookout for the beginning of trouble.

have moulding carved into it. This touch was common among gunsmiths of the golden age.

Half-Stock

Generally, the same overall stock parts observed on the full-stock are also associated with the half-stock, with the major exception being a much shorter forend. The half-stock rifle has a rib underneath the barrel to support the ramrod thimbles and may have an entry thimble and nose cap, as see on certain half-stock rifles built by the famous Hawken brothers.

Working with Stock Styles

No matter the style, keep in mind two things when working on or designing a stock: Replicating the original rifle, where the lines of the stock are vital to the correctness of the finished product, and working with stock modifications to correct a problem so the rifle can be fired with better aim, as well as shooter comfort. As examples of the latter, consider two commercial rifles, in finished and not kit form, that arrived with sharp cheekpieces. These literally cut into the face of the shooter. Careful filing and sanding of the offensive lines resulted in better shooting rifles.

Buttplate

This also affects authenticity and shootabilty. Early flintlocks, for example, tended to wide buttplates, while later designs were somewhat on the narrow side. These could deliver more felt recoil to the shoulder of the shooter. If building a custom rifle, remember that wider buttplates with more surface area are kinder to the shoulder. Also, where the modern muzzleloader is concerned, the addition of a top-grade rubber recoil pad is never a mistake.

LOP

An important stock consideration is length of pull (LOP). This is the distance in inches from the trigger to the center of the buttplate. It varies with the physique of the shooter—those with a long reach need a longer LOP, and vice versa. A short stock puts the shooter's thumb and nose in dangerous proximity. Also, the shooter has to scrunch up in order to properly mount and sight the rifle. On the other hand, an overly long stock may prevent the shooter from properly placing his face on the comb so he can see his sights clearly, as well as shoot in

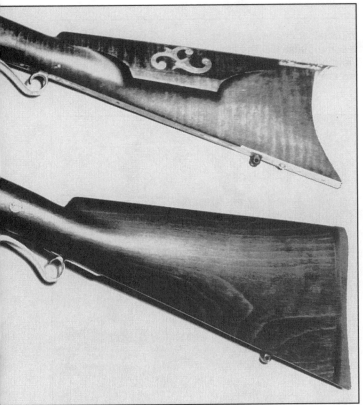

Here is an excellent example of two different buttplate styles, the top having the crescent or rifle-style buttplate with deeply curved line, while the lower stock has the flatter shotgun-style buttplate, along with a modern recoil pad and a more modern rounded bottom toe line.

tion known as the comb nose. The comb is at the top of the buttstock, which is the backmost part of the stock. The butt is usually, but not always, covered by a buttplate made of steel, brass or silver. In some instances, the lack of a buttplate suggests a utility firearm; however, certain high-class rifles and shotguns also go without them as a matter of style. The section of the stock running from the lower wrist to the buttplate is known as the toe line. The shape and width of the toe line often depends upon the type of buttplate used. If it is flat-bottomed, the toe line will be flat up to and including the trigger guard. On ornate rifles, the bottom part of the toe line may

This Thompson/Center modern muzzleloader shows a very straight comb with very little drop at the buttstock. The higher comb is ideal when a scope is mounted because it lifts the shooter's face so that his eyes are more in line with the center of the scope's ocular lens.

comfort. It forces the shooter into a poor stance, especially from the offhand position. Whether too long or too short, the condition can be corrected by cutting the stock or adding a piece of wood. The latter can be more difficult because matching color, grain and other properties of new wood to old is not easily done. Of course, the buttplate will have to be refitted in either case.

Drop

Besides LOP, another consideration is the stock's drop, the downward slope of the comb from an imaginary line that runs along the top of the barrel. The comb must support the shooter's face, giving the cheek a resting place and directing the marksman's vision to the sights for a clean sight picture. During recoil, the comb should not jam back into the cheekbone. There are always exceptions to standard stock dimensions; however, as a rule with a muzzleloader using conventional iron sights, drop is $1^1/_2$ inches at the comb nose and $2^1/_2$ inches at the buttstock.

Often, drop is affected by the specific sights mounted on the rifle. For example, if a scope is used, or if special double-aperture target sights are mounted, then the drop must be such that the shooter can mount the rifle normally, automatically gaining a reasonably good sight picture. With inadequate drop, the shooter must crowd his face down on the stock, which is not conducive to comfort during recoil. A lot of drop at the buttstock, with very little at comb, may cause a heavy recoiling rifle to drive directly into the cheekbone of the shooter.

Breeches

There are two basic breech styles in the muzzleloader that determine stock design in that region: the non-takedown with fixed tang and the hooked breech. The latter allows quick and facile barrel removal by driving out the wedges or pins holding barrel and stock together. The barrel wedge, also known as a key, offers a strong and reliable method of holding stock to

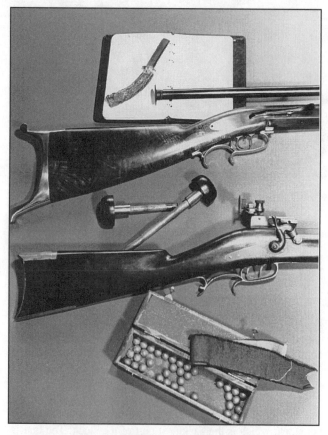

These two target stocks show very little drop. Both have target sights that are set quite high, and the modest drop at the comb allows the shooter's eye to line up accurately with the sights.

barrel. The problem with wedges is difficulty in positioning them on the stock. Beginners to muzzleloader gun building will probably find it no easy matter. Pins are easier to work with and are nearly as reliable. They stand up to medium, if not extremely heavy, recoil. I know of a 54-caliber half-

This Knight MK-85 modern muzzleloader clearly depicts the trend, which is function above any other criterion. The rifle has a black composite stock of thumbhole design.

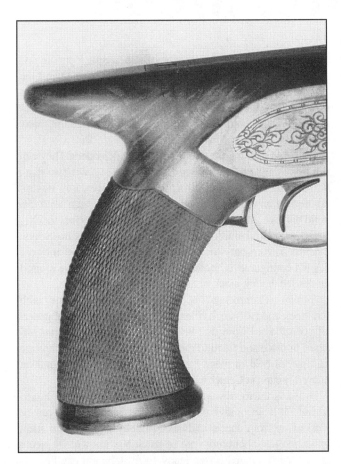

Here is a sawhandle pistol stock, an excellent stock style for target shooting because the web part of the hand between thumb and forefinger have an excellent resting place.

stock rifle using pins that has shown no tendency to fail in its twenty-year lifespan.

The hobby gunsmith must be able to recognize the different breech styles so he can intelligently and successfully disassemble these rifles for cleaning (see Chapter 21) or repairs.

Ultimately, personal preference and historical correctness dictate which stock design the hobbyist will wish to build, either in kit form or as a custom project, but practical considerations regarding shootability must be observed.

Modern Muzzleloader Stocks

The goal of this modern stock style is function more than anything else. Because the modern muzzleloader has no historical roots to worry about, anything goes, even thumbhole models. Materials, as noted elsewhere, can be wood or synthetic.

Shotgun Stocks

Single-barrel shotguns can wear stocks that are rifle-like. Double-barrel shotguns with one-piece stocks and hooked breeches may have a slight weakness in front of the breech due to the small size of the stock. In spite of this, though, seldom is a broken stock encountered. The wrist area of the double-barrel shotgun is also on the small side, especially considering the 12- and 10-bores, but due to a long tang on the trigger guard that offers support in this region, breaks are not common. If a break should occur, or for that matter a crack, Chapter 10 on wood repair shows how to deal with these problems.

Pistol Stocks

Choices in pistol stock design are somewhat limited to two basic styles: bird's-head and sawhandle, with some variations. The latter is ideal for the target pistol, incidentally, due to better contact with the web of the hand. These were also used on some duelling pistols. The bird's-head style is noted for its attractiveness and may be found on Kentucky pistols. Most blackpowder pistol kits have this particular style, but the hobbyist can modify it through judicious reshaping. And, as always, numerous embellishments as well as repairs are also possible on pistol stocks.

Muzzleloader Metals

WOOD AND METAL are the primary materials employed by the blackpowder hobby gunsmith. Woods have been discussed at length in previous sections of the book, and now metals get their turn. Muzzleloader metals are quite basic, but an understanding of their characteristics and uses is worthwhile for anyone interested in working with these firearms. While silver and gold are used for embellishments, and other metals like aluminum find their way into blackpowder gunsmithing and building, brass, steel and German silver are the three dominant metals for muzzleloaders.

Brass

An alloy of copper and zinc, brass is malleable (capable of being hammered or rolled out without breaking) and ductile (capable of being drawn into wire). Brass is harder than copper and, of course, quite strong.

It is used extensively in muzzleloaders for many pieces of metalwork. Bought in sheets of different sizes and thicknesses, brass can be stamped into muzzleloader parts, as well as sawed out and nicely finished. Easily worked by hand, brass can be soldered, if necessary, or engraved for decorative purposes. It is a very traditional muzzleloader metal.

Barrel wedges and certain types of pins need a metal device on the sides of the stock to protect the wood where they protrude through the forend. Such devices prevent early wood wear and guard against chipping of the stock when the wedges or pins are removed or replaced. Escutcheons serve this purpose, while also providing a small area of possible decoration, simple or elaborate—the latter requiring considerable engraving skill, partly due to the small surface on which to work. In a sense, escutcheons can be thought of as washers. They usually are of oval or elliptical shape, and some are round, although there are no set rules.

Along with the function of serving as a pass-through for pins and keys, some escutcheons (lock-screw escutcheons) support the head of a screw, giving it more bearing against the surface of the stock and preventing the head of the screw from pressing into the wood. Escutcheons are common on muzzleloader styles of both past and present, and are found in many current blackpowder kits.

Decorative inlays are common on muzzleloaders. They can run from simple oval pieces set into the top of a wrist, to stars, half-moon shapes, hearts or, for that matter, any design favored by an individual gunmaker. The hobby gunsmith can build his own inlays from sheet brass to add a personal touch.

Brass ramrod guides can be built in two distinct ways: machined from bar stock or stamped out and bent into the desired configuration. Both methods provide attractive ramrod guides for the full-stock or half-stock rifle or pistol.

Similar to ramrod guides, nose caps can be built into both full-stock and half-stock rifles. Full-stock nose caps are generally constructed from thin brass, with the end of the cap soldered in place and fitted to the barrel. Half-stock nose caps are cast pieces held in place by screws, as commonly found on many Thompson/Center muzzle-loading rifles.

Brass is an ideal metal for patch boxes and cap boxes because it is decorative in color, readily engraved and can be worked up from sheets. Advanced hobbyists can form sheet brass into just about any type of patch box known. Or precut and properly hinged boxes ready for installation can be purchased from outlets such as Don Eads' Muzzleloader Builder's Supply, an important source for blackpowder gunsmithing hobbyists. On the other hand, certain cap boxes are cast from heavy brass, as seen on some Thompson/Center rifles. With a minimum of tools, patch boxes handmade from sheet brass, preformed patch boxes, and cap boxes cast from heavy brass make an especially good addition to kits that do not already incorporate them.

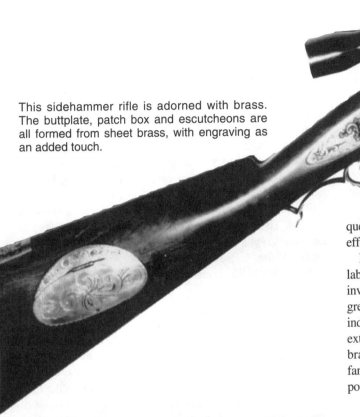

This sidehammer rifle is adorned with brass. The buttplate, patch box and escutcheons are all formed from sheet brass, with engraving as an added touch.

Many muzzleloaders employ toe plates to protect the stock from chipping. These functional brass pieces can be plain or ornate, depending upon the style of the gun as well as the desires of the gunsmith. The addition of a toe plate is worthwhile, and the project can be accomplished by the hobbyist.

Sheet brass has long been used for repairs or to cover a mistake that could not be readily hidden any other way. Just about every gun museum has old-time firearms showing a brass repair of a stock fracture. For example, while drilling a ramrod hole, the hole can go off course, breaking through the bottom of the stock and leaving a hole where there should not be one. In this case, the options are clear: start over with another stock or fix the hole. Sheet brass can be cut to form a decorative pattern, then inlaid over the mistake as if it were meant to be there all the time. The hole is covered, and the repair does not look like one.

Gunsmiths of yesteryear often cast buttplates from brass by melting the metal in the forge and making a sand casting. Today, brass is still used extensively for buttplates because it is rather easily cast into shape, plus it offers a good-looking, yet highly protective, fitting for the butt. Brass will not rust or deteriorate when exposed to inclement weather.

Brass also makes excellent trigger guards, which were often cast by early American gunmakers. Today's hobbyist will find a large variety of brass trigger guards offered by parts suppliers. These are high-quality castings, far surpassing what our forefathers had to work with. In kit building, the hobby gunsmith can substitute a brass guard more to his liking than the one supplied. The project requires some fitting, along with certain modifications to suit the particular contour of the stock in

question. However, the challenge is enjoyable and worth the effort.

Brass parts are easy to file and polish. Polishing by hand is laborious, but relaxing, and the end result is well worth the invested time. Power polishing wheels can speed the process greatly; however, there is more risk of washing out lines or inducing damage, especially for a hobbyist who does not have extensive experience with these high-speed machines. Certain brass parts embody graceful lines or curves, especially on fancy trigger guards, and these can be erased in no time on the power polishing wheel.

German Silver

German silver was once called electrum. It is a white alloy of copper, nickel and zinc, often used in the manufacture of cutlery. German silver is also known as nickel silver and albata. It may be used in place of brass for many parts—including escutcheons, inlays, nose caps, patch boxes, cap boxes, trigger guards and buttplates. The obvious difference is the color, German silver giving a white appearance, while brass has a yellow hue. Sometimes they are used together for a nice effect. German silver can be worked in the same manner that brass is formed to make gun parts. It is also sold in sheets, for example, and can be cast. German silver can also be engraved, although some claim this material tends to "grab" the engraving tool more than brass.

Casting German silver can be problematic, though, because it has a propensity to develop pits in the finished product. For large gun parts, such as buttplates and trigger guards, casters often replace German silver with white bronze. It casts easier and looks just like German silver. Also, casters often experience fewer reject parts with white bronze, a savings in time and expense.

Nose caps can be cast, instead of being made from sheet brass or German silver. The material used for this process is often tin, sometimes employed as an alloy by adding a little lead.

Steel

Steel is also an alloy, composed of iron plus carbon—the latter in varying amounts according to the specific kind of steel, of which there are many. It is extremely tough and, therefore, makes excellent gun parts. Steel can be somewhat malleable under certain conditions, while also having great hardness properties achieved through heating and sudden cooling. A high-carbon steel may contain as much as 1.5 percent carbon; softer steels contain far less.

Barrels, locks, tangs, triggers and numerous other parts are candidates for steel. Also, military blackpowder rifles of the past sometimes wore steel ramrods. These were of small diameter, but well-tempered and strong, ideal for battlefield conditions. We still find steel ramrods on many musket-type muzzleloaders replicated for today's market. Also noteworthy, thin steel pieces have been used for escutcheons, lock screws, toe plates, trigger guards, buttplates and other furniture. The original Hawken Brothers Plains rifle used steel for furniture. These rifles were said to be "iron mounted," with very little use of brass or German silver.

Because steel is such a hard metal, it is difficult to work or form into various shapes—as opposed to brass or German silver—but the finished part is also stronger. Furthermore, steel polishes well, takes on a good finish, and can be blued, browned and color case-hardened.

Heat-Treating

The hobby gunsmith will not venture into the more involved aspects of working with various kinds of steels; however, he can work steel in many different ways, from browning gun parts to certain types of heat-treating. As noted earlier, steel is composed of iron with carbon. Extremely soft steels cannot be hardened successfully, while those with higher carbon content can be made extremely hard.

But before going further, it's wise to stop and ask why we even bother to harden a metal that is already hard as it comes to us, as in a blackpowder gun kit. The reason for further tempering is additional strength and reduced wear. Lock parts, trigger parts and other working essentials of the muzzleloader can have life prolonged or hardness restored after repairs. Also, heat-treating is important in hardening the frizzen of the flintlock for improved sparking qualities.

The frontier gunsmith had a forge, but the modern gunsmith does not have to resort to a forge for his source of heat. For example, a propane bottle torch supplies heat for soldering with total convenience. A Prest-O-Lite acetylene torch delivers much more heat for larger parts, and the oxygen/acetylene torch provides the necessary heat range for welding, brazing and soldering.

For heat-treating parts, the oxygen/acetylene torch is required. These have various tips with orifices calculated to deliver different levels of heat. The serious hobbyist will find a number of uses for such a torch. The occasional blackpowder hobbyist may wish to rent a torch or have his heat-treating done for him.

Hardening

Oversimplifying the process, heat-treating means using an oxygen-acetylene torch to bring a piece of steel to bright cherry red. Temperature is in the neighborhood of 1400 degrees Fahrenheit. Temperatures higher than this rise above the high critical point of steel, which causes the metal to crystallize when quenched. Significantly lower temperatures do not bring the molecules of steel into proper motion for ultimate alteration of its hardness. Quenching oil is then used to drastically cool the heated steel within a relatively brief period of time.

As it is quenched, a vapor skin is formed on its exterior.

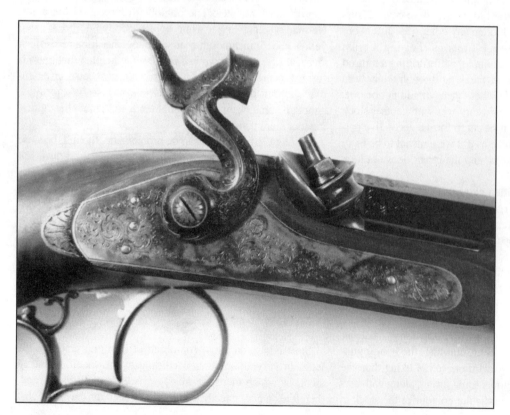

Steel, one of the most durable of muzzleloader metals, was used to make this lock, hammer, trigger and guard.

Incidentally, only true quenching oil is correct for the job. It is formulated to retard warpage of the heated piece of metal. Furthermore, quenching oil has a high flash point, so it will not readily burst into fire when contacting the heated part. Naturally, caution is still advised. Remember, the container of oil is open to accept the hot piece of steel, so anything can fall into it, including flammables. Safeguard the oil container from such contamination.

On the initial quench, the steel part should emerge so hard that a regular metal file will not cut into its surface. At this point, the steel is much too hard to be useful as a gun part, because its ultra hardness makes it brittle and prone to breakage. Therefore, it must be drawn back.

Drawing Back

To do this, the part must be polished bright so its colors can be observed when reheated. Now the part is reheated as evenly as possible, because uneven heating may cause it to warp

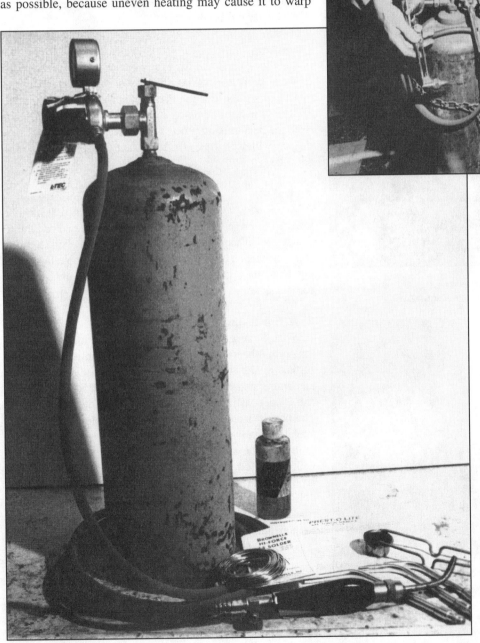

An oxygen/acetylene torch with an assortment of tips is a versatile heat source for the gunsmith.

A Prest-O-Lite acetylene torch with extra tips is an excellent heat source for the workshop. It will perform many services.

The color change of the heated part is obvious in this illustration.

Smoke emanates from the container of quenching oil, but due to its composition, the oil does not ignite.

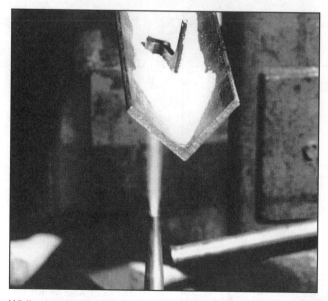

While drawing the temper of this sear, a bed of sand is used to evenly distribute heat.

when quenched. To help accomplish this, place the part on a bed of sand resting on a metal surface. Heat is applied to the metal surface, which transfers it to the sand, and then evenly heats the metal part. If this method is not possible, the part must be heated by torch with continuous motion from a steady and patient hand.

The hobbyist will not likely own a special heat-treating furnace, which brings the steel to a precise temperature; therefore, judgment by eye is necessary. With practice, this process works very well.

While drawing back, watch for color changes in the steel. First, the part will turn light yellow, and then deepen into a darker golden hue. In turn, this yields to a light blue, and then to a dark purple color, followed by a dull red, and finally a bright red. If the steel is heated beyond this point, it will turn white just before it melts. Because watching for colors is so important, draw the steel part in natural light. Avoid fluorescent light because it distorts the true colors of the steel, as far as the human eye is concerned.

Quenching

Most lock parts and triggers made of carbon steel will be drawn to a color somewhere between a dark straw yellow and blue, then quenched in oil. Parts not made of carbon steel will require case-hardening, as explained later. When all goes well, the heat-treating process ends here. If a problem arises, the part will need to be resoftened (annealed) and the process repeated.

Annealing

To anneal a steel part unsatisfactorily hardened, it must be reheated to bright red, then placed in a warm bed of sand to slowly cool. This produces a softened state. An abrupt temperature change, as by oil quenching, is not desirable in annealing. Now, the softened steel part is put through the hardening process again.

Case-Hardening

When a piece of steel does not contain adequate carbon for normal heat-treating, carbon must be introduced to the surface of the steel to make it harder. This is called case-hardening, and it is an excellent means of adding a harder and longer-lasting surface with a softer internal structure. The part is heated to a dull red color, coated with Kasenit, reheated again to dull red, and finally quenched in water (not oil). The surface of the steel part will be glass-hard with a mottled gray tone, while the interior will retain its original softness.

If a small part were hardened all the way through, it could break. But if it has a hard surface with a softer interior, it will be more durable.

Soldering

This uses a minimum of heat to join two pieces of metal with modest holding power. Not that soldering is an inferior method for joining parts; it's just not as certain as welding or brazing. The most common type of solder is standard

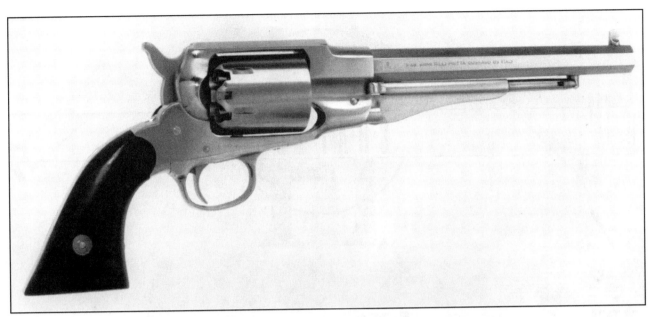

Although not strictly traditional, this replica 1858 Remington Civil War revolver is offered in a stainless steel version. The hobby gunsmith should know the merits, and demerits, of stainless steel, as well as all metals used in muzzle-loading.

plumber's formula, known as 50/50—half lead, half tin. While it has many uses, 50/50 solder is not the best for gunwork. For example, if parts joined with it are blued (with heated bluing tanks) in a bath of caustic salts, separation is likely. A better choice is Brownells' Hi-Force 44 solder, which bonds well and flows at a relatively low temperature, allowing the smith to work with a modest heat source. Also, metals bonded with Hi-Force 44 do not come apart when being blued in a hot caustic salt bath.

Stainless Steel

This is a newcomer to the world of muzzleloaders. It has been used in blackpowder shotguns, revolvers and rifles of many different types, including the modern muzzleloader. Stainless steel is excellent in its ability to resist corrosion and rust, but, as with all materials, it has drawbacks. Compared with carbon steels, stainless is softer, making it more vulnerable to scratches and wear. While it is important to exercise considerable care in protecting the barrel crown of any firearm, this is especially true of a stainless steel barrel. Ideally, a muzzle protector will be employed not only when cleaning, but also with the short starter. Furthermore, stainless steel is more prone to stripping a thread, so use extra lubrication when parts are removed for cleaning or gunsmithing. The blackpowder hobbyist is a source of information, as well as a builder, and therefore he should know as much as he can about these things.

Safety

As a reminder, working with metals at all levels, and especially during heat-treating or case-hardening, demands special attention to eye and skin protection. Wear goggles and gloves, covering up all skin that could be exposed to burns. Also, ensure adequate ventilation for the various pollutants—particle or chemical—that you may encounter.

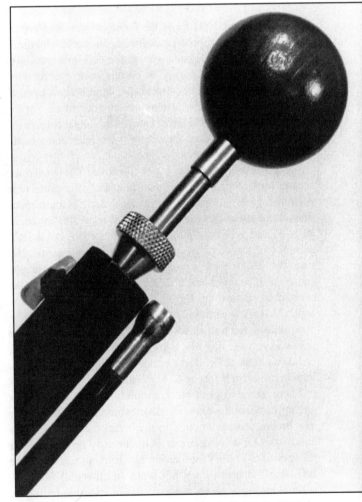

A muzzle guard accurately centers the ramrod in the bore, protecting the rifling and muzzle crown from ramrod or cleaning rod damage or wear. This one is in action on a short starter.

Bluing and Browning Metals

METAL FINISHING FOR the muzzleloader hobby gunsmith falls into two broad categories. Numerous methods require extensive equipment—even the full-time gunsmith often seeks specialized experts to do this work. On the other hand, there are a number of metal-finishing options open to the hobbyist that demand a minimum of equipment. For the sake of knowledge, sophisticated metal-finishing processes are discussed here. However, the hobbyist can learn some methods for the modest workshop setting.

Metal finishes serve two major functions. They make the firearm look complete, rather than raw, and offer protection. All finish types are usable for muzzleloaders. Modern metal finishes are just as at home on smokebelchers as they are on the latest bolt-action rifle. On the other hand, a replica of a 19th-century longarm deserves a finish that fits the time period. Hot bluing is definitely more modern than browning, for example, and even more up-to-date is Black T, or Black Teflon, a specialized proprietary finish from W.E. Birdsong & Associates, applied when a firearm is destined for severe weather use. This maximum protection finish may not seem appropriate on a frontloader, but if that rifle is used in wet conditions, Black T could be just the ticket. The muzzleloader can be sent through a local gunsmith to Birdsong & Associates for the job.

There are also possible combinations of finishes. For example, polished brass or silver combined with a slow rust brown process applied to the barrel can be especially handsome. Or a lockplate or buttplate may be sent off for professional color case-hardening. Remember, even the full-time gunsmith does not work in all metal finishes, often sending a piece away for color case-hardening or electrolysis nickel finish. Some smiths even use specialized deep blue finishes. But a finish is only as good as the surface of the metal it enhances. The more time spent preparing the metal before finishing, the better the finish.

Polishing

This is the first step to a good metal finish, necessary to most, but not all, types of finish. Polishing steel and non-ferrous metals is accomplished in various ways. The hobby gunsmith has the luxury of time on his side so he can lavish his attention on the polishing process before finishing. He does not have to meet the deadlines normally faced by the professional smith. That is why hand polishing and hobby gunsmithing go together so well. Hand polishing is still recognized as the best way to arrive at a near-perfect finish. It allows all corners to remain sharp and all flat areas to remain flat. Contours are kept clean. Of course, hand polishing is also the most time-consuming method. The process begins with hand filing parts to remove any rough spots left by machine work, as well as flashings, gates and generally rough moulds for cast parts.

Octagonal Barrel Polishing

All filing here is accomplished with care, and with the correct file. For example, an octagonal barrel may have boldly visible mill or shaper marks left in the metal. A smith should use a large 18-inch mill file to draw-file the flats for initial rough-filing, using clean, sweeping strokes. The big mill file cuts cleanly and quickly. Then, the smith may wish to turn to a 12-inch mill file to smooth out any rough areas. While it may seem like avoidance of duty, there truly is little reason to work long and hard on the three lower barrel flats when they will be hidden by the stock of the long rifle.

After the file work, turn to 80-grit abrasive cloth (or paper) wrapped on a flat wooden stick or file, then work in the same draw-filing style, up and down the flats in long sweeping strokes. This step removes all file marks. It's a progressive program: The next step uses 100-grit abrasive to remove

Mounting an abrasive belt on the Scott Murray Sanding Drum. Notice the wide selection of belts hanging on the wall behind it.

(Below) An octagonal barrel is draw-filed by hand. This is an extremely time-consuming process, but produces the best surface for metal finishing.

finishing process. Finish will not cover up scratches, and an unpolished barrel or other piece of metal will show up as a poor finishing job. There is no shortcut here. The hobbyist who wants the best possible finish on his metal will invest time and labor in polishing.

Power Polishing

Power polishing equipment is a terrific time-saver; however, the end result will not be as perfect as hand polishing. Furthermore, rough metal parts still require draw-filing, even when power polishing is used. However, some hobbyists will have the equipment at hand, and prefer this method. A handy piece of equipment for the job is the Scott Murray Sanding Drum. This unique, metal-flanged, rubber drum expands under rotation, holding a sanding belt firmly in place around the wheel. It also allows quick and facile belt changes. It's easy to lift off one belt and install another.

Abrasive sanding belts are available starting at 60-grit and running all the way to 600-grit. This special polishing wheel can be attached to an electric motor producing 1725 rpm, making it one of the most versatile polishing wheels available. While this tool will not handle every polishing operation, it does work for many projects. It is especially ideal for working flat surfaces. Of course, polishing at high speed demands extra attention. It's easy to make a mistake. Also, don't get caught up in the idea that the use of progressive grits is not necessary with power polishing. Starting out with a coarse grit and continuing with finer grits is *always* the proper technique. Using sequential grits actually requires less polishing time, too, and helps keep lines and flats intact. *Warning*: Power polishing requires experience, so using the Scott Murray wheel demands practice.

The Bead-Blast

Worthy of mention for the reader's knowledge is the bead-blast cabinet. After polishing, any steel part can be placed in

marks left by the 80-grit. The same draw-file motion is continued, progressing with finer and finer abrasive cloth, all the way to 600-grit. The latter is seldom required in pre-polishing metal for finishing purposes. Normally, running to 300-grit is more than sufficient.

Finer abrasive, down to 600-grit, may be necessary, however, to finely polish pieces of brass or silver. And, admittedly, there are a few rare cases where a particular piece of steel will benefit from finer than 300-grit abrasive. The goal is quite simple, yet extremely important—prepare the metal for the

one and blasted "hard" or "easy." Bead-blasting leaves a clean surface for browning and bluing solutions. The hobbyist will not normally own one of these, but there may be a professional gunsmith in the area who offers bead-blasting services.

Chemical Treatments

After all polishing is completed, it is time to chemically treat the metal to produce a brown or blue finish. No matter which finish is chosen, when treating a barrel, it is imperative to plug both ends of the barrel. This prevents bore damage. The market offers numerous solutions for metal finishing. Brownells has a long list of products to choose from, for example, as does Log Cabin Sport Shop. Ideally, the hobbyist will experiment with various brands and types until he arrives at the one he prefers to work with. Good news: If the finish is not what you expected, start over. It's a simple matter of polishing off the bad finish and applying a new one. Of course, this means extra time and involvement, but that is better than living with a finish you don't like. Here are a few finishes to consider.

Rust Brown

One of the easiest finishes to apply, rust brown is also durable and historic. The process requires a sweat box made of wood, into which water vapor is introduced, providing a damp atmosphere of about 80 to 85 percent humidity. The box must obviously be long enough to accommodate a gun barrel, and there must be a means of suspending the barrel or other gun part within the box. Sophisticated sweat boxes are available, but here is a practical sweat box any hobbyist can make.

A rectangular box with lid is built of plywood. Within the box, a barrel support is also built of wood using whatever design works best. Cover the bottom of the box with a thick

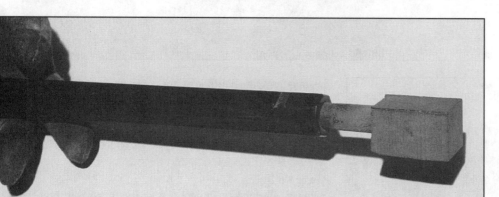

With any finishing method that uses rusting as part of the process, the barrel must be plugged to protect from chemicals and rust.

(Below) A bead blast cabinet, usually found only in the professional shop, is a big help when preparing steel parts for browning or bluing.

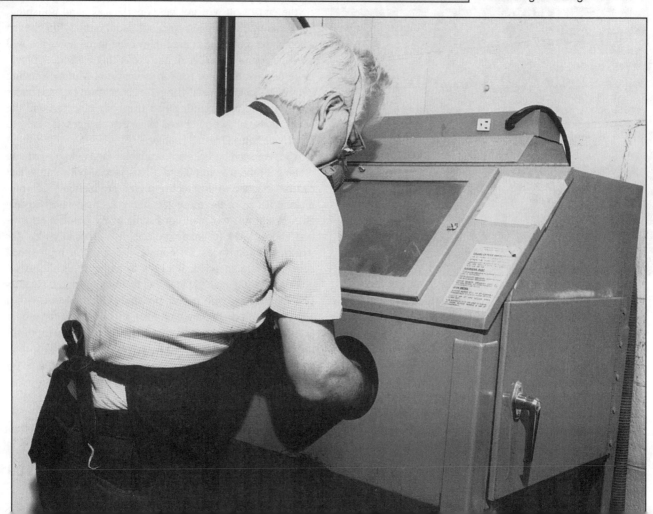

layer of sawdust or rags, soaked with water. An environment for rusting is now ensured.

Important: Steel wool is used in this process; however, the steel wool must be degreased carefully. If not done, grease from the steel wool will permeate the metal part to be finished, blocking both rust and chemicals. Steel wool can be degreased with acetone.

Rapid Browns

The old-timers called this express browning. The result of the process is a pleasing brown hue, but the effect is not as long-lasting as the slower rust-brown method. Birchwood Casey's Plum Brown is a good fast-brown solution. The idea is to heat the metal parts to a temperature that causes the solution to sizzle when it is applied, like drops of water on a hot frying pan. If the barrel is not heated evenly, the solution will spatter all over when applied, and the end result is a yellowish oxide on the surface of the steel. If this happens, remove the coating and start over. Follow the instructions supplied with the product. *Warning*: Do the job only in an area with adequate ventilation and do not breathe the fumes.

Polishing and degreasing are also important to this fast-brown process. The final finish will be only as good as the pre-finish. Also, careful heat control is vital to consistency. A propane torch can be used for smaller parts, while an oxygen/acetylene torch is better for large pieces, such as barrels. Suspend the barrel in order to heat it evenly. One way to do this is with a long wiping stick (see Chapter 19 on ramrods). Allow plenty of the wooden rod to stick out on both sides of the barrel (the breech plug is removed in this instance). Then, suspend wires from the ceiling that wrap around both ends of the wooden rod. This allows even heating. Here again, the first coating is vital. It must be even.

Ideally, the first coatings of rapid browning solution should be applied to the underside of the barrel, the part that will never be seen once it is seated in the stock's barrel channel. This allows the hobbyist to gain some practice, seeing how much liquid should be applied.

Three applications of solution are usually adequate. It takes about two hours to apply three coatings to a barrel, incidentally, so budget your time carefully. To stop the rusting action, apply a water and baking soda mixture to the metal, and then coat with paste wax. An alternative method, after the barrel is browned, is to place it in a sweat box, even though the rapid browning was used. This promotes a sort of aging process. Leave the barrel in the sweat box for about eight hours, then stop the rusting process as before with a water/baking soda and wax coating. The fast method of browning steel is quite acceptable and offers good results.

Rust Blue

Similar in practice to browning, this method imparts a blue/black color instead of brown. Once again, a solution is used to affect this finish, and Brownells offers different brands. A large tank of boiling water is necessary for this operation. Of course, that tank can be an old roaster heated on the stove if the part is small, such as a pistol barrel. But for rifle barrels, a much larger container is needed. Be certain to plug

A part is polished on a hard felt wheel. Proper safety equipment is used by the operator—glasses, gloves, respirator.

Hot caustic salt tanks are normally associated with the professional shop. Small parts are being lowered into the bluing tank. Rubber gloves and eye protection are a must.

barrels carefully, then follow the instructions on the bluing product. Naturally, polishing is vital to success once again, followed by careful degreasing. Rust bluing can be beautiful. In fact, some professional gunmakers of the hour prefer rust bluing to hot bluing. It is an old process, dating back well into the 19th century.

Instant Blue

This is also known as cold blue, and many brands are available. Proper metal preparation allows a reasonably good finish with cold blue, but it does not match hot blue methods for durability. For minor touch-ups, cold blue is acceptable. The process is rather simple, and the hobbyist need only read the instructions supplied with the product.

Hot Caustic Blue

The firearms industry uses this method almost exclusively, except for double-barrel guns where barrels are soft soldered together. Today, most commercial muzzleloaders, especially the modern ones, are hot-blued. Professional gunshops also use hot caustic bluing methods. The hobbyist is advised to prepare his project for bluing with a high-grade polishing job,

then take the pieces to a professional shop that does hot bluing. Those who wish to delve deeper into this process should read *Firearms Bluing and Browning* by R.H. Angier.

Color Case-Hardening

Beautiful—especially on lockplates, buttplates and other selected muzzleloader parts—color case-hardening is a job for a professional specializing in the process. It's a part of the gunsmithing world the hobbyist should know about, while letting a professional do it. Forget color case-hardening as a home project. Many have tried it and many have failed. True, old-time smiths once placed small metal parts in a mixture of burnt leather and powdered bone, apparently hardening the metal while imparting some coloration, but this is a far cry from color case-hardening.

The subject of metal finishes, surprisingly, is quite broad and complex, and too numerous to list. Those touched on here, however, are the major finishes of interest to the blackpowder hobby gunsmith. Fortunately, it is possible to produce a perfectly acceptable, even handsome, finish in the home workshop. And for those finishes that are not right for the hobbyist, there is always the alternative of having a pro do the work.

Rust-Browning a Barrel

Tools
Mill Cut File, 12-inch
Mill Cut File, 18-inch

Supplies
Abrasive Cloth, 80-, 100-, 300- and 600-grit
Acetone
Baking Soda
Birchwood Casey Degreaser
Commercial Browning Solution
Cotton Polishing Gloves
Cotton Swab
Paste Wax
Steel Wool
Sweat Box
Water
Wooden Plugs

Preparing the Metal

Polish the metal, as described in the chapter text, using progressively finer files and polishing cloths in a long, sweeping draw-file motion. Next, make well-fitting wooden plugs for the barrel and insert in both ends. The open ends of the barrel must be securely blocked, or rust and chemicals will ruin the rifling. Tap these wooden plugs in place, gently, but sufficiently deep to form a seal.

Degrease all metal parts with one of the many degreasing products on the market. Birchwood Casey offers a good one that is often found in sporting goods shops. Bead-blasting is also a means of degreasing, if a bead-blast cabinet is available. Parts must be grease-free or they will not rust evenly. Also, oils from the hands can thwart even rusting, so wear gloves when working with the parts. Brownells offers cotton polishing gloves. Use only a new pair that has not been contaminated and keep them perfectly clean throughout the operation.

Read all instructions that come with the browning solution, and be aware of all safety precautions. For those concerned about having toxic chemical solutions in the house, there is a non-toxic alternative offered by Laurel Mountain Forge called Barrel Brown & Degreaser, sold through blackpowder outlets. Even non-toxic chemicals should be treated with great respect. Especially, keep all chemicals away from children.

Applying the Browning Solution

The polished and degreased barrel is now ready for the browning solution. Fully dampen a

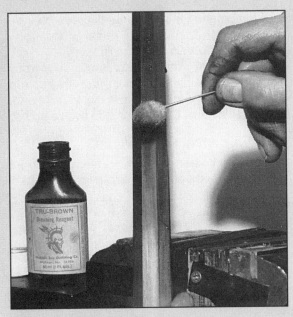

Browning solution is applied to a barrel for a rust brown finish.

cotton swab with the solution and apply it evenly to the barrel. This first coating is important, so make it even. If the initial coating runs or fails to coat evenly in any way, it's wise to stop the process here, repolish and try again.

Hand-polishing a barrel using wet/dry abrasive cloth wrapped around a file.

Rusting the Treated Metal

The sweat box interior should be warm, which it would be on a sunny summer day. If this is not the case, install a light bulb to raise the temperature. A warm atmosphere promotes humidity, and humidity promotes rust. You may wish to place a glass photographic thermometer in the box to check temperature.

In this sweat box, old blue jeans saturated with water are placed inside to provide a high humidity environment, which is necessary for rust-browning solutions.

A temperature of around 90 degrees Fahrenheit is good. If the box remains too cool, increase the wattage of the light bulb.

Leave the treated parts in the sweat box for the time prescribed on the instruction sheet for the particular browning solution chosen. This could be from three to twelve hours.

Carding with Steel Wool

When time is up, remove the piece from the sweat box and card with degreased steel

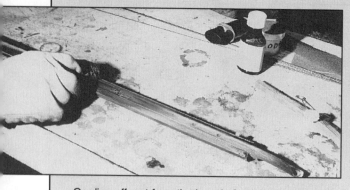

Carding off rust from the barrel after it is taken from the sweat box. Gloves prevent contamination of the barrel with oil or grease. The small stainless steel brush was used for carding off parts too small for easy handling. Degreased 4.0 steel wool is right for most carding.

wool. Acetone will remove grease from steel wool, but let it dry first. Do not allow grease of any kind on the metal. Rub the surface with steel wool to cut scale and rust. This prepares the metal for the next coating of solution.

Applying More Solution

Apply another coating of solution as before. Then, replace the metal in the sweat box for further rusting. The more evenly the browning solution is applied, the better. Repeat the coating/sweat box/carding procedure until the metal is dark.

Finishing Touches

When the metal is suitably dark, discontinue the rusting process by applying a baking soda/water mixture to the metal, then coat the metal with paste wax. Allow the piece to set overnight. Check in the morning to see if rust-

Applying baking soda with a water-soaked rag, a wash-down process that neutralizes the browning action.

ing has been halted. If it has not ceased, a rough-looking patch will be evident. Apply baking soda/water again, followed by paste wax.

Important: Do not attempt to stop the rusting process by placing the metal in boiling water because this can cause the surface to turn matte black.

Metal Embellishment

THIS IS ANOTHER knowledge chapter, more than a hands-on projects guide. While the hobby blackpowder gunsmith may be surprised at his own hidden talents in the art of metal embellishment, chances are quite small that any of us will emerge as an expert engraver. In the entire country, there are only a few truly professional engravers. Furthermore, no single chapter in a book can transform a person into an engraver, even the individual who possesses latent talent in the art. Therefore, this chapter is introductory in nature, designed mainly to show the reader a few options in metal embellishment and to serve as a basic guide for simple line engraving.

Nothing finishes a muzzleloader with more class than artwork, either in the wood or, in this case, on the metalwork. A few lines on a lockplate may suffice, metal inlays can be installed, or full-blown engraving may be considered on the furniture and lockplate, as well as treating the barrel to extensive engraving. Of course, overdoing any kind of embellishment can be gaudy, as with a rifle barrel engraved one end to the other; however, tasteful embellishment is never a mistake—when the job is done correctly. Incompetent work, on the other hand, reduces the value of the firearm instead of enhancing it.

As part of the introduction to engraving, designs are discussed, along with basic outlines for simple patterns. Perhaps a smoldering interest will ignite into a flame, and the reader may go forward as a hobby engraver. The best engravers in this country had to start some place, and most of them say they tried a simple piece first, found out they could cut a straight line into metal, then a curved line, and in time their talents emerged to full proportion. Those interested in furthering their knowledge on the subject of engraving may wish to look at *The Art of Engraving*, by James B. Meek. This text is available through Brownells.

Engraving

What parts of a rifle can be engraved? As noted earlier, the lockplate is a candidate, as well as the lockplate escutcheons, all screw heads, ramrod guides, nose caps, toe plates, patch boxes, cap boxes, buttplates, barrel wedges, barrel pin escutcheons, barrels, and decorative metal inlays such as cheekpiece inlays, destined for fitting into the rifle stock.

Timing

The engraving of certain parts should be done only after the firearm is completed, with inlays in place and wood finished. This is especially true of barrel pin escutcheons, nose caps on fullstock rifles, cheekpiece inlays, and other decorative inlays. Some parts, such as the patch box or cap box, can be removed from the stock and secured separately for engraving purposes.

Patterns

Engraving should be considered during the planning stage of custom rifle or pistol building. This way, engraving patterns will not appear to be an afterthought. Good books to consult for original patterns are *Thoughts on the Kentucky Rifle in Its Golden Age* by Joe Kindig, Jr.; *The Kentucky Rifle* by John G.W. Dillin; and *The Muzzleloading Cap Lock Rifle* by Ned Roberts. Though a modern-day engraver may not wish to copy original patterns, it's wise for him to study these for historical interest and to see what were used by professional engravers of yesteryear.

Pencil, paper and eraser constitute the first necessary tools for engraving, because a pattern should be drawn first. Professional gunmakers often draw a plan for the entire rifle before starting to build. The drawing is done on long locker paper so it is more or less to scale, with the outline of the rifle represented with considerable accuracy. Then, smaller pieces

Liz Dolbare, an accomplished engraver, transfers her pattern sketch from paper to patch box.

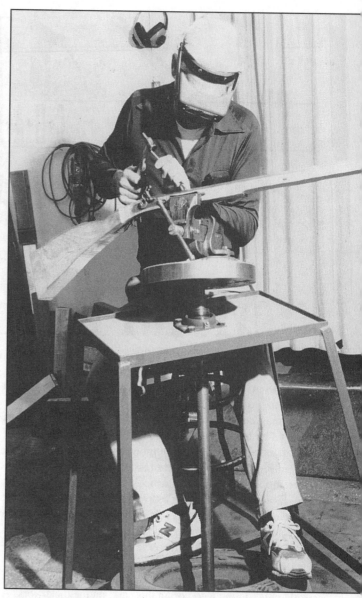

This is the engraving bench in use. An entire rifle can be held in the jaws of the vise. The operator controls tilt and rotation with his feet.

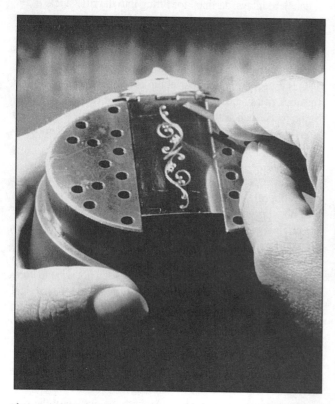

A patch box held in an engraver's block. This allows the engraver perfect control over the work.

This is a simple wriggle cut made with a flat graver. Both a straight and curved line are incorporated in this cut. A scrap piece of metal is used for practice.

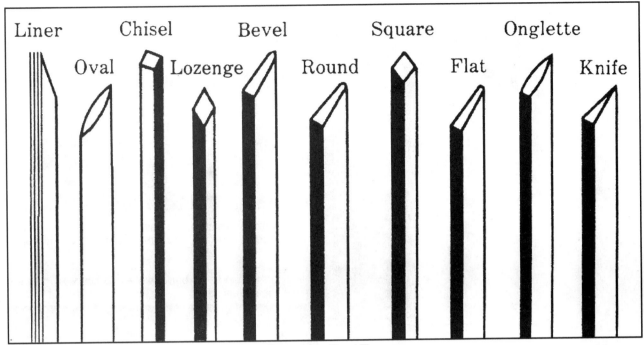

Engraving Tool Types

of paper are used to design inlays and metal furnishings. At first, patterns must be simple. For example, the weeping heart pattern, which dates back to early times, is composed of simple line engraving which can be cut with a single tool. Almost anyone can perform this type of cut.

Patterns with long, straight lines are not easy to accomplish, because the beginner has difficulty maintaining straightness, except for very short distances. Geometric patterns (those that repeat) should also be avoided by the beginner.

Remember engraving patterns should carry the same theme on a given firearm, maintaining a coordinated appearance on each part. For example, if a patch box has a scroll design, the toe plate should as well. A clever artist may get away with varying pattern designs; however, the beginner should stick to the same theme throughout.

Don Eades' Muzzleloader Builders Supply and Tedd Cash's Manufacturing Company offer excellent patch boxes, toe plates, inlays and other metal parts that are perfect for embellishment. Engraving patterns are also available.

It's wise to draw the pattern directly on the piece to be engraved. This allows the engraver to foresee any possible problems of incompatibility between the proposed pattern and the piece of metal, such as a curved surface that will not fluidly accept certain pattern lines.

Engraving Tools

Obviously, the piece to be engraved must be held solidly in place during the engraving process. One tool that fills the bill is the engraver's block. An example I've seen had the following specifications: a 28.5-pound round steel ball, 5³/₄ inches in diameter, with a built-in vise and a swivel base. The vise section of the block was designed to hold both regularly and irregularly shaped pieces. The block described here, and others

like it, are standard for professional engraving. Engraver's blocks do not have the capacity to hold a rifle.

Another tool is a special engraver's bench which looks like a potter's wheel and has the capacity to hold an entire rifle. It is a disc of solid steel, 18 inches in diameter and 1¹/₂ inches thick. Fitted to this is a shaft, which in turn is fitted to a bearing attached to a small bench built of angle iron. Connected to the bottom of the shaft is a discarded tire with a 13-inch rim. On top of the steel disc, a 6-inch vise is fitted. The gunsmith controls the vise by tipping the tire with his feet, turning it left, right or at angles.

Another unit that serves a similar function is a modified bowling ball. A flat spot is cut on the ball, and a simple drill press vise is attached. A round hole, smaller than the ball's diameter, is cut in a bench, and the ball is dropped into this hole. The ball can be revolved in the hole in any direction, and it is sufficiently heavy to remain stationary and hold the piece firmly in place.

Once the work area is set up, an engraving tool will have to be selected. The GRS Gravemeister or GRS Gravermax are air-driven engraving tools sold by Brownells, but these cost in the range of $1000. So the beginner should try Brownells' Hartliep Engraving School Starter Set. This hand engraving kit is not electric-powered, but includes a book, *The Basics of Firearm Engraving*.

Simple Engraving

Flat surfaces are easiest to work on, but rather than beginning on a gun part, start with a scrap piece of brass first, making practice cuts. Brownells also offers practice plates, good for drawing and using a pattern, as well as making cuts in metal.

The wriggle cut is a simple and a good one to begin with. Use the flat graver with a wooden handle from the beginner's

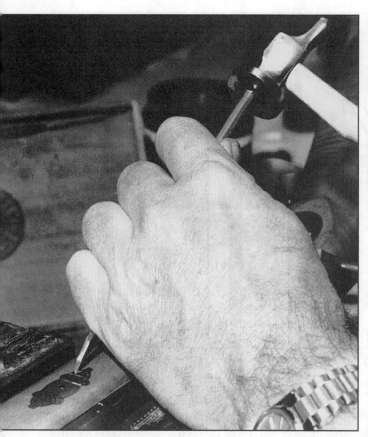

In this particular instance, the pattern has been drawn with a hard lead pencil directly upon the metal barrel pin escutcheon.

A finished double-acorn barrel pin escutcheon. All cuts are simple line engraving.

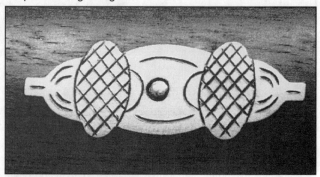

This is an onglette in use. Notice this right-handed engraver has the onglette in his left hand, with the chasers hammer tapping the top of the tool.

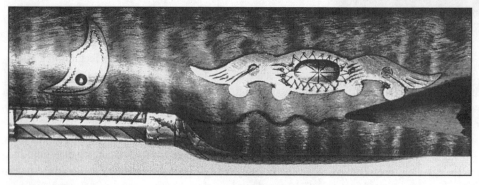

This particular metal embellishment was done by a beginner. However, the job definitely adds to, rather than detracts from, the rifle.

set previously mentioned. The wooden handle is held in the palm of the hand, while the index finger is placed along the top of the blade for control. Hold the tool at a 30-degree angle to the work and push forward and downward—hard enough so the cutting edge digs into the metal, creating a furrow. Without changing the angle between arm and hand, rotate or twist the graver clockwise, maintaining even hand pressure on the tool, then move it counterclockwise. Making a wriggle cut using these motions, the graver is "walked" over the metal surface, forming straight, curved or circular lines. Obviously, practice is necessary before even this simple cut can be mastered. Also, the graver must be kept sharp, or it may have a tendency to slip or not cut deeply enough into the metal. For sharpening, a diamond lap works well.

Tip: If a movable vise is used, it helps to move the piece of metal into the engraver, instead of always pushing the tool into

the metal. A combination of guiding the tool by hand, while at the same time moving the piece into the engraver, can promote smoother curved cuts.

The line cut can be executed with a square or onglette graver, or a die sinkers chisel. If you are right-handed, grasp the tool in your left hand as if you plan to stab it into the bench. The left hand controls the angle and position of the tool, turning the graver from side to side when metal shaving is desired. Held in the right hand, a chasers hammer supplies the force that drives the graver, using a tapping method on the topmost part of the tool. The hobbyist must practice not only the correct cutting angles of the graver, but also the force of the hammer on the graver, which dictates how deeply the tool cuts into the metal. Numerous light taps are best, rather than fewer heavier blows.

First, cut short lines in the simplest of patterns, then try

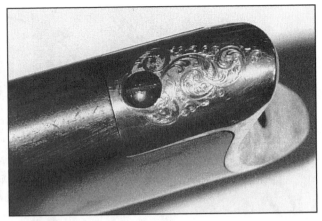

The buttplate and nose cap of this rifle are engraved with the same scroll pattern. It is another example of coordinated engraving.

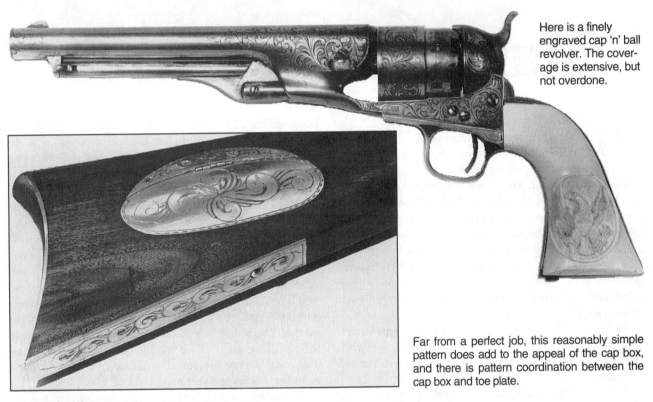

Here is a finely engraved cap 'n' ball revolver. The coverage is extensive, but not overdone.

Far from a perfect job, this reasonably simple pattern does add to the appeal of the cap box, and there is pattern coordination between the cap box and toe plate.

short curved lines. Master these cuts before attempting to cut a scroll pattern. While practicing curved lines, turn the graver from side to side to experiment with metal shaving, which makes the line look deeper and better defined. Three gravers were mentioned earlier for this section, but there are numerous types. The graver that works best is a personal matter, and the hobbyist is urged to try different tools to discover which works best for him. Often, the smith finds the tool that works best is the tool he uses most, turning to other gravers only for special cuts that his favorite tool will not accomplish.

Tip: Different types of metal require slightly different angles for the optimum graver cut, so use practice plates to determine which tool works best on which metal. This is a matter of personal experience and practice, so no specific statement can be made on what works best. Experience is the best teacher.

After *considerable* practice on flat practice pieces, the hobbyist can consider advancing to the firearm. Most kit guns come with inlays and barrel tennon escutcheons—small areas ideal for the kind of embellishment the hobbyist can generally handle. Naturally, the beginning engraver cannot expect immediate masterpieces. In all honesty, he should be satisfied when no major mistakes are experienced.

Hold on to the old practice pieces because they are excellent for comparison as engraving talent progresses. When you have an engraved piece that does not seem quite as good as hoped, compare it with those initial practice pieces, and you'll no doubt see that progress has been made. Nonetheless, the initial statement made at the beginning of this chapter stands firm: Engraving on a high level is a task for the masters. The hobbyist should be satisfied doing modest metal embellishment, trying the basic lines discussed here.

Muzzleloader Barrels

AS THE BARREL goes, so goes the muzzleloader. The action of a modern rifle may be its heart, but the average frontloader does not even have an action. It is, essentially, a barrel with a mechanism for ignition; therefore, the heart of the muzzleloader is its barrel. This is not the forum to discuss the many different types of steel used for blackpowder firearms over the years. Suffice it to say that today's muzzleloader barrels are made of high-quality steel well suited to the job. We are interested, however, in dealing with the breech plug, crowning the muzzle, and knowing what to ask a professional gunsmith to do for us on a barrel. A modest knowledge of rifling twist is also helpful, so the correct barrel can be used to stabilize a specific type of projectile.

There is no lack of quality blackpowder gun barrels today. Many barrelmakers are diligently working to provide the best possible products, and the "bad barrel" seldom surfaces nowadays.

Often, what is considered a poor barrel is, in fact, a condition of improper loading. Each barrel is a law unto itself. Despite the fact that two barrels are made by the same company with the same equipment, minute differences will exist. The hobby gunsmith must know this, because he will definitely come upon a muzzleloader not performing as expected, with groups being too large. Often, there is nothing wrong with the barrel, but it is simply crying out for a specific load chain that it "likes."

Barrel Configurations

Blackpowder barrels have been built in many configurations, but basically there are round barrels and octagonal barrels with "flats." Usually, we think of octagonal barrels as being traditional, for that style was popular with early gunmakers in Europe and America. Today's modern muzzleloader, by virtue of its up-to-date design, seldom if ever wears an octagonal barrel; however, replica and some non-replica muzzleloaders sold today do follow the octagonal tradition. An example is the extremely popular Thompson/Center Hawken, a rifle replicating no firearm from the past, yet its barrel is octagonal.

On the other hand, a stroll down the line at Friendship, Indiana, where the largest single gathering of muzzleloader target shooters occurs annually, will reveal "bench guns" with huge round barrels. These rifles are engineered for one thing: accuracy. A barrel diameter of 1.5 inches is not uncommon for a bench gun shooting slugs. The slug gun, as it is sometimes called, is loaded from the muzzle, usually with cast lead or swaged lead conical bullets and paper patches. So, round barrels on muzzleloaders are common, in spite of the fact that we consider octagonal barrels most traditional. Remember, round barrels were always the norm on military rifles and shotguns.

The hobby gunsmith must take his study of blackpowder barrel configuration one step further than the round vs. octagonal difference. For example, there is the tapered octagonal barrel. Rather than being straight-walled with each of the eight flats having the same width, this barrel type is smaller at the muzzle than at the breech. While this reduces barrel weight, it's probably correct to think of tapered octagonal barrels as more aesthetically pleasing rather than practical.

There also are "swamped" barrels. This old design is a double taper from both ends toward the center. The breech and muzzle ends are the same diameter, while the center is smaller than either end. Once again, the end result is weight reduction, but the true reason for swamping was, no doubt, artistic rather than funtional. Incidentally, a swamped barrel is more difficult to bed into the stock, which is quite understandable. Swamped barrels are still available, albeit at a higher cost than straight barrels. After all, they are more

Two heavy-barreled, scoped target rifles—the far rifle having a half-round/half-octagon barrel, the closer one a round barrel.

difficult to machine, and draw-filing is laborious and time-consuming, demanding several hours of extremely careful work with constant attention to dimensions.

Then there is the half-octagon/half-round barrel, which appears on some half-stock rifles, as well as some shotguns. In theory, this is another weight reduction measure, but if the reduced metal were weighed, the significance would be minimal. The half-round/half-octagon barrel is another measure of the gunmaker's art, and it did not die out with muzzleloaders. A number of custom cartridge rifles have been built with the same design. The part-round/part-octagon design is carried on in barrels that are not 50/50 in proportion. An example of this feature was found on a Cape gun that had an octagonal breech area, with the barrel going to round shortly after the breech. *Note*: The ramrod rib may have to be soft soldered on this barrel type, due to reduced barrel wall thickness.

Barrel Length

The hobbyist will definitely be confronted with choices in barrel length, not only for the building of a custom rifle, should he work at that level one day, but also in the event that a barrel shortening job comes up. Should that barrel be cut off? What will happen to the ballistics if it is? There is no specific formula that applies to muzzleloader barrel length and velocity, just as there is none that applies to the modern rifle barrel. The notion that a modern barrel loses 25 fps per inch of barrel is entirely false, as proved time and again by cutting a barrel down one inch at a time and chronographing the shots.

However, blackpowder does not burn in one fell swoop, and barrel length can make a difference in muzzle velocity. Rather than making a blanket statement concerning how long a barrel should be, it may be wiser to check chronographed figures, so guessing is eliminated. Here are two examples of long and short barrels, and their muzzle velocities with identical loads.

The first is a 32-caliber long rifle. When the barrel was a full 40 inches long, 30 grains of FFFg blackpowder behind a 45-grain patched round ball delivered a muzzle velocity of 2075 fps. When the barrel was cut down to 24-inch length, the identical load developed 1900 fps, a loss of 175 fps.

The trade-off is ease of carrying the gun in the field. The shooter demanding the most velocity from his 32-caliber squirrel rifle may wish to go with the longer barrel. There is one other factor to consider—using iron sights, the longer barrel has a longer sight radius. This is the distance between the rear sight and the front sight, and a long sight radius offers a clearer picture, especially for older eyes that have trouble focusing.

Caliber is an important factor in choosing barrel length. While 175 fps were lost between a 40- and a 24-inch barrel in 32-caliber, that does not mean the same holds true for other calibers. At 40 inches, the 50-caliber barrel produced a MV of 2025 fps with a 177-grain patched round ball and 100 grains of FFg blackpowder. When this barrel was cut to 24 inches, MV with the same load was 1900 fps a loss of 125 fps. Sight radius not withstanding, a shooter would be within his rights to

121

demand the shorter 50-caliber barrel, because percentage of velocity loss is not terribly significant between the longer and shorter barrel. Finally, remember that velocity per barrel length also varies with the bullet used, round or conical, plus all other load factors—the lube used, as well as differences in rifling style, condition of barrels, and so forth.

Twist

A chapter-long discussion of twist can be found in the *Gun Digest Black Powder Loading Manual*. While this is not the place to go into full detail on twist, suffice it to say that twist is not a matter of barrel length, in spite of the fact we note twist in regard to inches of barrel. While we use the term "one turn in 66 inches," that does not mean the rps (revolutions per second) of a projectile changes with barrel length. The rps is established by the *rate* of twist, plus exit velocity of the missile. If the rate of twist and MV of the bullet are identical, rps will be identical, regardless of barrel length.

For example, one bullet fired from a 20-inch barrel and another fired from a 30-inch barrel, both with a 1:24 rate of twist, will have identical rps if both leave the muzzle at the same velocity. Of course, barrel length is a factor in MV, although not as significant as somtimes thought. Therefore, exit velocity per barrel length will vary, causing rps to vary slightly. This factor is not very significant until the difference in barrel lengths is great. Of course, there is a difference between the pistol and the rifle. This is why pistols generally carry a faster rate of twist per caliber than rifles, not necessarily because of barrel length, but because of the great difference in exit velocity.

There is also the factor of bullet shape to consider. A round lead ball requires very little rps for stabilization. Therefore, muzzle-loading rifles designed to shoot patched balls have a slow rate of twist, say one turn in 66 inches, expressed as 1:66, which is more than adequate in a 50-caliber long rifle. Conicals demand more rps for proper stabilization; therefore, a 50-caliber conical-shooting rifle will have a *faster* rate of twist, perhaps one turn in 32 inches (1:32). Again, caliber also makes a difference. A larger diameter projectile has more mass and does not require the same rps for stabilization as a smaller missile. So a 32-caliber long rifle for round ball shooting may have a 1:40 twist, while a 50-caliber long rifle may have a 1:66 rate of twist.

Finally, it's extremely important for the hobbyist to understand there is no such thing as one perfect rate of twist for any given caliber. Bullet stabilization occurs within a *range*. For example, a 50-caliber round ball may be stabilized quite nicely in a 1:60, 1:66 or 1:70 rate of twist. Also bear in mind, the load itself will alter stabilization results. If the MV of a bullet has something to do with its rps, then as the load changes, and muzzle velocity changes, so does rps. That is why shooters may find a round ball stabilizes better from a faster twist barrel with a reduced load, because MV is lower with the reduced load.

And what about too much bullet spin? This is a difficult subject because proof is hard to find. Some barrelmakers feel a bullet can't spin too fast, and that may be true, but "stripping the bore"—an old-time term to denote a patched round ball riding over instead of being guided by the rifling—is a possibility. This may occur because the twist is too fast, and the round ball, which makes very little contact with the rifling, simply glides over the lands, rather than the lands gripping the ball. Of course, shallow lands would also contribute to the condition, failing to "bite into" the projectile.

Rifling

Another factor in barrel variation is rifling depth. The old rule of thumb, and it holds up fairly well, is shallow rifling for conicals and deeper rifling for round balls. Even though there is no single rifling groove depth that is perfect, a *range* of depth is the rule. However, fine accuracy has been proved with round ball guns having groove depths in the .010- to .012-inch range, while many fine-shooting conical rifles have proved their accuracy with groove depths of

A freshly faced barrel with sharp-edged rifling that runs all the way to the tip of the muzzle.

A good, smooth crown job on a round ball barrel, which facilitates the loading process. This type of crown will not cut patches.

Common Barrel Configurations

Manufacturer	Model	Caliber	Barrel Shape	Outside Muzzle Dim. (ins.)
CVA	Stalker Rifle/Carbine	50	Octagonal	$15/16$
CVA	Hawken Deerslayer Rifle/Carbine	50	Octagonal	$15/16$
CVA	St. Louis Hawken	50	Octagonal	$15/16$
CVA	Bushwhacker	50	Octagonal	$15/16$
CVA	Frontier Hunter Carbine	50	Octagonal	$15/16$
CVA	Frontier Carbine	50	Octagonal	$15/16$
CVA	Mountain Rifle	50	Octagonal	$15/16$
CVA	Hawken Rifle	50	Octagonal	$15/16$
CVA	Hunter Hawken	50	Octagonal	$15/16$
CVA	Plainsman Rifle	50	Octagonal	$15/16$
CVA	Blaser Rifle	50	Octagonal	$15/16$
CVA	Stalker Rifle/Carbine	54	Octagonal	$15/16$
CVA	St. Louis Hawken	54	Octagonal	$15/16$
CVA	Mountain Rifle	54	Octagonal	$15/16$
CVA	Hawken Rifle	54	Octagonal	$15/16$
CVA	Hunter Hawken	54	Octagonal	$15/16$
CVA	Trophy Carbine	50	Round	$7/8$
CVA	Apollo Rifle/Carbine	50	Round	$13/16$
CVA	Trophy Carbine	54	Round	$7/8$
Hastings	Remington 870	50	Round	$13/16$
Investarms	Hawken Rifle	50	Octagonal	$15/16$
Lyman	Trade Rifle	50	Octagonal	$15/16$
Lyman	Trade Rifle	54	Octagonal	$15/16$
Lyman	Deerstalker Rifle	50	Octagonal	$15/16$
Lyman	Deerstalker Rifle	54	Octagonal	$15/16$
Lyman	Deerstalker Carbine	50	Round	$15/16$
T/C	Renegade Rifle	50	Octagonal	1
T/C	Hawken Rifle	50	Octagonal	$15/16$
T/C	Hawken Rifle	54	Octagonal	1
T/C	Renegade Rifle	54	Octagonal	1
T/C	Pennsylvania Hunter Rifle/Carbine	50	Round	$7/8$
T/C	White Mountain Carbine	50	Round	$7/8$
T/C	Scout Carbine	50	Round	$7/8$
T/C	White Mountian Carbine	54	Round	$7/8$
T/C	Scout Carbine	54	Round	$7/8$
T/C	New Englander 24"/26"	50	Round	$29/32$
T/C	High Plains Sporter	50	Round	$29/32$
T/C	Tree Hawk Carbine	50	Round	$15/16$
T/C	New Englander 24"/26"	54	Round	$29/32$
Traditions	Frontier Rifle/Carbine	50	Octagonal	$15/16$
Traditions	Pioneer Rifle/Carbine	50	Octagonal	$15/16$
Traditions	Hawken Woodsman	50	Octagonal	$15/16$
Traditions	Hawken Rifle	50	Octagonal	1
Traditions	Hunter Rifle	50	Octagonal	1
Traditions	Pioneer Rifle	54	Octagonal	$15/16$
Traditions	Hawken Woodsman	54	Octagonal	$15/16$
Traditions	Hawken Rifle	54	Octagonal	1
Traditions	Hunter Rifle	54	Octagonal	1
Traditions	Buckskinner Carbine	50	Round	$7/8$

only .005- to .006-inch. Remember, when selecting a barrel, the hobbyist should tell the barrelmaker what bullet the barrel will shoot—round or conical. Then the appropriate barrel can be selected, not only in terms of twist, but also groove depth.

Obviously, when a barrel is selected by groove depth, this automatically translates the height of the land, because as groove depth inceases, the land of the rifling becomes taller. The taller land seems to "grab" the patched ball better, while the shorter land engraves the conical less aggressively with excellent stabilization and accuracy results. This is not to suggest that one will only work with the other. All of the remarks made here are of a general nature—it is *generally* the case that round balls "like" tall lands, while conicals "prefer" shorter ones.

Generally, there are two types of rifling: cut and buttoned (or swaged in). Both have been tested with accurate results. The hobbyist is advised to buy a barrel based on its maker's reputation, leaving the style of rifling up to the expert—the barrelmaker.

Lapping the Bore

When the hobby gunsmith encounters a bore that appears somewhat rough, he may wish to lap it. A lead slug is cast onto a cleaning rod, coated with lapping compound, and pushed back and forth through the bore, smoothing the lands and grooves. While knowledge of bore lapping is valuable to the hobbyist, the actual practice is questionable. In fact, shooting a new gun laps the barrel in its own way, and it is always wise to let a barrel "settle in" before thinking about lapping the bore. Moreover, Ned Roberts felt that the patch around the lead ball lapped the bore and wore the barrel more than the burning powder charge, and he may have been correct.

In the final analysis, bore lapping should be left to the barrelmaker. If the hobbyist comes across a bore that is rough, he should consider "shooting it in" first. If the bore refuses to respond, then a trip to the professional gunsmith or the maker may be in order.

The Barrel Crown

The crown, or recess at the muzzle of the barrel, affects accuracy, loading ease, and projectile or patch damage. A damaged crown may cause poor bullet grouping, scratching the shank or base of a conical, or cutting a patch during seating of the round ball. The crown also determines alignment of the conical projectile. If it's inserted crooked, accuracy generally suffers. The crown must be perpendicular to the bore, so the base of the elongated bullet is not tilted.

A recessed crown is excellent for the conical and will work with the patched round ball, too. A recessed crown is created by boring the muzzle to groove diameter about one-half the length of the proposed projectile. Should the bullet be an inch long, the recess would be about $1/2$-inch deep. This recess facilitates seating of the conical square to the bore. Also, the bullet slides downbore much easier. Plus, the rifling at the end of the barrel is protected from damage because the lands and

A modern version of the recessed crown, shown on a Gonic modern muzzleloader.

A modern muzzleloader showing a rather flat crown, with a slight chamfer to remove sharp edges.

grooves are now below the muzzle. The idea is not new, dating back at least to the 19th century.

Crowning, including the recessed crown, is properly done with a lathe, meaning it's a job for the professional gunsmith. However, the hobbyist needs to know all of his options so he can make a decision about what he wants, such as a recessed crown. Hand-crowning is a possiblity, of course, but is difficult, and the chance of getting a perfect job is remote. Custom barrels come crowned from the maker in a manner he feels is correct.

The False Muzzle

Used on target rifles, the false muzzle is an interesting attachment that provides not only perfect bullet alignment, but it also protects the rifling when the gun is cleaned by serving as a muzzle protector. See Chapter 21 on professional maintenance for more information on the muzzle protector. The false muzzle is used only during the loading

A barrel held securely by a four-jaw chuck of a lathe, being centered for crowning.

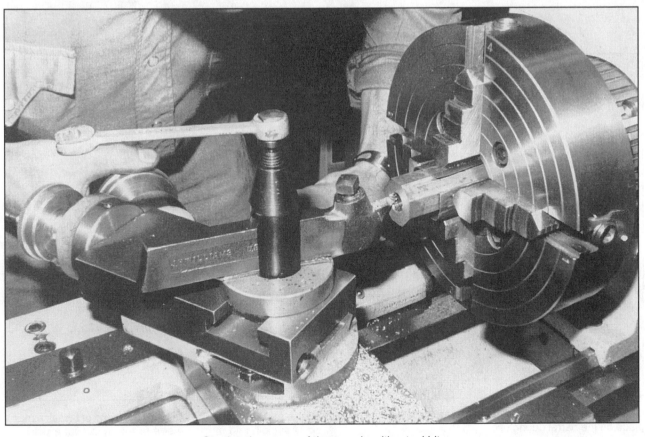

Starting the crown of the muzzle with a tool bit.

A false muzzle in place on a barrel. A sight block prevents
shooting the rifle with the false muzzle in place.

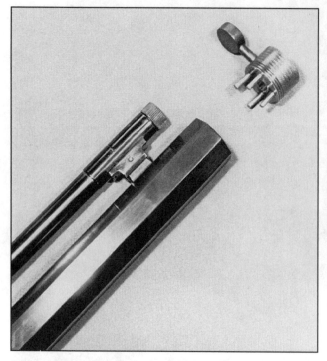

Observe the precision-fit pins that hold the false muzzle in
place on the barrel during use.

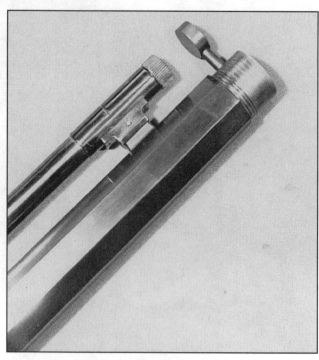

A false muzzle on a target rifle barrel. The end of the false muzzle is smooth and of groove size to readily accept a patched
round ball.

process, and is removed before shooting or it will be cast downrange. Its "bore" is smooth to promote easy loading of either a round or conical bullet. Sometimes an attachment is added to the false muzzle to prevent shooting with it still attached. This extension rises up and blocks the sight picture, alerting the shooter that he left the false muzzle in place. There are different types of false muzzles, including sophisticated two-part units for slug guns.

The Barrel Breech

The back of the barrel must be plugged somehow, because the muzzleloader is essentially a barrel with one closed end and a means of ignition. There are numerous types of breech plugs, including those on the modern muzzleloader which are readily removable so the gun can be cleaned from the breech end. As long as the breech plug does its job, containing gases, then it is difficult to argue about the specific design. Most custom barrels come from the maker with the breech end already plugged. The key to success is having the threaded section of the breech plug larger than the bore. Here is a chart of thread sizes available per bore size for proper plug fit.

Proper Plug Fit

Thread Size	Maximum Bore Size
$9/16$x18	up to 45-caliber
$5/8$x18	up to 54-caliber
$3/4$x16	up to 69-caliber
$7/8$x14	shotguns

The above thread sizes are standard with custom barrels; only a few commercial barrels have metric threads or odd sizes.

The Breech Plug

It is vital the breech plug fits precisely, inside the bore and at the back of the barrel. These two contact points must be on the money, with the top of the breech plug flush with the top barrel flat. This particular work is geared for the pro, who has depth measuring devices, such as a micrometer or caliper. Add to that a good vise, a sharp metal file and a proper-fitting wrench, and the smith is ready to fit a breech plug. B-Square sells a special wrench for fitting a breech plug, but the hobbyist can generally get by with an adjustable crescent wrench.

Fitting a Breech Plug

The plug must be firmly installed, of course, but too much force on the wrench can cause damage. Common sense must prevail. Once the plug is well secured in place, no further pressure is required. *Note*: While a normal crescent wrench can be used for fitting a new breech plug, removing one from an original firearm that may have been built 100 years ago demands a special wrench. In some instances, a wrench must be made just to fit the specific breech plug of an old gun.

As an illustration, the basic flintlock breech plug is a good place to begin, because the same surfaces that must match up on this plug must also match up on the hooked breech plug. As a broad and general rule, the length and diameter of a breech plug are the same. In other words, a $5/8$x18 breech plug has a $5/8$-inch threaded length. Exceptions are well-noted in catalogs. For example, consider a standard flint breech plug for a 54-caliber rifle, assum-

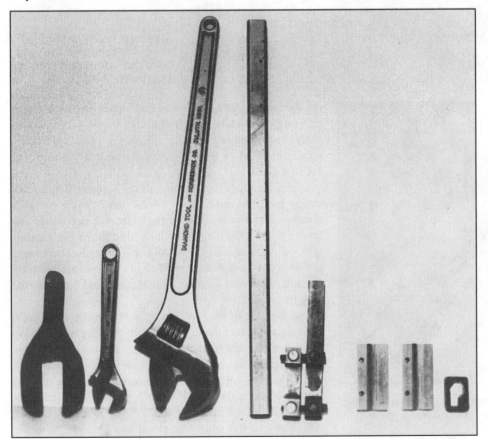

A selection of tools used to remove and install breech plugs. Left to right: homemade wrench, two adjustable wrenches, handles and special wrench by B-Square, aluminum jaws to hold the barrel in a vise, and a special adapter that fits a Thompson/Center plug for their Hawken rifle.

A flint-type breech plug, properly fitted. This is a drum and nipple setup, which is a good ignition system.

This is a neatly fitted takedown breech, with the joint between barrel and breech plug barely visible.

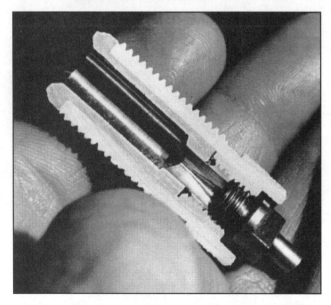

This is a cutaway view of the breech plug and nipple setup used on a Knight MK-85 modern muzzle-loading rifle with in-line ignition.

ing the barrel is already drilled and tapped 3/4x16 to accept this plug. Naturally, the dimensions of the plug must be such so its topmost part either matches or protrudes slightly above the level of the top barrel flat, but it must not fall below the flat.

Using a caliper, depth micrometer or other depth-measuring tool, the drilled and tapped recess in the barrel is measured and compared to the threaded portion of the breech plug. If the plug is too long to fit the recess, carefully file the end of the plug to the correct length. Then, place the barrel in a vise with padded jaws, lubricate the plug threads to prevent gauling and sticking, and screw in the plug by hand.

Pad the base of the breech plug with thin copper or brass sheeting to prevent damage, then turn the plug with an 8- to 10-inch adjustable wrench until snug. Do not over-tighten, which could deform the side of the breech plug. Ideally, the top of the plug will match the top barrel flat, creating a flat surface between the two. If there is not a correct matchup, remove the breech plug and check the end for score marks, which prove the plug bottomed out against the bore.

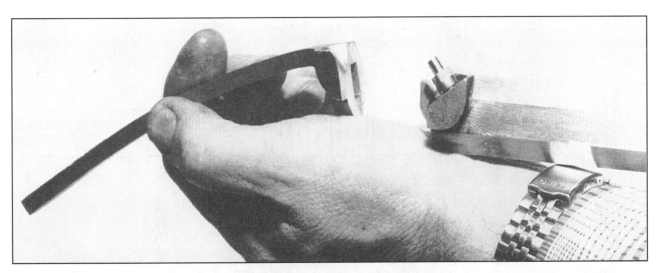

Here, the tang is removed from the breech plug.

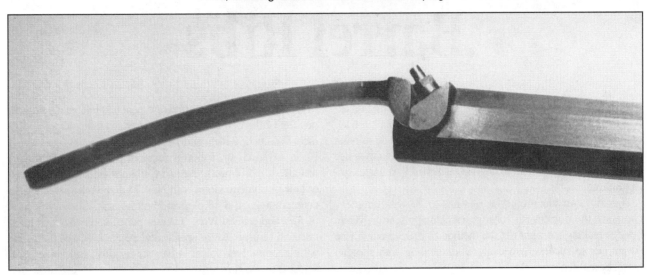

A hooked breech with the tang fitted to the breech plug.

Precision measuring equipment is ideal for all of this work; however, the job can be completed successfully by filing and matching.

If the breech plug did not bottom out, then the end of the barrel must be filed to remove some metal—very little at a time. Then, refit the breech plug. Continue this process until it does bottom out. On the other hand, suppose the breech plug was bottoming out correctly; however, the plug was not correctly aligned with the top barrel flat. In this case, an equal amount of metal is removed from barrel and breech plug ends to make a match. Be sure to lubricate the plug threads before refitting to prevent gauling.

Now the breech plug makes a perfect fit. Remove it one more time, apply anti-seize compound to the threads and install it once more. The anti-seize compound is not absolutely necessary, but should the plug require removal in the future, the compound will facilitate the job.

With breech plug properly installed, strike a couple witness marks on the bottom across the juncture of plug and barrel. These marks will always show the proper seating depth of the breech plug, should it be removed and replaced at a later date.

For a hooked breech, the same procedure should be followed—with a tight fit between plug and barrel, the shank of the plug tight inside the bore, and the flats perfectly aligned.

Although there are some exceptions, such as the excellent Thompson/Center Scout rifle and pistol, most modern muzzleloaders have breeches that are easily removed, generally with special tools provided with the gun. The removal of these breech plugs allows access to the bore for breech-end cleaning.

Draw-Filing a Barrel

An 18-inch mill file may be used to remove tool marks from the barrel flats. With the barrel firmly held in a padded vise, the file is controlled by both hands, held perfectly flat against the barrel, using an even push-pull motion. When the file loads up with metal particles, clean it with a stainless steel brush. A good file cleaner is also made from a flattened brass cartridge case. By working the flattened edge back and forth against the file, metal particles are cleared from the teeth of the file.

Barrel Ribs

A STUDY OF ribs is not the most exciting aspect of black-powder gunsmithing. Most of us would rather build a kit, heat-treat a metal part, brown a gun, or perform a multitude of other projects instead of working with ribs. However, a knowledge of the subject is important to anyone interested in muzzleloader smithing.

A major consideration with ribs has to do with choice—choosing the correct rib for a particular application. Then besides picking the right rib, the method of attachment is also paramount to success, especially when dealing with shotgun barrels versus rifle barrels.

The function of the rib is to hold ramrod guides in place, for housing the ramrod. A sturdy installation is essential to success. Although the ramrod itself weighs little, and exerts little force upon the ramrod guides, if the rib breaks, the ramrod guide is useless. So the rib ends up being the foundation for the ramrod, in an indirect way.

Shotgun Ribs

Ribs on a double-barrel shotgun are so specialized to install or repair that they must be handled only by an experienced professional blackpowder gunsmith trained in the art of soldering these special ribs and ramrod guides. For this reason, there is no project on the topic of shotgun ribs in our text.

Flat Barrel Ribs

A flat barrel rib is appropriate on the half-stock rifle—which has an exposed lower barrel surface—and on a pistol with octagonal barrel and exposed lower barrel flat. The bottom of the rib is, as the name implies, machined flat, thereby offering a matched surface for the octagonal barrel. The flat rib is of solid steel construction with machined sides, top and bottom, and a length of 24 inches. The flat rib comes in five different sizes to accommodate various barrel dimensions:

$13/16$-inch across the flats (measurement taken from the edge of one flat of the octagon barrel to the edge of the next flat), $7/8$-inch, $15/16$-inch, 1-inch, and $1^1/8$ inches.

An advanced workshop is required for working on ribs. A drill press, a drill press vise and C-clamps are needed for proper hole placement, along with Nos. 28 and 31 drill bits, a 6-48 counterbore, and 6-48 plug and bottom taps. Also, a selection of files and screwdrivers, a center punch and a 2-ounce hammer will be used. An oxygen/acetylene torch will be put to use with ribbon silver solder, silver solder flux, soft solder, soft solder flux and flux brush.

Fitting the Flat Rib

Ribs are fitted in two ways: One is to drill and countersink holes in the rib, after which the rib is attached to the barrel with small machine screws, or the rib can be soldered in place. Obviously, there must be corresponding tapped holes in the lower barrel flat to accommodate the machine screws, if that method is used. Either way, it must be held firmly in place, not only for holding the ramrod guides, but because, in some instances, the rib is also a repository for sling studs fitted on ramrod guides. The sling stud places an added burden on the guide, which in turn puts more stress on the rib. Why not use the two attachment methods in tandem, both soldering the rib in place along with screws? Because that's overkill. A good job of soldering or a good job of screw attachment will keep a rib intact.

Attaching a Rib with Screws

The rib is first measured and cut to the proper length. Then, it is laid upon the lower barrel flat for correct placement. The location of the ramrod guides is now determined. The screw holes are then placed as follows: one screw at the front of the rib, another at the rear where it meets the stock, and two more, each close to where the ramrod guide will be installed—but not right next to it. The guide itself will be held in place by solder or screws. This type of attachment can be seen on certain Thompson/Center muzzleloaders, where the guide is screwed onto the rib. Once proper screw location is decided, then each hole is centered on the rib and marked with a center punch. A commonly used screw size for this application is 6-48—a bastard size, in general, but readily found in the firearms trade. This screw size is all but universal for attaching scope bases to rifles.

Where marked, drill completely through the rib using a No. 28 drill bit. A drill press is recommended because it is very difficult to do this accurately with a power hand drill. Then, countersink each hole, just enough for the screw head to fit flush or slightly below. Use a counterbore made specifically for the screw head size. To maintain an even countersink depth, use the stop feature on the drill press.

Now, securely hold the rib to the barrel using a C-clamp or machinist's clamp. With a hand drill and a No. 28 bit, mark each rib hole to be made in the barrel with the tip of the bit. After that, the rib is unclamped, and at each drill mark on the barrel, a hole must be drilled and tapped to accept the machine screws that will secure the rib in place on the barrel flat.

There are four well-located spots marked by the hand drill. Place the barrel flat upon the drill press table. Since the barrel may be long and heavy, making it difficult to secure, a support of some kind will be necessary to control that portion of the barrel hanging over the drill press table.

There are various means of supporting the barrel during drilling. One workable device is a cord attached to the ceiling with a ring through it and the barrel placed through the ring. Or a unit can be built with pipe. A $1\frac{1}{2}$-inch nipple 6 inches long is fitted into a flange attached to the bench. A T-handle is made from a $\frac{3}{8}$-inch bolt and fitted to the pipe, acting as a lock screw. A second piece of pipe, $1\frac{1}{4}$ inches in diameter, is inserted into the $1\frac{1}{2}$-inch piece of pipe. The $1\frac{1}{4}$-inch pipe is fitted with a small flat anvil or a sling. You now have a jig that can be raised or lowered to fully support the weight of the overhanging barrel. Now that the barrel is fully supported, partly by the drill press table, and partly by the jig or ceiling cord ring, proper drilling of the lower barrel flat can be done.

The most important aspect of this job is proper hole depth in the barrel flat. Once that is determined, the stop on the drill press must be set so the proper hole depth is not exceeded. It must be deep enough for the screw to attach by a *minimum* of three complete threads. While it should go without saying, it is totally unacceptable to drill completely through the barrel and into the bore! A general rule of thumb calls for a remaining metal thickness of at least $\frac{1}{8}$-inch between the bottom-out of the screw hole and the bore of the barrel. On slim barrels with thinner walls, after starting the hole with a No. 31 bit, finish with a No. 31 bottom drill bit to fully complete the hole and not eat up any excess metal, preserving minimum barrel thickness.

Now each hole is tapped. To gain an accurate start for the tap, install a plug tap in the chuck of the drill press and turn

This rib was fitted with screws, which cannot be seen. The ramrod guide has been silver soldered to the rib, and the sling stud has been silver soldered to the guide.

Tapping a hole drilled into a rifle barrel for installing a rib. This is done by turning the chuck of the drill press by hand.

only by hand. Do not turn on the drill press. Finish tapping these holes by hand only. There will not be sufficient screw hole depth to use a starter tap. Once the plug tap hits bottom, back it out and finish with a bottom tap. This will provide a maximum number of threads for each hole. When finished, place the rib back on the lower barrel flat and install the screws. Loctite can be used on the screws to promote their integrity, but apply it only when all work on the firearm is completed, as it may be difficult to remove the rib after Loctite is used.

Attaching a Rib with Solder

The major reason for soldering a rib instead of screwing is barrel wall thickness. On more slender barrels, with lesser wall thickness, drilling holes may compromise the integrity of the barrel. Two types of ribs accommodate soldering. The first has a channel along the side that can be filled with solder, making attachment much easier. The other type is flat and does not have a channel. There are also ribs for round barrels that are slightly contoured.

All surfaces to be mated must be thoroughly clean and bright. Light draw-filing, or polishing with emery paper as coarse as 80-grit, is recommended. The goal is a dry, clean, bright surface that will offer a good bond for the solder. Next, a liquid flux is applied to the rib on all areas that will be soldered. Apply it neatly, and only where needed, rather than all over the metal parts. Remember, flux is normally acid-based. Wherever it is applied, solder will flow because the acid in the flux provides a clean and ready surface.

Secure the rib in a vise. Next, the rib is tinned by melting a light coating of soft solder onto the rib. A small flux brush is used to quickly and neatly apply additional flux only to those areas that will take the solder. Heat the bottom of the rib, not the surface to be soldered, with an acetylene torch and melt the solder. If an oxygen-acetylene torch is used, be careful not to overheat the rib. This type of torch is capable of generating tremendous heat and the rib can become too hot.

Remember that soldering uses a high heat source and molten solder. Great care must be taken to avoid getting burned by either. Wear safety glasses; flux may splatter when heated.

Tip: Plug the barrel with a wooden dowel to prevent flux or solder from accidentally finding its way into the bore. The wooden dowel may be scorched during the heating process, but this is no problem compared with a puddle of flux deposited in the bore.

The tinned rib is set aside. Now it is the barrel's turn to be cleaned and fluxed. After that, place the rib on the barrel flat and clamp it in place with C-clamps or parallel clamps. Since the rib has been tinned, only a bare minimum of additional solder will be required to ensure a good bond between the rib and the barrel flat.

Begin heating the barrel and the rib simultaneously. Move the torch up and down the length of the barrel, heating as evenly as possible. Have a flux brush dampened with flux ready and waiting. As the solder begins to melt, quickly and lightly run the flux brush along the joint formed between barrel and rib. The flux draws the solder along the seam for a per-

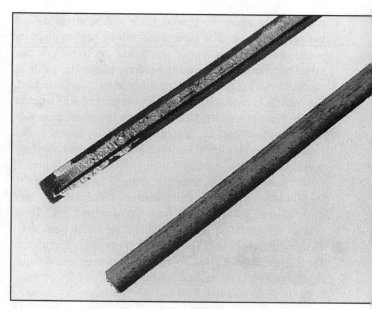

These ribs are for soldering in place. The upper one has a channel. Tinning has begun on this rib, which is designed for an octagonal barrel. The lower rib is concave in style, designed to fit a round barrel.

fect fit. Look for a bright line of solder appearing along the joint. This indicates a correct bond. Continue along the entire rib until it is fully bonded to the barrel at all points. Additional solder may be required here and there, but do not over-solder. It's easy to use too much, which then runs, making cleanup more difficult.

Do not cool the barrel with a damp cloth or any other measure. Simply allow it to air-cool.

Once cooled, all excess solder must be removed with a sharp pocketknife or a three-square file. The sharp corner of the file is pushed along the seam where rib and barrel are joined, cleaning up extra solder. Other optional tools for removing extra solder are a scraper made from a file or a Dremel tool with a polishing wheel attached. The latter is used only after heavy areas of excess solder have been attacked with knife, file or scraper. Yet another option is to take the barrel to a shop that has a bead blast cabinet, which removes some excess solder.

Caution: A barrel with a soft soldered rib cannot be run through the hot bluing process because the caustic salts will loosen the rib. Rust bluing or browning must be used.

Attaching Ramrod Guides

Next, ramrod guides may be attached to the rib or barrel by various methods. We will demonstrate one excellent procedure: soldering the guide directly to the rib. This requires a guide that matches the concave portion of the rib. In order to fit, the guide (also called a thimble) must have a flat filed into it. This makes the wall of the guide very thin; however, there remains just enough "meat" for soldering onto the rib. In turn, the rib is required to have a matching flat to accept the guide, so it fits flush on the rib. When there is a clean match between the flat of the guide and the flat on the rib, the area is cleaned, fluxed and soldered, using the technique previously described.

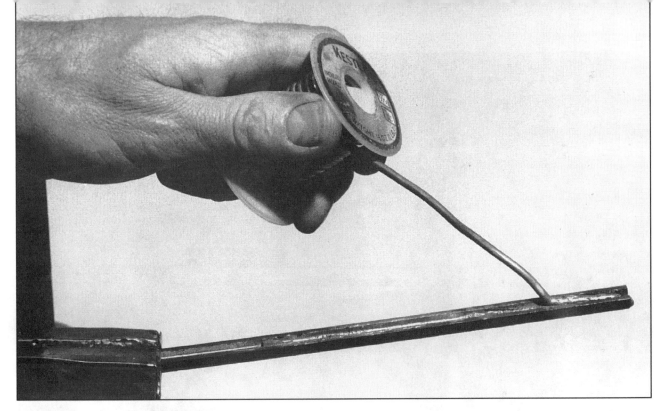

This rib, already heated by a torch, is being tinned, Once the thin layer of solder has been applied, it will be set aside while the barrel is cleaned and fluxed.

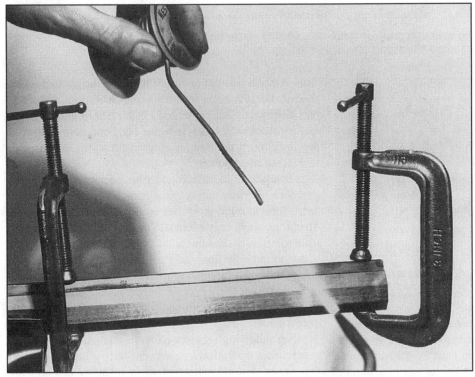

After tinning, the rib is attached to the barrel with C-clamps. Then, the barrel and rib are heated so the solder will flow and set.

Post-soldering cleanup is also required after the guide is soldered to the rib. This step removes superfluous solder and promotes a clean job.

The blackpowder hobby gunsmith may wonder how the guide is lined up on the rib so the ramrod fits properly. One way is to place a metal rod the same size as the ramrod through the guides before soldering in place. This ensures the lineup will be correct and the ramrod will fit. The rod is left clamped in place during the heating/soldering cycle. *Do not*

allow excess solder to inadvertently attach the metal alignment rod to the ramrod guides.

Silver Soldering Ramrod Guides

This is an alternate method of attachment, especially if the rib has been screwed to the barrel and not soft soldered in place. This method requires very high heat, which could detach a previously soft soldered rib. Silver solder is especially useful when a sling stud is attached to a ramrod guide or a rib.

Soldering a ramrod guide on a rib. After cooling, excess solder can be removed with a sharp pocketknife or three-square file.

This ramrod guide is silver soldered directly to the barrel. Note the small depression milled into the barrel to match the guide.

Its extra strength helps hold the stud in place. Silver soldering does require an oxygen/acetylene torch for melting. The ramrod guide is aligned and held in place on the rib, as previously described. If the hobbyist has access to a milling machine, the flats on the rib may be milled into place. If not, careful filing does a good job.

Be sure to remove the rib from the barrel before proceeding with the silver solder operation.

Silver soldering is similar to soft soldering, as far as method of operation is concerned. The mating surfaces must, once again, be completely cleaned and readied for flux. This time, a special silver solder flux is applied to mating surfaces. Brownells offers a special low-temperature ribbon silver solder that is highly recommended. As its name suggests, the silver solder is supplied as a thin ribbon or strip. A section is cut to match the exact length and width needed. Everything is securely clamped in place with perfect alignment. The guide and rib are heated with a torch, melting the ribbon of silver solder and bonding the guide to the rib. There is no need for excessive heating—just enough to melt the silver solder.

Should additional silver solder be required to fill a small gap between the ramrod guide and the rib, use it in wire form. Bear in mind that silver solder is difficult to remove. Therefore, apply only enough to make a neat bond. It is possible to actually do damage to the rib and/or ramrod guide when scraping or filing away excess silver solder because gouges may be left in the metal. Careful filing is often required to get the job done correctly. As previously suggested, a bead blast cabinet can be helpful in removing excess solder.

Silver soldering requires patience and care. As with so many other operations, however, ability increases with experience, and a good job of silver soldering can be done by a dedicated hobbyist.

Silver soldering is conducive to many kinds of metal finishing, including hot bluing. Silver solder is not affected by the caustic salts of the hot bluing tank.

Silver Soldering Sling Studs

A sling stud may be silver soldered to a ramrod guide, and ribbon silver solder is especially useful for this operation. The methods already described prevail, including metal preparation and careful attention to keeping the stud in proper alignment.

Metal Castings

CASTINGS HAVE BEEN an essential part of muzzle-loading for centuries. Early gunsmiths used sand castings for trigger guards, buttplates, sideplates and other appointments often made of brass. Today's level of technology has escalated castings from an art to a science, with methods far beyond the dreams of early day smiths.

Today, cast parts include buttplates, trigger guards, nose caps, sideplates, cap boxes, functional lock parts, underlugs, keys, front and rear sights (including peep sights), triggers, breech plugs, tangs, even flat springs, and this list is not all-inclusive. The result is the availability of more parts for gunsmiths, from full-time professionals to hobbyists.

A few purists continue to enjoy doing it the "old way" by making their own sand casting mould, melting brass in a forge, and forming their own parts. While this is a romantic venture, it lies beyond the domain of the general home hobbyist, who does not have access to a forge. Remember, melting lead is one thing; melting brass is quite another. The latter requires heat levels far higher than lead, which can be turned from solid to liquid over a campfire. The same goes for silver. Forget the Lone Ranger casting his own silver bullets by his evening fire. Melting silver demands a lot more heat than fireside coals normally provide. And while we may not have the proper equipment to form our own castings, there are many fine parts available through a number of outlets, such as Log Cabin Sport Shop. It's important for the hobby blackpowder gunsmith to know how to select and use castings in the process of modifying or building a muzzleloader.

Casting Metals

Brass, silver, white bronze and steel are the metals most used in casting, with German silver available, but not as popular. Brass is most prevalent because it casts well, results in a fine-looking product, and is historically correct in many instances. Brass was widely used during the golden age of muzzleloader building because it was easy to work with, due to its malleability. Furthermore, brass fittings are handsome, either polished or allowed to age naturally to a finish known as patina. Hand tools suffice for working this soft metal. A modest selection of files along with abrasive papers clean up brass castings and polish them well.

As noted, German silver is not as popular as brass for muzzleloader metalwork. Many cap boxes offered on muzzleloaders manufactured today, such as the Thompson/Center Hawken, are usually made of brass. Cap boxes from aftermarket suppliers are generally of brass as well. But a few parts cast of German silver are available, generally for smaller items.

White bronze is an alternative to German silver for castings. It looks like German silver, but costs less and casts better. A high rate of loss contributes to the cost of German silver, whereas white bronze results in fewer casting mistakes. White bronze castings can also be worked like brass due to malleability. It files and polishes similarly, making it a good choice for the hobbyist.

Steel and iron castings have enjoyed a place in the muzzleloader trade for a long time. Many rifles and pistols are "iron-mounted," especially in the later percussion era. The Jaeger rifle, which was brought to America by early gunsmiths, is an example. The trend is especially seen in the Plains rifle, epitomized by rifles today known generically as "Hawkens" because the Hawken Brothers built the 19th-century originals that gained considerable fame among the mountain men of the Far West. Obviously, steel is durable, taking a great deal of abuse without bending, scratching or breaking. Due to such heavy-duty service, military arms were often iron-mounted, as were a number of shotguns that saw heavy use in the field. All the same, steel is more difficult to work because of its hard-

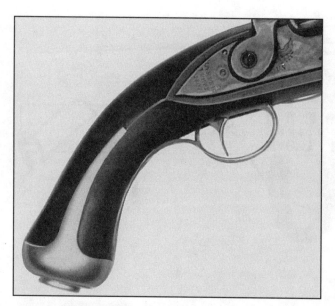

The long, slender portion of this pistol grip cap and the trigger guard challenge the mould maker and his casting talents.

ness. Also, steel parts must be finished after polishing, generally with some form of bluing (see Chapter 14 on finishing metals). In spite of certain drawbacks, steel castings are readily available and often historically correct, as on the Plains rifle, for example. These parts include trigger guards, buttplates, nose caps, as well as a few cap boxes.

The hobbyist working on a period firearm should take special note concerning original metal appointments. It is not appropriate, for example, to use brass castings on a firearm that originally had iron mountings. When adding cast parts to a kit gun, the object is to match the metal already used for the kit. Obviously, adding a toe plate, buttplate, cap box or patch box of steel when the kit already uses brass is not the way to go.

Investment Casting

For the reader's knowledge, it is worthwhile to take a brief glance at investment casting, which is most frequently used today. It is not a new process, but rather dates back a few thousand years. Museums displaying the work of lost civilizations often show implements that were made by investment casting,

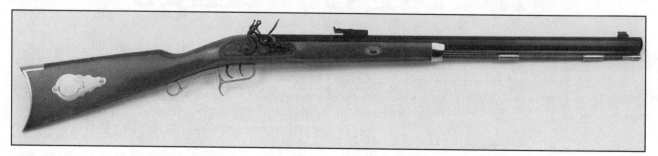

Castings on this rifle include the buttplate, cap box, trigger guard, certain lock parts, rear sight and forend cap. These high-quality appointments would considerably drive up the price of the rifle if they had to be built from bar stock.

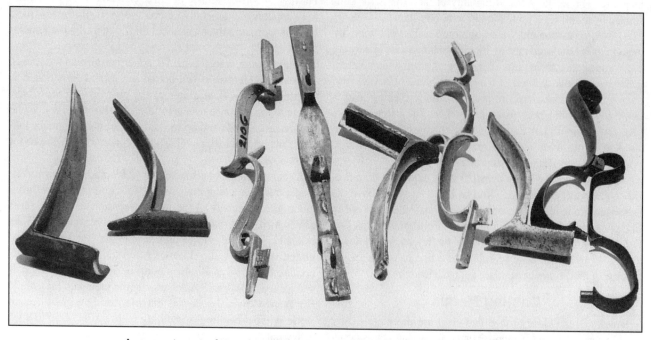

An assortment of cast buttplates and trigger guards—note that gates and flashings are still in place and must be filed off. Then the parts have to be polished before use.

also referred to as the lost wax process. The lost wax process prevails today in many industries such as firearms, textiles, medical equipment, vehicle parts, even pieces used for space exploration.

Modern technology has elevated investment casting to a process precise enough to allow parts to be used "as cast" without further finishing. Even engraving patterns can be duplicated with remarkable precision.

Here is a brief, and simplified, description of the lost wax process as it applies to mass-production:

A master is built. The master part is created out of metal to specific dimensions; these dimensions being as close as possible to what the finished part should be, with consideration given to shrinkage of the various materials to be used (the wax as well as the actual metal being used).

A mould is built. Once the master part is made, obviously it must be copied to produce the many duplicates for production casting. To do this, a wax "casting" is made of the master. Using something similar to a two-piece bullet mould, each mould block has a matching cavity to produce a complete part.

One at a time, each half of the mould is filled with an epoxy material and the master part laid into the cavity half-way, leaving behind an exact impression. Then, the two mould halves are properly vented to allow air to be displaced as the mould is completely filled.

Hot wax is injected into the mould. The wax must fill every nook and cranny to exactly duplicate the master part. The mould is then allowed to cool, which hardens the wax. When the mould is opened, the wax form is removed, giving the pattern that will soon become a metal part. A wax image is used for each and every part made. After removal from the mould blocks, each wax part is attached to a "tree," clustered together in an appropriate number for the foundry. Thus assembled, the wax parts (tree and all) are dipped in a cleaning solution, then into a wetting agent.

The wax parts are ceramic coated. The idea here is to coat them with a very fine slurry of lime powder that contains a blended binder. The consistency of this initial slurry is vital to the finished product because it determines the finished surface of the part. Once dry, the trees are repeatedly dipped in a coarser

Wax is being poured into a master mould. Once it has cooled, the resultant wax part is dipped in a slurry, forming a ceramic coating.

Molten metal is poured into a ceramic mould tree. Once the metal has cooled, the mould is broken away, leaving a precision cast part.

slurry until enough of the material is built up to be sufficiently strong and self-supporting. Think of this as a wax part covered with a ceramic shell. The shell varies in thickness according the the part to be cast, and some can run up to 1/4-inch.

The coating is heated. When the final dip has dried, the trees are placed in an autoclave, a special furnace for melting the wax out of the moulds. The shell is baked until all traces of wax are gone, and then held there at temperatures of perhaps 1200 to 2000 degrees Fahrenheit. The ceramic mould is now ready to accept the molten metal.

Molten metal is poured into the heated ceramic mould. Once cooled, the shell is broken away from the cast part, and the part removed from the tree with cut-off wheels. After stress-relieving, the part has any remaining gate material, or flashing, cut or machined off. If necessary, the part may be sand-blasted to remove any scale left from the heat-treating process, giving a clean and even finish. At this point, the metal is totally unprotected from rust so it receives a light coat of oil to prevent deterioration until it's ready to be used.

The lost wax process is used industry-wide, and makes it possible for even smaller operations to produce their own quality parts, such as locks or sights, on a scale large enough to enter the marketplace with a competitive product of reasonable cost.

The overall quality of investment-cast parts is high, making them ideal for the gunsmith at any level, professional to hobbyist. Unfortunatley, specific parts have come and gone from the market, so if you find specific castings that suit your work, it may pay off to buy a modest supply for future use, just in case your favorite parts become unavailable.

Good investment-cast parts require a minimum of preparation for use because they clean up readily. Siler locks are a fine example of high-quality investment-cast parts. Refer to Chapter 5 on locks for details; however, be aware that certain softer steel parts in this particular lock kit demanded heat-treating to harden them. If made individually of bar stock, Siler lock parts would escalate in price considerably, whereas casting them keeps the price of the kit within reach of the hobbyist—a perfect example of how important castings are to all who wish to work on muzzleloaders.

Muzzleloader Ramrods

ONLY A SLENDER rod of metal or wood, the ramrod is nonetheless one of the most important elements of the blackpowder firearm. Without a ramrod, the muzzleloader is rendered useless, as many shooters have learned on the range and in the field. Substitutes often fail to get the job done and can sometimes cause damage.

As a newcomer to muzzle-loading, a youth who would one day become a blackpowder gunsmith searched for ways to fix broken gun parts when dollars were short. Defunct ramrods were replaced with hickory, not always perfectly straight, but hickory all the same. Instead of a handsome and functional brass base for these rods, a spent cartridge case of the right diameter was crudely pinned in place. These homemade ramrods worked, but there was no way to swab the bore in the field with them because they did not accept jags, worms or screws.

Today, ramrod selection is excellent, with many examples of wood and metal, as well as the newer synthetic varieties which are nearly indestructible. I've seen a demonstration of the latter's strength which included bending until both ends met, yet the rod did not break. Each ramrod has its unique place. Steel rods were often found on military firearms; today's replica muskets generally follow suit. Wooden ramrods were common on sporting rifles in the past, and are still popular today. Of course, synthetic ramrods were not invented until modern times; however, they are well-suited to modern muzzleloaders, and they also make excellent part-time ramrods for any firearm used in the field. The original wooden ramrod can be temporarily replaced with the unbreakable synthetic unit. Then, after shooting, the wooden rod is reinstalled for cosmetic purposes.

Wooden Ramrods

Without doubt, the wooden ramrod is still the most popular, in spite of space-age materials. One reason for their staying power is success: Wooden ramrods work well and they always have. The wood of preference, hickory, is strong, lightweight, and can be shaped or tapered to fit any kind of blackpowder firearm. It is also fairly straight, and that's important for every ramrod, of course, or it will scrape the bore. Abrasive materials embedded in the wood could cause bore damage with enough use.

The hobby gunsmith should understand how to wisely and safely use the wooden ramrod, as well as pass this information on to others who may rely upon his judgment. For example, allowing the rod to bow during the seating of a projectile is asking for trouble. It may break, and it's not impossible for the sharp broken end to jam into the shooter's arm. Wooden ramrods tend to break when oversized bullets require too much force for seating. They also break when bores are fouled so heavily that it's nearly impossible to push a patched ball or lead conical down into the breech. A broken ramrod should not be repaired, even with today's excellent wood glues. Instead, it should be replaced.

Selecting a New Wooden Ramrod

Never choose a soft wood dowel from the local hardware store as a replacement ramrod. These are for furniture building and repair, as well as other applications, but they are not right for ramrods as they lead to breakage. Hickory is the better choice. As this is written, unfinished 48-inch hickory rods are available from Dixie Gun Works for only $8 per four-pack, plus shipping charges. In selecting a hickory rod, look first for *straight grain*. This is important. When the grain pattern trails off to one side or the other, the rod can be expected to break at that point. Obviously, you won't have a chance to look at mail-order rods, so you may wish to order several hickory sticks at one time, knowing that not all will be perfect. The perfect sticks can often be cut for shorter ramrods, however.

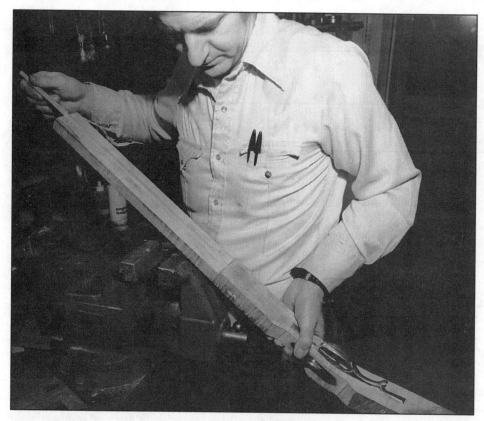

Dale Storey checks a newly built ramrod for proper fit. The ramrod must fit the recess in the stock so it stays put, but it must also be easily removed for use.

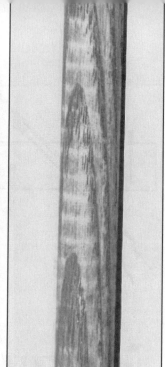

This hickory ramrod shows grain cutting out at the side. This condition makes for a weak rod. In a ramrod, the grain should be as straight as possible. For appearance, a straight-grain ramrod can be candy-striped.

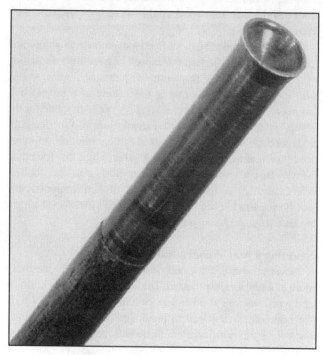

This tip is belled to more closely match the contour of a round ball, for seating without damage to the lead projectile.

Check over the ramrod to ensure it's straight, but do not expect perfect straightness. It just won't happen. Simply go for the straightest one possible. A crooked rod may not thread its way through the ramrod guides. The other side of the coin is the perfectly straight ramrod that fits loosely in its guides, con-

tinually sliding out. This condition is sometimes remedied by a small spring that applies tension to the rod, holding it in place. Finally, the correct size rod must be ordered. Dixie offers four diameters: $5/16$-, $7/16$-, $3/8$- and $1/2$-inch.

Going back to the spring arrangement that holds a ramrod in place, be advised that most original rifles did not have the spring. Accurately copied modern replicas of these originals also lack the spring-hold feature. Therefore, if a very straight ramrod continues to fall out of its guides, a slight bend in the rod may be necessary. This can usually be accomplished by heating the rod and warping it slightly by hand. To heat the wood, use a clean cloth wrapped around the rod and rub vigorously with the cloth to create friction heat. Then, gently bend the rod by hand to create a slight warp.

Making a New Wooden Ramrod

Hickory ramrods can be rendered slightly supple, which can promote longevity, because they will bend and not break from reasonably applied pressure. Hickory ramrod material comes to the hobby gunsmith in a dry, non-flexible state. Dixie notes an average of 8 percent kiln-dried moisture level because the wood has to be dried before it can be cut into rods. So, it is prone to breakage because it is somewhat brittle. It is very easy to correct this condition. Some old-time gunsmiths soaked a new ramrod in coal oil or kerosene to limber it up. These liquids readily permeate the wood, making the rod more supple. Linseed oil and finishing oils do not work well because they dry and/or congeal on the surface, rather than penetrating.

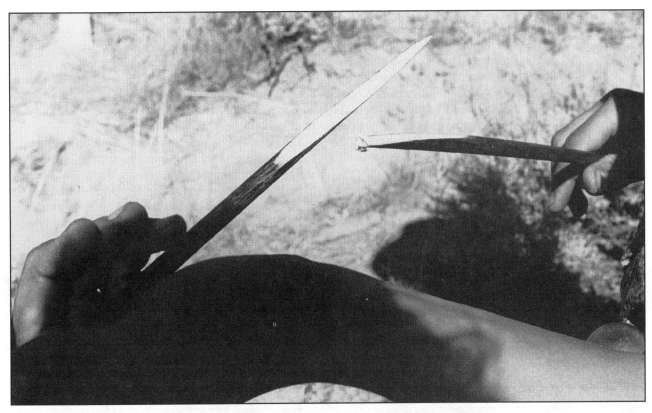

It is easy to see how a broken ramrod like this can be dangerous to the shooter.

While coal oil and kerosene work, Neat's-foot oil is safer to use, and therefore comes highly recommended. The ramrod is soaked in Neat's-foot oil for a week or two, resulting in the necessary suppleness. A good way to soak a rod is to plug one end of a length of pipe, plastic or metal, then partially fill it with oil. Be careful not to overfill because the oil will be displaced when the rod is inserted in the pipe. Hickory ramrods soaked in Neat's-foot oil have good longevity.

There is one catch: A ramrod so treated will not take on a finish later, because finishing oils cannot penetrate the wood. This is not a big problem because the rod can be stained before soaking.

Candy-Striping

Now and then, a natural tiger-striped ramrod turns up; however, these curly grained hickory rods are hard to find, and it takes effort just to sharply bring out the grain pattern. Furthermore, naturally figured rods are not always strong, due to uneven grain direction. Fully figured ramrods are nice for show, but they should be kept for that purpose only, replacing them with stronger units for range and field use. A compromise is the candy-striped ramrod—good looking, but strong and functional.

There are at least two ways to stripe a rod. One involves wrapping the rod with masking tape in a spiral pattern. Choose a narrow-width tape for this work. Then apply a dark brown stain to the rod. Of course, only the exposed wood is treated, thereby leaving a candy-stripe pattern when the masking tape is removed. Then, finish and soak the rod.

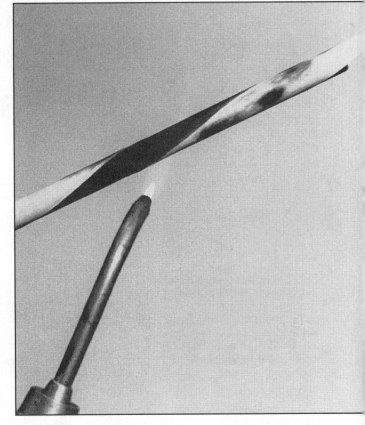

After wrapping with masking tape, a torch flame is used to scorch the surface of the ramrod, leaving a candy-stripe effect.

Another method also requires an initial masking tape wrap. The pattern may be as tight as a barber pole, or more lengthened in style, depending upon how the tape is applied. Then, use an oxygen-acetylene torch to scorch the exposed wood, but not burn it. When the tape is removed, the scorched portion contrasts with the bare wood for the candy-stripe effect. The rod is then finished and soaked in Neat's-foot oil. The scorching method is more difficult to do than the staining, and it takes more time. However, it is more permanent than the stain, and it accepts any type of finish without fading.

Shaping and Tapering

Shaping a hickory ramrod with a knife or piece of broken glass is a painstaking process. A homemade scraper can be made that saves time. A piece of 1/8-inch steel plate, sufficient-ly large to be held in a vise, is drilled, with holes slightly larger in diameter than the ramrods to be tapered. A large plate should be chosen, because several holes of various diameters can be drilled, allowing different sizes of rods to be tapered using that single plate. After drilling, the holes are counter-bored with a regular 60-degree counter bore forming a sharp edge around the circumference of each hole. Next, harden the plate so that the edges remain sharp.

The ramrod is drawn through the appropriate hole in the plate, using downward pressure to shape it. This method creates a rounder ramrod, whereas a knife edge or glass edge often leaves flat spots. The rod is worked back and forth through the cutting hole, revolving it all the while to maintain uniformity. Once the rod is taken down to near final dimensions, finish with sanding.

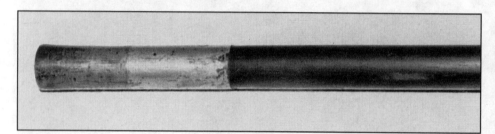

(Left and below) This is a unique ramrod arrangement found on an original 19th-century percussion muzzleloader. The end is removeable, exposing a screw to remove a stuck ball. With the end in place, the ramrod is suited to drive projectiles downbore.

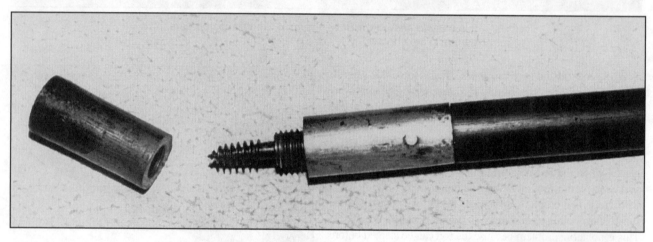

Uncle Mike's thread adapter set, shown in the center of this photograph as three units, offers the blackpowder hobbyist a means of employing a wide variety of cleaning accessories on various rods.

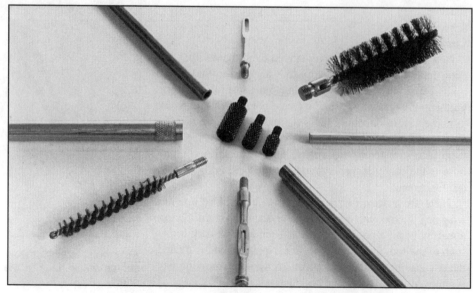

The shotgun ramrod is very often tapered. The job can be tedious. However, another method of tapering the wooden ramrod can be used: sandpaper plus the power drill. The end of the ramrod is held in the chuck of a power hand drill. Coarse sandpaper is held around the other end of the rod, angled to provide a tapering effect when the drill is turned on. The whirling rod is quickly reduced in diameter by the sandpaper. After the majority of wood is removed with coarse 60-grit paper, progressively finer paper is used to smooth the surface. A variable-power hand drill makes this method even more workable because turning speed can be controlled.

Fitting the Base of the Ramrod

Do this before soaking. If the base is fitted after soaking, the adhesives used may not bond correctly because the rod is already permeated with the Neat's-foot oil. Brass pins are also used to connect the tip. The pin is important insurance. Due to the oil soaking, gluing alone cannot be trusted.

The adhesive can be glue, epoxy or hot-melt ferrule cement, which comes in a stick and is available at the local sport shop, hobby shop or hardware store. Adhesive is used to initially secure the tip in place before $3/32$-inch hole is drilled through the tip and rod. A $3/32$-inch brass pin is then inserted through this hole. The pin will protrude slightly on either side of the rod, so place the ramrod end on a flat hard surface, such as an anvil or vise top, and with a small hammer peen the ends of the pins over. Then file the tiny lumps of brass smooth to match the surface of the tip. This dresses the ends of the pins. If the job is done right, the tip will be securely in place and properly aligned, which is especially important when using

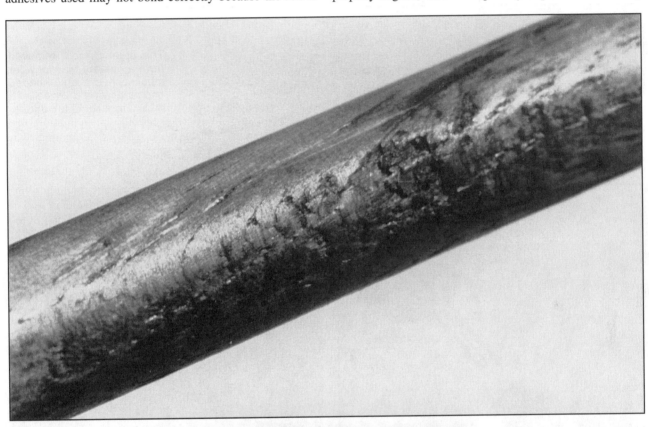

(Above) A clear example of chattering, where damage was done to the side of the ramrod during tapering. Chattering occurs when the ramrod is scraped against the grain, rather than with it.

(Left) A ramrod base tip is drilled so a pin can anchor the tip in place.

143

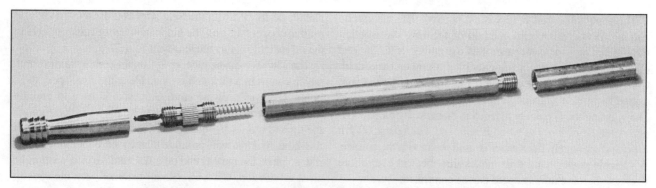

This ingenious jag set came from the Hawken Shop. It incorporates many implements in one unit, from extension to screw with bullet drill and a multitude of jags. The little drill is used to create a hole in the projectile to make a clean entry for the screw.

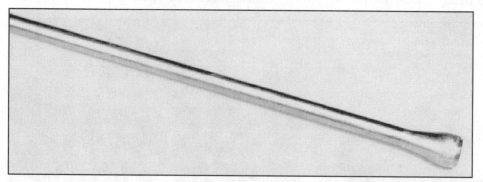

This steel ramrod, removed from a military blackpowder musket, has a bulb-shaped end for seating a projectile. It is not threaded for accessories.

A steel ramrod cannot damage the bore when a bore protector is used. The protector centers the rod in the bore so the rod does not touch the rifling.

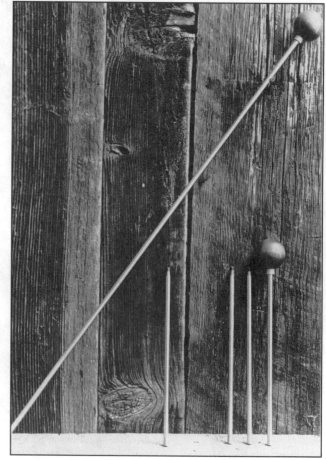

Uncle Mike's stainless steel ramrods in one-piece and breakdown styles. The ball handle is removable.

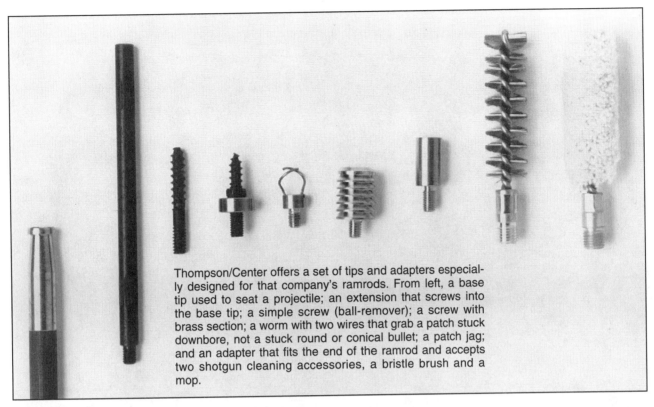

Thompson/Center offers a set of tips and adapters especially designed for that company's ramrods. From left, a base tip used to seat a projectile; an extension that screws into the base tip; a simple screw (ball-remover); a screw with brass section; a worm with two wires that grab a patch stuck downbore, not a stuck round or conical bullet; a patch jag; and an adapter that fits the end of the ramrod and accepts two shotgun cleaning accessories, a bristle brush and a mop.

threaded tips that hold cleaning jags and other removeable accessories.

An improperly fitted, or aligned, tip can work loose during the loading process or a cleaning session. Sometimes this means a tip plus jag stuck downbore. An example of this occurred recently with a rifle that was accused of having a ball stuck downbore. A checkup with a wiping stick proved there were 4 inches of something stuck downbore. This fact was easily assessed by measuring bore/length with the rod on the outside of the barrel, marking it, and then inserting the rod downbore. If the bore were clear, the ramrod would have fallen all the way down to the marked spot on the rod. Instead, the mark rested 4 inches above the muzzle of the rifle.

The problem was first attacked by removing the drum and nipple, upon which powder flowed out from the open orifice. As a safety precaution, oil was poured through the drum hole to kill the powder charge. All of the powder could not be worked free through the drum hole, so the breech plug was removed next. The remainder of the charge was fished out from the breech, after which solvent was used to clear the breech fully of any powder residue. In this case, a solid brass $3/8$-inch ramrod was used to drive the obstruction from the debreeched barrel. What came out? A patched round ball, but not only that. It had a screw (ball-puller) driven into it, with the screw still attached to a base, which had come off of the end of the ramrod. The base of the ramrod had not been properly attached with both pin and adhesive.

The Wiping Stick

The hobby blackpowder gunsmith will want to have on hand several wiping sticks. These are basically long ramrods, generally 48 inches in length. They can be readily made from Dixie Gun Works raw hickory rods. Fitted with proper tips, wiping sticks do an excellent job in heavy-duty professional-type blackpowder gun cleaning. The long ramrod provides a good hand grip. Many adapters can be used with the wiping stick, including jags, worms, screws, breech scrapers and so forth. The wiping stick is a workhorse ramrod.

Metal Ramrods

When ultra strength is demanded, metal rods come to the fore. As noted, military muskets of the past often carried steel ramrods, as did military pistols, such as the Harper's Ferry model. These are normally small diameter rods. Coupled with a muzzle protector, steel rods will not damage or even touch the bore. These are also at home on some shotguns, although synthetic rods are becoming more common. While steel ramrods can be threaded to accept accessories, some are simply bulged on the end and finished with a cup section for ramming projectiles downbore. Stainless steel is also used for making one-piece rods, as well as sectioned cleaning rods. The latter are handy for field use, accepting many different accessories. An excellent one is Uncle Mike's $5/16$-inch diameter unit which breaks down into three 10-inch sections, takes a variety of tips and has a large wooden handle.

Steel is not the only metal used for ramrods; solid brass is also a possibility. Brass rods are generally of relatively large diameter, with fairly hefty weight to match. These are often used for loading at the shooting range, rather than in the field. For range use, it is convenient to have a separate rod, rather than using the one that is fitted in the firearm's pipes. A long brass rod is also an asset in the shop, where its strength is appreciated. And maybe most importantly, a brass ramrod will not scratch the rifling.

Thompson/Center's Polymer-Coated Fiberglass Ramrod is the perfect example of a high-tech rod, composed of an extruded fiberglass core with a non-abrasive polymer sheath. In the above demonstration, this rod was placed against a rock, and a 4000-pound truck was driven over the rod, bending but not breaking it.

Synthetic Rods

There are far too many synthetic ramrods offered by numerous manufacturers to make a complete listing here feasible. The unbreakable synthetic ramrod is not detrimental to bores, which can't be said for some earlier fiberglass rods which lapped the rifling lands. Synthetic rods are very much at home on modern muzzleloaders and are extremely workable on blackpowder shotguns as well. The march toward better synthetic materials continues, too. For example, Thompson/Center offers a synthetic ramrod with a core of solid fiberglass, but an outer sheath of polymer. The result is a tough, strong, nearly indestructible ramrod that at the same time is non-abrasive.

Another rod currently available, and worthy of inclusion here, is the Super Rod. Its name is not an overstatement. It is more rigid than some previous synthetic units, which promotes easy seating of projectiles, as well as shotgun wad columns, while at the same time being virtually unbreakable under normal use. It is also non-abrasive. Furthermore, the Super Rod seems almost immune to varying temperatures. It does not get brittle when it is cold, nor does it become too flexible when it is hot. Finally, the Super Rod is also impervious to oils chemicals. This model is readily available through blackpowder suppliers, such as the Log Cabin Sport Shop.

The blackpowder hobby gunsmith should have on hand several ramrods of different design and construction to match various tasks, from wooden types that rest in the pipes of the muzzleloader, to wooden wiping sticks, long metal rods for shop work, and synthetic units for heavy range and field use. The hobbyist should be able to build his own wooden ramrod, cut it to proper length (sometimes a little longer is better so the end can be gripped when it's in its guides), finish it neatly (perhaps with a candy-stripe effect), and tip it appropriately.

Muzzleloader Sights

"A RIFLE IS no better than its sights." That's a cliché, but it's also the truth—not only for rifles, but pistols and revolvers as well. There are even shotguns that have sights, either a second bead mid-barrel to aid alignment or full-blown rifle-type irons, if not a scope. The blackpowder hobby gunsmith should know quite a bit about sights because they can cause a lot of trouble. It is not merely a matter of replacing a broken sight. The smith should also be able to match sights to guns for specific functions and specific shooters. A great sight for one shooter may be nothing more than a millstone about the neck of another.

Scopes

There is a vast array of gunsights suited to frontloaders, from the simplest fixed open iron arrangement to the modern scope. We'll begin with scopes because they are the most familiar to modern shooters, and a multitude of blackpowder fans are turning to glass sights on their muzzleloaders. It's well worth looking into the story of scope sights as part of the hobbyist's education. They are nothing new. The glass sight was born far from the shores of this land, and nowhere has it found more success, although it took a long time before scopes caught on. While nobody can pinpoint each nuance of gunscope history, the story certainly begins with the regular telescope, which magnified distant objects. Who made the first telescope?

It appears that Johann Lipperhey of Middleburg, Holland, a spectacle maker, came up with the first working model in 1608. It was a crude instrument of no particular value until Galileo, the famous Italian astronomer and scientist, upgraded the invention from playtoy to viable instrument. Therefore, Galileo gets credit for creating the first workable telescope. Later attachment of the terrestrial telescope to the rifle was as

natural a progression as using wheels on a car, but the first riflescope and its inventor are lost in a far-away niche of gun history.

The terrestrial telescope, carried by adventurers of land and sea, was held in constant association with firearms. The famous mountain man, Jim Bridger, carried one to look for "squalls" from lofty places in the Far West. As far back as the Continental Congress of 1776, there are notations pertaining to the purchase of telescopic rifle sights; however, some historians believe these to be tube sights without lenses. Perhaps, but why did our founding fathers call them telescopes? Many trailblazers carried telescopes. That one of them stuck a scope on a rifle is not a quantum leap in reasoning.

Certainly, the American Civil War era saw limited, but important, use of riflescopes. In his book *Modern American Rifles*, A.G. Gould observed that, during the Civil War, a number of Whitworth muzzle-loading rifles with telescopic sights were shipped to America from England for Confederate snipers. The Union Army was not without the scope sight, either. Hiram Berdan, chief of the U.S. Sharpshooters, gave a demonstration of long-range shooting prowess to President Lincoln. One of Berdan's snipers put every bullet fired into a man-sized target at 600 yards.

While we do not know the inventor of the riflescope, we can treat its inception as we have the telescope, giving credit to the first (or at least one of the first) inventors who made it a *practical* tool. That would be William Ellis Metford of England, in the year 1824. I trust the dates of firearm and scope invention as I would a rattler in the bottom of my sleeping bag, but we are stuck with the dates that research provides, so 1824 it shall remain. Metford designed and perfected a scope sight which was fitted by Colonel George Gibbs to an experimental rifle. Of 8x magnification (approximately), the

This heavy blackpowder slug gun uses modern telescopic rifle sights to realize its accuracy potential.

Storey Sidehammer custom rifle is fitted with a powerful B&L scope sight for purposes of testing. Scopes are used on some blackpowder firearms and are now more popular than ever.

scope worked quite well. It had very unique and worthwhile adjustment capability and was built like a fine scientific instrument. Metford could prove to anyone, with scope in place, the rifle was far more capable of delivering its full accuracy potential to the target.

Many of the 19th-century American buffalo runners used the riflescope, a perfect example of a glass sight on a black-powder firearm, albeit a cartridge rifle. Colonel Frank H. Mayer remained our best link with that particle of past history. He died in Fairplay, Colorado, in 1954 at age 104. Mayer said the good buff rifle cost a hundred dollars or more, "not including the necessary telescopic sight." Mark the word necessary. Mayer obtained his first buffalo rifle from Colonel Richard Irving Dodge (who also wrote about buffalo hunting, incidentally). It was a 40-90-420 Sharps, a 12-pounder topped with a 20x target scope made by A. Vollmer of Jena, Germany, a geographic area noted for fine optics. Mayer had an additional horizontal wire added to the scope, thereby producing a stadia wire arrangement for judging range. But the scope sight, still longer than a bad dream and with a small field of view, did not catch on among the grassroots hunters of the 19th century. There was much distrust of the glass sight.

Not adopted by sportsmen, nor even the bulk of target shooters, after the Civil War, nor following the age of the bison hunters, the scope sight was also eschewed by the general shooting public prior to and during World War I. In between the two great wars, however, many scope designs were set forth. The poor-quality American sniper scope used in "The War to End All Wars" had not been touted as a piece of high-class military technology and made no impact. But there was an explosion of interest in scope development between the wars.

When the attack on Pearl Harbor rocked America, the rifle scope was still not commonplace as a piece of shooting hardware—not on the target range, and certainly not in the hunting field. Initial distrust lingered. The American rifleman glanced ever sideways at the glass sight. Fremantle, in *The Book of the Rifle*, explained how he set up his scoped rifle for the field, "the tube of the telescope is only 8 inches long and is conveniently carried in a little leather case on a belt." When a long-range shot presented itself, the rifleman attached the scope on the spot, in the field. Also, scopes were mounted to the side, so as not to deter the shooter from using his trusted iron sights. Fremantle considered it foolhardy and thoroughly American to mount the scope directly over the bore in competition with the regular metallic sights of the rifle. Those old-time notions remained fixed in shooters' minds for more than a little while.

However, after WWII, the scope began to find favor with the broad base of target shooters, as it had much earlier among a limited number of paper-punchers. The art of benchrest shooting, strictly an American pastime, especially demanded a magnified target and a precise aimpoint. Target shooting with the glass sight had always been deemed a pretty reasonable venture anyhow. Now, the leaders of the hunter/writer community—Keith, O'Connor, Whelen, Paul Curtis, Stewart Edward White, and many others whose pens scratched out stories of the sport hunting world—began to write glowing reports applauding the glass sight. Their stories upholding the riflescope were, at first, looked upon with guarded reservation. Switching to glass sights was still a risky business, rightfully so in some instances; scopes continued to suffer many design and mechanical problems.

From distrust to full trust, the scope sight progressed to become America's number one aiming instrument. Interestingly, the blackpowder progression is a minor reflection of the big picture—for the muzzleloader began with no sights at all, progressing to crude open iron sights, then to more sophisticated open iron sights, to aperture or peep sights, tube sights, and finally to the scope. Today, scopes are mounted on muzzleloaders where appropriate—not on Pennsylvania long rifles, to any degree, but certainly on modern muzzleloaders, as well as a few custom rifles, such as the Dale Storey Buggy Rifle.

Scope Mounts

Before leaving scopes, it's imperative to mention that a scope is, in the long run, no better than its mount, for if the scope is not attached securely and accurately to the firearm, it may become more detriment than value. Many mount styles have come forth over the years. Today, we have a great number of excellent scope mounts to choose from, including detachable as well as permanent fixtures. The Warne Detachable is an excellent example of an innovative scope mount, because it incorporates a peep sight in its rear base. A system of this nature demands the front sight match the peep sight with proper height. The gunsmith must check this out carefully with a collimator, or at the shooting range. Properly set up, the Warne Detachable sight gives the rifleman a choice: peep or scope on the same rifle. That's flexibility.

Sight Types

Among the various sight choices, how does the shooter know which to choose? Muzzleloaders must be fitted with sights that meet the requirements of shoots and hunts. Many blackpowder

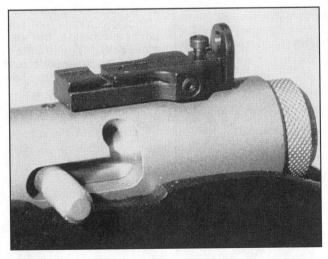

This is a side view of the Warne Detachable scope base/peep sight mounted on a modern muzzleloader.

target matches are for iron sights only; some specify only open irons, in fact. There are special blackpowder-only hunts that do not allow the use of scope sights on muzzleloaders.

Fixed Open Iron Sights

Fixed or non-adjustable open sights generally consist of a notched rear sight mounted in a dovetail notch, combined with a blade front sight also mounted in a dovetail notch. Fixed and non-adjustable are misnomers, however, because this simple open sight can be adjusted for windage by sliding the rear sight in its dovetail notch in the direction the shooter wants the next bullet to hit on the target; or for the front sight, sliding it in its dovetail notch to the right to make the next bullet hit to the left on the target and vice versa. Also, the front sight can be filed down so that the bullet hits higher on the target, or a taller front sight can be installed to make the firearm group lower on the target. Because of these possible adjustments, easily accomplished by the hobby gunsmith, the fixed open sight is, in fact, not fixed.

The majority of today's fixed sights are investment cast and of high quality, most of them fitting a standard ³/₈-inch dovetail notch. There are many different dovetail sizes, however, and the hobbyist may have to file or recut a dovetail to accommodate a new sight not of standard dimension.

Various styles of fixed open rear sights exist, including flat-top and curl-top, where the sides of the sight curl upward from the base of the sight. Either type forms a shallow "V" notch which visually matches well with a front sight blade.

The semi-buckhorn rear sight is a variation of the design, where the curl-top extends higher, giving the appearance of horns. The same kind of front sighting blade can be used with the semi-buckhorn as with other styles of rear sight.

Buckhorn or full buckhorn rear sights carry the concept of upward-rising horns further, resulting in even higher projections. In some instances, the two curls roll inward and almost touch. The hobby gunsmith may consider removing full buckhorn rear sights in favor of other styles, because the horns can sometimes block out part of the sight picture. Perhaps, but a lot of good shooting has transpired with buckhorns.

Adjustable Open Iron Sights

While the front sight on this system generally remains stationary in a dovetail notch on the barrel (or affixed on a ramp), it is the rear sight that provides adjustment. The sight is tapped left or right for horizontal bullet placement, called windage adjustment. Vertical movement is called elevation adjustment, accomplished by the use of an elevator bar or a sliding element that can be loosened, moved and then retightened into place. The higher the rear sight is set in its notches, the higher the group strikes the target. Sometimes adjustment is accom-

The hobby blackpowder gunsmith must have a full understanding of sights, not only concerning style, but also mechanical construction. Here is an adjustable rear sight disassembled to show its parts.

plished with a screw turned to either raise or lower the rear sight. There are far too many variations of adjustable iron sights to give all of them attention here. However, many different iron sights are illustrated for this chapter.

Receiver Sights

The blackpowder gunsmithing hobbyist has a multitude of different receiver sight options available today. Also known as peep sights, the various models attach in different ways, some directly to the breech of the rifle. These provide an excellent sight picture because the shooter does not have to consciously align the front sight in the center of the peep or hole of the rear sight. The human eye does that automatically, seeking the point of greatest light, which is in the center of the hole. Therefore, the shooter need only look *through*, not at, the peep, aligning the bead or blade of the front sight on the target.

There are numerous fine receiver sights for muzzleloaders, some of them quite sophisticated. A simple, but highly effective, one is the Storey peep sight, adjustable for windage and elevation. Since adjustments are not quickly made, this is a field sight. Lyman's 57SML is another fine receiver sight, fully adjustable and readily adaptable to most blackpowder rifles. It's a good target sight because it adjusts quickly. Williams makes several excellent receiver sights. So does Thompson/Center, with different models to

Williams offers a rear sight that attaches to the octagon barrel, as shown here. It's suitable for a number of blackpowder rifles and is fully adjustable.

(Left) A simple fixed iron rear sight, which, in fact, is adjustable for windage by sliding it in its dovetail notch.

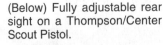

(Below) Fully adjustable rear sight on a Thompson/Center Scout Pistol.

Another fully adjustable rear sight, this one on a Thompson/Center muzzleloader.

The Lyman 93 Match front sight (left) comes with several optional inserts, as shown. Five of these are of the aperture type, and two are posts.

This Williams adjustable peep sight fits neatly on a modern muzzleloader.

An excellent, yet simple, aperture rear sight is this design by Dale Storey. It is mounted on the tang of the rifle.

Lyman's 57SML Micrometer Sight is a precision instrument that attaches to the tang of a muzzleloader.

Called a tang sight because it mounts on the tang, as shown here, this particular model is a long-range Creedmoor style. It has great latitude for elevation adjustment.

choose from. A little gunsmithing know-how, plus a touch of ingenuity, allows the fitting of different peep sights to a multitude of muzzleloaders. Also, sights not originally intended for frontloaders can be adapted. For example, the Redfield Palma Target Sight has been fitted to muzzleloaders, but special bases may have to be professionally machined.

The hobby gunsmith must remember that many receiver sights accept different sizes of apertures. Shooters who complain about "ghost ring," which is a fuzzy outer sight picture with a peep sight, should try different aperture sizes to see if that solves the problem. Of course, the important part of the peep sight picture is the center. However, especially for field work, a larger aperture is often desirable. The Merit Master Disc No. 3 has an adjustable opening, from .022- to .125-inch. This iris-type system is versatile, offering the shooter various apertures in one sight for different situations. Merit also has a No. 4 sight disc with an iris opening of .025- to .155-inch. This field model is more compact than the target model.

Vernier Tang Sights

The hobbyist should know about this sight because he will run across one at some time in his life, and because it was quite popular in its era. This sight mounts only to the tang. Its use is optional because it may be flipped up for sighting or rested flat against the tang, out of service so an open iron rear sight may be used. The tang sight is held in position either by a spring detent or a lock screw. This sight is valuable for long-range shooting and was encountered on both muzzle-loading and cartridge blackpowder rifles.

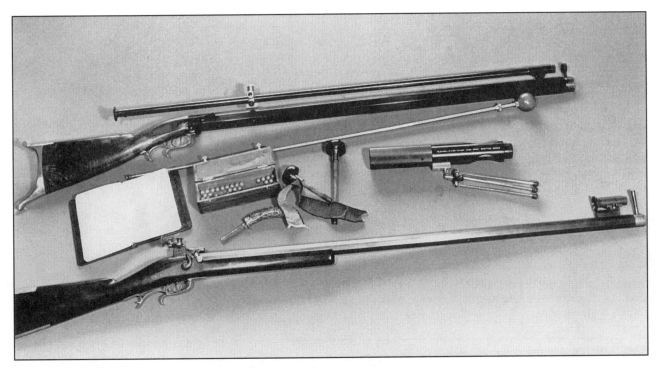

The top rifle is a benchrest round ball shooter with tube sight. The lower rifle is a light benchrest rifle with double aperture sights.

Tube Sights

The tube sight is simply a long tube without lenses. It uses external mounts with apertures fitted to the rear and front of the tube. The tube sight is mainly for target work, and very accurate shooting can be accomplished with it. The tube sight may extend from the wrist section of the rifle all the way to the

The front portion of this tube sight retains different inserts. The large disk in front of the sight reminds the shooter to remove the false muzzle before firing the rifle.

muzzle. It's especially useful on warm days because it helps eliminate mirage caused by heat waves rising from the barrel.

Front Sights

Not much has been said about front sights; however, the variations are many. The job of the gunsmith is to match up the right front sight with the rear sight, not only in proper height for obvious sight-in reasons, but also in terms of historical propriety. A front sight from one era matched with a rear sight from another may work fine, but the gun owner may not appreciate the mixing of time frames.

Silver-hued blade front sights were common on many original muzzleloaders, often mounted on bases of brass, copper or steel. The base materials are not important, except to note that softer metals may fatigue if driven back and forth in the dovetail notch too many times. Then it's difficult to keep the sight in place. Incidentally, the bright silver blade has the advantage of standing out in dim light; however, it may also reflect light, making a sight picture difficult. So, the smith may wish to darken the sides of the blade through bluing or browning.

The list of other front sight options for muzzleloaders is seemingly endless, including the Patridge style, which is thick, flat on top, and mated with a square notch rear sight. It's sometimes called a "partridge" sight as well, but since its inventor was E.E. Patridge, that spelling should stand as correct. This sight presents a rectangular picture.

The bead front sight is entirely different because the picture is round. There are dozens of different bead sights made of numerous materials from steel to colored plastic. The smith's job is to match the size of the bead with the rear sight notch, if the rear sight is of the open style. Also, bead size is important

This is a globe front sight sheltered by a hood. It has a windage adjustment knob, and is typically used with a Vernier tang rear sight.

(Above) This is a semi-hooded front sight, another option.

(Left) This front sight presents a rectangular view. Note that it is fitted on a ramp screwed to the barrel.

(Below) Here is a front sight with a bead formed from the parent material of the sight—just one more option among many.

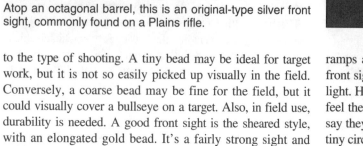

Atop an octagonal barrel, this is an original-type silver front sight, commonly found on a Plains rifle.

to the type of shooting. A tiny bead may be ideal for target work, but it is not so easily picked up visually in the field. Conversely, a coarse bead may be fine for the field, but it could visually cover a bullseye on a target. Also, in field use, durability is needed. A good front sight is the sheared style, with an elongated gold bead. It's a fairly strong sight and reflects light well.

Ramp front sights are sometimes fitted with hoods that provide shade for the blade. For example, Williams Streamlined ramps are slotted to accept hoods. As noted above, a bright front sight is ideal in low light, but can cause trouble in bright light. Hoods are often a matter of preference. Some marksmen feel the hood blocks out part of the sight picture, while others say they never see the hood at all when they take aim—only a tiny circle, visually, around the front sight.

The globe sight has taken on several meanings over the years. In fact, the first globe sights were so-named because they were perfectly round front sights, shaped just like a globe

A traditional-style pistol with fixed sights.

or ball. The globe sight was found on some original muzzle-loaders, especially those used for target shooting, but it is also useful in the field. The Lyman 93 Match is a fine front sight referred to as a globe type. With a series of interchangeable elements or target inserts, the 93 is quickly detachable. Its diameter is $7/8$-inch with bases of .860-inch (European) or .562-inch (American) hole spacing. Height is .550-inch, measured from the top of the dovetail to the center of the aperture. It's known as an aperture sight because it has optional fixtures with holes in which the target is centered.

Hooked Breeches and Sights

The smith may have a problem attaching certain sights to firearms with hooked breeches. The barrels on these guns are quickly removable for cleaning; however, if the peep sight is fitted to the breech, it may not return to its precise previous location when the gun is taken down and put back together a number of times. The solution is a very tight-fitting breech offering little slack. Sometimes glass-bedding the barrel, so it has a hard surface on which to rest, is useful in maintaining sight alignment.

Pistol Sights

Many of the early boarding pistols, as well as pistols worn in the belt or sash, and those used primarily for extremely close-range shooting, truly had no sights at all. Sometimes a lump of metal up front was considered an aiming point, but it was of little use in producing an accurate sight picture. However, these days, blackpowder pistols can wear any number of different sights—including scopes, if their owners wish. The most common pistol sight is a combination of front blade with rear straight slot for the 6 o'clock hold, which means the bullseye is visually perched on top of the front blade, rather than being obliterated by it. Exchanging fixed sights for adjustable types on a pistol is a sure way to improve groups.

Choosing a Sight

Buckskinners, and all other shooters interested in the originality of firearms, may have to choose sights based solely on

Here is yet another option from the world of blackpowder sights, a pistol with an open rear sight that is adjustable for elevation via a screw with a large head.

historical correctness. This is not always conducive to hitting the target, for some older sights leave much to be desired. However, a good set of open sights, as found on many original guns, works far better than we sometimes wish to believe. It's often a matter of learning and practicing how to get a good sight picture.

There are also individual considerations. After all, eyesight is not a constant. As we get older, our ability to see well gener-

Sighting in a rifle is sometimes a job for a hobby gunsmith, especially if the firearm will be used with two different loads—one for target, the other for the field.

ally declines. Good sights for a twenty-year-old shooter may not be good for a sixty-year-old, not to mention eyesight varies greatly from person to person. While it may not prove historically correct, peep and scope sights often save the day when a shooter demands less strain from his eyes. The human eye must focus on three levels in open sight shooting: back sight, front sight and target. The peep sight reduces this to two levels: front sight and target, since correct use means looking through, not at, the rear sight. Focus is on a single plane with a scope. The reticle, or sight, is visually pasted right on the target.

The blackpowder hobby gunsmith may find himself building a full-blown custom rifle someday, but if not, perhaps he will put together a kit, or many kits. Most of these firearms will need sights, although a few pistols will not wear sophisticated aiming devices. Furthermore, the maker of the firearm will often be obligated to sight-in these guns. Scope sight adjustment is simple: The turret cap is removed and the dial is changed the correct number of clicks or line marks in the proper direction. Open iron sight adjustment was previously men-

tioned. Peep sights are also easy to move in the right direction for sight-in. What has not been discussed is how different loads affect the aiming point. The gunsmith has to know what load will be used before he can sight-in the firearm. This is especially true for rifles that will be asked to perform on the target range as well as in the field. In some instances, sights will have to be altered when loads are changed. For example, a 60-grain charge of powder for target work will demand one sight-in, while a 100-grain field charge will need another. Fixed sights are difficult to adjust quickly, but all other sights handle the two-load problem efficiently, if the gunsmith is aware of the situation. A scope, for example, can enjoy two settings, one for each powder charge. The shooter adjusts the scope to match the situation. The same can be done with adjustable iron sights as well.

The modern blackpowder hobby gunsmith needs to familiarize himself with a multitude of sights, because, as promised in the beginning of this chapter, he will run across numerous options the longer he works on blackpowder guns.

Professional Muzzleloader Maintenance

EVERY BLACKPOWDER GUNSMITH, professional or hobbyist, will hear the words, "This gun used to shoot well, but now it doesn't." Modern rifles can go sour due to copper fouling in the bore, which can turn a tackdriver into a rifle that groups like a scattergun. Once the copper fouling is completely cleared, the rifle shoots well again. Muzzleloaders never get copper fouling because they do not shoot jacketed bullets, but they can go sour, and the blackpowder hobby gunsmith should know how to fix inaccuracy due to a caked or fouled bore.

Blackpowder is hygroscopic, with a "g," meaning it attracts moisture. Blackpowder is also corrosive, meaning it will eat into metals. The first property mentioned is the worst one, because blackpowder is not nearly as corrosive, all by itself, as many shooters believe. Residue left downbore can wreak havoc with the steel. So, the first thing to look for when a muzzleloader fails to function properly is fouling, not only in the bore, but in the nipple seat area, the touchhole of a flintlock, or even in the lock itself—anywhere the firearm functions.

Pyrodex does not demand cleaning between shots. However, it does require the same kind of after-shooting cleanup associated with blackpowder. The blackpowder hobby gunsmith needs to know this because there has been confusion on the subject.

A fouled bore can cause a rise in pressures because the bore actually becomes smaller in volume as it cakes up. A clean muzzleloader, in other words, is safer than a dirty one. Pressures do not rise to astronomical levels; however, the wise shooter keeps his blackpowder gun clean not only for its preservation and accuracy, but also for overall safety.

The term "fouling the bore" should be thought of as "dressing the bore." The hobbyist who testfires his own or someone else's firearm should consider dressing the bore before shooting a group. The squeaky clean bore is ideal for storage, but not always ideal for consistency in grouping. This is especially true with Pyrodex. But remember, with Pyrodex cleaning between shots is not recommended.

A bore light is useful in checking for fouling, and the hobby gunsmith should have one handy at all times. In severe cases, including a ring in the bore, the firearm may have to be debreeched for inspection and cleaning, meaning the breech plug must be removed with a large wrench while the barrel is secured in a vise. Never remove a breech plug without trying to clear the bore of fouling first. Removing the breech plug is a last resort on a firearm that is severely fouled.

Cleaning the Muzzleloader with Water

Over the years, only one kind of cleaning method has been popular, and that's the water method—using cold or hot water to flush the bore of the frontloader. Blackpowder residue contains many different types of salts, and water breaks down salt beautifully. That is why plain H_2O works well in getting the gunk out. On the other hand, muzzleloaders can also be cleaned without water, using bore solvents. Combining the two methods is exceptionally effective and recommended for a blackpowder firearm that has not been cleaned properly.

Cleaning the Muzzleloader without Water

The hobbyist may wish to adopt this method of cleaning for the removal of bore fouling. With this method, solvent, rather than water, is used to break down blackpowder residue.

It is worth mentioning here that when using a bore brush and solvent, it's best to either use an eyedropper to apply solvent to the brush or pour a little into a shallow dish and dip the brush into that. By dipping the brush into the fresh solvent bottle, you'll only contaminate the whole bottle of fluid with the dirty brush. Some solvents come in a squeezable spout-topped bottle, which makes the job easier.

Advanced Maintenance

Basic cleaning methods work most of the time. However, there are special cases where harsher measures are demanded, especially when a vintage original muzzleloader is encountered. Perhaps the old gem's bore hasn't seen a cleaning for a half-century. Also, it's unfortunate, but some frontloaders, only a few years old, may have seen neglect and abuse. These require extra cleaning effort as well.

These advanced cleaning methods for crusted, caked and badly fouled bores, as well as rusted bores, will restore certain barrels to operational level. However, some bores, sad to say, can never be restored.

Maintenance Tools

As with so many of the specific tasks discussed in this text, it may be necessary to find help if the hobbyist does not have the right tools on hand. These are a large wrench, a solid vise, a copper bristle brush, cleaning patches, a cleaning rod, a toothbrush and pipe cleaners. The maintenance methods are described here for the hobbyist's knowledge. If he does not have these tools, or help is required for breech plug removal, the hobby gunsmith can go for help, knowing what the professional has to do and why he has to do it.

Certain firearms require special wrenches to remove breech plugs. For example, Thompson/Center has special wrenches that fit the breech plugs for their Hawken-type firearms. Using the wrong wrench may result in damage to the firearm. So find out if there is a special wrench for the gun you're trying to debreech. B-Square also offers special wrenches for a variety of breech plugs.

Warning: When removing a flintlock rifle or pistol breech plug, it is important to remove the lock from the stock first, along with lock screws, because often the top lock screw goes through a hole in the breech plug, and if this screw is not removed, getting the plug out will be a problem. Also, remove the tang screw.

Disassembly for Maintenance

While it may seem overly obvious, the barrel should be removed from the stock before any debreeching is attempted.

Special Hints for Muzzleloader Care and Handling

The fouling shot and common sense. Use the fouling shot (dressing the bore) for target shooting and for accuracy tests (shooting groups), but do not foul the bore if the firearm will be carried for a while without further shooting. Instead, ensure the bore is completely dry of any oil. An oily bore can cause a projectile to go astray.

Disassembly. When taking a muzzleloader apart for cleaning, be careful that pinned stocks (barrel and stock held together with pins) are not split by careless removal of these pins. Also be careful with the full-stock when separated from the barrel. Striking a hard surface may crack or break these slender stocks.

The flush bottle. It is simply a small container with a plastic tube that connects to the nipple of the percussion firearm. A tight damp patch is run up and down the bore creating a vacuum that draws water from the bottle and then pushes it back into the bottle. The flush bottle works well in the field and is also useful for preliminary cleaning in the shop. Water or solvent can be used in the bottle.

Hot or cold water? Boiling water is unnecessary. There is no proof that boiling water removes more bore fouling than simple hot water. The heat from the water warms the barrel, which later helps to dry remaining water from the bore. *Caution:* A muzzleloader barrel cleaned with very hot water can get hot enough to burn the hand.

The bristle brush. This is highly recommended because the bristles get down into the grooves of the rifling, which helps to remove fouling from this region.

Remove the cleanout screw. The removal of this screw allows a flow of water or solvent, promoting cleanup.

The cleaning rod. Special cleaning rods for muzzleloaders are available, properly sized for the bore. Use a muzzle protector to center the rod in the bore and prevent lapping of the rifling.

Hot, but not boiling, water is poured downbore to flush the barrel, loosening bore fouling.

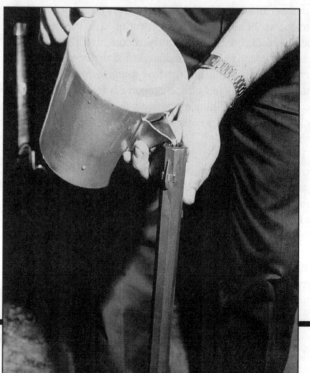

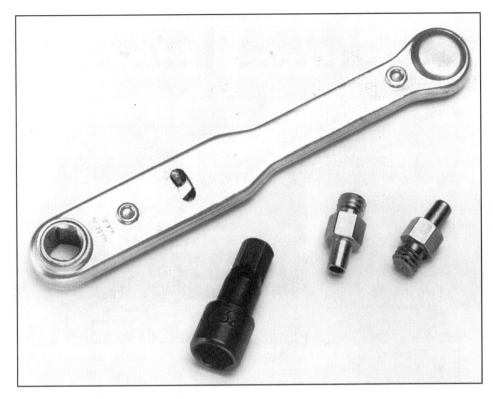

Most modern muzzleloaders require special tools for proper disassembly of the firearm. This Nipple Pack with Ratchet Wrench is for CVA's Apollo rifle.

Barrel pins or wedges are driven out first. It is wise to always drive a pin out from left to right, as some are tapered in this direction, and to drive them in the reverse direction may split the stock. Wedges are obvious; they come out only one way. Make note of where each pin and wedge came from and replace them in their original positions in the stock. Often, wedges and pins are individually fitted. Also, be certain to replace the wedge right side up. Do not reverse it upon its return to the stock, as it may not fit correctly.

In separating a barrel from its stock, a strong ramrod or cleaning rod can be used, but carefully. The rod is inserted downbore, leaving a few inches protruding from the muzzle. The rod is then used to lever the barrel away from the stock by judicious pressure, pressing down on the forearm with fingers. Never use force. If the stock barrel will not part, something is wrong, so find out if a pin was left in place. Using a lot of force to separate barrel and stock may result in a cracked stock. If a barrel will not come free with modest pressure, the best avenue is to seek professional help.

There is no such thing as perfect uniformity in how barrels and stocks are attached to each other. Careful inspection is essential to prevent damage. For example, one fullstock rifle had screws going up through the ramrod guides to attach the barrel to the stock, and they had to be removed for disassembly.

Ideally, muzzleloaders will receive good treatment. Heirlooms should be kept unloaded and clean in a dry environment. After shooting, all frontloaders should be cleared of fouling and left with a film of protective oil until the next time out to the range or field. However, the ideal is not always the case. When a muzzleloader requires more than a normal clean-up, that's the time for professional-type maintenance to come to the fore. The blackpowder hobby gunsmith is perfectly

capable of providing most of this level of service in muzzleloader cleaning.

Note: The cleaning of shotguns, pistols and revolvers follows the same general pattern as rifle maintenance. Of course, disassembly and assembly vary gun to gun, but the same major steps apply.

Testing Bore Condition

A bore light, as well as a tight feeler patch, will help the smith determine the final condition of the bore he has been working on, using vision and feel to locate bad spots. However, there is another way to see if the bore is worthy of service, and that's by shooting groups at the range. *Remember that some abused muzzleloaders are unfit to shoot. Never shoot one that is obviously damaged. Do not shoot a muzzleloader if the bore is badly pitted.* In testing bores returned to reasonably safe condition, use only target loads. The restored barrel will probably never deliver top-notch accuracy if it had to be returned from such a state of ill repair. However, the firearm may supply reasonable hunting and/or plinking accuracy. Many original muzzleloaders have been returned to the field in safe shootable condition, but their bores needed reconditioning.

Plastic Fouling

Another type of fouling encountered in the bores of black-powder firearms is plastic fouling. An extremely smooth bore, with polished lands, or a shiny shotgun bore may never develop any serious plastic fouling. But the use of plastic sabots and shotgun wads can foul some barrels. Shooter's Choice solvent and a bristle brush usually serve to clear plastic fouling. Follow the directions on the container.

Cleaning With Water

Tools

Nipple Wrench or Large Wrench
Screwdriver Set
Small Mallet or Hammer
Vise

Supplies

Accragard Metal Preservative
Blackpowder Bore Solvent
Boiled Linseed Oil
Canned Air
Cleaning Patches
Cleaning Rod
Copper Bristle Bore Brush
Flitz
Hot and Cold Water
Pipe Cleaners
Soft, Dry Cloths
Toothbrush

A toothbrush with solvent is used to remove fouling around nipple area. The tootbrush is also useful in cleaning the interior of the lock.

Setting Up

Be certain the firearm is completely unloaded. Always do this before working on any firearm. Then, using the appropriate tools, disassemble the muzzleloader.

Flushing the Bore

Thoroughly flush the bore with cool water, then follow with a hot water flush. This should begin to loosen caked residue. Next, use a copper bristle bore brush to scrub the grooves of the rifling. Afterward, remove the cleanout screw, if your firearm has one, and flush again with fresh, hot water through the cleanout screw hole. Be careful. Don't promote further decay by allowing streams of dirty water to invade the niches and crannies of the gun.

Scrubbing the Fouling

Use a toothbrush doused with blackpowder bore solvent to scrub the hammer nose, snail area, metal parts around the lock, nipple seat, nipple threads and other exposed metal parts. Use a pipe cleaner to swab the vent of the nipple, as well as the nipple seat of the firearm, or the touchhole of the flintlock.

Flush with cool water by simply pouring downbore. This begins the cleaning process.

A copper bristle brush is ideal for working the fouling out of the rifling grooves.

The clean-out screw is removed with a screwdriver that fits the head snugly. The wrong screwdriver may a strip the head.

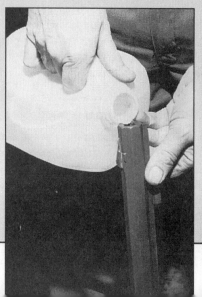

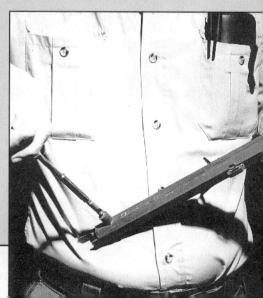

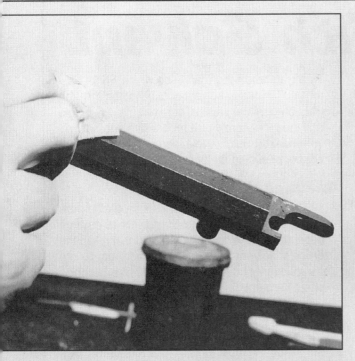

A piece of clean cloth soaked with solvent is useful in removing fouling from exterior metal parts.

Swabbing the Bore

Using cleaning patches, swab the length of the bore. Scrubbing with a bristle brush loosened the fouling, but now that fouling must be picked up on a patch. After each pass through the bore, use new patches. Your first patches will be wet and dirty. Continue until a patch emerges white—or at the least light gray. Then finish by wiping out all channels, cracks and crevices with dry pipe cleaners.

Cleaning the Firearm

The cleaning process itself will deposit some

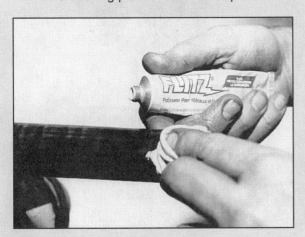

The brass forend cap of this stock is brightened using Flitz on a cloth. Other products intended for cleaning brass may also be used.

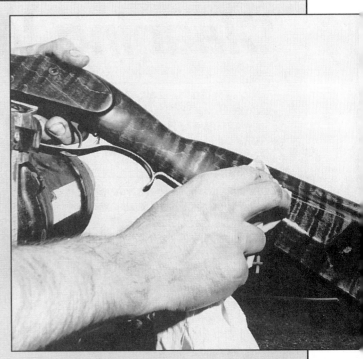

Wood can be touched up with cloth and a dab of linseed oil, as shown here.

dampness on the exterior metal of the firearm. Clean off any dampness with a solvent-soaked cloth. You don't need much solvent. Give the wood the same treatment, but do not use the solvent-cloth—that's for the metalwork. Instead, use a clean cloth with a few drops of pure boiled inedible linseed oil on it. Now, go over the entire firearm one more time with a soft, clean cloth—no solvents or oils—to pick up any excess solvent or oil left on either metalwork or wood.

If the firearm is going into dry dock for a while, run a cleaning patch through the bore with a little metal preservative on it, such as Accragard. *Important:* Be certain to remove any preserving oils from the bore before firing the muzzleloader again.

Apply a light coating of metal-preserving chemical to the outside of the barrel and lock.

Cleaning the Lock

Now and again, the lock will need a special cleaning. Remove it from its mortice in the stock. Blow dirt out of the workings with canned air or an air hose. Use a toothbrush to flick away stubborn dirt.

Polishing Metalwork

Brightwork, such as brass fittings, may be cleaned up with a little bit of Flitz on a cloth. Then, follow with a clean, soft, dry cloth.

Cleaning With Solvent

Tools

- Nipple Wrench or Large Wrench
- Screwdriver Set
- Small Mallet or Hammer
- Vise

Supplies

- Accragard Metal Preservative
- Blackpowder Bore Solvent
- Boiled Linseed Oil
- Canned Air
- Cleaning Patches
- Cleaning Rod
- Copper Bristle Bore Brush
- Flitz
- Pipe Cleaners
- Soft, Dry Cloths
- Toothbrush

Setting Up

Be certain the firearm is completely unloaded. Always do this before working on any firearm. Then, using the appropriate tools, disassemble the muzzleloader.

Scrubbing the Fouling

Soak a cleaning patch with blackpowder bore solvent and attach it to the cleaning rod. There are many good solvents on the market today, so try a number of them and see which works best for you. Run the solvent-soaked patch through the bore several times. Then, remove the nipple and cleanout screw and repeat with another solvent-soaked patch. Next, scrub the bore with a copper bristle brush for several strokes.

Swabbing the Bore

Run a couple of dry patches through the bore to see what they look like. If the patches emerge dirty, employ the bristle brush again, only dip the brush in solvent first. Then, use more dry patches following bore scrubbing. These patches should emerge fairly white now.

Cleaning the Firearm

Clean the rest of the firearm as shown in the hot water method, only forget the water. Use only solvent on the patch or cloth.

The same pipe cleaner and toothbrush tricks used in the hot water method are used in the no-water process. The nipple can be cleaned by dropping it in a small container with solvent. Use a pipe cleaner to clear the nipple vent and a toothbrush to clean the nipple's threads. The same protective film of metal preservative can be used in the bore, but, of course the same precaution of removing oils before firing is once again suggested.

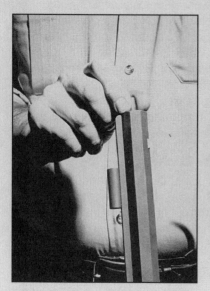

Ensure that the firearm is unloaded before cleaning it. Check this by inserting a ramrod into the bore to see if it is empty.

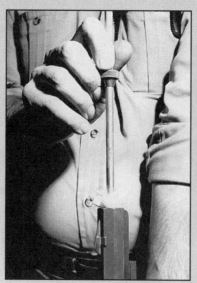

Swabbing the bore with cleaning patches on a jag. The cloth patch is used to soak up water and/or solvent, and to help remove fouling from the bore.

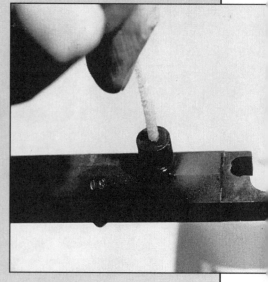

A solvent-laden pipe cleaner is used to swab out the drum area on a rifle. Pipe cleaner is also used to wipe out any hard-to-reach spot on the muzzleloader.

Cleaning the Revolver

The blackpowder revolver can bind when dirty, as this revolver did. Fouling causes the failure of cylinder rotation.

Tools

Nipple Wrench or Large Wrench
Screwdriver Set
Small Mallet or Hammer
Vise

Supplies

Accragard Metal Preservative
Blackpowder Bore Solvent
Boiled Linseed Oil
Canned Air
Cleaning Patches
Cleaning Rod
Copper Bristle Bore Brush
Flitz
Hot and Cold Water
Pipe Cleaners
Soft, Dry Cloths
Toothbrush

Setting Up

Be certain the revolver is completely unloaded, checking each cylinder chamber. Always do this before working on any firearm. Then, using the appropriate tools, disassemble the gun, including removing all nipples from the cylinder.

Flushing the Bore

Thoroughly flush the bore and cylinder chambers with cool water, then follow with a hot water flush. This should begin to loosen caked

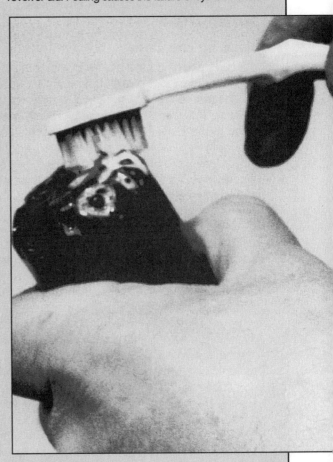

A toothbrush is excellent for removing fouling from the cylinder.

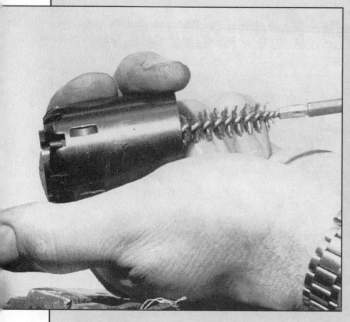

Cylinder chambers are scrubbed with a bristle brush.

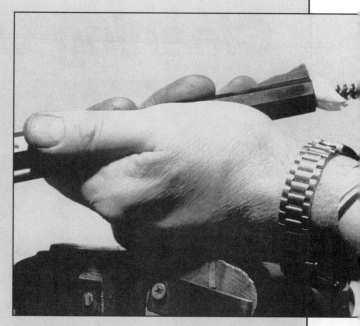

Cleaning patches attached to a bristle brush are run down-bore—scrubbing the bore and removing the fouling.

residue. Next, use a copper bristle brush to scrub the bore. Using a toothbrush, scrub the cylinder and cylinder chambers.

Swabbing the Bore

Using cleaning patches, swab the bore and cylinder chambers. Scrubbing with a bristle brush loosened the fouling, but now that fouling must be picked up on a patch. After each pass through the bore and cylinder chambers, use new patches. Your first patches will be wet and dirty. Continue until patches emerge white—or at the least light gray. The cylinder nipples should be cleaned out with pipe cleaners.

Cleaning the Firearm

The cleaning process itself will deposit some dampness on the exterior metal of the firearm. Be certain that no water has invaded the workings of the revolver. If you suspect it has, the revolver will have to be fully stripped and all moisture removed. Parts may be dried in the oven on low heat. Clean off any dampness with a solvent-soaked cloth. You don't need much solvent. Give the wood the same treatment, but do not use the solvent-cloth—that's for the metalwork. Instead, use a clean cloth with a few drops of pure boiled inedible linseed oil on it. Now, go over the entire firearm one more time with a soft, clean cloth—no solvents or oils—to pick up any excess solvent or oil left on either metalwork or wood.

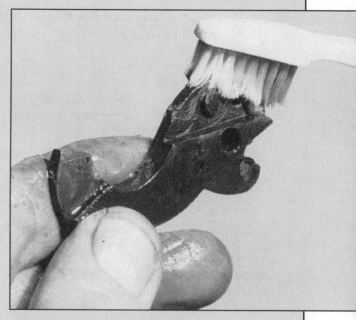

Professional-type cleaning includes complete disassembly of the revolver, including the hammer, shown here being scrubed with a tootbrush.

If the firearm is going into dry dock for a while, run a cleaning patch through the bore with a little metal preservative on it, such as Accragard. *Important:* Be certain to remove any preserving oils from the bore before firing the muzzleloader again.

Apply a light coating of metal-preserving chemical to the outside of the barrel and lock.

Advanced Cleaning

Tools

- Large Wrench
- Nipple Wrench or Vise Grips
- Screwdriver Set
- Small Mallet or Hammer
- Vise

Supplies

- Blackpowder Bore Solvent
- Cleaning Patches
- Commercial Bore Solvent
- Copper Bristle Bore Brush
- Flitz
- Gun Oil
- JB Bore Cleaner
- Steel Wool

Setting Up

Check the gun for a load. As noted elsewhere, it's not at all impossible to run across an original muzzleloader that was charged decades ago without firing. Currently manufactured muzzleloaders are also subject to this condition—loaded and left that way. Naturally, the loaded firearm must be made safe before any cleaning is attempted.

Removing the Nipple and Breech Plug

The nipple should come free with the use of an ordinary nipple wrench; however, in severe cases, a small wrench may have to be employed, and in some cases, plenty of solvent and Vise Grips may be needed. This may ruin the nipple in the process; however, if it is so badly frozen in the seat that such measures are required to free it, the nipple is no good anyway. The nipple seat will have to be redrilled and retapped.

Using a large wrench, while the barrel is held in a strong vise, the breech plug can be removed. This is not a do-it-always procedure. Only remove the breech plug when absolutely necessary to remove serious fouling. However, once the breech plug is removed, the gunsmith can do two things: first, he can see directly into the bore to accurately study the condition of the rifling, and second, the bore can be vigorously and completely cleaned.

Note: If the nipple is, or seems to be, rusted in, or if the firearm is in an obvious state of rust inva-

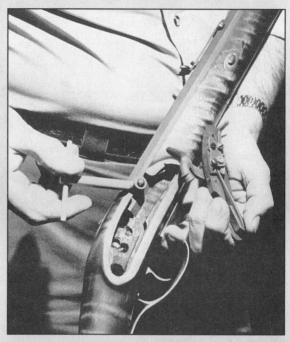

The firearm is disassembled appropriately for cleaning. In this instance, the lock is removed, as well as the nipple from the drum.

A good bore solvent, like this one from Birchwood Casey, will go a long way toward loosening crusted fouling.

sion, go to the next step *before* attempting to remove either the nipple or the breech plug. A solvent soak may help to remove rust or fouling from the threads of the nipple and/or breech plug, making removal of either a much easier task.

Soaking with Solvent

Especially if the firearm did not have to be debreeched, a soak with commercial bore solvent is an ideal way to attack internal rust and fouling. Simply pour the bore full of any standard

Dale Storey locks a barrel in a vise for some heavy-duty bore scrubbing using solvent on a bristle brush.

solvent and allow it to do its work for several hours, maybe even overnight.

Following a soak with standard commercial bore solvent, repeat the process using a commercial blackpowder solvent, because many solvents that cut rust will not effectively attack blackpowder residues (salts).

Scrubbing the Bore

With the barrel held securely in a vise, use a strong cleaning rod with a bronze brush coated with blackpowder solvent to attack the fouling. A hundred passes with the bronze brush through the bore may not be nearly enough. Also, a little waiting in between attacks on the bore is not a bad idea, allowing the solvent to work on its own.

Swabbing the Bore

Sometimes a water-soaked patch follow-up is a good idea, giving the gunsmith an idea of how effective his efforts are. If the wet patch comes out dark, that means fouling remains in the bore. It may always, by the way, come out on the brown side; however, it should eventually emerge near-white, if not plain white, indicating the bore is quite close to residue-free.

Visually inspect the bore. If it still looks like the inside of a factory chimney, repeat bore scrubbing.

Using Bore Compound

Now a bore compound is put to use. For the purposes of this work, JB Bore Cleaner and Flitz were the two compounds used. Both remove lead and fouling quite well, especially when applied with a bronze brush and plenty of elbow grease. Following the use of either product, a patch saturated with gun oil is run through the

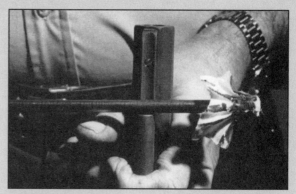

This is a clear illustration of the cleaning patch at work. Note the heavy fouling picked up by patch.

bore several times. Then, the bore is dried with clean patches. Remember to remove all oil before shooting.

Inspecting by Feel

After all of the above steps have been conducted, run a test by feel. A tight cleaning patch is used to detect irregularities in the barrel. These can be felt as the tight patch is slowly run through the bore. If the bore is pitted, that damage is there to stay, but an admittedly drastic measure can be taken to further eliminate crusted bore fouling.

Scrubbing with Steel Wool

Only as a last resort, a wad of fine steel wool is wrapped on a bristle brush, treated with solvent, and run through the bore several times. *Never use steel wool on good, sharp rifling. Steel wool is a last resort only for barrels that are already severely damaged. Steel wool can harm a good barrel.* Follow the steel wool treatment with another round of bore compound. Be certain to clear the barrel of all compound, as well as oils, before shooting.

Understanding The Modern Muzzleloader

THE BLACKPOWDER HOBBY gunsmith should have a working knowledge of the modern muzzleloader because this particular blackpowder firearm is here to stay. The modern muzzleloader offers few opportunities for gunsmithing projects; however, it may require repairs, and there are a few refinements that can be made on this type of frontloader. But first, what is a modern muzzleloader and what makes it tick?

There is no chiseled-in-concrete list of criteria that absolutely defines the modern muzzleloader. Yet, the modern muzzleloader is entirely recognizable as a specific genus and species. The difficulty in pigeon-holing this breed of gun is determining the difference between a muzzleloader that's modern from a modern muzzleloader. Each one deserves distinct attention.

Many muzzleloaders that are modern have shorter-than-usual barrels. They can be fitted with telescopic sights. On the light and handy side, they do not replicate any original firearm of the past. An example of a muzzleloader that's modern is the currently offered Thompson/Center White Mountain Carbine. In calibers 45, 50 and 54, this little rifle has a short 21-inch barrel, tastefully stepped down from octagonal to round where the forestock leaves off. It has an adjustable open rear sight and a blade front sight. Wearing a rubber recoil pad, the 6^{1}/$_{2}$-pound carbine is equipped with studs for quick detachable swivels and comes with a sling. The White Mountain Carbine has a single trigger, as opposed to a double-set or multiple-lever system. (See Chapter 7 on triggers.) The rifle has a rapid rate of twist for a muzzleloader: 50-caliber is 1:20; calibers 45 and 54 carry a 1:48 twist. In every regard, this is a muzzleloader, yet it is obviously well-removed from the rest of the ilk by virtue of its appointments and design.

Another good example of a muzzleloader that is modern, as oppposed to a modern muzzleloader, is Thompson/Center's Scout in both rifle and pistol. Once again, no rifle or pistol from history looked like a T/C Scout, let alone behaved precisely like one. From a distance, the rifle appears to be a Model 94 Winchester without a lever—sort of—and the company makes no bones about it. "It comes up to your shoulder with the speed and feel of a lever-action rifle," T/C says of the Scout. The semi-buckhorn adjustable rear sight is reminiscent of a lever-action carbine, and the front sight is a blade. But the Scout is also drilled and tapped for a scope sight, and it is sling ready. It parts in the middle, takedown fashion, for easy transportation. This model does not clean from the breech, but due to the short barrel and breakdown feature, it spiffs up in a hurry with no trouble. The Scout has in-line ignition—the flame from the percussion cap darts directly into the breech because the nipple is mounted where a firing pin would normally rest, if this were a lever-action deer rifle. It also has a rebounding hammer with a hammer block that prevents accidental discharge. The vented breech plug coupled with double-angled side ports bleed gas off in a forward direction away from the shooter. In both of its calibers, 50 and 54, the 21-inch barrel of the Scout Carbine has a fast 1:20 rate of twist, as opposed to the much slower rates of twist associated with muzzleloaders of the past. Takedown requires only a screwdriver and ^{3}/$_{16}$-inch hex wrench. The T/C Scout Pistol looks very much like the rifle and functions in the same manner.

Identifying the Modern Muzzleloader

While there is no rule that precludes calling these two examples modern muzzleloaders instead of muzzleloaders that

Here is a look into the breech area of the Shannon modern muzzleloader, showing a striker and nipple. With in-line ignition, the nipple is virtually a part of the breech plug. The striker behind the nipple flies forward to detonate the percussion cap. The wing on the right-hand side of the "action" is a safety. Also, note the peep sight.

are modern, for our purposes, five criteria identify the "true" modern muzzleloader.

1. Uses in-line ignition.
2. Can wear a scope without modification to the firearm.
3. Has a fast rate of twist.
4. Cleans up from the breech end, for most models.
5. Follows the lines and design of cartridge rifles. Some even have bolts; stocks are shaped in the modern fashion; safeties are generally of modern firearm style; recoil pads and slings are common; most are drilled and tapped for easy mounting of scope sights.

These traits are arbitrary, but they help the hobby gunsmith determine the type of firearm he is dealing with. Essentially, there are six broad categories of muzzle-loading *rifles* encountered today: original, replica, non-replica, double barrel, musket and modern.

Originals abound, many of them in shooting condition, although most are wisely relegated to a safe place for collection, rather than field work.

Replicas are copycats. They copy, at least to a degree, a rifle from the past. Replicas were introduced so the modern blackpowder enthusiast could enjoy shooting original-*style* rifles without risking the real thing to wear and possible field damage.

Non-replicas are the most prevalent muzzleloader style of the hour. The T/C Hawken is a perfect example of the clan. This well-made frontloader carries an old-fashioned name, and it works just like the original, but it does not copy the original in style.

The double rifle is not common now, although there are a few modern-made blackpowder double guns around; however, the English double-barrel sporting rifle was quite popular in the 19th century.

Muskets are blackpowder rifles of military origin, although some muskets, such as the Whitworth, also have great target shooting ability. They make rugged, powerful hunting rifles.

This see-through Williams scope mount allows the use of iron and telescopic sights on one modern muzzleloader. Pre-drilled and tapped holes make the addition of a scope no problem for the hobby blackpowder gunsmith.

Then there is the modern muzzleloader. These vary among models—barrels can be short or long, triggers may be modern or traditional, and the rifle may or may not have a modern safety.

In-Line Ignition

These days, in-line ignition means the percussion cap is mounted at the back of the breech so that, in effect, the breech plug itself contains the nipple. Flame from the cap is directed forward into the base of the powder charge. However, in a more general sense, in-line ignition is nothing new. Underhammer rifles and pistols employed in-line ignition. Sidehammer models also used it. In-line ignition simply means the flame from the percussion cap has a direct route to the powder charge in the chamber of the gun. In a sense, the revolver always had in-line ignition,

Ready to fire, the Knight MK-85 modern muzzleloader has its cocking piece fully drawn to the rear. When the trigger is pulled, the cocking piece will fly forward, sending a striker against the percussion cap.

since the percussion cap is mounted at the back of the cylinder directly behind the powder charge in the chamber.

Bullets for Modern Muzzleloaders

Sometimes the role of the hobby blackpowder gunsmith is that of mentor to other shooters. That's why understanding the modern muzzleloader is important, and part of the modern muzzleloader plan is a quick rate of twist, which means stabilizing conical, rather than round, projectiles. The modern muzzleloader has helped to promote some interesting projectiles—not to say there is a direct cause and effect, because Buffalo Bullet Company produced what we call modern muzzleloader bullets before the rifle type was well known. However, dozens of companies have come forth with elongated projectiles crafted for fast-twist muzzleloaders.

These bullets are often modifications of the old Minie style with hollow base, modest shank and various nose configurations—generally round-nose, sometimes with a hollowpoint.

These CVA lead pistol bullets are used with plastic sabots. The sabot transfers the spin of the rifling to the projectile, then it falls away as the bullet is put into flight.

Also, the sabot is back. The idea of shooting a smaller-than-bore-sized bullet is hardly new. Remington has had its Accelerator ammo for quite some time in 30-30 Winchester, 308 Winchester and 30-06 Springfield, firing a 55-grain, 22-caliber projectile that is encased, as it were, in a plastic cup that transfers the impetus of the rifling to the smaller caliber bullet. The bullet spins because the cup spins. The sabot falls away in front of the muzzle, but the bullet continues to spin its way to the target. As we know, rotational velocity is much more constant than forward velocity, so these saboted bullets stay on their axes all the way to the target, over normal shooting distances.

Sabots have been around a very long time. They were once made of wood, some sources report, and perhaps other materials as well. Lexicographers reveal the word comes from the French language and pertains to "shoe." Today, the sabot concept is strongly associated with the modern muzzleloader for shooting jacketed pistol bullets. In certain modern muzzleloaders, accuracy is excellent with the sabot/bullet combination. The hobby gunsmith troubleshooting a modern muzzleloader that is not producing good groups should try the sabot, along with as many other bullet types as possible, to find the projectile the firearm "likes" best. Even a round ball may work in some firearms, in spite of the fast rate of twist, but usually with light loads only. Revolutions per second of the missile depends on rate of twist and exit velocity of the bullet. Get the velocity down, and the round ball can shoot well from a fast rate of twist.

Modifications to the Modern Muzzleloader
Glass-Bed the Recoil Lug

On some modern muzzle-loading rifles, it is possible to glass-bed the recoil lug area to prevent the stock from splitting under recoil.

Fit a Scope

This is simply a matter of choosing the correct scope mount and using the existing pre-drilled and tapped holes to mount the

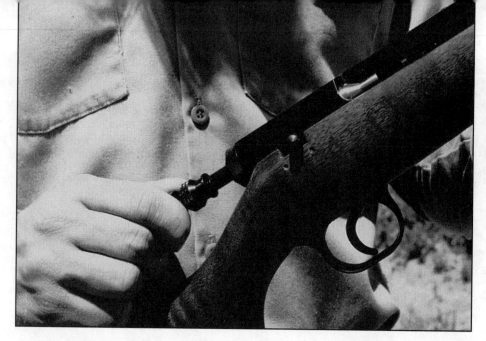

The cocking piece is being withdrawn. The knurled end on the cocking piece can be turned to change the travel length of the striker.

scope. A variable scope works well on the modern muzzleloader, especially one in the 2-7x or 2.5-8x range. The higher power is ideal for improved bullet placement on game in the field.

Fit a Sling

When the modern muzzleloader is not sling-ready from the factory, one can be mounted rather easily using Uncle Mike's blackpowder sling eyes and detachable mounts. Although, some gunsmiths may wish to use their own individual and unique methods of mounting sling swivels.

Refinish the Metal and Stock

Most modern muzzleloaders are blued. However, if the blue finally wears thin from field use, the modern muzzleloader can be treated to a browning job. See Chapter 14 on browning steel.

Wood stocks can be refinished, as described in Chapter 9 on that subject, and synthetic stocks can be painted.

Fit a Recoil Pad

Fitting a recoil pad to a modern muzzleloader without one is a useful addition. Also, some hobby blackpowder gunsmiths may wish to replace a factory pad with a different model, such as the highly recommended Pachmayr Decelerator pad. First, pads are fitted by cutting off the stock at the proper length. The length of pull—distance from trigger to buttstock—can be altered at this time. Remember to consider the additional thickness of the pad as part of length of pull. Excess material is removed via a grinder or sander. Then, screw the pad in place. This project is for the advanced hobbyist only, with a well-equipped shop and special tools.

Another way to fit a recoil pad is by using a jig. This is generally a job for the pro, however, and is the method used in the gunshop.

Timing and Striker Adjustment

Most modern muzzleloaders with a striker can be adjusted by screwing it in and out to shorten or lengthen the dis-

Uncle Mike's Super Swivel for Muzzleloaders has a patented SwivelLock system for extra security against accidental opening of the swivel. The Super Swivel is detachable.

tance of travel. If the striker hits the percussion cap with more force than necessary for detonation, or not enough force, it can be timed by adjusting its length of travel to strike the cap just right. Repeated trial-and-error shooting will prove this out.

The Custom Modern Muzzleloader

It is entirely possible to build a muzzleloader based on the modern style, using the barrel and action of a modern muzzleloader and building a custom stock to fit. Also, there are custom muzzleloaders that are modern, as opposed to being modern muzzleloaders. One is the Dale Storey Buggy Rifle design, which is a takedown model, breaking in the middle. It uses a sidehammer lock for ignition. The custom Dale Storey Buggy Rifle readily takes a scope, or it can be ordered with iron sights. The advanced hobbyist who reaches the level of custom gunbuilding may wish to design his own version of a modern muzzleloader.

Glass-Bedding a Rifle

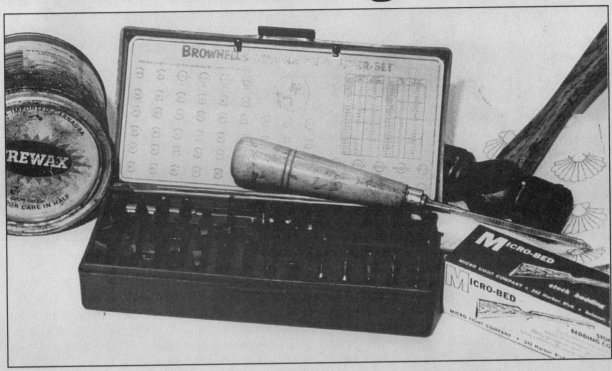

These are the tools necessary for glass-bedding: screwdriver set, chisel, epoxy bedding kit, mallet (plastic and rubber head), paper towels, and wax for a release agent.

Tools

Chisel, 1/4-inch
Epoxy Kit
Rubber Mallet
Screwdriver Set

Supplies

Gun Oil
Paper Towels
Wax

Setting Up

After checking for a load, remove the breech/barrel from the stock. No further disassembly is required. Slip the ramrod from its guides, remove the two tang screws and lift the "action" from the stock. Then, using 1/4-inch chisel, fresh-up and remove a little wood from the back section of the recoil mortice in stock. Freshened wood helps create a better bond for the epoxy.

Apply the release agent to all parts that will be subjected to epoxy, including screws. A release agent is normally supplied with the epoxy kit. It prevents the epoxy from sticking where it shouldn't.

Using a 1/4-inch chisel to enlarge a mortice before glass-bedding epoxy is applied.

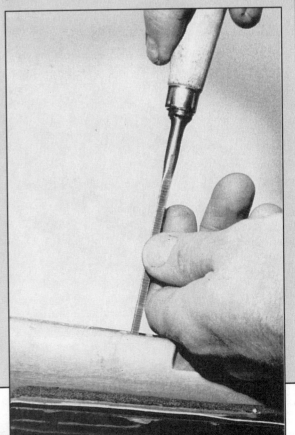

After mixing the epoxy, per kit instructions, apply it to the enlarged recoil lug area.

After the epoxy is evenly applied, the barrel/breech is reassembled into place and left to cure.

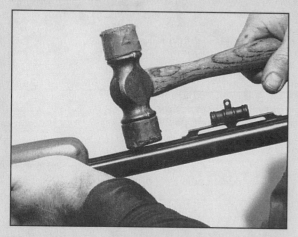

After curing, remove the barrel/breech from the stock with light raps from a rubber-headed mallet.

The glass-bedding job around the recoil lug of a modern muzzleloader is complete. The recoil lug is now entirely set in epoxy.

Applying Epoxy

Mix the epoxy according to its instructions. If adding flock or fiber, add enough to give the epoxy the consistency of thick grease. Then, using a mixing stick, apply epoxy to the recoil lug mortice. Common sense dicates how much to use. The goal is to fill the area where wood was removed, plus a bit extra.

Fitting the Assembly

Lower the barrel/breech assembly into place and tighten the tang screws. If any epoxy oozes out from the juncture of barrel and stock, wipe this off with a paper towel right away. *Tip:* If the epoxy gets on your clothes, clean them with white vinegar. It can also be used for general cleanup of uncured epoxy.

Allow the epoxy to cure for twenty-four hours in a warm place.

Cleaning the Firearm

Disassemble the barrel/breech from the stock. A rubber mallet may be used to strike the bottom of the barrel at the front of the stock to break it loose. Then, clean areas of unwanted cured epoxy using a 1/4-inch chisel.

Clean off the release agent from metal parts and wood, if necessary, and apply a light coating of oil to all metal parts. After reassembly, the rifle is ready to shoot. Now, there is no question that the fit between recoil lug and stock is perfect, and recoil will be distributed to the stock without fear of splitting it.

Fitting a Recoil Pad

Selection of pads and hard plates.

Tools

Disc Sander
Double Cut File, 8-inch
Hand Wood Saw
Jig (B&R Recoil Pad Fitting Jig, or equivalent fitted to a disc sander table.)
No. 32 Twist Drill Bit
Pin Punch, 3/16-inch
Power Hand Drill
Screwdriver Set
Scribe
Sharp Knife with Thin, Pointed Blade
Small Ballpeen Hammer, 2-ounce
Vise with Padded Jaws

Supplies

Emery Cloth, 80-grit
Flexible Straightedge, 6-inch
Gun Oil
Masking Tape
Paraffin
Pencil
Recoil Pad or Flat Plate of Choice
Sanding Paper
Tape Measure

Cutting the Stock

Remove the barrel/breech assembly; you'll need only the stock for this project. In measuring the proper length of pull, remember to include the thickness of the recoil pad. Then, using the flexible ruler, mark the stock with a pencil to show where it will be cut.

Remove the old buttplate or recoil pad, if there is one, along with the screws. Next, saw off the

Sawing off the end of the buttstock after marking it. The saw is slightly angled, as described in the text, with the handle leaning toward the front of the stock or forearm.

stock at the marked line with a hand saw. *Tip:* Angle the saw handle toward the front of the stock. In this position, if the saw tears wood on the off-side, it won't matter, as this can be cleaned up on the sander.

Sanding the Stock

Now, take the stock and new recoil pad to the disc sander and square up the angled saw cut. The back of the recoil pad is also squared up on the sander.

Marking Screw Holes

With the 3/16-inch punch inserted into the top hole of the recoil pad from the back, push the punch until it forces the surface of the rubber pad outward. The tip of the punch will show the location for the wood screw. Now, the tip of a sharp

Using a drift punch to locate the screw hole in the recoil pad which will be installed on a modern muzzleloader. The sharp X-Acto blade in the photo will be used to make a cross-slit at the point where the screw will enter.

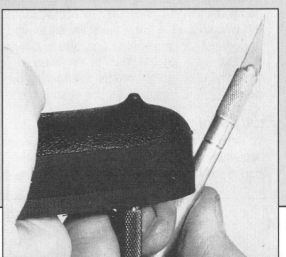

knife is pushed through at the point indicated by the tip of the punch, making a 1/4-inch vertical slit. Repeat this procedure for the bottom hole to locate the position of the lower screw.

Put one drop of gun oil into each slit in the recoil pad, and insert one screw into each hole until its tip reaches the front surface of the pad.

Next, position the pad on the butt of the stock and, with a small hammer, strike the head of each screw so its tip marks the wood, providing location points for drilling. If the screw strikes an existing hole which cannot be used due to size or location, then that hole must be plugged. (Refer to Chapter 10 on wood repair for instructions on how to plug a hole.)

Drilling the Holes

With a power hand drill and a No. 32 twist drill bit, drill each pilot hole into the buttstock. Be sure to hold the drill square to the butt.

Then, remove one of the screws from the pad (remember, they were left there) and tap each hole with that screw, using a little paraffin on the threads of the screw.

Now, screw the pad to the buttstock.

Sanding the Pad

With a sharp scribe, mark around the perimeter of the stock on the hard backing of the recoil pad.

Then, remove the pad and attach it to the special adapter that is part of the recoil pad fitting jig. The jig provides proper alignment for sanding the excess material in a precise manner. According to directions, adjust the jig to the top of the comb. This adjustment can vary with individual stocks. Attach the special adapter to the arm of the jig mounted on the disc sander table, as illustrated.

Sand the recoil pad carefully and slowly to the scribed line on the hard backing of the pad. Sand from the top of the butt halfway down each side of the pad, but no further at this point.

Remove the special adapter along with the pad from the arm of the jig and reset the adapter, this time on the toe line of the stock, establishing the correct sanding line for final sanding. Now, sand from the toe line down to the mid-point of the recoil pad. This completes the sanding process.

Final Fitting of the Pad

Remove the recoil pad from the adapter and screw it to the buttstock. Check the alignment of pad to stock. Minor adjustments can be made at

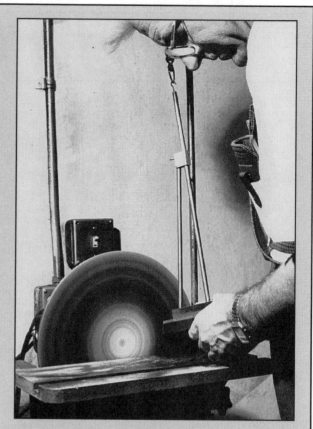

Sanding the toe line of the recoil pad on the disc sander. Note that the pad is controlled by a special adapter, which, in turn, is attached by hook and eye on the jig.

Final cleanup using a double-cut file.

this point, because the pad will slide against the stock, in spite of screws. The pad's screw holes are oversized as they come from the factory.

Where the pad overlaps the wood, use a double-cut file to trim the surface to a perfect match. Take care to avoid scratching the stock wood finish with the file. A layer of masking tape over the wood will help protect it from the file and let you know when you file too hard.

Finally, using 80-grit emery cloth, sand around the hard backing of the recoil pad to remove any disc sanding scratches.

The Muzzleloading Shotgun

THIS IS A knowledge chapter more than a working chapter. That is because blackpowder shotgun gunsmithing, especially with regard to barrels, requires considerable knowledge, experience and, in many instances, specialized tools and equipment. Only a well-trained blackpowder gunsmith who works with blackpowder shotguns, especially double barrels, such as the late V.M. Starr, has any business working on these guns extensively. Myron Olson, for example, continues Starr's work, including the fine art of jug-choking—one of the many jobs that cannot be handled by the hobbyist and, in fact, is beyond the scope of most professionals.

The blackpowder front-loading scattergun played an important role in firearms history, here and abroad. These days, the versatile shotgun takes a back seat to rifles and handguns. Nonetheless, the blackpowder hobby gunsmith must have *knowledge* of the muzzle-loading shotgun because, in spite of its third-place ranking, it remains a highly useful blackpowder firearm for target and field use.

The hobbyist must understand that a properly loaded blackpowder shotgun renders excellent power, with the possibility of a dense pellet pattern at normal shotgun ranges. Pattern density depends somewhat upon choke selection, just as the choke determines patterns for modern shotguns shooting self-contained shells. The blackpowder shotgun also offers a wide range of loads—all in one gun. The shooter merely alters the load the way he wants it, within the confines of safety and prudence, of course. Therefore, although the hobbyist cannot do a great deal of high-level work on the blackpowder shotgun, he should go forth with at least a basic knowledge of the gun itself.

The hobbyist should also be familiar with shotgun lock time: The time elapsed from the release of the sear to detonation of the main charge of powder in the breech. Lock time for blackpowder guns is somewhat slower than for modern smokeless guns, across the board. This fact holds true for the blackpowder shotgun, but it is a marginal difference at best, and the percussion shotgun's lock time is fast enough to provide excellent results on trap, Skeet or in the field. This is not quite so true of the flintlock shotgun. It has a slower lock time than the percussion shotgun, which puts it into its own category. To make hits, the shooter has to learn how to sustain his lead with the flintlock. Ideally, swing is not slowed down at all until shot is on its way out of the barrel.

After-shooting cleanup for the blackpowder shotgun is the same as for other muzzleloaders. Chapter 21 on professional cleaning techniques applies well to the shotgun, with special attention given to the use of modern one-piece plastic wads, which can leave plastic wash in the bore. This film of plastic is best reduced and removed with a solvent, such as Shooter's Choice, coupled with a bristle brush and followed by cleaning patches. Because of its smooth bore, as opposed to a rifled one, the blackpowder shotgun cleans up quickly and efficiently.

Original Shotguns

These are not widespread, but neither are they impossible to locate. As an example, an E.F. Bulhel & Mehlis 20-gauge side-by-side blackpowder original muzzleloader recently showed up. It was a percussion gun with Damascus barrels and inlaid silver. Its owner was interested in shooting the gun, but due to possible collector value, he was dissuaded. The blackpowder hobby gunsmith may find himself in a position

Clay bird shooting for fun or competition is just one application for the blackpowder shotgun. That is why the hobby smith should know about this muzzleloader—because it is a highly useful gun in its own right.

storage, could render a Damascus barrel weak and possibly dangerous.

Checking Barrels

The hobby smith cannot do this job directly; however, the professional gunsmith does not normally do the job, either. It is knowledge that counts here, knowing how barrels are tested. As an oversimplification, barrels are tested by first giving them a magnetic charge. Then the barrels are covered with, or submerged in, a solution that contains very fine iron particles. If there are cracks in the metal, a magnetic field will set up and those cracks will become visible. A specific test many of us might recognize is called Magna Flux. Barrels may also be inspected by a remote visual process with an optical probe lowered into the barrel, exploring the surface of the bore. Many major cities have laboratories that can perform these inspections.

Proofing Barrels

Proofing is a direct method of barrel-testing, and it can result in a ruined barrel. The only reason for mentioning it is the hobby gunsmith will hear about this method, if he has not already, and he should know what it entails. Although proofing has long been used by gun factories, it should be strictly avoided by the hobbyist. In brief, the method uses a load much stronger than ordinary, the theory being that if the gun holds up under that overload, it must be all right. There are several problems in proofing, not the least of which is ruining a firearm. There are also inherent dangers. If a gun does erupt, someone could get hurt. Furthermore, while a firearm may hold up to a proof load, or even several proof loads, such heavy charges could cause unseen damage that may show up much later when the gun is fired with normal loads. For these reasons, proofing at the blackpowder hobby gunsmith level is decidedly *not* recommended.

to give advice concerning original shotguns. He should always refer the owner of the shotgun to an expert collector. Many original muzzle-loading shotguns are of no particular collector value, but some are. Also, if the hobbyist can see any problem whatsoever with the gun, he should recommend that it not be fired. And even if he thinks the gun is in shooting condition, such decisions should be left to a professional.

Damascus Steel

Modern methods of making this type of steel do not entirely coincide with original methods, and, in fact, certain knife blades of Damascus steel are strong. However, the hobby gunsmith should recognize that twist steel of the past did not produce a terribly strong barrel. Strips of iron and steel were heated, twisted and forged around a mandrel—a laborious job. When everything went just right, with each ribbon of metal perfectly welded to the next piece on the mandrel, the Damascus barrel was relatively strong and durable. Sometimes the match-up of metal strips was so close that the grain was difficult to see. However, any imperfection in the continuous welds resulted in a less-than-perfect barrel. A lot of shooting, especially without benefit of proper cleaning, plus years of

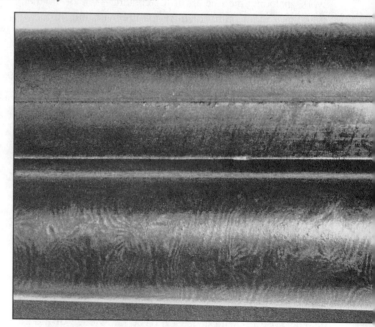

Spotting a twist steel or Damascus shotgun barrel is no problem. Note the swirls in the metal of this fine old shotgun.

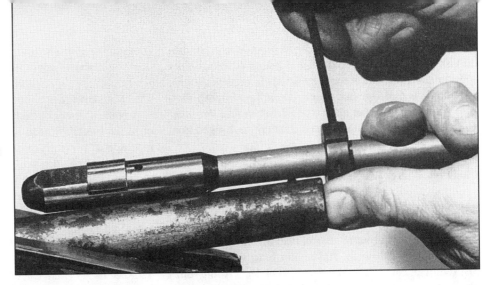

Distance is set by hand measurement on a dent removal tool. The anvil portion is aligned with the dent in the barrel.

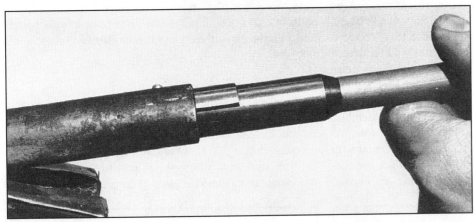

Inserting the dent removal tool into the muzzle of the shotgun barrel.

Rough Bores

Original blackpowder shotguns, as well as modern-made guns not properly cared for, may have rough bores. In some cases, pitting may have taken its toll, ruining the gun. In less severe instances, these bores can be returned to safe shooting condition. Chapter 21 discusses cleaning methods, but it should be noted the use of steel wool on these smoothbores may remove rust that otherwise would not come out. Also, it may be possible to polish the shotgun bore with emery cloth attached to a dowel rod. Ideally, this job is accomplished on a lathe with the breech plugs removed—probably another job for the pro.

However, the hobbyist should be able to tell if bore polishing will help restore a shotgun to safe shooting condition. The way to tell is to visually inspect the bore for deep rust and pits. A rule of thumb: If a cleaning patch saturated with solvent cannot freely run up and down the bore without damage to the patch, polishing is in order. *Caution:* Some original shotguns have a choke taper built into the barrel. In such cases, care must be taken when polishing so the choke is not polished out.

Fixing Dents

Original, and many modern-made, blackpowder shotguns may have barrel dents. Older guns often do. Fortunately, a hydraulic dent remover is now available from Brownells. Testing showed this device works as advertised. The tool has an enlarged mandrel on one end and a tube with a handle on the other end. On the mandrel, a small anvil protrudes when an Allen wrench is inserted into the handle and turned. The system works by hydraulic force, and the tool is quite powerful. Because of this, it must be used with great care. If not, what was once a dent in the barrel can be reversed to a bulge. This is an expensive tool, and one must be purchased for each gauge. It is, therefore, recommended only for the hobbyist who would get continued use from the tool. At the very least, however, the blackpowder hobby gunsmith should know such a tool exists.

Missing Ramrod Guides and Loose Ribs

Ramrod guides may be missing or ribs may be loose. These conditions can be remedied by the hobbyist who has faith in his soldering skills. First, find a metal tray long, wide and deep enough to hold the barrels. Place the barrels on supports in the tray. Then, fill the tray with water, up to the mid-point of the barrels. Of course, heating and soldering takes place above the water line. Soldering ramrod guides or ribs without water to keep the barrels cool can result in a disaster. *Important:* Clean all areas to be soldered, and also flux these areas properly. The best flux for this project is resin flux. Acid-base flux can become trapped underneath a rib, for example, where it cannot be neutralized. In time, the acid flux can eat out the metal in this region. While this job is not an easy one, the advanced hobbyist with soldering skills should be able to handle it.

If the rib of the shotgun happens to be silver-brazed, then the task of soldering a ramrod guide is simplified. Many older Belgian shotguns, and some German-made models as well, had barrels brazed together. Rarely do we find English shotguns with anything other than soft-soldered barrels. *Warning:* The original color or patina of the metal may be changed from the heat.

Checking Barrel Wall Thickness

Certain shotguns, for one reason or another, left the factory with rather thin barrels. The blackpowder hobby gunsmith should check for this condition as part of his normal shotgun inspection routine. Barrel wall thickness should be a minimum of .040-inch. Any major bore work, such as rust removal, can reduce barrel wall thickness. At the muzzle and a short distance downbore, thickness can be checked with an inside dial caliper or Brownells' Barrel Caliper. The hobbyist who has even the least concern about the safety of a shotgun due to barrel wall thickness, or lack thereof, should defer to a professional. Sometimes a hobbyist's best job of smithing is done when he delegates to the pro. But to correctly do so, the hobbyist must know all he can—including what he can't do. Remember, certain barrels must be inspected with a magnetic particle test, checking for various types of damage. Combined with barrel wall thickness inspection, these tests reduce the normal element of risk involved when shooting an original

shotgun, or any shotgun that seems to have undergone heavy use, abuse or lack of proper maintenance.

Checking Breeches

A point of deterioration that should be checked is the interior of the breech, next to the breech plugs. While a shotgun may appear perfectly intact in this region, removal of the breech plugs could reveal another story. One blackpowder shotgun I know of looked perfect on the outside, but when the breech plugs were removed, it was obvious that considerable deterioration of metal had occurred around the threaded section of the barrel. This gun was not safe to shoot. Removal of double-barrel shotgun breech plugs requires a special wrench that the hobbyist probably will not have. However, the informed hobby smith can take a shotgun to a professional and have the breech plugs removed for inspection. Single-barrel shotguns have breech plugs similar to those of rifle barrels and, in some cases, these plugs can be removed safely by the hobbyist.

Checking Nipple Seats

The nipple seat—in other words, the threaded recesses that accept the nipples—should be checked on an original blackpowder shotgun, as well as any shotgun that has seen less than adequate cleaning. Years of use, storage or neglect may cause the threads to deteriorate to the point where nipples are loose and cannot be tightened in place. If the area seems intact, and

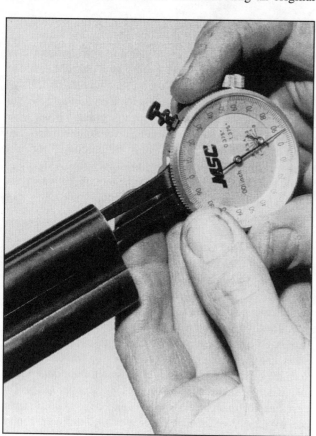

An inside dial caliper is used to measure the inside diameter of a shotgun bore.

Here is the nipple seat of a blackpowder muzzle-loading shotgun. With the nipple removed, visual inspection is easily accomplished.

the problem is minor, oversized nipples can be purchased and installed by the hobby smith. These seat tightly, forming a proper gas seal.

Beyond Barrel Inspection

If the barrels of the shotgun are sound, then the obvious next step is inspection of the rest of the gun. The lock must have positive half-cock and full-cock notches for safety. The stock should be tight and intact, as cracks may result in a break that could cause injury to the shooter.

Steel Shot

Perhaps it is wise to bring up steel shot before going any further. Even though tests have shown some blackpowder shotguns—Beretta's over/under; CVA's side-by-side; Navy Arms' Fowler, Classic and T&T; plus Euroarms' Cape Gun—are capable of handling steel shot, this was only with specific loads and a certain type of shot. Tom Roster, a shotgun expert, ran a series of tests proving these guns survived steel shot; however, in many instances, steel shot scored the barrel walls and, in general, caused damage. The blackpowder hobby gunsmith is advised to consider steel shot a possible threat to the welfare of the muzzle-loading shotgun. *Do not under any circumstances shoot steel shot in an original blackpowder shotgun!*

Currently, shotguns specially designed for steel shot are either on the drawing board or already available, such as Navy Arms' side-by-side double barrel. Tests with this gun show plastic one-piece wads from Ballistic Products, Inc., holding 1¼-ounces of steel shot worked well. If the hobby gunsmith wishes to pattern steel shot in the Navy Arms gun, as well as in others that may appear in the future, understanding the relationship between choke and steel shot is highly important. A Modified choke generally produces Full choke patterns with steel shot. Naturally, each individual gun must be patterned. Many are temperamental—they like one size of shot better than another.

New Blackpowder Shotguns

Modern-made blackpowder shotguns have an advantage over the old-timers because the new guns are made with fluid steel barrels, just like modern shotguns. This does not mean they will all handle steel shot, but it does ensure strength. After all, until recently, modern shell-shooting shotguns were not intended for steel shot either.

Also, many newer shotguns have barrels that are silver-brazed, meaning they will not come apart when blued. This is not a blanket statement, however, and it does not apply to all shotguns. To check for silver-brazed barrels, do the following: With a sharp scribe, and in an inconspicuous place so the gun won't be marred, make a tiny scratch along the rib where it is joined to the barrel. If a little shred of white material is scraped out, then the barrels are soft-soldered. If the scratch shows a very light yellowish color, the barrel could be brazed. Unfortunately, this test is not entirely foolproof. However, in general, it will be much easier to produce a visible scratch on a soft-soldered barrel as opposed to a brazed one. Remember, if

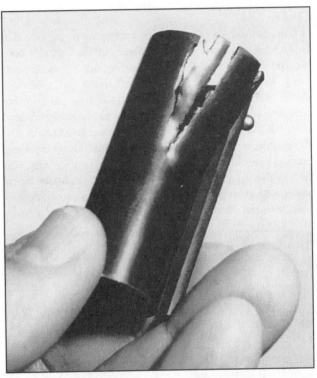

Steel shot may have a disastrous effect on a barrel.

Cabela's modern-made blackpowder side-by-side Turkey Special has chrome-lined barrels. Optionally, it comes with a shooting kit that contains steel shot in sizes No. 2 and BB.

the test results are wrong, and a barrel is soft-soldered rather than brazed, when placed in a hot bluing tank with caustic salts, the rib may fall off.

Beads

These are often made of brass or aluminum, in various sizes and colors, so the shooter can select what suits him best. The center bead on most shotguns helps position the shooter's head. The shooter settles his face on the stock so when looking downbore the front bead seems to sit atop the center bead. Then, leaving his head in place, the shooter ignores the center bead while the clay pigeon is airborne. Competition shotguns often have white Bradley-type beads or fluorescent orange Ray-Bar beads, but many other colors are also used, including white, brass or silver.

Choke

Blackpowder shotguns are not exceptions to the rule that choke makes pattern. While it is true certain Cylinder bore blackpowder shotguns do shoot steel shot into reasonable patterns, because steel shot patterns relatively well with less choke than demanded by lead shot, the best patterns are obtained with choked muzzleloaders, especially with lead shot. While choke is basically no more than constriction near the muzzle, it can work wonders for patterns. Generally, there are two kinds of choke the smith should be familiar with. The first is the tapered choke, where the bore gradually tapers about 8 to 10 inches behind the muzzle to a point approximately 1/2-inch from the muzzle. Final constriction is actually

The front bead of a double-barrel blackpowder shotgun with a white center for visibility.

This is the center bead on a shotgun. It is more for correct placement of the face upon the stock than for aiming.

measured in thousandths of an inch. The nearby chart shows a relatively standard measure of constrictions per degree of choke, from Full to Cylinder.

The second type of choke the hobbyist should know is called jug choke or recess choke—because that's what it truly is. A short section approximately 1 1/2 to 2 inches from the muzzle is literally hollowed out, leaving a recess in the bore larger than the muzzle diameter. The results of this choking style can be quite impressive, including tight Full choke patterns. Mentioned earlier, V.M. Starr was noted for working with jug chokes. He was a South Dakota gunsmith who perfected the art. From his shop in Eden, Starr choked many shotguns that produced random patterns when he got them and excellent controlled patterns after he was finished. From the 1940s to the 1970s, Starr choked a great number of blackpowder shotguns with the recess choke. He was the best in the business. Today, he is followed by his protégé, Myron Olson, who uses the same jug choke system Starr employed. Jug choking is an art and a skill. It also requires special tools. While the hobbyist and, for that matter, the ordinary professional gunsmith will never jug-choke a gun, knowledge of the choke type is important.

Choke Tubes

Choke tubes offer several constrictions on one barrel because they can be screwed in or out at the muzzle. Therefore, one gun can have from Cylinder bore to Extra Full choke. Some blackpowder shotguns made today offer choke tubes, while other guns can have them installed if there is enough metal at the muzzle for threading. If there is not

V.M. Starr, in his later years, working at his lathe. The blackpowder hobby gunsmith should know the name of this person. He was one of the greats in choking muzzle-loading shotguns.

Bore and Choke Dimensions

Ga.	Bore Dia. (ins.)	Constriction (ins.)						
		Full	IM	Mod.	Skt. 2	IC	Skt. 1	Cyl.
10	.775	.035		.017		.007		.000
12	.729	.035	.025	.019	.012	.009	.005	.000
16	.667	.028	.020	.015	.010	.007	.004	.000
20	.617	.025	.019	.014	.009	.006	.004	.000
28	.550	.022	.016	.012	.007	.005	.003	.000
410	.410	.017		.008		.004		.000

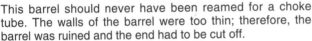

This barrel should never have been reamed for a choke tube. The walls of the barrel were too thin; therefore, the barrel was ruined and the end had to be cut off.

This choke tube came from a barrel with too large a bore diameter. Choke tubes must match up perfectly with barrels.

enough "meat" to accommodate the threading for tubes, the barrel can be ruined. Tooling is expensive, and most hobbyists will not wish to invest; however, there are several different makes of choke tubes, and each manufacturer offers the proper tools for threading shotgun muzzles. Brownells also offers such tools. The hobbyist should know this type of choke is available, and armed with this knowledge, he can seek out a professional who can install them.

Bore and Choke Dimensions

Another piece of knowledge the hobbyist should have on hand is a list of dimensions for the various chokes in different gauges. Over time, the specific dimensions assigned to various chokes have changed, but the nearby chart is a reliable set of figures with which to work.

The blackpowder hobby gunsmith will find that muzzle-loading shotguns are often unique in function, especially in patterning. Different shot sizes, as well as different wad types and columns, can greatly affect patterning. The amount of shot used is also a factor, as is the amount of powder. Always bear in mind there are limits. The blackpowder shotgun is a machine, and its limits can be exceeded.

Volume-for-Volume Loading Technique

One way to load a blackpowder shotgun, for example, is with the volume-for-volume method. This has nothing to do with weighing shot or powder. Weights of shot and powder charges are not figured in this system. The load is prepared with a volumetric charger, whether a powder measure or a shot measure. For example, if a powder measure is used to pour 90 grains, then the same setting is used to pour the shot.

Standard Bore Sizes*

Ga. No.	Bore Dia. (Ins.)	Ga. No.	Bore Dia. (Ins.)
A	2.000	20	.615
B	1.938	21	.605
C	1.875	22	.596
D	1.813	23	.587
E	1.750	24	.579
F	1.688	25	.571
1 (one)	1.669	26	.563
H	1.625	27	.556
J	1.563	28	.550
K	1.500	29	.543
L	1.438	30	.537
M	1.375	31	.531
2	1.325	32	.526
O	1.313	33	.520
P	1.250	34	.515
3	1.157	35	.510
4	1.052	36	.506
5	.976	37	.501
6	.919	38	.497
7	.873	39	.492
8	.835	40	.488
9	.803	41	.484
10	.775	42	.480
11	.751	43	.476
12	.729	44	.473
13	.710	45	.469
14	.693	46	.466
15	.677	47	.463
16	.662	48	.459
17	.649	49	.456
18	.637	50	.453
19	.626		

*Table above is the full listing of English shotgun bore sizes as given in the Gun Barrel Proof Act of 1868.

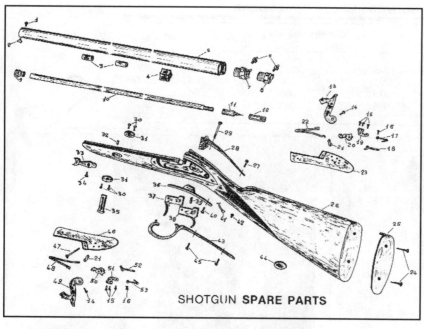

13	Hammer, Right	
14	Hammer Screw	
15	Tumbler Support Plate Screws (3)	
16	Sear Spring Screw	
17	Sear Spring, Right	
18	Sear, Right	
19	Tumbler Support Plate, Right	
20	Tumbler, Right	
21	Tumbler Stirrup	
22	Mainspring, Right	
23	Lockplate, Right	
24	Buttplate Screws (2)	
25	Buttplate	
26	Stock	
27	Rear Tang Screw	
28	Standing Breech	
29	Front Tang Screw	
30	Wedge Escutcheon Plate Screws (4)	
31	Wedge Escutcheon Plate (2)	
32	Wedge Retaining Pin	
33	Forend Tailpipe	
34	Forend Tailpipe Screw	
35	Wedge	
36	Trigger Plate	
37	Trigger, Right (Front)	
38	Trigger, Left (Rear)	
39	Trigger Axis Pin	
40	Trigger Plate Screw	
41	Trigger Spring	
42	Trigger Spring Screw	
43	Trigger Guard	
44	Escutcheon Plate	
45	Trigger Guard Screws (2)	
46	Lockplate, Left	
47	Lockplate Retaining Screw	
48	Mainspring, Left	
49	Hammer, Left	
50	Tumbler, Left	
51	Tumbler Support Plate, Left	
52	Sear, Left	
53	Sear Spring, Left	

SHOTGUN **SPARE PARTS**

1	Front Sight Bead		**7**	Breech Plug, Left
2	Ramrod Stop		**8**	Breech Plug, Right
3	Ramrod Pipes (2)		**9**	Ramrod Head
4	Wedge Lug		**10**	Ramrod
5	Barrels		**11**	Ramrod Worm
6	Nipples (2)		**12**	Ramrod Worm Cap

This gives a volume-for-volume load. This load is safely adjusted by using the same powder charge and *less* shot. Another adjustment is to leave the shot charge intact while using less powder. The latter approach often improves pellet patterns—a little less powder with the same shot charge.

Blackpowder is an excellent propellant for the shotgun because it burns at a rate conducive to good shotgun ballistics, while maintaining a reasonable pressure level. Naturally, the muzzle-loading shotgun can be overloaded, which destroys the pattern and could be potentially dangerous to the shooter. The shotgun should never receive more powder/shot than allowed by the manufacturer of the gun.

The use of Fg and FFg blackpowder is recommended, as well as Pyrodex CTG and Pyrodex RS. Fine-grain powders are not especially useful in blackpowder shotguns, not so much because they blow patterns as often thought, but because such powders can generate higher pressures that result in minimal gains, and they can also cause damage to felt wads and other wad materials that can be burned through. Once the wad above the powder is destroyed, the pattern can go, too, if that wad is supposed to support the shot column. The hobbyist may be called upon to pattern a blackpowder shotgun. He should bear in mind the use of proper wad columns is a must and maximum loads established by the manufacturer should never be exceeded.

Patterning the Shotgun

A good way to pattern a shotgun is with a large sheet of paper that has a large aiming point (dot) in the center. Aim only for that dot. After firing at 40 yards, walk up to the pattern, place a 30-inch-diameter cardboard disc over the most dense portion and trace a circle around it using a felt-tip pen. Next, count the holes within the circle, and then divide by the number of shot in the load—giving you a pattern percentage. If the shot charge held 150 pellets, and 100 pellets landed inside the 30-inch circle, that would be about a 67-percent pattern. This is usually referred to as Full choke. Here is one reference to pattern percentages and chokes.

25% to 34% = Skeet No. 1
35% to 44% = Improved Cylinder
45% to 54% = Modified
55% to 64% = Improved Modified
65% to 75% = Full
Over 75% = Extra Full

Remember, patterns can be altered dramatically by changing wad columns, so only use those recommended by a reliable reloading source or the gunmaker. The wrong wad column can cause trouble. Patterns are also changed with different shot sizes and types—steel, lead, copper-coated and so forth. Patterns also vary according to the amount of shot or powder used in a load. Remember, adjust these two components only within the framework of approved maximum loads. Never use more shot or more powder than allowed by the gunmaker.

Caution: If a wad column fits downbore so tightly it cannot readily move upbore the instant the gun is fired, this could result in a damaged gun, with possible injury to the shooter. Pressure rises significantly the instant blackpowder detonates, and the volume of gas must be allowed to move upbore. A restrictive wad column will not allow this movement. Always use acceptable wad types only in the proper wad column arrangement.

Tuning
The Caplock Revolver

TUNING PROVIDES SMOOTH, reliable operation of the caplock revolver, which in turn promotes better shooting. A revolver can be tuned in a number of ways. First, the trigger should have a crisp, clean letoff with reasonable weight of pull—not a "hair" trigger, but a safe one—usually about 2.5 pounds. Target pistols, especially those with double-set triggers, may have a much lighter letoff. But whether target or field, the goal is the same—a good trigger to enhance shooting ability.

Second, the revolver should load easily, without too much lead shaving on the lip of the cylinder chamber. A tiny circle of shaved lead does not destroy accuracy, but obvious slicing can be a problem. A well-tuned revolver exhibits little or no lead shaving.

Third, the timing should be correct, so the gun's moving parts are synchronized. When the hammer is cocked, the movement should feel smooth and clean. The cylinder should be properly aligned, so the projectile enters the barrel's forcing cone accurately. These and many other features of caplock revolver tuning need to be understood by the competent blackpowder hobby gunsmith before beginning work.

Tuning is done on both new, finished revolvers and those built from kits. Original revolvers are not candidates for tuning due to their historical and collector value; however, if a shooter insists, it can be done. Normally, an original revolver has been "worked in" so thoroughly that parts are self-polished. In theory, a modern replica revolver may eventually work in through long service, but tuning puts things in order right away, plus it improves aspects of the revolver that no

amount of working in will cure, such as shaving of the lead projectile, alignment of the cylinder and hardening of certain lock parts.

The hobbyist may wonder why a new revolver, fresh from the factory or built from a kit, would require tuning of any kind. The vast majority of new revolvers are well-made and of high quality, but if hand-tuned at the factory, the added cost would drive the price out of the range of many buyers. However, the hobby gunsmith can do his own tuning, making his revolver all the better for absolutely minimal expenditure of time or money. Plus, tuning will give the hobbyist a better working knowledge of his newly aquired gun.

A few tools are required for tuning the caplock revolver: a good set of gunsmithing screwdrivers, just as called for in so many other projects; stones for polishing, such as a medium Arkansas and a hard Arkansas; abrasive cloth or 400- and 600-grit wet/dry sandpaper; chamfering tool; vise; power hand drill; and 4-inch smooth mill file. Also needed are a wooden dowel rods, one very close to the bore size and another one for polishing chambers. The latter can be slightly smaller in diameter than the former, and it should have a slot cut into the end of it.

Tuning a blackpowder caplock revolver is an interesting process, and one that can be accomplished with a minimum of time, tools and handwork. It is an excellent Kitchen Table Level project that offers the possibility of great reward and satisfaction. Furthermore, after doing the job a few times, a hobbyist can become quite proficient at this type of gunsmithing, making him an expert caplock revolver tuner.

Correcting Revolver Timing

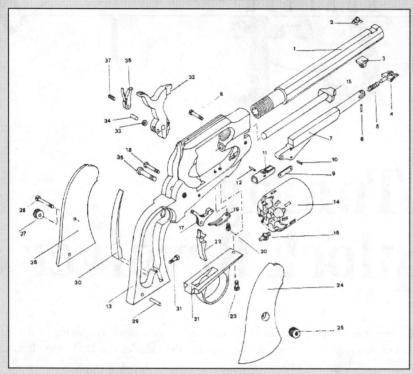

1	Barrel
2	Front Sight
3	Loading Lever Retainer
4	Loading Lever Latch
5	Latch Spring
6	Latch Pin
7	Loading Lever
8	Loading Lever Screw
9	Link
10	Link Pin
11	Rammer
12	Rear Hammer Pin
13	Frame
14	Cylinder
15	Cylinder Pin
16	Nipple
17	Cylinder Bolt
18	Cylinder Bolt Screw
19	Trigger & Bolt Spring
20	Trigger & Bolt Spring Screw
21	Trigger Guard
22	Trigger
23	Trigger Guard Screw
24	Right Grip
25	Right Grip Nut
26	Left Grip
27	Left Grip Nut
28	Grip Screw
29	Grip Pin
30	Mainspring
31	Mainspring Screw
32	Hammer
33	Hammer Roller
34	Hammer Roller Pin
35	Hammer Screw
36	Hand & Spring
37	Hand Pivot

Tools

Chamfering Tool
Drill Press or Hand Drill
Forcing Cone Reamers
Smooth Mill File, 4-inch

Supplies

Arkansas Stones, medium and hard
Sandpaper, Wet/Dry 400- and 600-grit
Small Box for Parts
Wooden Dowel Rod

Examining the Gun

Be certain that the revolver is unloaded before doing anything. Bring the hammer back to the fully cocked position. The cylinder bolt should fall into place to lock the cylinder at the same time the hammer engages the full-cock notch. That is what timing means—synchronization. If the cylinder locks up prematurely, and the hammer has to be forced to reach full-cock, the hand is too long and must be carefully shortened. This problem may occur on a new gun, or a gun that is fitted with a new hand. The cure is a matter of adjusting the length of the hand to promote proper timing.

Adjusting the Hand

Careful polishing with a stone can slightly shorten a hand that is too long. Of course, it is impossible to add length to a hand that is too short, which can also be a problem. If the hammer reaches full-cock, but the cylinder is not rotated far enough to lock the gun into battery (firing mode), then the hand is too short. The only cure is to replace the hand with a longer one, and it may have to be polished for a perfect fit.

Checking the Cylinder Bolt

Be certain the cylinder bolt spring operates correctly, so the bolt locks the cylinder. As the hammer is cocked, the bolt should quickly release the cylinder, while not touching the cylinder again until just before it falls into place, locking the cylinder for the next shot. If the cylinder bolt does not function correctly, check to ensure it is not broken. Then, exam-

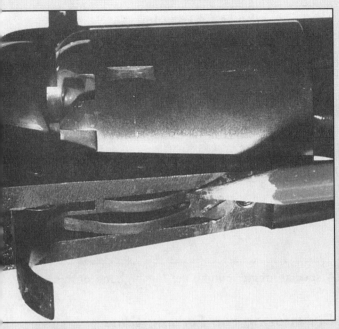

The cylinder bolt spring must be checked to ensure proper revolver tuning.

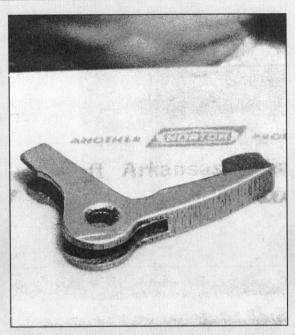

Polishing the cylinder bolt after it was removed from the revolver.

ine the cylinder bolt spring and the section of the hammer that actuates the bolt to be certain they are not damaged. If the cylinder bolt does not function properly, odds are one of these parts are broken and must be replaced.

Checking the Loading Lever

Ensure the loading lever works properly. Set the revolver on half-cock, rotate the cylinder to align with the loading lever, and then work the lever so the rammer falls into the cylinder chamber. The rammer should cleanly enter and depart. Anything less means a problem. The usual cure is a new rammer, as it may have become damaged. Loading lever and rammer problems are rare, but this checkup is another aspect of tuning that must be accomplished for a complete job.

Chamfering Nipples

Hand chamfering the nipples of the revolver will provide a bevel on the cone (end) of the nipple so caps fit snugly. In fact, the chamfered nipple can promote better ignition if the nipple was peened over, preventing a snug fit of the cap on the cone. Also, the chamfer provides a better angle for cap debris to escape from the nipple cone after detonation. Excess cap debris can cause cylinder lockup. A fired cap that clings to the cone of the nipple is virtually rotated with the cylinder, ending up between the frame and the cylinder. It's better to have the fired cap fall away when

Checking the loading lever for proper alignment with the cylinder chamber.

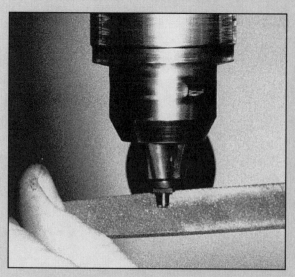

Chamfering a nipple with a file. The nipple is installed in the chuck of a drill press on slow speed.

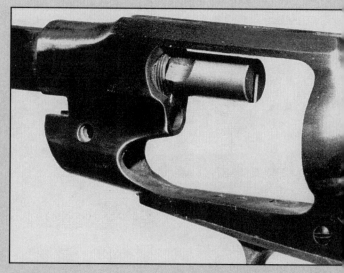

A special reamer cutting the forcing cone of this revolver.

the cylinder is revolved for the next shot, and the chamfered cone promotes this action.

Using a small sharp file, the hobbyist can put a slight bevel on the cone of each nipple. The major problem is securing the nipple in a vise to work on it without crushing the body of the nipple. A better way to chamfer nipples is with a drill press, inserting the nipple in the chuck. Then with the drill press on at low speed, a file can be held at the correct angle for a bevel on the nipple. Another way is with the nipple held in the chuck of a hand drill. But the hand drill must be secured in place so, when the file is held against the cone of the nipple, the cut will be consistent. If the drill moves during the operation, the angle will be altered.

Incidentally, the angled or chamfered nipple cone also improves cap installation, another positive aspect of tuning the revolver, because it makes shooting the gun a little easier.

Chamfering the Forcing Cone

Check the forcing cone at the end of the barrel. If its angle is minimal, it can be chamfered with special reamers from Brownells to cut a proper forcing cone. If it is rough, it can be lapped with a special tool also available from Brownells. This is another of those steps the hobbyist needs to know about for his own body of knowledge, but the work is best accomplished by a professional. If the forcing cone looks rough or minimal, have your gunsmith improve this area, as it could make a difference in accuracy.

Checking Chamber Alignment

Now run a wooden dowel rod down the muzzle and into a chamber of the cylinder, checking alignment of bore to chamber. Check all chambers for alignment, not just one. If there is a mismatch, the dowel will hang up on the cylinder chamber. If it does,

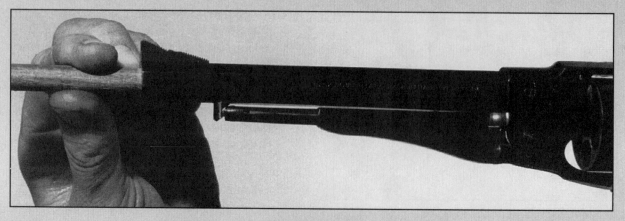

Using a wooden dowel to check barrel/chamber alignment.

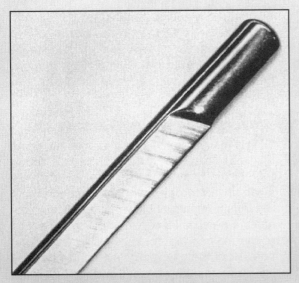

A cylinder pin after polishing with 600-grit wet/dry sandpaper.

The star of the revolver cylinder with all burrs polished and removed.

The chambers are being smoothed with a chamfering tool.

the remedy is not one for the hobby gunsmith's shop and, in fact, may not be correctable at the local professional shop. In that case, the revolver should be returned to the factory. While the hobby gunsmith cannot fix this problem, it is important for him to be able to find the problem, and the simple wooden dowel, well-fitted to the bore, will do the trick.

Checking Cylinder Motion

The well-tuned revolver has clean, smooth cylinder motion. With the revolver in half-cock mode, turn the cylinder to check operation. If it binds, check the cylinder pin for straightness. A pin that is only slightly bent will impair the smooth function of the cylinder.

Also, using 600-grit wet/dry sandpaper, lightly hand polish the cylinder pin to improve fit. Simply brighten the surface and do not try to remove metal.

Removing Burrs on the Cylinder Star

Take the cylinder out of the revolver and check the star or back section for burrs. If burrs are found, remove them using a hard Arkansas stone. Do not remove any parent metal in the process—only the burr. You don't want to change the fit between the cylinder and the barrel or damage the star.

Chamfering Chamber Mouths

The mouth of each cylinder chamber can be carefully hand beveled using a chamfering tool. The idea is to only remove the sharp edge from the chamber mouth, reducing lead shaving of the projectile when it is being seated.

Polishing Each Chamber

Using a slotted dowel and a power drill, each chamber can be polished. Attach the unslit end of the dowel in the chuck of the hand drill, and then place a piece of 400 wet/dry sandpaper through the slit in the dowel. Run the dowel into the chamber, then turn the drill on low speed and polish. Smooth chambers will enhance loading ease. Don't remove any metal—simply polish each hole.

Polishing each chamber with 400-grit wet/dry paper on dowel, using a power hand drill.

Polishing Working Parts

Completely disassemble the revolver, laying the parts in a small box where they will not be misplaced. Carefully polish each *working part* (mating surface) with a hard Arkansas stone, being certain to hold the part flat against the stone so angles are not altered. The task is to polish these parts, not to remove metal or change part shape because functioning could be altered. Bolt, trigger, hand and hammer are good candidates for polishing.

Reducing Mainspring Tension

This is an optional step and does not come fully recommended by the authors. It is important for the hammer spring to have adequate strength for proper function, especially in delivering a hammer blow that positively detonates a percussion cap. Lightening the action of the mainspring could result in weak ignition. Nonetheless, some shooters prefer a lighter mainspring action, and for those the following is offered: On guns that have a leaf mainspring (not a coil type), the spring can be filed down with a smooth mill file to make it thinner, which will lighten the action. Before attempting this maneuver, be certain to have an extra spring on hand to replace the original should it break, or should you wish to return to greater spring strength.

Checking for Cylinder Gap

Although the hobbyist cannot do anything about this problem, he should know how to check for it. Hold the revolver so light shines through the point between the cylinder and the barrel. If this gap looks excessive upon visual inspection, the revolver should be taken to a gunsmith to have him check it with a feeler gauge.

As noted in the text, there is nothing a hobbyist can do about an overt gap in between cylinder and barrel; however, it is important as a point of inspection. The gap on this particular cylinder is not excessive.

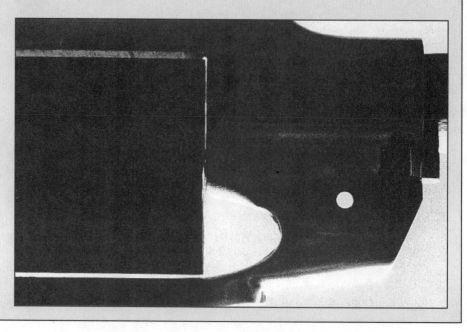

Improving Trigger Function

Tools

Oxygen-Acetylene Torch
Smooth Mill File
Soldering Iron

Supplies

Arkansas Stones, medium and hard
Hi Force 44 Solder
Quenching Oil
Sand with Metal Container
Short Lengths of Wire

Setting Up

The trigger should positively engage half-cock and full-cock notches. The notches are on the hammer, and the best way to repair non-functioning notches is to call the problem to the attention of a professional gunsmith. However, the advanced hobbyist can do the job by carefully filing the notches for positive engagement with small polishing stones. These stones must, obviously, fit well into the notches in order to make them square for full engagement.

However, this step demands precision work, and the hobbyist must be willing to take responsibility for his work because *a botched trigger job can result in a dangerous situation.*

Polishing the Trigger

Carefully polish all engaging surfaces on the trigger using a hard Arkansas stone, removing all tooling marks. Maintain all angles, and do not remove metal or change the shape of a part. Especially clean and sharpen the surfaces of the trigger that engage the full-cock notch of the hammer.

Hardening the Trigger

Also, the trigger may be hardened, if its metal is soft. A soft trigger will wear quickly, which can later be unsafe. To check for hardness, run a file over an inconspicuous spot on the body of the trigger, rather than an engaging surface, which could alter the shape. If a file removes metal readily, the trigger is too soft and must be hardened. Case-hardening is the process used; however, if the trigger has a thin portion where it engages the hammer—such as the Colt Model

Stoning the trigger surface that engages half-cock and full-cock notches on the hammer.

1860 revolver and some other single-action blackpowder revolvers—over-hardening may make this area brittle, at which point, it may break. The correctly hardened trigger will take a reasonable amount of pressure without breaking. Naturally, fast-draw use, which is discouraged with a blackpowder revolver in the first place, can put pressure on a hammer that will cause a trigger to break, even when it is properly hardened. Instructions for proper hardening techniques can be found in Chapter 5.

Polishing the Hammer

The full-cock notch on the hammer should be carefully polished so trigger matchup remains clean and breaks with no creep. For

Stoning the full-cock engagement on the hammer.

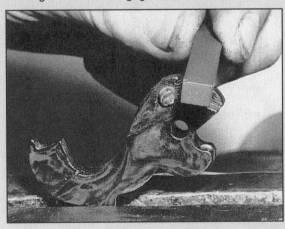

Checking the full-cock notch for positive engagement by applying pressure to the cocked hammer.

safety, engagement is never reduced to that point where the hammer is not held securely at full-cock. *Do not change the angle of the full-cock notch.* This is extremely important. The surfaces should be polished with a sharp-edged fine-cut stone, but should not be overworked. Polishing is once again the byword. Removal of metal here is incorrect.

Hardening the Hammer

The hammer may also be hardened, just like the trigger. If the surface of the hammer files easily, this test shows that it is too soft, and must be case-hardened. Instructions for hardening techniques can be found in Chapter 5.

Checking Positive Engagement

Next, check the trigger and hammer after reinstallation to ensure positive engagement of the full-cock notch. Make sure the gun cannot be forced off of full-cock by pushing forward on the cocked hammer. If it can, take the revolver to a gunsmith or send it back to the factory for repairs. Also, the trigger should fully engage the half-cock notch and not come out when the trigger is pulled. When testing this condition, do not apply undue force to trigger, which could break something.

Testfiring

Finally, fire the revolver and make sure the hammer does not end up in half-cock after the gun goes off. If it does, this indicates the full-cock setting is too light. Or, in the case of the Colt 1860 and similar blackpowder revolvers, the trigger could be broken.

Tip: On the Ruger Old Army revolver, reduce the full-cock engagement by soft-soldering a piece of thin shim stock onto the bottom of the full-cock notch, effectively reducing the depth of that notch. If too much metal is removed from the top of the full-cock notch, the trigger will fall into the half-cock notch when the gun is fired. Take care and use a very low temperature solder, like Hi Force 44, so the temper of the hammer will not be affected by overheating.

Building the Blackpowder Gun Kit

THERE ARE A number of excellent reasons to build a blackpowder gun kit—rifle, pistol or revolver. Building a kit is a great way to get started in blackpowder gunsmithing. No major tools are required, and sophisticated lathe and mill work have been completed by the manufacturer. For example, barrel tennon dovetails and sight dovetails are cut; the breech plug perfectly fits the barrel; the tang screw holes are drilled and counterbored; the lock screw is located, drilled and tapped; and stocks are primarily shaped and inletted for most major parts. For an increased understanding of kit building, the hobbyist should also see Chapter 26 on building the custom rifle. Making a custom rifle is far more sophisticated than building a kit; however, the hobbyist will gain an appreciation and understanding of this kit-making chapter by studying, in general, the process necessary to complete a custom rifle. So, look over the custom chapter before building a kit. It is an exercise well worth the effort, and the only time you will be advised to read ahead in this book.

Kit building does not demand high skill or deep gunsmithing knowledge and experience, with the exception of certain advanced models. Furthermore, kit-building saves money. Kits are priced under finished firearms. With a minimum of tools, and in a relatively small work space, a shooter can assemble and finish a kit to be proud of—a muzzleloader for the target range or field shooting, or a gun to fill in a missing niche in a collection. Historians may assemble kits for club reenactments, the Brown Bess kit being a perfect example. Kits may also be built as decorations to hang over a fireplace.

Another good feature of the kit is there are few to no extra parts to buy. Most kits come complete and ready to build. A few finishing materials may be required, but certain examples, such as Mountain State's Mountaineer, are provided with finishing supplies. The kit also has a final sight-in advantage over a scratch-built muzzleloader. The hobbyist does not have to concern himself with the alignment and matching of front and rear sights. They are usually well-placed at the factory.

Although the usual kit is simple enough for the beginning blackpowder hobbyist to complete, there is enough work left for both entertainment and learning. Every kit is a teaching tool and learning experience. For example, the kit builder will become acquainted with terms that may be unfamiliar. However, the mystery will quickly be lost if the reader follows this simple pre-building plan: Open the box containing the kit, remove all parts, and lay them out on a clean surface. Then, pick up each part and identify it by comparing its shape with the schematic supplied in the kit.

Some parts are obvious. Everyone knows what a barrel is, or a stock, a trigger, sights or a ramrod, and so forth. Chapter 5, on building lock kits, provides a wealth of information concerning specific lock parts. For example, the hobbyist now knows what a fly in the tumbler is or, for that matter, what a tumbler is. He has learned about lockplates, sears, frizzens, frizzen springs, bridles, sear springs, and so forth. Those parts and other lock parts will not be discussed here. However, there are a few parts that may bear odd-sounding or unfamiliar names for a beginning blackpowder gunsmithing hobbyist. Let's stop right here and discuss these parts before going forth into kit-making. This will familiarize the kit builder with the language he will need to understand and the parts with which he will be working.

Sometimes called a barrel lug, the **barrel tennon** is a piece of metal attached to the barrel through which a wedge passes to hold the barrel to the stock.

The wedge is a flat piece of metal, usually steel, that passes through the stock and barrel tennon to secure the barrel to the stock.

Brass or steel **pins** are used to hold the stock and barrel together. Like a wedge in function, it is rod-shaped instead of a flat piece of metal.

Of various shapes, **jags** are used to secure a patch on the end of the ramrod or cleaning rod, so it can be pushed down-bore.

Also known as a screw, the **bullet puller** is a tip that installs on the end of a ramrod or cleaning rod to remove a ball from the bore. It's shaped like a wood screw without a head.

Also called a worm, a **patch puller** is a metal corkscrew used to withdraw a stuck patch from the bore. It is attached to the end of a ramrod, cleaning rod or wiping stick. For more information, see Chapter 19 on ramrods.

Ramrod guides are also known as thimbles or pipes. They are brass, German silver or steel loops through which the ramrod fits and is held in place. Normally, ramrod guides are attached to the forearm of a full-stock rifle or the rib of a half-stock rifle. The same applies to pistols.

Made of brass, German silver or steel, the **escutcheon** is a metal inlay through which wedges, pins or screws are held in place. In effect, it acts like the washer with a bolt.

The **patent breech** is found on a percussion rifle. The breech plug and nipple seat are cast as a single unit.

The **breech plug** is a threaded metal plug screwed into the breech end of the barrel to seal the rear of the chamber. It is, in effect, just what its name implies: It plugs the end of the barrel that forms the breech.

A **hooked breech** has an extension at the plug end which forms a hook and fits into an integral receptacle built into the tang. The entire barrel can be removed from the stock by dis-engaging the hook from the receptacle when the barrel is lifted upward at the muzzle.

Also noted as a tube in the past, the **nipple** retains the cap on a percussion firearm. The cone of the nipple holds the cap, while the vent of the nipple directs the cap flash into the breech, igniting the powder charge.

The **flash hole** is a small hole in the side of the barrel flat that leads to the powder charge in the breech of the flintlock

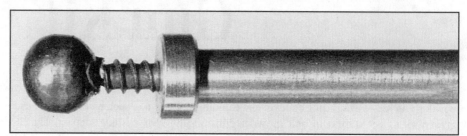

This is a bullet puller attached to the end of a ramrod (here screwed into a ball).

A barrel wedge, in the lower right-hand corner, is used to secure the barrel to the stock.

rifle. It's also known as a touchhole. The flash from the pan darts through the touchhole to reach the powder charge.

Also called a touchhole bushing, the **flash hole liner** is a small threaded tube that acts as a liner when inserted into a touchhole that has been drilled and tapped to accept it. Normally of stainless steel, these replace burned out touch-holes.

The **tang** is a metal extension on a breech plug or takedown breech normally located on the top of the grip area of the pistol or rifle. It is usually held in place by screws.

Also known as a forend or forearm cap, the **nose cap** is a metal cup at the end of a gunstock. It serves as a receptacle for a ramrod on the half-stock rifle or pistol. On a full-stock rifle or pistol, the nose cap protects the fragile wood at the end of the stock. On half-stocks, it is usually attached with screws, or it can be cast in place.

The **patch box**, usually made of brass, silver or wood, is in the buttstock of the rifle. Usually, this box holds lubricated patches for round balls. However, small accessories such as nipples and nipple picks, as well as flints, have been found in the patch boxes of original rifles.

Normally smaller than the patch box, the **cap box** is found

At the bottom is a touchhole liner, used to replace burned out touchholes.

A patent breech has its breech plug and nipple seat cast as a single unit.

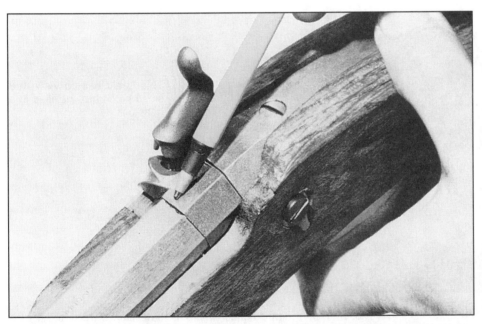

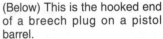

(Below) This is the hooked end of a breech plug on a pistol barrel.

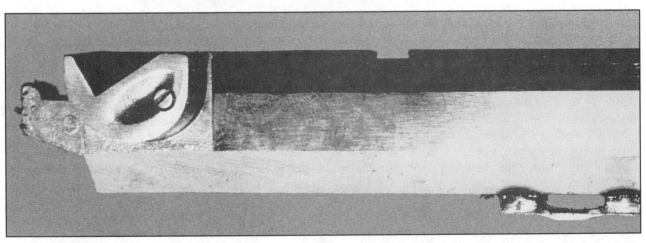

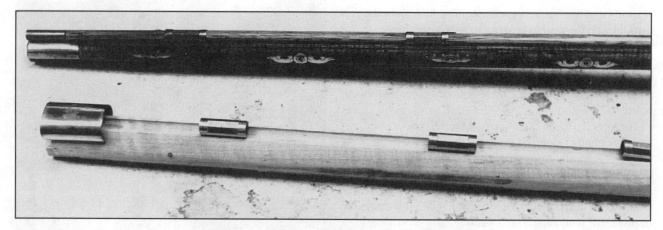

Ramrod guides are clearly shown on the lower stock. The stock above is finished.

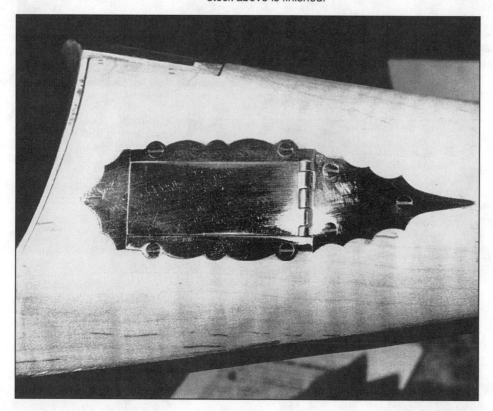

This is a close-up view of a small patch box installed in a buttstock.

in the buttstock of a rifle and holds percussion caps. It is often made of brass, silver or steel.

Besides learning new terms, it may be helpful for the reader to understand a basic procedure used in kit-building. Inletting black is used to fit numerous parts of the muzzleloader, including locks and lockplates, tangs, trigger assemblies, escutcheons, nose caps, buttplates, trigger guards, and other parts. See Chapter 26 for examples of the use of inletting black when building guns.

Inletting black is a paste product, black in color, applied with a brush to any metal part fitted into wood. The part to be inletted is coated with a film of inletting black. Then, the part is fit into an existing mortice or set onto the wood where it will be fitted. Next, the part is lightly tapped with a small rubber or plastic hammer, which transfers a black impression of the part on the wood. The black impression is, in effect, a pattern showing the builder where he must remove wood in order for the part to fit.

Although each kit project is different, at the same time every kit contains similar functions. So, if shaping a cheekpiece appears photographically in one project, it probably will not be illustrated for every other kit. Some of the operations common in kit building are securing the tang with a screw, installing rib and guides, mounting sights, removing excess wood, and so forth. Final stock finishing is not discussed, since this process enjoys a full discourse in Chapter 9. Also, certain extremely basic functions, such as fitting pistol grips, which is no more than installing a screw, were not illustrated, as they are self-evident. Furthermore, as suggested, the reader should turn to the custom section in Chapter 26, which is full of illustrations depicting the many functions that also pertain to kit building.

Building Navy Arms' Brown Bess Rifle Kit

Tools

- Center Punch
- Drift Punches, 1/16- and 1/8-inch
- Inletting Black with Brush
- No. 40 Drill Bit
- Power Drill
- Rubber or Plastic Mallet
- Screwdrivers
- Small Hammer
- Vise
- Wood Chisel, 1/2- and 1/4-inch
- Wood and Metal Files

Cleaning Up Metal Parts

All steel and metal parts must have their gates and flashings removed. All burrs must also be cleaned up. This means careful filing of each part. Pay close attention to part shape, maintaining all lines and contours as intended. Any alteration of shape may cause problems. If there is any question at all regarding what appears to be excess metal, *do not remove it* until the part is ready for final fitting. Then it will be easy to see what is excess and what is essential. Be careful with the sides of parts. Careless filing here may destroy proper metal to wood fit, leaving unsightly gaps.

Installing the Barrel

Secure the barrel to the stock with the furnished pins. All holes are pre-drilled in the stock and barrel tennons, so the pins are simply drifted in place.

Installing Ramrod Guides

Position the ramrod guides in their proper mortices and install them with the pins provided with the kit.

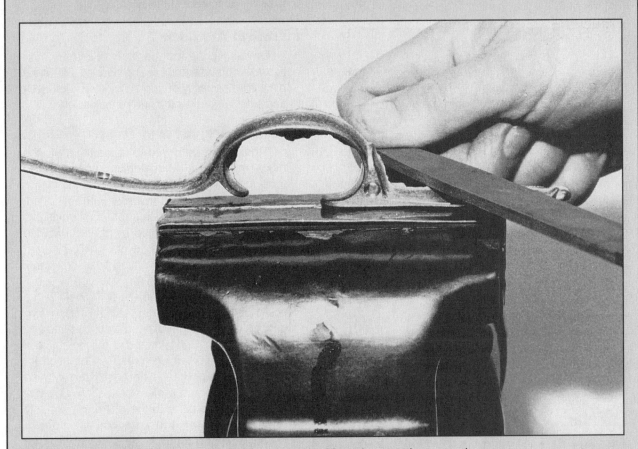

Using a file, flashing is removed from the cast trigger guard.

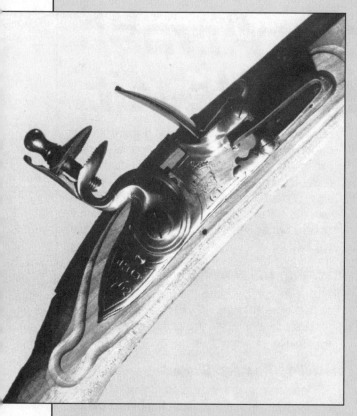

No extra inletting was required to fit the lock into its mortice.

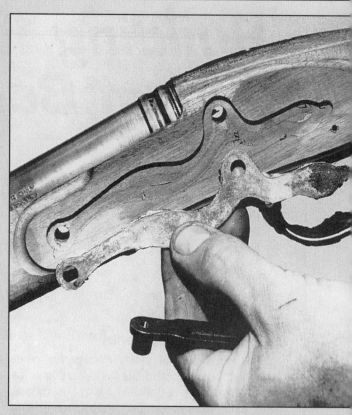

The sideplate requires filing and careful cleanup, but fits well into its mortice in the stock.

Installing the Lock

On this kit, the lock perfectly fit into the mortice with no additional inletting needed. The sideplate also perfectly fit into its mortice. Both lock and sideplate were attached by lock screws.

Installing Trigger and Trigger Plate

A hole must be drilled to fit the trigger to the trigger plate. But before drilling, inspect both parts to locate the correct position of the trigger so it properly engages the sear when installed, and so the trigger will also freely pivot on its pin, rather than being restricted by contact with the trigger plate too early in its cycle. This can retard the trigger's motion, preventing sear movement when the trigger is pulled.

Once located, mark the site of the hole with a sharp center punch. Then, slip the trigger into position on the trigger plate, clamp the plate in a drill press vise, and slowly drill the hole with a No. 40 bit. Ideally, a drill press will be used for accuracy of alignment. The hobbyist may wish to take this job to a professional shop. Use cutting fluid on the bit, with the drill press set only one step faster than its lowest speed. Remember, the smaller the bit diameter, the faster it turns.

The trigger plate and trigger are drilled for the trigger pivot pin.

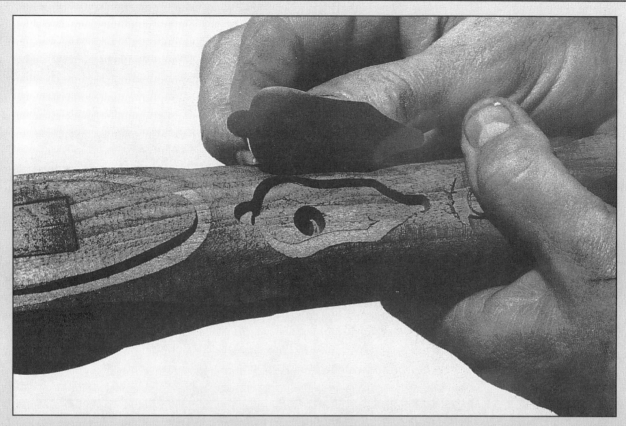

Typical of the Navy Arms Brown Bess kit, the metal inlay fits well in its stock mortice.

Installing the Trigger Assembly

Place the trigger assembly in its mortice and secure it with the tang screw. At this point, cock the lock and test the trigger for proper function. Do not dry fire the gun—retard hammer fall with your thumb. Normally, the falling hammer is retarded by the frizzen on this lock, but during this test of the trigger action, the frizzen is not set. So do not dry fire.

Installing the Brass Inlay

The brass inlay that goes on top of the wrist is now installed, which requires minor inletting. Use inletting black as a guide, along with a sharp chisel. This is a short task. With the inlay fitted into the wrist, insert the screw that runs from the bottom of the wrist into the inlay.

Fitting the Trigger Guard

The trigger guard demands very little, if any, inletting. Simply fit it into place with the appropriate pin.

Fitting the Buttplate

The stock is rough inletted for the buttplate, but final fitting is required. Use inletting black and sharp chisels to perform this step. This

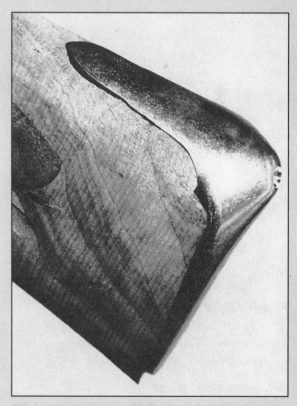

The buttplate demands the most inletting and fitting. Adequate wood should be left around the buttplate for proper stock shaping.

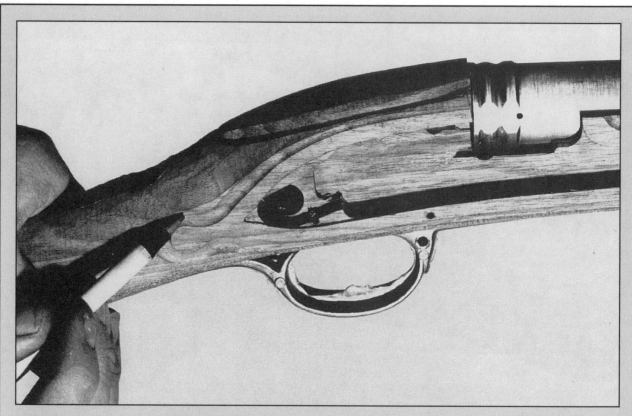

Note the excellent inletting of the lock mortice. The pen points to extra wood that must be shaped by filing to match the contour of the stock. All panels and moulding are well-defined on this kit.

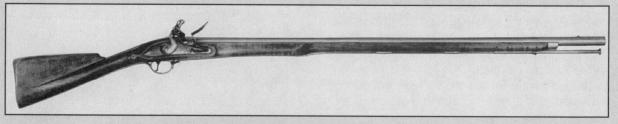

A completed Navy Arms Brown Bess. Finishing this kit requires minimal work, with the exception of the buttstock and buttplate area, which demands extra shaping.

demands careful attention and patience, so go slowly. When the buttplate perfectly fits the stock, it is secured by two screws.

Fitting Sling Swivels

Attachment of the sling swivels is self-explanatory. They can only fit one way in their proper locations and are secured in place.

Shaping the Stock

The Brown Bess stock is well shaped from the factory, but does demand some work, especially at the butt. Also, there is extra wood around the lockplate that needs removal. This allows an especially good metal to wood fit when the excess is carefully removed.

Finishing the Stock

Both wood and metal require finishing. Consult Chapters 9 and 14, respectively, for instructions on these projects.

Overall Impressions

This is an excellent kit for the historian or collector, because it allows ownership of a replica Brown Bess musket at a reasonable price.

Building Thompson/Center's Hawken Rifle Kit

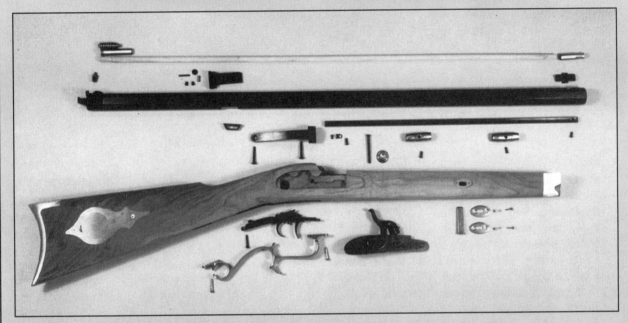

All the parts for the Hawken Rifle kit are laid out, ready for installation.

Tools

- Brass or Nylon Drift Punch
- Drill (hand or power)
- Drill Bits: No. 33, No. 46 and No. 50
- Flat, Smooth Mill Cut File with handle, 10-inch
- Garnet Paper or Sandpaper, 80-grit
- Round Bastard Cut File with handle, 10-inch
- Sanding Block
- Screwdrivers
- Small Hammer
- Vise with Padded Jaws
- Wood Gouge, 3/8-inch

Securing Tang to Stock

The tang fits easily in place in its appropriate mortice. Hold the tang firmly in position, properly aligned, and mark the location for the tang screw hole to be drilled. Pilot-drill the hole with a hand drill and a No. 33 drill bit. Using a screwdriver that fits the screw slot correctly, and with a touch of paraffin on the screw threads, install the tang screw firmly in place. Do not worry about excess wood rising above the level of the tang. That problem will be confronted later in the project.

Installing the Barrel

Insert the barrel into the stock. It should easily fall into place in the barrel channel, because of excellent kit construction. If minor inletting is required, refer to Chapter 26 about the custom gun for instructions.

Installing Forend Escutcheons

Next, remove the barrel and install the two forend escutcheons into their respective mortices in the stock with the shoulder portion facing downward into the mortice. They will not fit flush with the surface of the wood. The two escutcheons are identical, so it makes no difference on which side of the stock you start. Secure each escutcheon with the two brass wood screws provided. As always, use the cor-

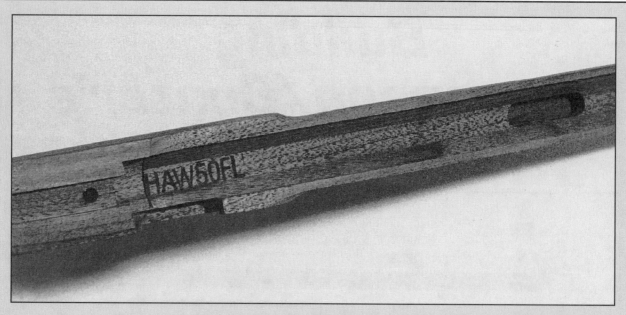

Good machine inletting is clearly visible on this Hawken kit.

rect size screwdriver for the screw slot, and put a touch of paraffin on the screw threads to facilitate seating. Don't torque these screws down; simply seat them firmly. Overtightening these screws may strip them out of the stock.

After the two forend escutcheons are mounted, hook the barrel into the tang and lower it into the stock channel. Press the single forend wedge (key) into place through the escutcheons you just installed. The barrel is now secured.

Installing the Lock

Drive the barrel wedge out with a drift punch and remove the barrel once again for further work. Next, place the lock into its mortice in the stock. On the sample kit, the lock readily mounted in place. The breech plug portion of the barrel is notched to fit over the top of the lockplate. With the lock in place, install its screw and bushing. The lockplate screw bushing, which is mounted on the opposite side of the lock, does not fit into a mortice in the stock, but rests on the surface of the wood. After the lock is installed, replace the barrel in the stock by gently tapping the barrel wedge through its channel with a small hammer.

Fitting the Trigger Assembly

Align the trigger plate with the front tang screw. This will show the location of the rear trigger plate screw hole. Mark this hole by centering the screw in the trigger plate hole and softly striking the head with a small hammer.

Building the Thompson/Center Hawken Rifle kit, with a newcomer to kit-making taking instructions from a pro. At this point, the ramrod guides are being installed.

Then, drill the hole with a No. 50 bit and firmly install a steel wood screw in place. With the trigger assembly mounted, press the trigger guard in its respective location and thread the front tang screw into the trigger guard. This screw holds both the front of the trigger assembly and the trigger guard. Next, install the front and rear trigger guard screws. Be sure to pre-drill the holes with a No. 46 or No. 47 bit. If the holes are not pre-drilled, there is a chance the heads will be twisted off of these brass screws.

Installing Rib and Ramrod Guides

The buttplate and patch box come complete from the factory on this kit, as does the nosecap. Now, it is time to install the rib and the ramrod guides. The holes for these are pre-drilled and tapped. *Option*: On our particular sample, an Uncle Mike's ramrod guide with integral sling stud was attached. While a sling may not be a traditional muzzleloader appointment, one was desired on this rifle for its practicality. This option does not have to be followed, of course, as T/C provides two guides with the kit. *Note*: The front screw that attaches the rib to the barrel was too long, and had to be shortened. This is an easy job of filing or grinding.

Tip: For extra security, Loctite can be used on the screws that attach the rib and ramrod guides. Purple Loctite should be used, as the red type will set up too hard and the screws will be too difficult to remove. Bear in mind, however, that if these screws have to be removed later, the job will not be easy.

The small spring that comes with the kit is used to retain the ramrod in position. This is a small flat spring and its location is obvious.

Mounting the Sights

The rear sight base is positioned on the barrel over the pre-drilled and tapped holes and secured with two screws. The use of Loctite as insurance against loosening is recommended. Then, install the elevation spring and slip the rear sight blade assembly into position. Now, drive the pin through the base assembly using a drift punch. Finally, insert the sight elevation screw into the blade base and twist into place. The rear sight is now installed and ready for both windage and elevation movement. Now, turn to the front sight and, with a brass or nylon drift punch, install it.

Installing the Ramrod

Both ends of the ramrod are threaded for tips, making installation simple. For a solid hold, use a dab of epoxy on the threads before installing them. These tips should also be pinned, and information on this precedure can be found in Chapter 19.

Replacing Screws

T/C includes replacement brass screws for those who wish to use them instead of the steel screws that are factory installed in the buttplate, patch box and nosecap. This is a simple matter of removing the steel screws and installing the brass ones.

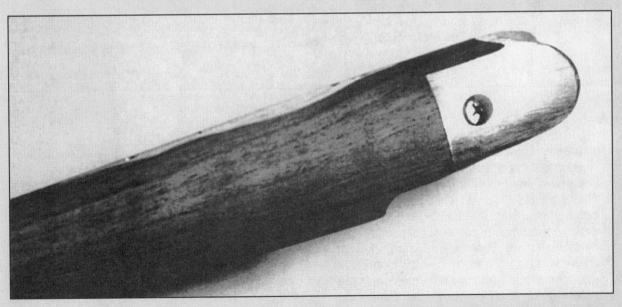

This kit comes with a nicely finished buttplate, well-installed.
Little to no fitting is required.

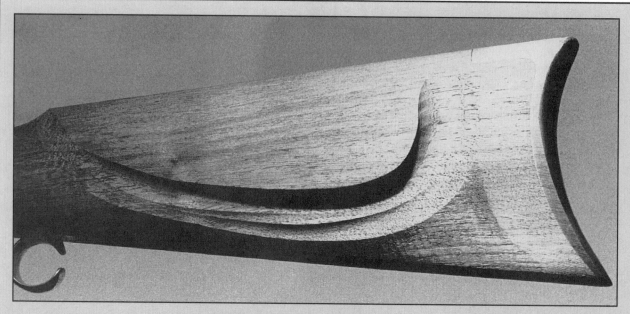

The Hawken stock, straight out of the box, has some shaping to do on the cheekpiece.

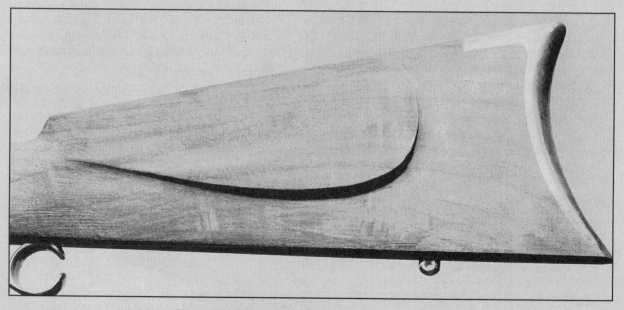

The cheekpiece is now shaped, ready for sanding and finishing.

Removing Excess Wood

By visual inspection, the hobbyist can readily see where excess wood needs to be removed. Files are used to reduce wood from the appropriate areas. Start with bastard cut files, later switching to smooth mill files. Remember, the metal parts are finished, so file carefully or these will be marred. It is wise to protect exposed metal surfaces with masking tape before going to work, especially around the tang and above the lockplate—areas normally associated with excess wood. Next, check the hammer. Does excess wood interfere with hammer motion? If so, correct the situation with careful wood removal until the hammer functions freely. To find where lock parts may be hitting the wood, inletting black is used. Coat the lock parts and reinstall the lock back into the stock. After cycling the lock, a black mark will show where wood is interfering and needs removal. Another area noted for excess wood is the cheekpiece. Use your judgement. It is possible to incorporate personal taste when shaping the stock, but be very cautious. You

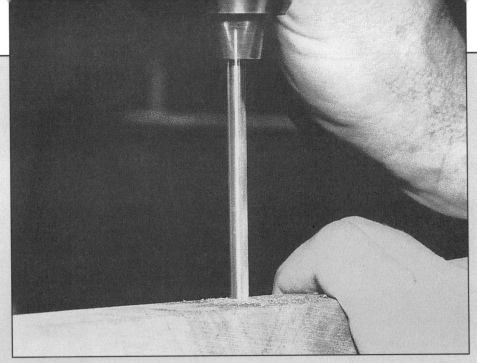

Using a $5/32$-inch bit, a hole is drilled for the sling stud.

can't put wood back on after you have filed or sanded it off.

Sanding the Stock

After wood removal by file, sand the stock using 80-grit paper. Use a sanding block for flat surfaces and bits of paper to work contours, keeping all lines sharp.

Installing the Rear Sling Stud

Recall that the front sling stud, in this case one with integral sling eye, was previously mounted. It is now time to mount the rear stud. Find the center of the stock's toe line about 3 inches in front of the toe of the buttplate. Using a $5/32$-inch bit, drill a hole the depth of the threaded portion of the stud. Then, counterdrill this hole with a $7/32$-inch bit. The larger hole will prevent wood splitting when the stud is installed. Using a drift punch inserted through the eye of the stud as a handle for turning, twist the stud in place. In this case, an Uncle Mike's rear stud was used to match the front stud. Remember, this stud does not come with the kit, but is bought separately as a set in either brass or blued steel finish.

Finishing the Stock

The stock is now prepared for final finishing. Use the instructions provided in Chapter 9 on the subject of wood finishing.

Options

The option of studs with sling eyes was already covered, but there are other things that

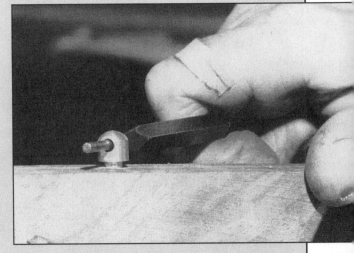

A drift punch is used to turn the sling swivel stud into the stock.

can be done. The breech area can be glass-bedded for better recoil distribution. Or, forend escutcheons can be inletted into the stock, flush with the wood. This requires the barrel wedge to be shortened, or too much of it will protrude. Also, a brass toe plate can be added to the stock, or inlays can be fitted in the stock, especially on the broad surface of the cheekpiece.

Overall Impressions

This is a high-quality kit requiring a minimum of tools. It's a good beginner's choice that should result in a highly serviceable rifle. Although the kit is easy to assemble, there remains a good deal of finishing work to do in terms of final stock shaping and wood finish. A job well-done should take several hours.

Building Mountain State's Mountaineer Rifle Kit

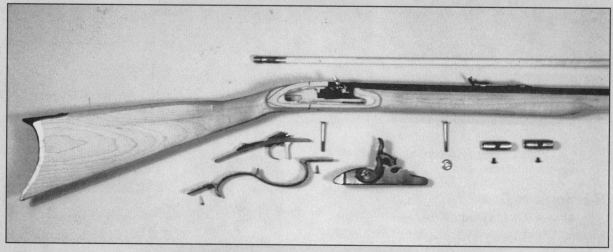

The Mountaineer Rifle kit and its various parts are spread out for assembly.

Tools

Bastard Cut Round File with handle, 10-inch
Bastard Cut Round File without handle, 10-inch
Flat, Smooth Mill Cut File with handle, 10-inch
Screwdrivers
Wood Gouge, 3/8-inch

Removing Excess Wood

Remove all excess wood protruding above the level of the metal parts. The trigger plate requires special attention. This is initially accomplished with bastard cut files, changing to a smooth mill file for the final strokes, then 80-grit sandpaper. *Caution:* Avoid making contact with the metal during this step. Since this rifle kit comes in the white, light file and sandpaper strokes will not harm the metal. Obviously, any heavy-duty marks caused by file work will require polishing out.

No final sanding is attempted in this step. The idea is to reduce high wood. Also, the stock is provided with a panel around the lock, initially a bit large and nondescript. Lines drawn on this oversized panel offer a guide for shaping that a novice builder can readily follow. Since this work is essentially one of excess wood removal, it is not considered a separate step.

Shaping the Stock

The cheekpiece and comb could be left as they come from the factory; however, a little effort refines these lines. The hobbyist is encouraged to use his own judgment and critical eye in making a slight design change on cheekpiece and comb. Draw pencil lines on the wood to indicate the final shapes of both.

First, the cheekpiece: The general style of the cheekpiece must remain the same, which is the small squared-off type found on early long rifles. There is ample wood for a functional and good-looking cheekpiece to be shaped out. Use a 3/8-inch gouge to rough out the edges of the cheekpiece, then shape it from the bottommost line toward the top of the comb with a bastard cut file. The rear line of the cheekpiece can be shaped to gracefully curve upward to the beginning point of the buttplate.

The front portion of the cheekpiece should flow toward the comb with a clean line. The hobbyist may use his own discretion in this matter, or fol-

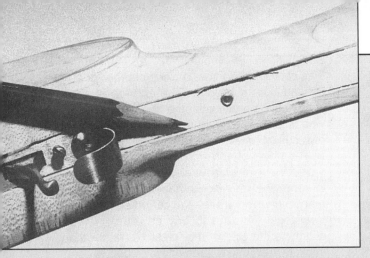

Extra wood needs to be removed at the trigger plate.

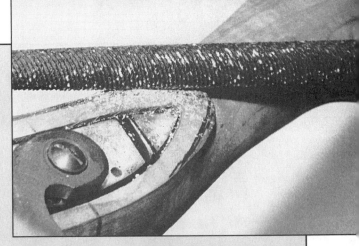

The panel around the lockplate is shaped.

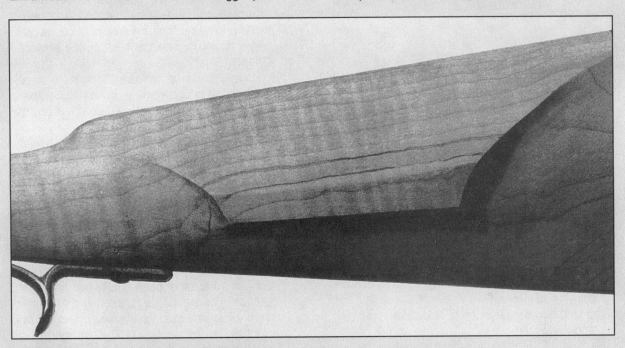

The sanded cheekpiece is fully shaped and ready for finishing.

low the line illustrated. Partial shaping of the cheekpiece is complete along the sides. Now, a bastard cut round file is used to work the bottom into a clean radius, a transition line from buttstock to cheekpiece, after which 80-grit sandpaper, both with a block and as free, small pieces, cleans up gouge and file marks. Maintain those lines meant to be straight, under the cheekpiece and where there is subtle blending at that point in front of the cheekpiece, behind the wrist.

While working this latter portion of the cheekpiece into shape, sharpen the lines at the point of the comb. Don't make the comb too thin by oversanding. On this rifle, the comb is already quite thin and should be reduced very little. Remove only a minimum of wood, just enough to clean the machine marks left in the wood at the factory. The off-side of the stock may show gouges left from the stock duplicator. Use a sanding block to keep flat surfaces flat, and straight lines straight. Small pieces of sandpaper can be used to smooth out all contours in the stock.

Finishing the Stock

After the stock is fully shaped, including sanding of the long forearm, it is ready for finishing. Refer to the Chapter 9 on stock finishing, choosing the type of finish you prefer for your own Mountaineer Rifle.

Finishing the Metal

The Mountaineer, as pointed out, comes to the hobbyist assembled. Therefore, metal finishing is done quite early in the project. Study Chapter 14 to learn how to brown the metal for an original appearance.

Checking Ramrod Guides for Burrs

The kit we completed had burrs on the interior of the ramrod guides. These were eliminated

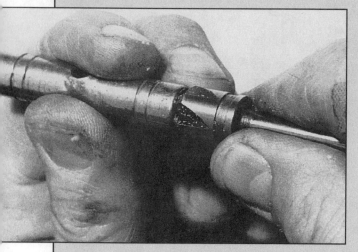

A burr is removed from the ramrod guide using a countersink to bevel the edge.

using a countersink to bevel the ends of the guides.

Shortening Screws

In this kit, both screws holding the barrel to the stock had to be slightly shortened, as the screws were too long for a tight fit between barrel and stock. These screws are accessible through holes in the bottom of the ramrod guides and take an Allen wrench. Be careful not to strip these small screws. This system of holding the barrel to the stock is unique to this rifle.

Options

Several options are possible on the Mountaineer kit. One is a lock screw escutcheon, purchased from a supplier such as Mountain State or handmade on a lathe. The advanced hobbyist may wish to make his own round escutcheon, inletting it into the stock and making the screw head flush with the surface of the wood.

Another option is the addition of a toe plate. This can be made from a piece of brass or purchased from a supplier. The addition of a toe plate is good practice for the beginning hobbyist who is looking forward to someday building his own custom rifle from scratch.

The fitting of a rear entry thimble is another project within the parameters of this kit. The job is somewhat advanced, however, because of marginal wood where the ramrod enters the forestock. Be sure to buy an entry thimble matching the size of the forestock, rather than trying to fit an overly large unit in place.

A nosecap may also be added to the Mountaineer, but this must be done before wood and metal finishing. For instructions on fitting a nosecap, see the custom rifle section in Chapter 26.

Inlays are also possible options. A cheekpiece inlay is appropriate, for example. Inlays can also be installed where barrel pins are normally placed.

Finally, glass-bedding may prove beneficial in the breech area. This helps protect against recoil damage to the relatively slender breech and wrist areas.

Overall Impressions

This entry-level rifle requires only basic tools. The end product is a no-frills shooting piece. The lock and trigger were not highly polished, but proved to be of good quality and gave good service. The sights are functional, with the rear sight easily adjusted for elevation, and the front sight drifted for windage. Pay attention to the screws attaching the ramrod guides and barrel to the stock; however, unless the rifle is abused, these screws should hold up. Overall, wood to metal fit is good. Wood quality was better than average on the sample rifle, showing some fiddleback figure, and took a nice finish.

Tip: The most difficult aspect of building this kit is metal finishing. The hobbyist who wants bluing, instead of browning, or who does not wish to bother with metal finishing at all, can have the job done professionally.

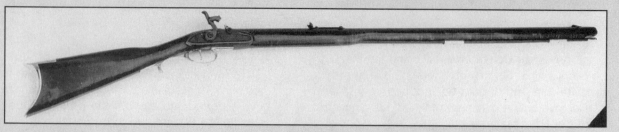

The Mountaineer Rifle has been fully assembled and finished.

Building Traditions' Deerhunter Rifle Kit

Tools

Drift Punch, 1/8-inch
Screwdrivers
Small Hammer
Three-Square File with one edge ground
safe, 8- or 10-inch

Fitting Barrel Parts

Fit all the parts on the barrel, which include the front sight, rear sight, underlug and ramrod guide. The dovetails for the sights and barrel tennon need a little file-fitting, using the three-square file. Ensure a snug fit by filing only enough to allow entry into dovetail notch. File a little, try the fit, and repeat until it's right.

Installing Tang, Trigger and Lock

The tang and trigger are installed in their respective mortices in the stock. Secure the tang in place with the appropriate screw provided. Place the lock in the stock mortice and twist in its screws.

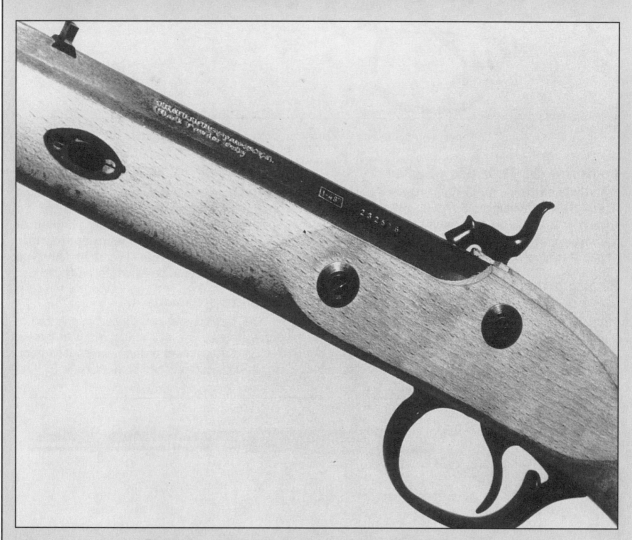

The lock screw escutcheons in this kit lie on the surface of the wood. As an option, these can be recessed into the wood. The offside panel of this rifle kit is nicely shaped out of the box, requiring little extra work.

The ramrod guide and sling swivel are easily installed as one unit. It is attached to the barrel with two screws.

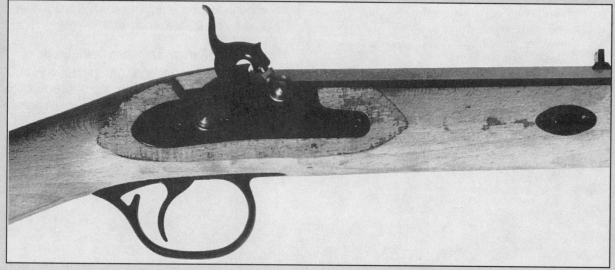

The lock on this rifle kit fits its mortice with no extra inletting.

Installing the Rear Sling Swivel

Center the sling swivel on the toe line about 2½ to 3 inches from the end of the stock. Drill a pilot hole the same size as the shank of the swivel screw, then lubricate the threads with paraffin before screwing in the sling swivel.

Finishing the Stock

The rifle is assembled at this point. Shaping the stock, which requires mainly sanding, is done now, followed by finishing. Both wood and metal require finishing. Follow instructions provided in Chapters 9 and 14, respectively.

Options

The usual glass-bedding option in recoil areas is possible. Also, the muzzle can be recrowned, and sights can be modified or changed by simply choosing appropriate replacements and installing them. And, as always, the lock can be tuned, as in Chapter 6.

Overall Impressions

The Traditions kit can be built in only two or three hours. The lock that came with this kit required adjustment of the sear engagement, which was accomplished *professionally*.

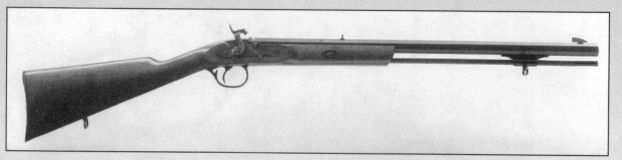

After building and final finishing, the Deerhunter Rifle is ready to shoot.

Building Lyman's Plains Pistol Kit

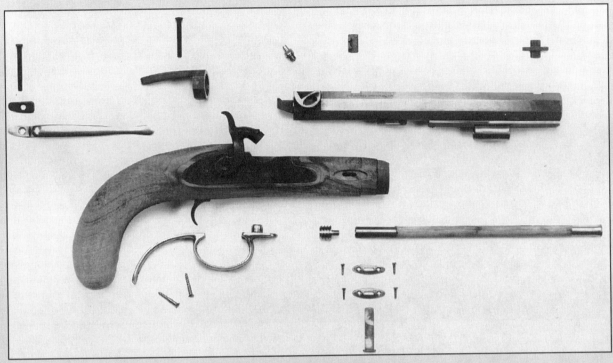

The Lyman Plains Pistol with all its parts laid out.

Tools

Brownells Screwdriver Set
Drift Punch, 1/8-inch
Half-Round Bastard Cut File without Handle,
    8- or 10-inch
Inletting Black and Brush
Jeweller's File
Rubber or Plastic Mallet
Scribe, Awl or Very Small Ice Pick
Small Hammer
Smooth Mill File, 8-inch
Wood Chisel, 1/4-inch
Wood Gouge, 1/4-inch

Setting Up

Remove all parts and check them against the schematic drawing that comes with the kit. Make sure everthing is complete. Before starting read all instructions included in the kit.

Fitting Tang and Escutcheons

Place the tang in the stock and install its screw. Then, fit the escutcheons into their precut mortices and secure with two wood screws.

The tang screw is installed.

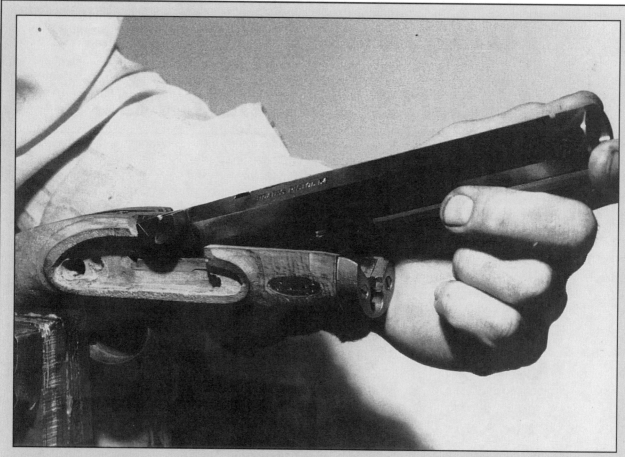

The barrel is lowered into its mortice, being careful not to split the stock in the process.

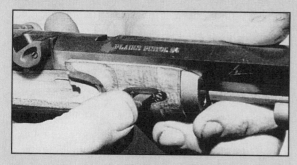

Fit the barrel wedge from right to left only.

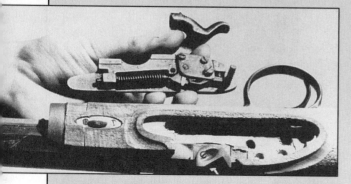

This is a view of the lock from its interior side, next to its lock mortice.

Use an awl or ice pick to start the holes so the screws will not split the stockwood.

Fitting the Barrel

Be especially careful in this step. If the barrel does not fall into its mortice without force, undertake a minor inletting job to ensure when the barrel is fitted it will not split the stock. This kit comes with a written notice that states: "Do not force the barrel into the stock. This will result in cracking the stock and voiding the warranty." Minor inletting is done with inletting black and a 1/4-inch chisel.

Installing the Barrel Wedge

Insert the barrel wedge into the stock. The key goes through the escutcheons, as usual; however, if key fits too tightly, use a jeweller's file to neatly enlarge the barrel wedge holes. Remember, insert wedges right to left only.

Fitting the Lock

Once again, if the lock does not fit into the mortice without force, a modest inletting job is needed. Use inletting black and brush, along

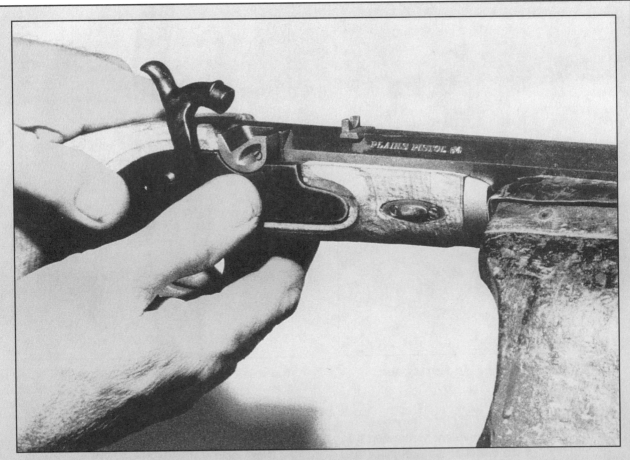

The lock fits well into its mortice in the stock.

with a 1/4-inch chisel, to perform this task, which is a simple matter of cutting away a bit of wood to allow proper lock fit.

Choosing Escutcheon Options

At this point, the builder makes a choice between a belt hook or a lock screw escutcheon; however, even though this choice is made now, the decision can be reversed later. So do not lose the extra part. You may wish to change your mind and use it later.

Lock Screw Escutcheon: Install the lock screw escutcheon into its proper mortice in the stock. This is a simple fit with finger pressure.

Belt Hook: First, remove the lock screw and lock screw escutcheon from the stock. Replace the escutcheon with a belt hook and re-install the lock screw, which holds the belt hook in place.

Installing Sights

Drive both front and rear sights into their notches from the right to the left. Should either sight fit loosely, use a thin brass sheet, cut to fit, as a shim, so the sight is tightly held in place.

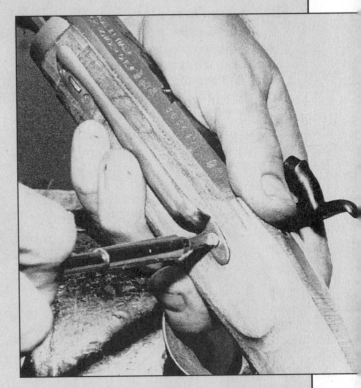

Installing the belt hook, which is optional because a lock screw escutcheon may be used.

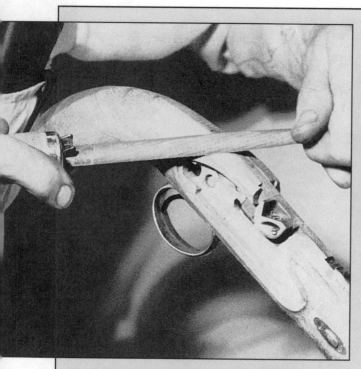

Final shaping of the stock around the lock area.

The nose cap is fitted to the pre-inletted region on the stock.

Installing the Rib

The rib is installed by simply screwing it to the bottom of the barrel in the pre-drilled and tapped holes.

Fitting the Nose Cap

The nose cap is already pre-inletted into the stock. The nose cap is secured to the stock with two brass screws mounted from the front of the nose cap into the forend. Use an awl to pre-punch these two holes, then the screws will not split the stock.

Shaping the Stock

Use files to shape the stock where needed. These points are relatively obvious. For example, the kit stock required minor filing of the handle to form a smooth surface and matching lines.

Final Finishing

Carefully sand and finish the stock as described in Chapter 9 on wood finishing. Also, finish the metal as described in Chapter 14 on the subject.

The Lyman Plains Pistol, fully assembled and finished.

Building CVA's Hawken Pistol Kit

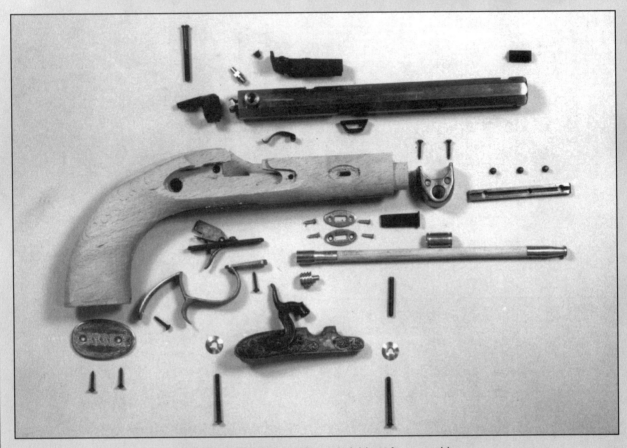

The Hawken Pistol kit and its parts laid out for assembly.

Tools

Awl, Ice Pick or Scribe
Brass or Nylon Drift Punch
Drill Bits: $1/16$, $1/8$, $3/32$, $9/64$ and $1/4$-inch
Flat Smooth Mill File with Handle, 8-inch
Garnet Paper or Sandpaper, 80-grit
Half-Round Bastard Cut File with Handle,
    6- and 8-inch
Inletting Black with Brush
Screwdriver Set
Small Chisel
Small Hammer
Three-Square File (one edge ground safe),
    8-inch
Vise

Setting Up

Remove all parts and check them against the schematic drawing that comes with the kit.

Make sure everything is complete. Before starting, read all instructions included in the kit.

The parts fit well without further filing or polishing on this kit. Minimal inletting was required; however, specific kits may vary. Therefore, inletting tools are listed in the tool section. The lock, sights and grip cap are final-finished. Other metal parts, and wood, require finishing. CVA's pre-packaged finishing kit can be used. It is complete, except for the lack of a few extra sheets of sandpaper in various grades. *Tip*: Discard the wedge plate screws that come with this kit, because they lack points. Regular brass wood screws of the same size were purchased at a hardware store and substituted.

Installing the Barrel Tennon

The barrel tennon dovetail slot was slightly undersized on the sample kit. Therefore, a few

The barrel tennon dovetail may have to be enlarged with a three-square file with one edge ground safe.

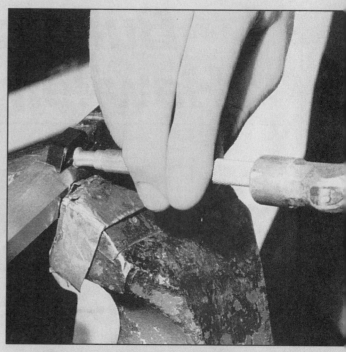

Driving the barrel tennon into the dovetail using a brass-tipped punch, which will not damage the steel.

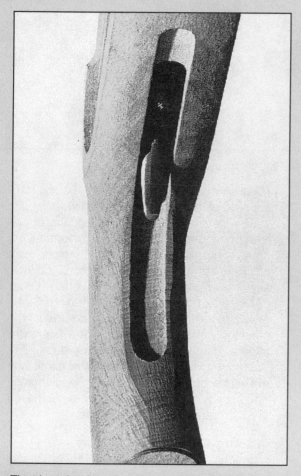

The trigger has been installed and screwed to the tang.

strokes with a three-square file enlarged the notch. Do not remove too much metal. A tight fit is necessary. The edge ground safe rests in the bottom of the tennon, where its smooth surface would remove no metal. Metal should be removed only from the sides of the dovetail notch.

Fitting the Rear Tang

With the barrel tennon firmly in place, the rear tang is installed in its pre-cut mortice. Do not alter its location. Changing tang placement can affect how recoil is delivered to the stock. It can also alter the relationship between hammer and nipple.

The tang is held in place by the tang screw, which is secured to the trigger plate. The tang screw may have to be shortened, as on the sample kit. The correct tang screw length is easily determined by screwing it into place and marking the portion of the screw that protrudes above the trigger plate—that much of the screw must be taken off. Count the number of threads to be removed, and file or grind from the tip of the screw.

Fitting the Barrel

Hook the barrel into the tang. The hooked breech makes this a simple matter of carefully lowering the barrel into the stock with its hook

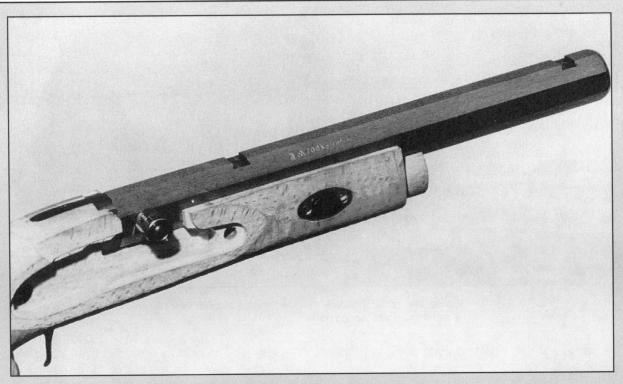

The barrel has been fit into the stock.

end fitted into its receptacle in the tang. This kit required no extra fitting of the hooked breech. However, minor metal removal may be necessary on other samples of this kit, or other kits. Where to remove metal is obvious, as the portion of the hook that is binding will be shiny from rubbing in the tang receptacle.

Installing Barrel Escutcheons

The barrel escutcheons properly fit into their mortices in the stock. They were attached with brass wood screws purchased from a hardware store, rather than the originals that came with the kit. Use an awl to pre-punch the holes for these screws, about $1/16$-inch. Also, paraffin on the screw threads eases installation.

Fitting the Lock

With escutcheons installed in their stock mortices, and the barrel in place, the lock is fitted into its mortice in the stock. No inletting is required. The holes are pre-drilled, and the lock is held in place with two screws and two lock screw washers.

Installing the Trigger Guard

Fit the trigger guard into its stock mortice. No further inletting was required on the sample kit. Two brass wood screws secure the trigger guard. Mark the holes with an awl to start the

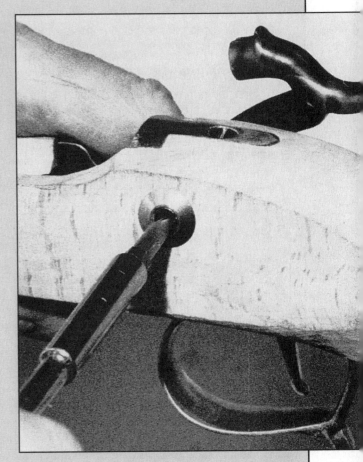

A lock screw is inserted through the lock screw escutcheon.

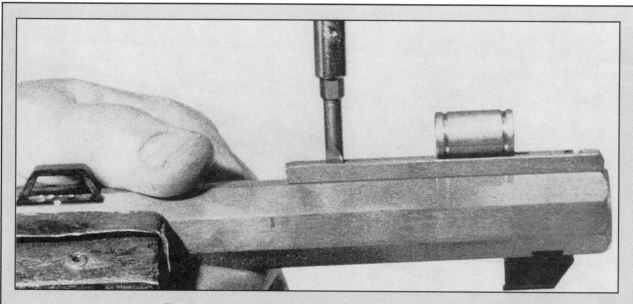

The rib, with its guide already mounted, is screwed into the barrel's pre-drilled and tapped holes.

screws, or drill a pilot hole with a $^3/_{32}$-inch drill bit.

Fitting the Nose Cap

Remove the barrel from the stock. Then, fit the nose cap on the end of the stock using the two screws supplied.

Fitting Thimble and Rib

First, the ramrod thimble is attached to the rib with screws, and then the rib is screwed onto the barrel. All holes are pre-drilled and tapped.

Installing the Sights

No further adjustments are necessary for installing the sights into their dovetail notches on this kit. The sights are simply driven into place. *Tip*: If other samples of this kit, or other kits, have dovetail notches that are too large to securely hold the sights in place, a thin shim can be cut from brass and placed in the bottom of the dovetail notch. This takes up space and offers a snug fit for the sights.

Fitting the Grip Cap

Center the grip cap on the pistol grip of the stock and mark hole alignment. Then, drill or punch holes to accept the screws. Afterward, screw the grip cap onto the stock with wood screws. Excess wood protrudes beyond the edges of the grip cap, and this wood will have to be removed during final stock shaping.

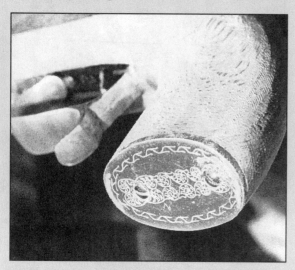

The pistol grip cap is fitted, with the stock final-shaped for good metal to wood fit.

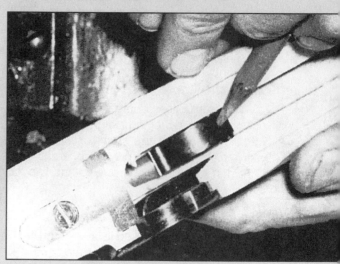

The ramrod tension spring has been installed in the stock.

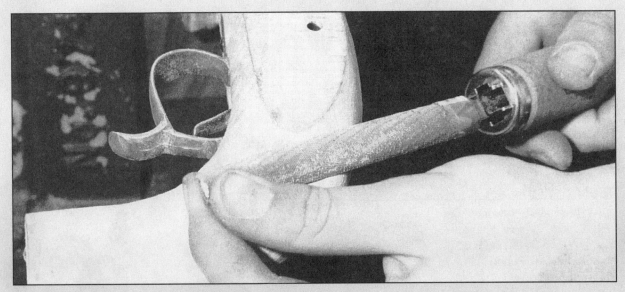

An 8-inch half-round bastard cut file with handle is used to shape around the moulding of the stock.

Installing the Ramrod

To install the ramrod retaining spring, first remove the barrel. Then, loosen the front lock screw and pull it halfway out. Slide the loop of the spring over this screw with the small "coil" facing the bottom and rear of the barrel channel. Next, tighten the lock screw and reinstall the barrel.

Now, the ramrod is ready for insertion with no further finishing. If the ramrod fits too tightly, the retaining spring can be bent to adjust tension.

Shaping the Stock

Final stock shaping is done by removing excess wood so metal and wood profiles blend. Keep all lines sharp. Read Chapter 9 on wood finishing.

Finishing the Metal

CVA has a finishing kit that contains all the supplies needed for completing this step. Follow the instructions carefully. Also, read Chapter 14 on metal finishing.

Options

The stock wood can be stained to darken it. Also, the sights can be altered. More traditional sights may be used in place of the ones that come with the kit.

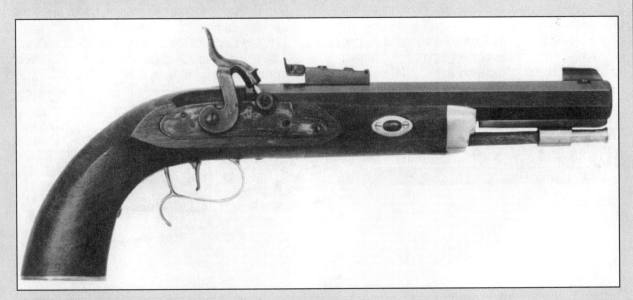

Ready for use, the Hawken Pistol is fully assembled and finished.

Building Navy Arms' 1860 Army/Reb '60 Revolver Kit

Tools

Brownells Screwdriver Set
Chisel, 1/4-inch
Inletting Black and Brush
Nylon Drift Punch
Rubber Mallet
Smooth Mill File, 6-inch

Setting Up

Remove all parts and check them against the schematic drawing that comes with the kit. Make sure everything is complete. Before starting, read all instructions included in the kit. Both revolvers are essentially the same, the only difference being barrel length. The two kits were built simultaneously.

Installing the Front Sight

Drive the front sight into place using a nylon-tipped drift punch and a small hammer.

Installing Loading Lever and Cylinder

The loading lever and plunger are assembled according to the schematic drawing. Then, slide the cylinder onto the base pin. Next, insert the complete barrel assembly with loading lever onto the base pin, aligning the two pins on the frame. After the barrel wedge has been tapped in place, install its retaining screw.

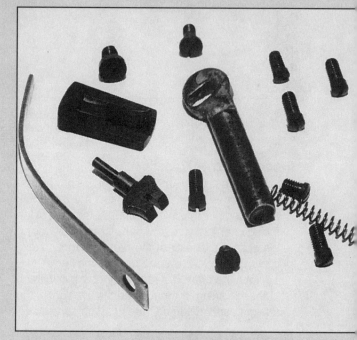

All of the unassembled parts for the kit.

Checking Cylinder Rotation

The cylinder must, of course, rotate freely for proper operation. If the cylinder is too tight, slightly back out the wedge. If cylinder is still too tight, the revolver may have to be taken to a professional smith for further attention. The

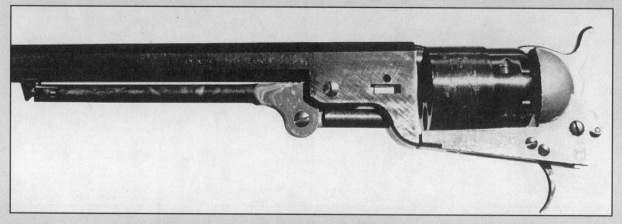

The barrel assembly with loading lever and cylinder in place.

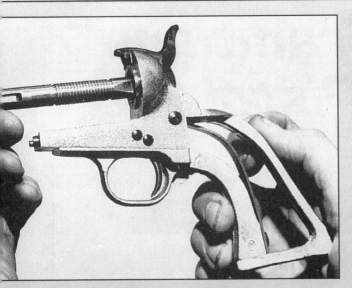

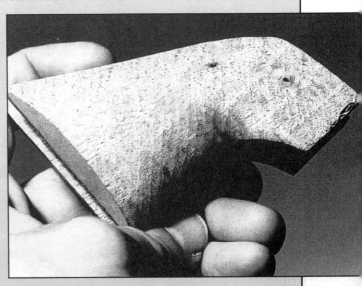

The backstrap has been fitted to the frame, and the trigger guard is in place, as well.

The wood grips are well-made to fit the backstrap and trigger guard; however, shaping and finishing is required.

smith will have the proper tools to make further adjustments so the cylinder will rotate freely, although this condition is highly unlikely.

Installing Trigger Guard and Mainspring

Using the appropriate screws, install the trigger guard into place.

Next, hook the end of the mainspring under the small wheel on the back of the hammer. Tighten this screw carefully, to avoid stripping the threads.

Checking Backstrap Fit

Inspect screw hole alignment because it may be necessary to slightly bend the backstrap to correct alignment. Place the backstrap in a strong vise with padded jaws and apply pressure by hand. With the holes aligned, fit the grips to the trigger guard and install the backstrap. Only *start* the two top frame screws and

the single screw for the trigger guard. Once all the screws have been started and aligned, then they can be tightened.

Shaping the Wood Grips

Using files, shape the wood grips to fit the brass backstrap and the trigger guard. At the same time, file away any flashings or gates from the brass backstrap. The goal of this step is to match the surfaces of the wood handles and the frame of the revolver.

Final Finishing

Finish the wood and polish the brass pieces. Both of these processes are discussed in Chapters 9 and 14, respectively.

Tip: The success of this kit depends upon careful workmanship to avoid scratching the already finished surfaces. The beginning hobbyist may wish to seek help in bending the backstrap for proper fit.

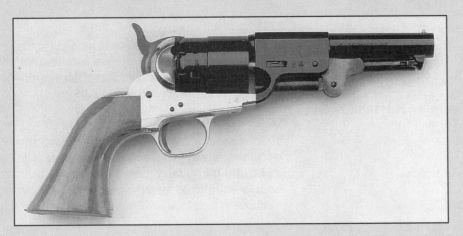

This is the Navy Arms Reb '60, fully finished.

Building Traditions' Trapper Pistol Kit

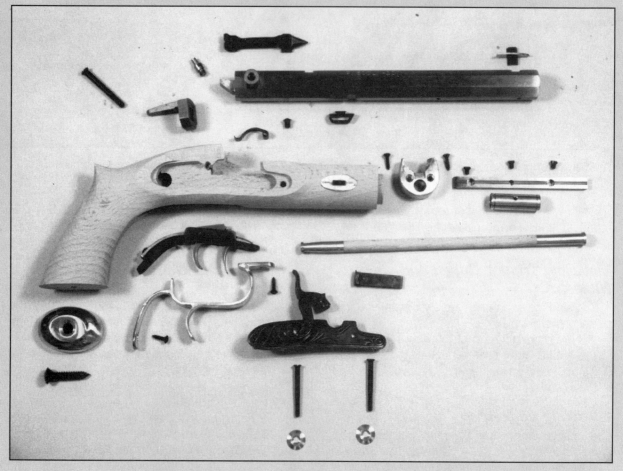

Here are all the kit parts for the Trapper Pistol.

Tools

Brass or Nylon Drift Punch
Chisel, 1/4-inch
Drift Punch, 5/32-inch
Drill Bits: 5/32-, 1/4-, 11/32-inch
Half-Round Bastard Cut File with Handle,
    6- and 10-inch
Inletting Black and Brush
Power Hand Drill
Round Bastard Cut File without Handle,
    6- or 10-inch
Rubber Mallet
Screwdrivers
Scribe, Awl or Very Small Ice Pick
Small Hammer
Square, 4-inch or 12-inch
Three-Square File (one edge ground safe)
    8- or 10-inch
Wood Gouge, 3/8-inch

Setting Up

Remove all parts and check them against the schematic drawing that comes with the kit. Make sure everthing is complete. Before starting, read all instructions included in the kit.

Fitting Metal Parts

The stock is already shaped, and the escutheons are installed. The first task is to install the barrel tang, barrel tang screw, and double-set trigger assembly into their proper mortices in the stock.

The barrel is fully assembled and ready to fit into the stock.
It is shown here supported only for visual reference.

Fitting Barrel and Lock

Next, lower the barrel into the stock and secure it with the barrel tennon. Then, place the lock in its proper mortice in the stock and secure it with the lock screw.

Fitting the Trigger Guard

Fit the trigger guard into its respective mortice and secure it with the appropriate screws. Each screw hole should be started with an ice pick or awl, so the screw threads into the wood without damaging it. Also, apply paraffin to the screw threads for easy entry.

Fitting the Sights

On the barrel, each dovetail notch for the sights must be slightly enlarged using a three-square file with one edge ground safe. File until there is a snug fit. The sights themselves are drifted into place with a brass or nylon drift punch and a hammer.

Fitting the Ramrod Thimbles and Rib

Before proceeding, file burrs from any metal parts that may have them. Then, attach the ramrod thimbles to the rib with the appropriate screws. Next, the rib is fitted to the barrel with two screws.

Fitting Nose Cap and Ramrod

Remove the barrel from the stock and fit the nose cap to the pre-inletted portion of the stock. While the barrel is out of its channel, remove the front lockplate screw and place the ramrod spring on the screw. Then, replace the barrel and try the rod for fit. If it does not fit freely, a little filing with a round file in the nose cap hole should cure the problem. Visually check for any

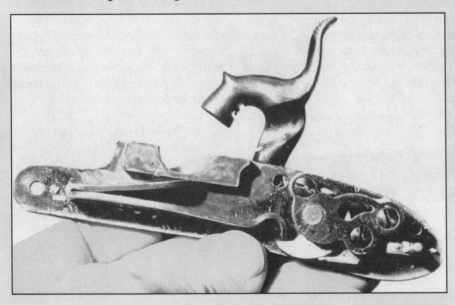

The lock from the Traditions Trapper Pistol has a sear/tumbler adjustment hidden behind the bridle. This feature is not present on all locks. Also, note that this is a percussion lock with a flint-type mainspring tumbler engagement.

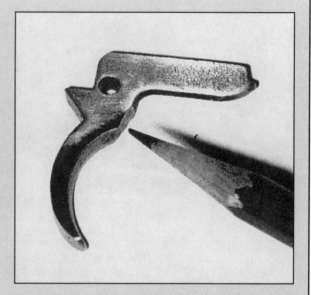

The hammer was improperly aligned with the nipple cone. The problem was corrected by cold-bending the hammer in a vise using an adjustable wrench.

Minimal filing was required to remove excess metal, increasing trigger arc.

spots where the ramrod may bind in the stock, and correct the problem with judicious filing.

Fitting the Grip Cap

This is a simple matter of placing the grip cap on the pistol grip of the stock, which is pre-inletted. Thread a wood screw through the pre-drilled hole to secure the grip cap.

Final Finishing

At this point in the project, the pistol is ready for final shaping of the stock, plus metal and wood finishing. Refer to Chapters 9 and 14 on wood and metal finishing.

Options

The recoil area, where the tang fits in the stock, may be glass-bedded, as well as the pistol grip cap, to ensure stability. Also, lock adjustment is possible with this kit; however, the reader should refer to the instruction sheet because the process is clearly defined there. If there is

ever any question concerning lock adjustments, contact a qualified gunsmith to properly adjust the lock or trigger. An improperly adjusted lock or trigger could prove dangerous.

Overall Impressions

The hammer was not formed at the correct angle in this kit. It required slight bending for perfect alignment with the nipple. To do this, the hammer was removed from the lock and secured in a vise with protected jaws. Then, the hammer was bent cold, not heated, with a crescent wrench. If the hammer required considerable bending, it would have been heated with an oxygen-acetylene torch.

Also, the rear trigger would not travel high enough to engage the sear when the trigger was in the set mode. To increase the trigger throw, a tiny bit of metal was ground off from the front of the trigger where it makes contact with the trigger plate, as shown. Once this was done, the trigger and lock functioned correctly.

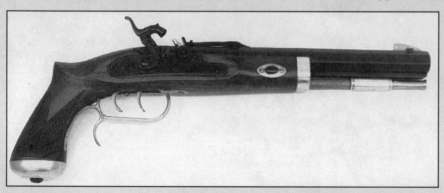

Fully assembled and finished, the Trapper Pistol is ready for action.

Building Traditions' Derringer Kit

Tools

Brass or Nylon Drift Punch
Chisel, 1/4-inch
Drift Punch, 5/32-inch
Drill Bits: 5/32-, 1/4-, 11/32-inch
Half-Round Bastard Cut File with Handle,
    6- and 10-inch
Inletting Black and Brush
Power Hand Drill
Round Bastard Cut File without Handle,
    6- and 10-inch
Rubber Mallet
Screwdrivers (including a very small
    regular one)
Scribe, Awl or Very Small Ice Pick
Small Hammer
Square, 4- or 12-inch
Three-Square File (one edge ground safe)
Wood Gouge, 3/8-inch

Setting Up

Remove all parts and check them against the schematic drawing that comes with the kit. Make sure everthing is complete. Before starting read all instructions included in the kit.

Fitting Tennon to Barrel

The tennon dovetail is precut, but requires minor enlargement with a three-square file that has one edge ground safe. Insert the file into tennon and remove metal carefully. After enlarging, the tennon is driven into the notch with a hammer and drift punch for a snug fit.

Fitting Barrel to Stock

This step requires the use of inletting black, plus a 3/8-inch gouge and 1/4-inch chisel, to provide a good fit. The barrel, with inletting black applied, is tapped into its mortice in the stock,

The barrel is fitted into the stock recess after inletting black was applied.

(Below) A 3/8-inch gouge is used to remove excess wood marked by inletting black in barrel channel.

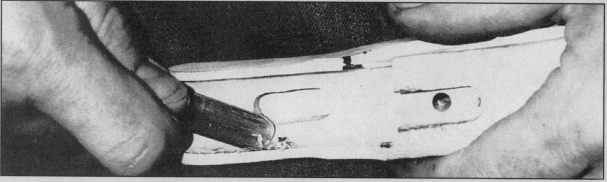

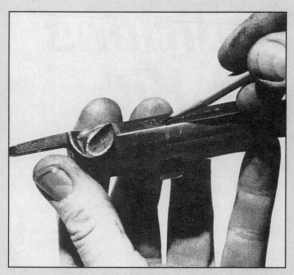

Using a pencil, the location of the barrel tennon is marked on the barrel.

Using a square, measure the location where barrel pin will be drilled in the stock and barrel tennon.

leaving black marks on the wood. Then, remove excess wood until the barrel fits.

Marking Barrel Tennon Location

On this kit, the barrel tennon and the stock were not pre-drilled for the stock pin. The precise location of the pin hole has to be marked. With a pencil, mark the tennon location on the side of the barrel. Fitting the barrel into the stock, transfer the barrel marking to the stock.

Remove the barrel and with a square, measure from the top of the barrel to the point on the tennon to be drilled for the barrel pin. Place the

barrel once again into the stock and, using the square, transfer the above measurement to the stock as accurately as possible. The point established on the stock locates the point where stock and tennon will be drilled for the barrel pin. Center-punch the hole to be drilled. Using a power hand drill and a $5/32$-inch drill bit, drill a hole through both stock and tennon. A power hand drill suffices for this step, although a drill press and drill press vise facilitates accuracy of the hole.

After the hole is drilled, the barrel pin is driven into place with a small hammer. The pin should

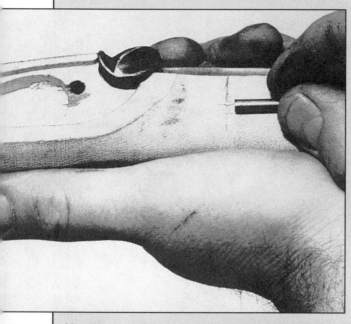

Here is where the barrel pin will be fitted after drilling.

The barrel pin hole is drilled with a power hand drill.

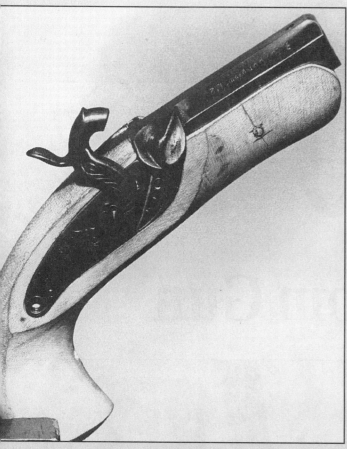

This is the Traditions Derringer with barrel pin in place and lock installed. From this point, final metal and wood finishing is required.

protrude from the side of the stock. Do not shorten the pin at this time. It will be shortened later.

Fitting Trigger Assembly to Stock

The trigger assembly is fitted to the stock, and the tang screw is inserted to hold the assembly in place. The tang screw provided with this particular sample kit was too short. There are two options to correct this problem: inlet the trigger assembly deeper into its recess or replace the screw with a longer one. The latter was chosen. A 10x32 screw, a common thread, was purchased at a hardware store. When a new screw is used, the screw head must be properly countersunk in the tang, or the screw head made to fit the existing countersink. In this instance, the former was chosen.

Fitting the Lock

The perimeter of the lock mortice was in good shape; however, the sear struck the wood on the inside, which meant deeper inletting of the lock mortice for proper functioning of the sear. A touch of inletting black on the sear showed where wood had to be removed. After that, fit the lock into the mortice and install the lock screws. At this point, cycle the lock to ensure it functions properly, with full-cock and half-cock notches engaging positively.

Fitting the Trigger Guard

With the lock properly functioning, the trigger guard is installed. Extremely minor inletting was required to fit the trigger guard in its mortice in the stock. Each screw hole was started with an awl to prevent breakage of the small screws when twisted into place.

Fitting Tennon Escutcheons

Barrel tennon escutchons are fitted to the *surface* of the stock, not inletted. They are held in place by tiny screws that are easily broken. A very small screwdriver is required to install these screws. The barrel pin, which was left long, must now be filed flush to the escutcheon face. The escustcheons will have to be removed later for stock finishing.

Fitting the Front Sight

The front sight is installed on the barrel by carefully filing the stud until it can be driven into place with a brass hammer using mild strokes. To ensure it remains in place, a bit of epoxy can be dropped in the hole before the sight is driven home.

Final Finishing

All assembly is completed at this point. The stock is ready for final shaping of wood to metal fit, as well as stock and metal finishing. The only metal part requiring finish is the barrel. Refer to Chapters 9 and 14 for appropriate wood and metal finishing instructions.

Options

This small pistol offers few options. However, the following refinements are possible. First, the barrel pin escutcheons can be inletted into the stock. Next, since the barrel comes uncrowned, the hobbyist may wish to have his local gunsmith do this to facilitate the loading process. If the pistol is not going to be fired, but used for collection or decoration, this step is superfluous. Finally, if the pistol is going to be fired often, the recoil area of the breech can be glass-bedded to ensure recoil is properly distributed to the stock.

The Custom Gun

THE APEX OF the blackpowder hobby gunsmithing world is handmaking a custom firearm, either pistol or rifle. In this section, building a rifle is addressed. There are numerous methods of rifle building. This is just one of them. Even though countless muzzleloader gun styles have existed over the past centuries, the hobbyist must decide for himself which to build. We selected a half-stock Plains rifle for this particular section. These rifles are popular and have been for a long time. The sidehammer lock was chosen for its direct ignition quality, and because this lock style is a favorite of the authors. However, the reader may select whatever lock style he prefers.

Important: Portions of other rifle building projects are included in this section to give the reader experience with various types of muzzleloaders. Generally, these different guns are included photographically so the reader can visualize specific construction directions for various types of rifles. This broadens the scope of this section and further aids the reader in dealing with a specific muzzleloader he may wish to build.

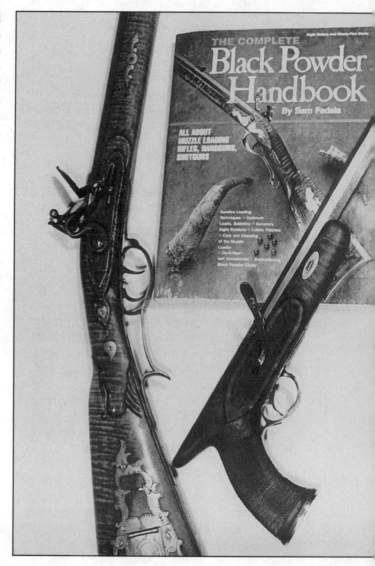

Two examples of the gunmaker's art, both built by Dale Storey of DGS, Inc., Casper, Wyoming.

Building a Custom Rifle

Tools

Ballpeen Hammer
Bench Disk Sander (optional)
Bench Vise
Block Wood Planes, Large and Small
Cabinetmaker's Rasp
Calipers
Carpenter's Square
C-Clamps, 6-inch
Center Punch
Chisels: $1/8$-, $1/4$-, $1/2$-inch, plus 2-inch Butt
    Chisel
Drift Punch set
Drill Bits, Fraction Set
Drill Press
Drill Press Vise
File Handles
Gouges: $1/4$- and $3/8$-inch
Hacksaw and Extra Blades
Half-Round Bastard Cut File, 10-inch
Hand Drill, Manual or Electric
Inletting Black and Brush
Metal Scribe
Needle-Nose Pliers
Oxygen-Acetylene Torch
Plastic or Rubber Mallet
Round Bastard Cut File, 10-inch
Sanding Block
Screwdriver Set (Brownells Master Mag)
Sharpening Stones
Smooth Mill File, 10-inch
Taps and Dies, 10x32, 8x32 and $1/4$x28
Three-Square File, 8-inch
Try Square, 12-inch
Wood Brace

Supplies

Abrasive Cloth, 80- and 120-grit
Eraser
Garnet Paper, 80-, 120- and 320-grit
Glass Bedding Kit
Gun Oil
Layout Blue (Dykem)
Linseed Oil
Metal Straightedge, 12- and 36-inch
Soft Lead Pencil
Soft Solder
Soft Solder Flux
Turpentine
Wet/Dry Sandpaper, 230- and 400-grit
White Paper, 60 inches x 18 inches

Dale Storey exhibits a custom rifle built by hand. This particular rifle is a fullstock model. The gunmaker has a multitude of options in building his own custom muzzleloader.

Parts Needed

Barrel, good quality with proper rate of twist
Flint Breech Plug with Tang
Nipple, $5/16$-inch shank
Barrel Tennons (2)
Rib
Ramrod Guides (2)
Forearm Cap
Barrel Pins, $1/8$-inch (2)
Front Sight
Rear Sight
Tang Screw, wood type
Front-Action Sidehammer Lock
Lock Screw
Lock Screw Escutcheon
Single Trigger with Trigger Plate
Trigger Guard
Buttplate
Ramrod with Tip
Plank of Wood
Assortment of Brass or Steel Wood Screws
Toe Plate

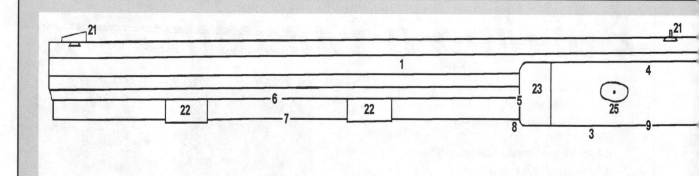

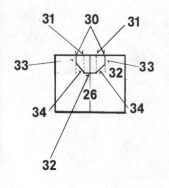

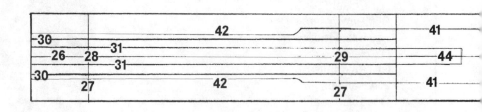

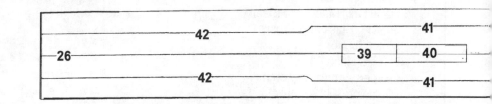

Drawing the Custom Rifle

All parts are gathered for the job. The tools are readied. Now, it's time to draw a plan of the custom rifle. At the same time, assemble the lock because it is actually placed upon the drawing to locate the sear.

Note: The drawing is divided into four parts: top, middle, middle-left and lower. The top drawing represents a layout of the left-hand side of the rifle, with cheekpiece. The middle drawing is a layout of the top of the stock blank before any inletting or shaping is done, and the middle-left drawing shows the layout of the barrel channel from the front before inletting of the barrel. The lower drawing shows the bottom of the stock blank before shaping. The trigger plate mortice and trigger guard mortice are indicated on the lower drawing.

Starting at the left side of the paper, sketch in the barrel (noted as 1) in exact dimension. Draw lines to indicate the barrel flats. Take the measurements from the barrel and transfer these to the drawing. The muzzle appears on the left-hand side of the paper; the breech on the right.

Draw a dotted line (2) from the top of the barrel, breech end, to the right edge of the paper. This line is a reference for the stock's drop and will be erased later when the sketch is finished.

Decide on the length of the forearm (3). This should be about 13 to 14 inches, depending upon barrel length. For a 30-inch barrel, 13½ inches is about right. The length of the forearm on the drawing is 13 inches.

Establish where the forearm will meet the side of the barrel and draw a line (4) from the middle of the barrel flat back to the breech, gracefully angling the line upward until it meets the breech.

Take a measurement of the thickness of the rib. Draw a straight line (5) down at a right angle from the very end of the forearm. This is called a layout line.

Measure the depth of the rib and draw it on the barrel back to the layout line. This line (6) forms the rib in the drawing.

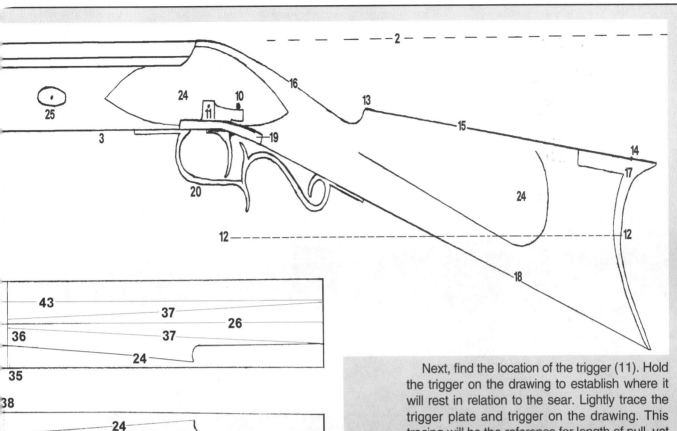

Take the diameter of the ramrod, which in our case is $^7/_{16}$-inch, and add this to the bottom of the drawn rib. Now, sketch the ramrod onto the paper (7). *Important:* If the ramrod guides are going to rest on top of the rib, as some do, the small gap between the ramrod itself and the rib must be taken into consideration. If the ramrod lies against the rib, there will, of course, be no gap. In the sample rifle, the ramrod rests flat against the rib.

Then, add $^1/_8$-inch below the ramrod. This establishes the total depth (8) of the forearm.

Continue the bottommost line (9) on the drawing, which forms the lower line of the forearm. Continue the line back toward the breech to represent the entire forearm. *For now, stop this line at the breech.*

Take the lock and place it upon the drawing as close to its final correct position on the finished rifle as possible. Figure where the sear will rest (that portion of the sear engaged by the trigger). Make a prominent dot on the drawing (10) to note the location of the sear.

Next, find the location of the trigger (11). Hold the trigger on the drawing to establish where it will rest in relation to the sear. Lightly trace the trigger plate and trigger on the drawing. This tracing will be the reference for length of pull, yet to be established.

From the trigger, measure rearward toward the buttplate to establish length of trigger pull. The length of pull on the sample rifle is 14 inches, so draw a dotted line (12) on the paper starting with the trigger and going to the right.

From the breech end of the barrel, measure 6 inches rearward and $1^1/_2$ inches down. Make a reference mark (13) to note the point of the comb.

Using dotted line 2 as a reference, measure downward to a depth of $2^1/_2$ inches and make a dot (14), as noted on the drawing. This establishes drop at the buttstock, $2^1/_2$ inches from the top of the barrel.

Connect dot 14 to dot 13. This line (15) is the top of the comb.

Lightly sketch in what will be the top of the wrist (16). This line is drawn free-hand from the top of the breech down to the point of the comb.

Lay the buttplate (17) at the end of the line (12) that establishes the length of pull. Trace around the buttplate to give an idea of how it will fit onto the buttstock.

With a straightedge, draw the line (18), that forms the toe line of the stock.

Hold the trigger plate (19) on the drawing and see how it fits the lines of the schematic. A little bit of erasing and redrawing may be necessary.

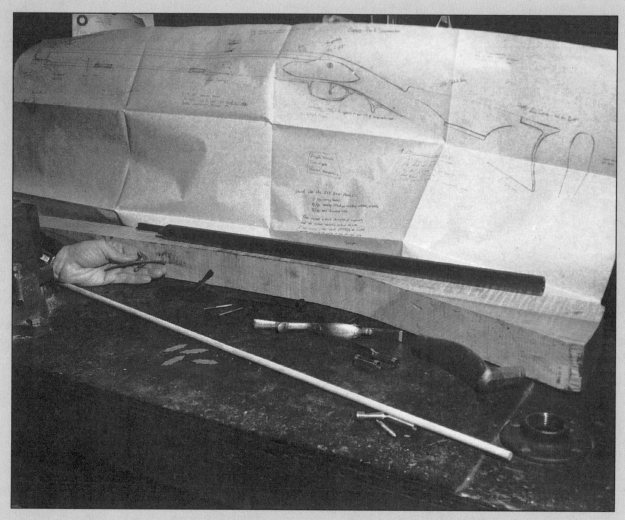

The schematic, with all parts laid out.

The idea is to establish clean lines that form the future rifle.

Place the trigger guard (20) on the schematic and sketch it in.

Figure the location of the front and rear sights (21) and draw them in place. This is a simple sketch to show where they will fit on the barrel.

Draw the ramrod guides (22) in place on the schematic. Then, draw in the prospective nose cap (23) at this point. Next, draw the cheekpiece and offside lock panel (24). Finally, draw the barrel tennon pin locations, as well as inlays (25).

Use an eraser to remove location dots and the dotted line that represented the reference point for the top line of the stock. In short, clean up the drawing to look like a rifle.

Note: This is a standard layout for iron sights. Some of these dimensions can be altered to suit the individual. Dimensions may also be altered for scope sight use, whereby there will be less drop in the stock. Also, specific lines will vary depending upon actual dimensions of the parts used to build the muzzleloader. From this point, the drawing is used only as a reference. All marks are actually made on the stock blank. Remember that the drawing is the road map. Place it where it can be seen clearly as you work. *Important:* The right-hand side of the rifle need not be drawn. It serves no purpose unless a patch box is used, and one was not used on the sample rifle.

Fitting the Breech Plug

At this time, the breech plug is fitted to the barrel. Refer to Chapter 16 on barrels for instructions as to how this is done.

Draw-Filing the Barrel and Rib

The draw-filing of a barrel is covered in Chapter 14 under the heading of "Octagon Barrel Polishing." The task, generally speaking,

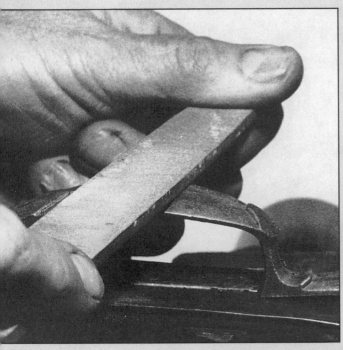

Pre-layout work includes cleaning up castings, such as filing this trigger guard.

A maple plank is squared up with a block plane.

is to bring the barrel to final dimensions by filing the flats. The rib can also be draw-filed at this point. This removes machining marks, making the final metal finish better.

Rough-Filing the Metal Parts

If any parts are sand castings, clean them up by filing off flashings, gates and overall roughness. This is not final finishing. File enough, however, to make a smooth surface on all appropriate parts.

Truing the Plank

Now, the plank must be trued-up. The plank arrives, normally, in a planed condition on both sides. Using a try square and block plane, the object is to make the top of the plank square to its right-hand side. This is an important step because the entire layout of the plank is based upon its original trueness, including the establishment of the centerline. If the plank is crooked at the start, it's likely to result in an improperly dimensioned stock.

The left-hand side of the plank can also be trued. It is not a necessity, but neither is this a useless step because the left surface will serve for stock layout.

Note: Reverse these procedures for a left-hand stock. True the top to the left-hand side of the plank first, then true the right-hand side.

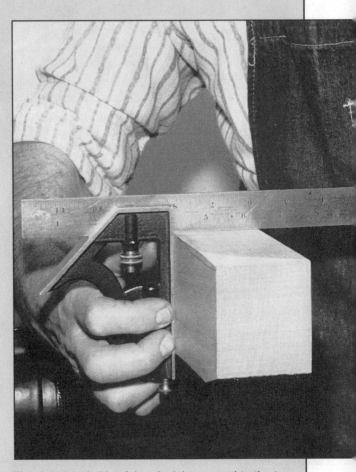

The right-hand side of the plank is squared to the top with a try square.

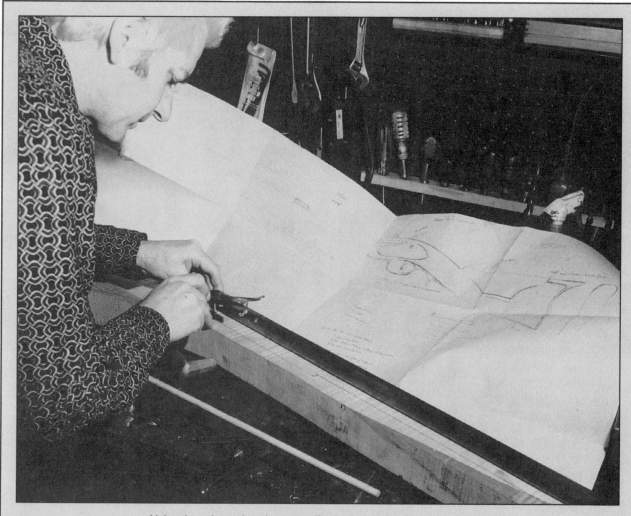

Using the schematic to lay out a rifle. In the photo, the custom rifle is a fullstock. However, the process is exactly the same for a halfstock. Specifically, the location of the trigger assembly is established here.

A try square is used to lay out the bottom line of the forearm.

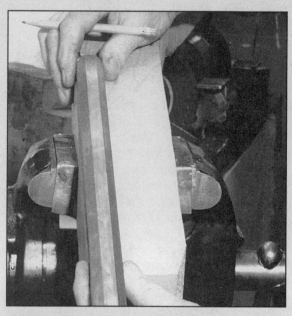

Using the barrel of the rifle as a guide to start layout.

Transferring Pattern to Plank

Place the barrel directly upon the wood plank. Here is where the drawing pays off. Now follow, step by step, the layout you did on the drawing, only this time the parts will be indicated on the plank in their proper position. Using a pencil and try square, draw the lines of the barrel and other parts onto the plank. Remember, the top of the plank serves as a reference point for the entire gun.

Important. Some planks are straight across the entire length of the top; others may slope downward toward the rear of the stock. To work with the latter, a carpenter's square is used to establish the point of the comb, as well as drop at the point of the comb and the top of the buttstock.

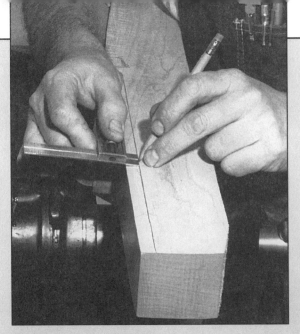

The top of the forearm is established on the blank using a small try square.

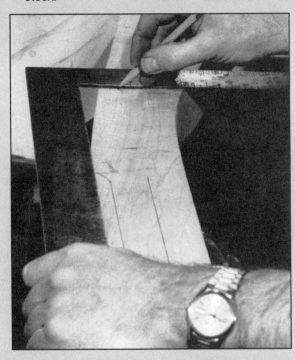

The point of the comb is laid out using a carpenter's square.

The trigger assembly is marked on the blank.

The stock is completely laid out on the blank with black pencil lines.

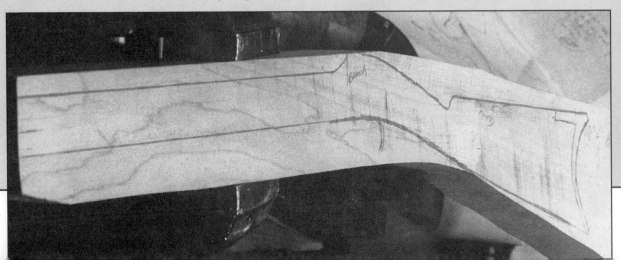

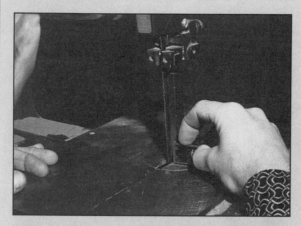

Check the band saw blade to ensure the table is at a right angle to the blade before cutting begins.

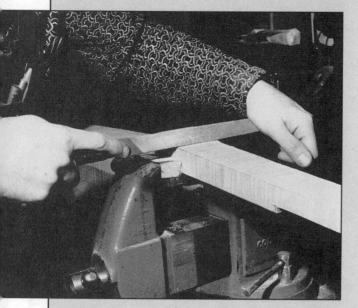

The stock blank is squared using a half-round bastard cut file.

The top of the comb is trued with power disk sander.

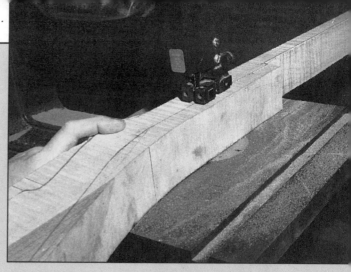

Using a bandsaw, the plank is cut into a stock blank.

Cutting the Plank

Cut out the plank on a bandsaw, being certain that the blade and the table are at a right angle for true lines. A skip-tooth blade makes sawing easier and quicker. First, cut from the top of the plank to the top line of the forearm. Then, cut the top of the barrel channel. Next, cut down from the top of the plank to the point of the comb. The top of the pistol grip is cut, followed by the top of the point of the comb to the buttstock. Then, shape the top line of the buttstock. Finally, cut the toe line from the tip of the forearm to the toe of the buttstock.

Do *not* cut out the profile of the buttplate at this time. Instead, leave a little extra wood, which will also leave a bit of extra length, on the butt to allow later adjustment for length of pull when fitting the buttplate.

Truing Saw Lines

Progressively using a wood rasp, a half-round bastard cut file and a smooth mill file,

Using a small try square and pencil, draw the centerline of the blank.

reduce wood down to the layout lines. A power disk sander can be used to sand those lines it can reach. Be certain the table of the sander and the sanding disk are at a right angle to maintain true lines.

Establishing the Centerline

Using a 12-inch try square and hard lead pencil, at least a 4H, establish a centerline all the way around the plank. Be sure this line is accurate. Use the right-hand side of the stock to establish all measurements. *This centerline is the reference point for the remainder of the project.* Make a notation of the distance in inches of the centerline from the right-hand side of the plank so, if part of the line is lost at any time, it can be accurately redrawn. For example, if the plank is 2½ inches wide, the centerline will be at 1¼ inches. This line (26) is used to align barrel, trigger plate, trigger guard, buttplate, toe plate, and for stock shaping, indicated on the lower drawing.

Establishing Barrel Channel Parameters

Refer to the middle drawing on the schematic for reference to the following:

The width of the barrel for this project is 1-inch across the flats. Looking down on the stock blank, with the forearm facing left, there is a centerline (26) that runs directly down the stock. Now draw two lines at right angles to the centerline. The first line (27) is 2 inches back from the tip of the forearm, and the second (27) is 2 inches in front of the breech end of the barrel. These two lines should intersect the centerline, making two crosses (28 and 29).

Using a pair of sharp dividers set at ½-inch, place one leg of the divider at one cross (28) and make a dot by pressing the other point into the wood on the cross-line (27). Do this again for the other side. The result is two marks, each ½-inch from the centerline. Do the same for the other cross (29). Now, drawing parallel to the centerline, connect the marks pressed into the wood. You have now established the outside parameters of the barrel channel width (30).

Locating the Bottom Flat of the Barrel Channel

Now, measure the width of the flat on the barrel that you are using for your custom rifle. For example, assume the width of a single flat on your sample barrel to be 7/16-inch. Then, divide 7/16 in half, which is 7/32-inch. Set the

divider at this measurement and repeat the previous step, placing the leg of the divider at the line intersection (27) and making two marks on either side of the lines (28 and 29). Using these marks as reference points, draw lines the length of the stock establishing the bottom flat of the barrel channel (31).

Laying Out the Barrel Channel

For this step, we are trying to establish the depth of the barrel channel. The barrel will be inletted into the stock to a depth one-half the thickness of the barrel. Since, this is a 1-inch barrel, measure down from the centerline of the blank ½-inch using a try square. Working at the forearm of the blank, and looking directly into the end of it, draw a horizontal line (32) parallel to the top of the blank. This line, which cuts directly across the forearm portion, represents how deep the barrel channel will be.

Next, set the try square at the top of the stock where lines 31 end. Scribe two lines downward to line 32. These two lines now establish the width of the bottom flat of the barrel channel.

Remember, the barrel is inletted half-way into the stock, which means the side flat of the barrel is inletted into the stock one-half the width of that flat, which is 7/32-inch. These two lines (33) mark where the side flats of the barrel are inletted in the barrel channel.

At this point, two barrel flats inside the mortice are not accounted for. Connect the end of Lines 33 with ends of Lines 32 on each side, forming the two lower, angled barrel flats (34).

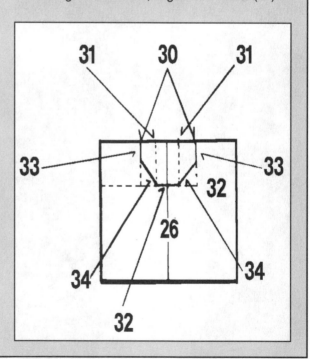

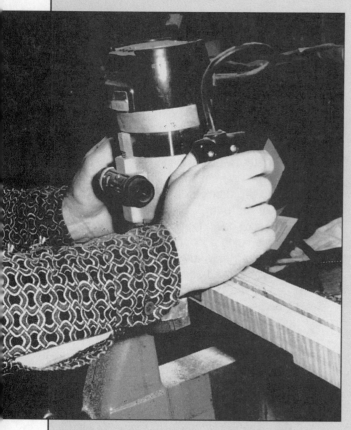

Using a router to begin barrel channel inletting.

A good job of inletting for the barrel channel and tang.

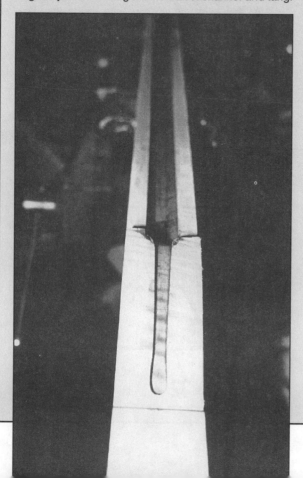

The barrel channel is inlet by hand with a chisel.

Inletting the Barrel

The outside parameters of the barrel have now been defined in the stock. The builder now knows exactly where the barrel channel mortice lies in the stock blank, so the barrel can be inletted into the stock. There are two ways to remove wood: A router can be used to perform a great deal of the labor, or the entire operation can be accomplished by hand.

Router: Using the router, remove wood from the bottom flat area to the proper width and depth as drawn on the stock blank. Stay slightly inside of the layout lines to avoid over-inletting—final fit is done by hand. The router base will butt against the breech end contour of the stock. From this point back, the bottom flat must be inletted by hand. Next, rout the two side flats into the barrel channel. At this point, the mortice has a stair-step shape, since it has three relatively square cuts. From here on, the barrel mortice is finished by hand. The stair-step section will be shaped by hand with a $1/4$-inch chisel to match the contour of the barrel flats.

Hand Inletting: Using chisels, cut the bottom flat first, as the router did previously. A try square set at $1/2$-inch (since the 1-inch barrel is inletted half-way into the stock) is used to check the depth of the channel. Then, chisel the side flats into the stock using the layout lines as guides. Stay slightly inside of the lines for initial "hogging out" of wood. Remember, use the try square continually to check for proper inletting depth. The stair-step is again removed by hand to match the slanted contour of the barrel.

From this point forward, whether a router was used or not, the remainder of the work is accomplished by hand.

Using inletting black with a brush, plus a rubber or plastic mallet and chisels, the barrel channel is finished. Apply inletting black to the part of the barrel that fits into the stock mortice. With a mallet, tap the barrel into the mortice to transfer the inletting black to the channel. Remove the barrel from the stock, and dark lines will indicate where wood must be removed. Repeat this process until the inletting black shows all parts of the barrel are in contact with the channel. *Note*: The barrel tang, at this point, is left straight and unbent until the barrel mortice has reached full depth in the blank.

Bending the Tang

Using a vise with padded jaws, close the jaws until they are slightly wider than the thickness of the tang. Slip the tang between the jaws of the vise and pull the barrel toward you, bending the tang very slightly downward. Check the contours of the tang. Working slowly, bend again and again, until the tang contour matches that of the stock. Then, apply inletting black to the tang and rap it into the tang mortice with a mallet to mark the stock, showing where wood must be removed. Continue this process until the tang is fully inletted into the stock. *Note*: Do not remove too much wood which will create a gap. Work slowly and carefully here. If the tang ends up slightly above the level of the wood, it can be filed to match the surface of the stock for a perfect fit.

Glass-Bedding

As an option, the barrel channel and tang can be glass-bedded. Follow the instructions from the glass-bedding kit to the letter. Also, take note of Chapter 22 pertaining to glass-bedding.

C-clamps are used to hold the barrel when glass-bedding into the barrel channel.

Apply layout blue to the barrel to establish the location of the barrel tennon dovetail.

The depth of the barrel tennon dovetail is measured with a try square.

Figure the dovetail depth on the barrel using a try square.

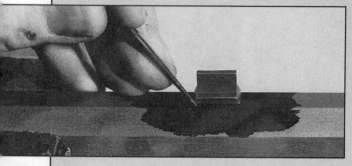

Mark the top of the dovetail on the barrel using a scribe—one end only.

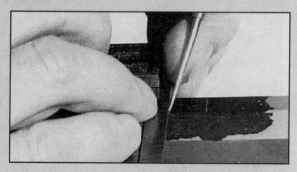

Scribing layout lines for the top of the dovetail. These lines show where to remove metal for the dovetail.

Installing Barrel Tennons

A decision is made to use wedges or pins at this point. For this project, $1/8$-inch pins were selected, as they are simplest to install, while at the same time offering adequate holding power. The barrel tennon used here is the dovetailed type. Refer to the schematic for the location of the barrel pins. There are two ways to install the dovetailed tennons: A milling machine may be used or it can be done by hand.

Milling Machine: Measure the dovetail depth of the tennon. This is the base section of the tennon that will enter the female notch in the barrel. Now with a dovetail cutter in the milling machine, cut the notch into the barrel.

Minor final hand fitting may be required for a perfect fit.

Hand Fitting: Apply Dykem (layout blue) to the top flat of the barrel and each flat on either side, where the dovetail notch will be cut into the barrel. Then, measure the depth of the notch to be cut into the barrel using the try square. Mark the cutting depth by resting the try square on the barrel flat and pulling the square along the flat, which scratches a mark into the Dykem (blue area). Do this for both sides of the barrel. Placing the tennon on the flat of the barrel for further measurement, make two marks where the top of the dovetail will meet the barrel.

Now, both the depth and length of the tennon

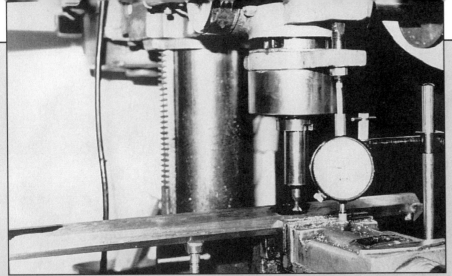

A mill is used to cut the dove-tail notch.

Keep all scarfing cuts made with a hacksaw inside of the layout lines.

Using the blade of the hacksaw to remove scarfing cuts. This removes metal quickly.

A three-square file with one edge ground safe is used for cleaning up the barrel tennon dovetail.

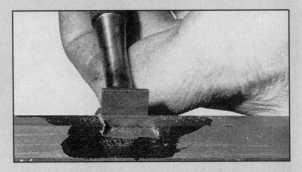

Using a drift punch to drive the barrel tennon into the dovetail.

are established. Using a hacksaw with a sharp blade, cut downward, nearly to the marked line, with several cuts. Then, turn the hacksaw sideways to make perpendicular cuts in the barrel, sawing out as much material as possible. Next, using a three-square file, with one edge ground safe (smooth), remove material from the dovetail. The edge of the file cuts corners for the dovetail notch.

Fit both tennons in place. This should be a snug fit, but not one demanding hammering. Then, shorten the tennons to match the rib height (1/4-inch). Finally, inlet the tennons into the stock. A Dremel tool may be used; otherwise, hand chiseling is necessary.

A Dremel tool with a small carbide bit is used to inlet the barrel tennon into the stock blank. The Dremel tool makes narrow inletting easier.

The pencil mark drawn on the barrel will be transferred to the stock.

The pencil mark drawn on the barrel is then transferred to the top of the stock.

Drilling Barrel Pin Holes

Using a soft lead pencil, mark the center of the tennons on the side of the barrel as illustrated. Then, place the barrel back into its mortice and transfer the line onto the stock blank, showing where the tennon will rest in the wood. Securely clamp the barrel in the stock with a C-clamp of the proper size. Set the try square at $1^1/_{16}$-inches, which is the distance from the top of the barrel to the center of the barrel pin hole, and mark the drilling site.

Using a drill press with $1/_8$-inch bit, drill the barrel pin hole. This can be done with a power hand drill; however, it is more difficult to drill straight. A drill press is more accurate.

Pins, which can be made from any steel rod of the proper size, including welding rod, are now ready to install. The pins will be a little long at this time, but will be shortened later to fit.

Fitting the Lock

The next step is to figure the position of the nipple. With a sidehammer, the nipple is drilled and tapped directly into the barrel. Since the

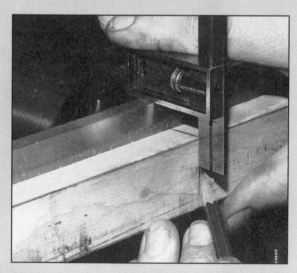

This illustrates the precise location where the barrel pin hole will be drilled. Measuring with a try square on top of the barrel flat gives the precise location.

The barrel pin hole is drilled using a drill press with a $1/_8$-inch bit. A C-clamp firmly holds the barrel in the stock mortice while drilling.

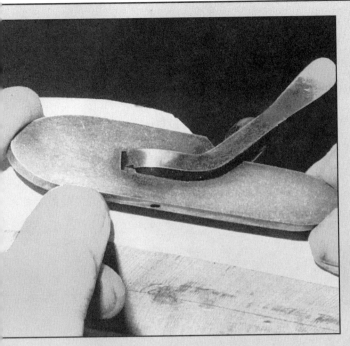

Locating the lock on the stock.

Tap the lock with a rubber mallet to transfer the inletting black to the stock, showing where wood must be removed to create the lock mortice.

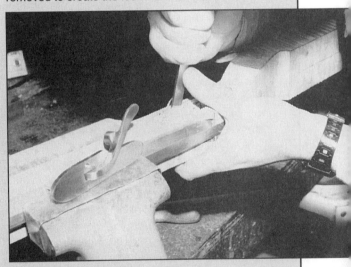

Black indicator marks left by inletting black are removed.

barrel has been inletted to one-half of its depth into the stock mortice, the nipple will be located in the center of the barrel, right in front of the breech plug. Assume the use of a $5/8$x18 breech plug. Now measure $5/8$-inch forward of the breech plug, plus $3/16$-inch, and mark a line on the stock.

Strip the lock of all parts, with the exception of the hammer, and place it on the stock, with the hammer nose resting where the nipple will be installed.

You can now see where the lock must be inletted into the stock. Use inletting black with a brush and coat the lock. Place the lock back on the stock at the proper location and tap it with a rubber mallet to transfer black to the wood. The marks are guides for inletting. Inlet the lockplate and hammer to the correct depth, within $1/4$-inch of the side flat of the barrel. As lock depth continues to fall below the level of the stock, the excess wood above the lockplate must be removed.

After the lock is completely inletted to the correct depth, it is reassembled with all its parts. Locate that point where the sear will be inletted into the stock. Its position is obvious by visual inspection, since the sear protrudes and is readily seen. Using a $3/8$-inch bit, drill a hole down to the center of the stock, plus $1/4$-inch more. This hole accommodates the sear.

Blacken the internal protruding parts of the assembled lock and, using inletting procedures

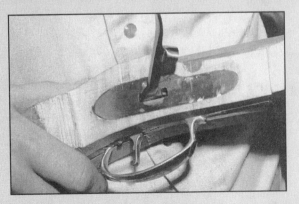

With the lock and trigger completely fitted, it is important to check the proper function of both.

A ¼-inch diameter hole is drilled into the bottom of stock to expose the sear mortice.

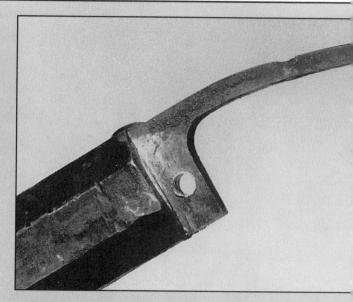

A hole had to be drilled through the web of the breech plug in order to accommodate a lock screw.

described earlier, inlet the lock entirely into the stock.

On the bottom of the blank, find the internal location of the sear. Use the knowledge you gained in building kits as a guide here. With a ¼-inch bit, drill into the stock until you strike the sear cavity. The function of this hole is to allow manual tripping of the sear with a drift punch or small screwdriver, and not the trigger, which is not yet installed. Remember, the lock is removed from the stock before this drilling.

Now, replace lock into its mortice and try to cock the hammer. If the hammer will not cock, this is an obvious indication that more wood must be removed to free the motion of the hammer. This step is a matter of careful use of inletting black, with minimal removal of wood, repeating the process until the hammer will cock. Once the hammer works freely, the lock can be tripped using a small screwdriver or drift punch.

Next, find the location of the lock screw, which holds the lock in place. In order to do this, look over the lockplate to see where the screw can be positioned. Remember, we do not want the screw to strike any part of the lock that will impair function. Once this location is established visually, the correct point must be transferred to the outside of the lockplate. *Note*: In some instances, the hole for the lock screw may fall at the location of the back, or web, of the breech plug. This is a common practice and should not alarm the builder. If this is the case, a drill press should be used to make the hole through the breech plug web.

This hole should not make contact with any portion of the plug that is threaded into the barrel. With the lockplate returned to its mortice, center-punch the lock screw hole location. A 10x32 screw is used, so the hole is drilled with a No. 21 bit. Place the stock on the drill press table and drill a hole all the way through the lockplate, stock and breech plug end (web), if necessary. Drill slowly, especially if the breech plug web must be drilled. After the hole is drilled, thread the lockplate with a 10x32 tap. Make the threads by hand and do not use power on the drill press. Remove the lock from the stock and set it aside. Use a No. 8 bit to enlarge the lock screw hole *in the stock*, allowing clearance and preventing binding of the lock screw.

Next, replace the lock and lock screw. Test the lock for function—it should work smoothly at this point.

Note: If two lock screws are used, as is the case with certain locks, be sure to use a smaller front lock screw. This screw must go between barrel and ramrod, avoiding contact.

Remember, no two custom rifles are exactly the same. Therefore, the builder must use his knowledge and ingenuity with regard to different locks and rifle styles.

Fitting the Trigger

Sear location was established earlier, as seen through the guide hole in the bottom of the stock. A single trigger was selected for this specific rifle. The extended portion of the trigger (the bar) must make contact with the sear for best

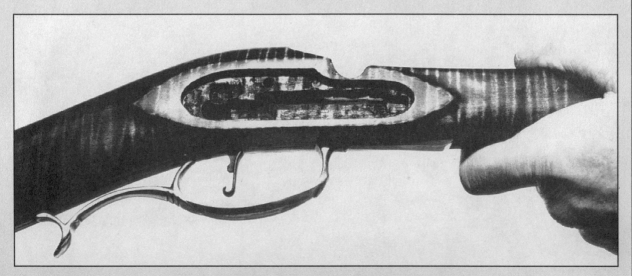

This completed lock mortice on a finished stock clearly illustrates the value of careful work in this area. The lock will rest in its mortice with excellent wood to metal fit.

leverage. Hold the trigger in position to visually determine correct placement. Then, remove the trigger from the trigger plate by driving out the pin. Now, inlet the trigger plate into the stock, aligning it so the rear of the trigger bar makes contact with the sear.

As always, use inletting black and the procedure normally followed to inlet any part. Keep chisels sharp for faster, cleaner inletting.

The trigger plate is inletted. Then, remove the plate from its mortice and reinstall the trigger. Inlet the trigger bar at this time. If the trigger bar is too high, it can be filed down to proper height. Every firearm is different.

Securing the Trigger Plate

There are two different ways this can be done. Before undertaking either option, remove the trigger from the plate once more and temporarily secure the plate to the stock with a C-clamp.

Option One: The trigger plate can be secured with a screw from the tang through the stock and threaded into the plate. To do this, find where the screw must go through the tang to reach the trigger plate, transfer this point to the trigger plate itself, and mark it with a center punch. Place the stock in a drill press vise and align the hole. With a No. 21 bit, start drilling the

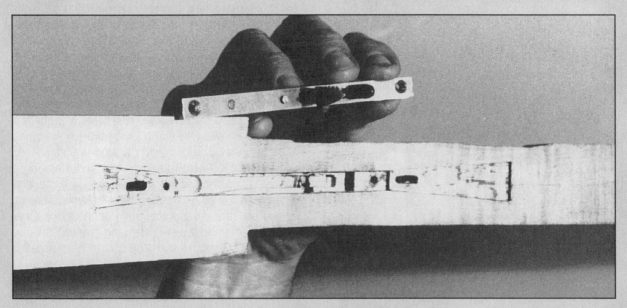

The trigger guard is inletted. The trigger plate, in hand, will fit neatly into its mortice.

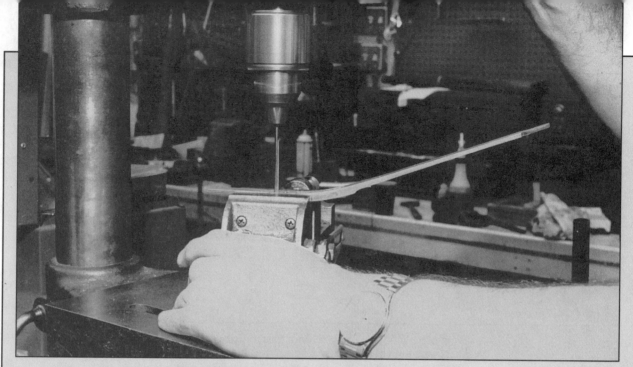

Using a drill press and a No. 21 bit, the trigger plate is drilled for a tang screw.

hole for the screw, down from the top of the stock (tang area). Stop when you are halfway through the stock. Now, turn the stock over and align the stock and bit. Drill from the mark on the trigger plate back toward the tang, until the two holes meet. Do not drill the hole all the way through from the top, because the hole may end up off the mark on the trigger plate.

Remove the trigger plate from its mortice and drill down from the top of the tang with a No. 8 bit, running it through all the way so the hole is straight to accept the screw. This part of the procedure ensures screw clearance.

Replace the trigger plate into its mortice. Then, using a 10x32 tap inserted into the top of the stock, thread the trigger plate hole. Next, countersink the screw head in the tang. The rear of the trigger plate is also screwed to the stock, but this is with a small wood screw. Drill through the rear of the trigger plate, countersink the hole so the screw will rest flush, and install a wood screw. Pre-drill a pilot hole for the wood screw so it does not split the stock wood.

Option Two: This is a simplified method for installing the trigger plate. Both the front and rear of the plate are secured with wood screws, as the rear portion was secured in Option One. If this method is used, the tang requires a wood screw to secure it to the stock, because the aforementioned tang screw will not be used.

Note: Double-set triggers are fitted in the same manner as the single trigger; however, the trigger plate is longer, and two trigger bars must be aligned to properly engage the sear for function.

Hand-starting a tap in the drill press.

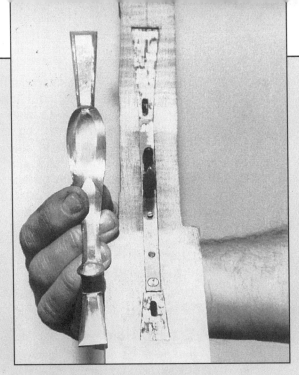

The trigger guard mortice is completely inletted with tennon holes.

Installing the Trigger Guard

Visually establish the proper location of the trigger guard on the stock. The guard must be positioned to allow space for a finger in front of the trigger, yet enough room for trigger movement rearward. Using the centerline on the stock, find the location for the trigger guard. It has two tennons rising upward that must be inletted into the stock, using the same inletting methods previously used. Different style guards require different inletting depths. Normally, the extensions of the trigger guard are inletted halfway into the stock.

The trigger guard is secured to the stock with pins that run through the tennons. The two pin holes must be carefully located using a try square, measuring from the edge of the trigger guard to a point about halfway up the tennon. Then, with a pencil, mark this location on the stock.

Since a $3/32$-inch pin is used, the hole is drilled with the same size bit. It can be hand drilled, although a drill press is preferred for accuracy. Be certain to clamp the trigger guard to the stock before drilling to guarantee a perfect fit.

The front trigger guard pin normally emerges within the lock mortice on the right-hand side of the stock. Therefore, remove the lockplate from the stock before drilling this hole.

At this time, install the trigger guard with front and rear extensions in their respective mortices in the stock blank, and secure the guard with the two $3/32$-inch pins.

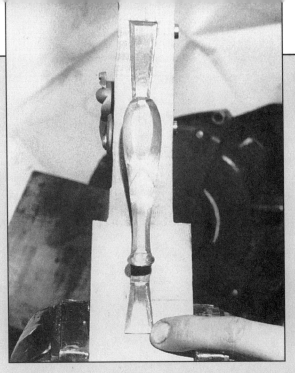

Align the trigger guard with the centerline on the stock.

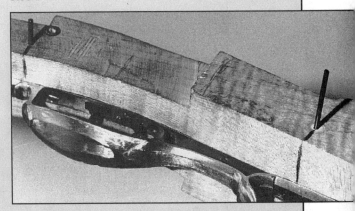

The trigger guard is held in place with pins that extend through the stock. The pins are aligned with layout lines and are driven through the stock at this time.

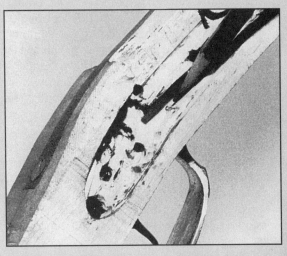

This is where the trigger guard pin is located in the lock mortice.

Trace the buttplate on the blank before cutting the wood and fitting the buttplate.

Installing the Buttplate

Remember, extra length was left on the butt during plank cutting. Now, final length of pull is established, measuring from the center of the trigger to the center of the butt. Mark the buttstock with a pencil to note the measurement. The average LOP is 13.5 inches. Depending on body shape, this may have to be adjusted longer or shorter. Your best bet is find a rifle that fits and measure its LOP. Then, hold the buttplate on the stock and scribe around its perimeter with a pencil to mark its location. The buttplate tends to wander on the stock, so do your best to hold it in place while drawing.

Next, remove the lock and barrel and, using a bandsaw, cut the buttstock off at the pencil mark just outside of the layout line, leaving adequate remaining wood for final inletting.

Using inletting black and chisels, fit the buttplate to the buttstock, using the centerline for proper location.

After inletting, secure the buttplate with two wood screws—one on the top, one near the bot-

tom. Then the screw heads are countersunk. Brass or steel screws can be used.

As an option, the buttplate can be glass-bedded in place. A thin film of glass is spread over the butt, after applying release agent to both buttplate and screws. Then the buttplate is installed and left to cure. When the buttplate is removed, the glassed-in area offers a perfect fit and moisture seal. However, glass-bedding should not be considered a substitute for good inletting work.

Fitting Rib and Ramrod Guides

The procedures used to fit the rib and ramrod guides were described in Chapter 17.

Drilling the Ramrod Hole

A special drill must be made to correctly accomplish this task, or the gunmaker will have to go to a professional shop. Since a $7/16$-inch ramrod hole will be drilled, a $7/16$-inch drill bit is required. This bit is attached to a $7/16$-inch rod of adequate length, about 42 inches to accommodate long barrels. Attachment is done by drilling a female hole into the end of the rod and, on a lathe, turn the shank of the drill bit to match the hole. Then, soft solder the bit to the end of the rod. The end result is simply a very long drill bit. Mark the bit with masking tape to show the proper drilling depth.

Important: The drill bit for this operation is specially ground using a combination of a grindstone and a Dremel tool, as shown nearby. This special shape promotes a straight hole, regardless of wood or grain structure. A standard bit tends to wander, resulting in a crooked hole.

Using a wood brace, drill 15 to 20 revolutions only, then pull the bit out, with continuous right-hand revolutions. This cleans the hole during cutting. Do not turn the bit counter-clockwise at any time. If the cleaning process is not observed, the bit can overload and go off course or it can get stuck.

If the forward trigger guard tennon protrudes into the ramrod channel, the bit will strike the tennon, which will be felt. In this case, the tennon may have to be shortened slightly for drill clearance.

Fitting the Forearm Cap

A precast nose cap was used on the project rifle, similar to the one on the popular Thompson/Center rifle. The cap must be installed on the forearm before making final layout lines. The nose cap will serve as a guideline during stock shaping of the forearm. Fit is rather obvious, as the nose cap is the end of the forearm. Furthermore, fitting the nose cap is the same on full-stock or half-stock rifles when a pre-cast cap is used.

The first step is to hold the nose cap in place on the forearm and draw a line around it with a pencil. Then, using chisels, the cap is inletted onto the forearm. Inletting black is used to determine wood removal and fit. On a half-stock rifle, the nose cap is secured with wood screws. On a full-stock gun, the cap can be secured with epoxy.

Drawing the Stock Shape on the Blank

Although all markings are made on the stock blank at this point, reference to the middle drawing of the schematic is helpful.

Guidelines are drawn on the stock blank to provide direction in shaping the stock. Using a try square, mark a line (35) perpendicular to the centerline at the point of the comb. The width of the point of comb is established with these lines.

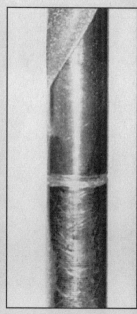

A properly ground and sharpened bit (left) for drilling the ramrod hole, as discussed in the text. This specially ground bit ensures straight drilling of this important channel, once attached to the end of a long rod (right).

Using a brace, the ramrod hole is drilled with the special bit attached to a long rod. In this particular instance, a fullstock is drilled, which requires special care in order to maintain a straight hole.

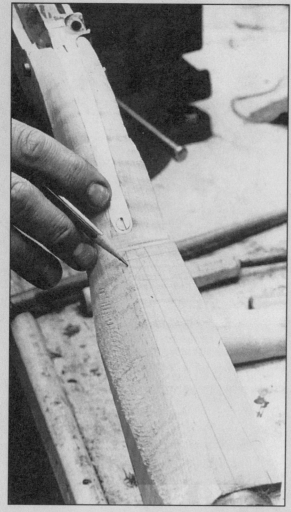

Note the layout lines on the buttstock. These lines are followed when shaping the stock.

A piece of welding rod lying alongside the barrel acts as a guide to establish the width (thickness) of forearm.

If a $1/4$-inch point of comb is desired, dividers are set on the centerline and two lines are drawn $1/8$-inch on either side, giving a $1/4$-inch point of comb (36).

Using a straightedge, draw a line (37) from the buttplate to each of the two lines just established. These two lines define the comb of the stock.

Lay the stock on the right side (for a right-handed shooter) and, using a pencil, draw in the desired cheekpiece (24). This is a freehand operation.

Turn the stock to expose its belly and draw a perpendicular line (38) to establish the width of the toe line. The width of the toe line is the same as the width of the bottom of the buttplate. Using the centerline for guidance, along with dividers, establish the width with pencil marks that end at the right-angled line.

Note: On the drawing, 39 represents the trig-ger guard mortice and 40 is the trigger plate mortice.

Now, lines of the buttstock have been established, so panel and moulding lines around the lock are drawn freehand. Then, turn the stock over and transfer the matching pattern to the off-side of the lock.

The moulding width is already established on the lock side, so the same width of wood must be noted for the offside. The thickness of the stock at this juncture is related to the bottom and top of the stock.

How thick should the forearm be? See the illustration with a section of welding rod, $1/8$-inch wide resting alongside the barrel. The welding rod is used to establish the width of the fore-stock, $1/8$-inch on each side of the barrel. Transfer this line to the bottom of the stock with a try square, since the width of the forestock will be the same on top and bottom.

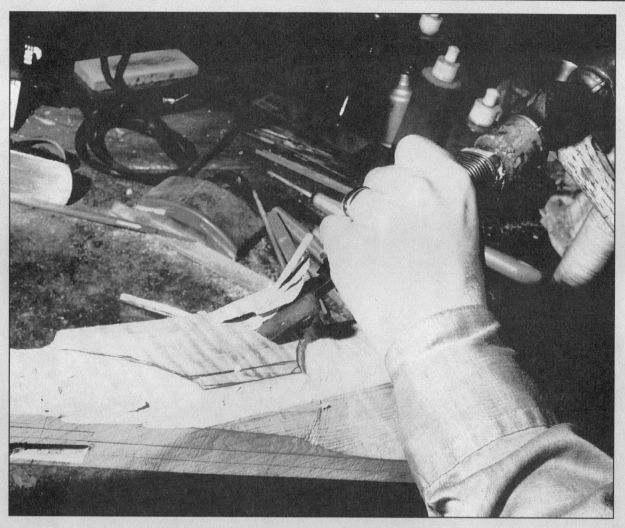

A 2-inch butt chisel with mallet can be used to remove wood quickly. This is not recommended for the beginner.

Shaping the Wood

At this point, the stock takes shape using gouges, chisels, rasps, files and sandpaper. Straightedges are used to check progress in specific locations on the stock.

Starting on the cheekpiece side of stock, using a 1/2- or 3/8-inch gouge, remove wood on the perimeter of the cheekpiece to establish its lines. Considerable wood is removed at this time, working to the layout lines and following the contour of the buttplate and toe line. As wood is removed around the perimeter of the cheekpiece, it begins to emerge, while at the same time, excess wood is removed to the level of the buttplate. The buttplate, in this instance, is a guide for final stock shape.

Work underneath the cheekpiece, as well as forward about halfway into the wrist. Heavy removal of wood, as noted above, is done with gouges. The beginner may find a rasp easier to

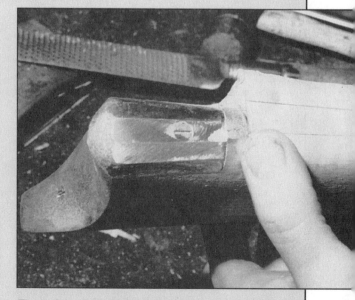

The surface of the stock is brought down to the level of the buttplate. A wood rasp is used for quick wood removal.

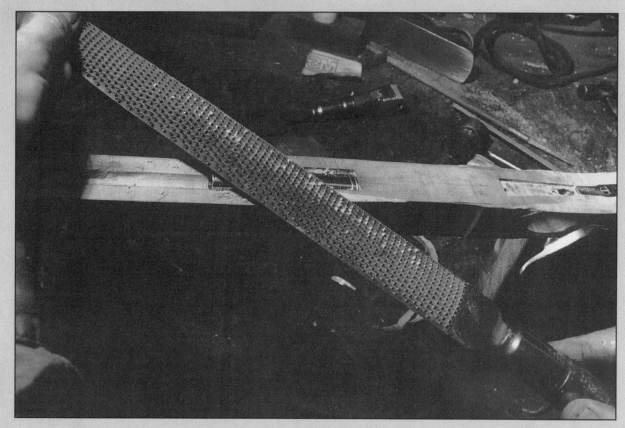

A cabinetmaker's rasp quickly removes wood from the forearm of the stock blank.

work with, since a gouge is capable of "hogging out" a lot of wood quickly. A half-round bastard cut file is substituted for the rasp as the level of the wood comes closer to the finished lines. Work around the cheekpiece in an effort to create a smooth profile. A round bastard cut file is extremely useful to create the curved lines in this region.

Final stock shaping is done with a smooth mill file, leaving a relatively smooth surface that can be final-finished with sanding. The amateur is advised to have a finished rifle on hand as a model, if possible. *Note*: Where possible, a small hand block plane is useful. The plane maintains straight lines, especially along the toe line, top of the comb, forearm, and any flat surface of the stock, even under the cheekpiece.

Tip: Use a 12-inch straightedge to check the flatness of surfaces. The straightedge will quickly reveal bumps that can be smoothed out by filing. Once the cheekpiece side of the stock is shaped, turn the stock over and shape the other side, again using the guidelines as well as the buttplate as a pattern.

After the buttstock is shaped to about mid-wrist, it is time to work forward. Remove the

trigger and guard, but not the trigger plate. The lock should be disassembled, with only the lockplate remaining in the stock. On the lock side, using a gouge, remove wood around the lock molding in the same fashion as wood was removed around the cheekpiece. Of course, not as much wood is removed in this region, so care must be taken with the gouge. Turn the stock over and repeat the process on the other side, again following guidelines for accuracy. *Note*: Although it takes only moments to read about shaping a stock, the procedure is time-consuming, requiring patience and care. Go slowly.

Continuing forward, progress is made along the forearm, once again shaping to established lines. Gouges are not used here, and shaping is best accomplished with wood rasps, files and block plane. Avoid going against the grain, especially with the plane, as this may tear out pieces of figured wood, leaving a pit in the surface of the stock.

After the forearm is shaped, move to 80-grit sandpaper for rough sanding. Using both a sanding block and small sections of sandpaper held by hand, lines and surfaces are well-main-

After removing a lot of wood, a bastard cut round file is used to shape around the cheekpiece.

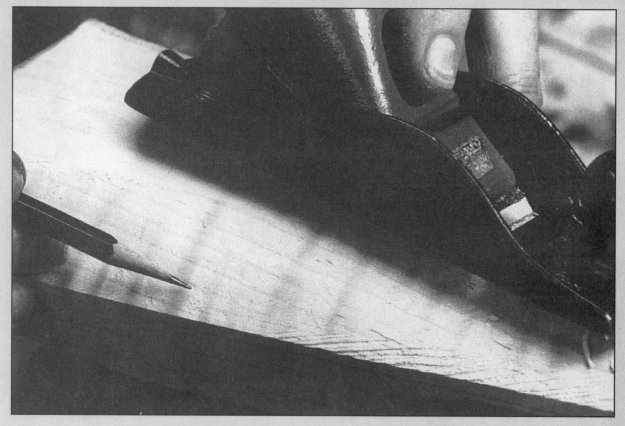

A small block plane is used to remove wood from the stock blank, keeping lines straight.

As mentioned in the text, a piece of shotgun barrel and a steel rod can be used to bend a metal inlay before inletting.

tained. The sanding block is especially important on flat surfaces, where hand-sanding may make ripples in the wood. Where the sanding block does not fit, small bits of sandpaper get into those tight places, such as the cheekpiece, wrist area, lock moldings, and so forth. When rough sanding, the builder can often feel uneven spots, or see them with a straightedge. Additional filing may be required to remove wood in these problem areas. The most difficult areas are around the cheekpiece, as well as the transition areas near lock mouldings.

Stop your work at this time. Study the stock with a careful eye. Look for any area that demands further correction. Don't forget to use your model rifle for comparison.

If stock lines look good, it's time to sand the entire stock with 120-grit sandpaper. Maintain sharp, straight lines at all times. After that, sand the entire stock again, this time with 220 paper.

Preparing the Inlay

A double-acorn pattern was used on the project rifle stock as a barrel pin inlay. Mark and drill a hole in the inlay where the barrel pin will be inserted. Then, the inlay is shaped using a homemade two-part tool: a piece of shotgun

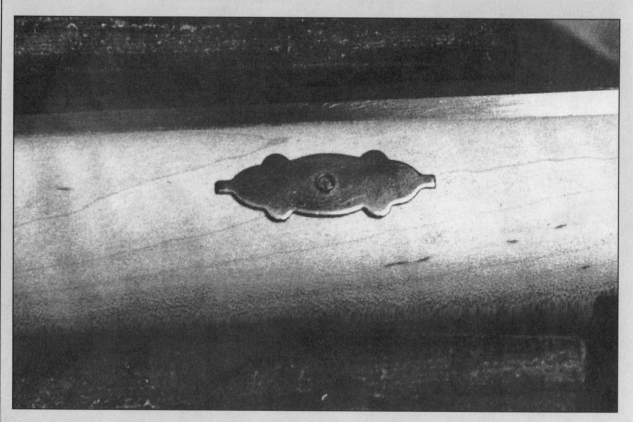

This inlay has been shaped to fit the contour of the stock. It is now ready for inletting into a mortice.

barrel cut lengthwise into a small section, coupled with a steel rod that closely fits the contour of the shotgun barrel piece. The inlay is placed inside the piece of shotgun barrel, and the steel rod is placed on top of the inlay. By gently rapping the steel rod with a hammer, the inlay begins to take on the contour of the shotgun barrel piece. Do not fully form the inlay because final contouring must take place on the stock itself, so it perfectly matches. Some surfaces will be nearly flat, others quite rounded. So bend the inlay with needle-nose pliers to match the stock's contour. Carefully mark each inlay with a scribe to denote location and direction on the stock, such as RR with an arrow (right, rear, arrow pointing direction of muzzle). Once inletted into the wood, the inlay will fit no other place.

Next, push the stock pin out beyond the surface of the stock until it protrudes by 1/8-inch. Check the inlay hole against the pin. If the pin does not pass through, enlarge this hole with a small jeweler's file.

Forming the Inlay Mortice

The mortice outline for the inlay is formed by coating the back of the inlay with inletting black, placing the inlay back on the barrel pin, firmly

The impressions left by inletting black clearly show up on stock wood.

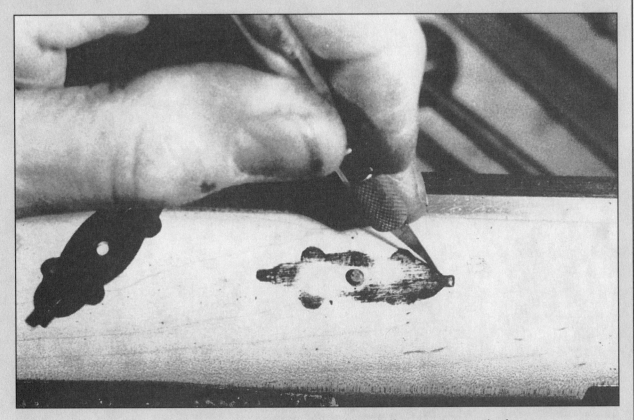

Initial cuts are made with a sharp-pointed X-Acto knife to create a mortice for the inlay.

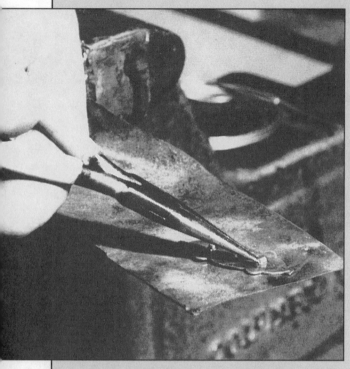

Small pieces of solder are placed on the underside of the inlay with a pair of needle-nose pliers.

Small brass wood screws are soldered to the back of an inlay.

The inlay is fully inletted and shaped to the contour of the stock.

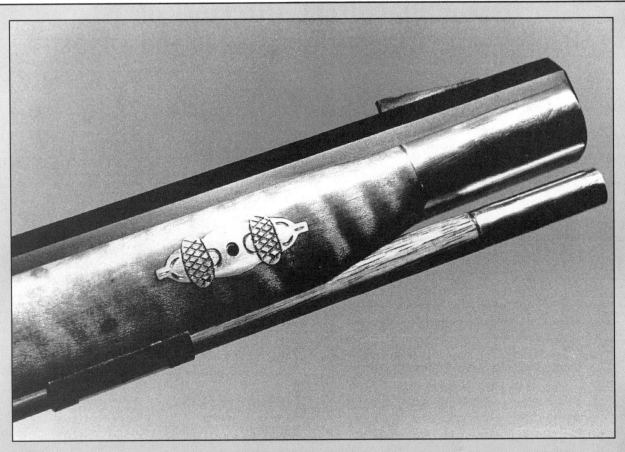

After engraving, the double-acorn inlay is quite attractive.

sliding it down on the surface of the stock, and gently tapping the inlay to transfer the pattern to the wood. The outline will not be completely black, as the surface of the inlay will not make full contact with the wood. However, a pattern will be established.

With an X-Acto knife (sharp, pointed blade), plus small chisels, remove wood to create a mortice for the inlay. Continue the process of removing a little wood at a time, blackening the inlay, pressing the inlay into place, then removing more wood until the inlay rests flush.

Installing Inlay Screws

The object of this step is to solder two tiny brass flathead wood screws to the inside surface of the inlay. Clean the back of the inlay with emery cloth, but do not destroy the identification marks made earlier. Once clean, place the inlay on a sheet of brass or copper, with the backside of the inlay facing up. Place a drop of solder flux on the inlay where each brass wood screw will be soldered in place. Then, tiny pieces of 44/40 solder are placed in the same spots. Remember to flux the head of each screw as well. Using a torch, heat the under-side of the copper or brass sheeting. When the drops of solder melt, place a wood screw, head down, on the melted solder using needle-nose pliers. The screws serve as pillars, so each inlay mortice must have holes inletted for these screws. The inlay is then epoxied into its mortice, with the screws permanently anchoring it in place.

Final Fitting of the Inlay

In this step, using a smooth mill file, the inlay is filed flush with the surface of the stock. Do not file the inlay below the surface of the wood. Maintain the contour of the stock.

Note: Any decorative inlay, such as a cheek-piece inlay, is handled in the same manner. A toe plate may also be used on the stock. It is inletted in the same way as an inlay. However, the toe plate is attached to the stock with wood screws.

Final Finishing of Metal and Wood

These procedures are amply covered in Chapters 14 and 9, respectively. Also, refer to Chapter 15 on metal embellishment for engraving of the inlay.

Manufacturers' Directory of Blackpowder Gunsmithing Tools and Supplies

Ackermann & Co.
16 Cortez St.
Westfield, MA 01085
Phone: 413-568-8008
Hickory dowels for ramrods.

Allen Manufacturing
6449 Hodgson Rd.
Circle Pines, MN 55014
Phone: 612/429-8231
Iron castings.

American Pioneer Video
P.O. Box 50049
Bowling Green, KY 42102-2649
Phone: 800-743-4675
Videos on building muzzleloaders.

Bauska Barrels
105 9th Avenue West
Kalispell, MT 59901
Phone: 406-752-7706
Muzzle-loading gun barrels.

Blue and Gray Products
34 W. Main St.
Milo, ME 04463
Phone: 800-231-8313
FAX: 207-943-2416
Replacement ramrods and supplies.

B-Square Co.
P.O. Box 11281, 2708 St. Louis Ave.
Ft. Worth, TX 76110
Phone: 817-923-0964
Phone: 800-433-2909
FAX: 817-926-7012
Various gunsmithing tools.

Birchwood Casey Laboratories, Inc.
7900 Fuller Rd.
Eden Prairie, MN 55344
Phone: 612-937-7933
FAX: 612-937-7979
Finishing and cleaning products

Birdsong & Associates, W.E.
4832 Windermere
Jackson, MS 39206
Phone: 601-366-8270
Black-T (Teflon) metal finish.

Brownells, Inc.
200 S. Front St.
Montezuma, IA 50171
Phone: 515-623-5401
FAX: 515-623-3896
Gunsmithing tools and supplies.

Cash Manufacturing Co., Inc.
P.O. Box 130, 201 South Klein Drive
Waunakee, WI 53597-0130
Phone: 608-849-5664
Brass and silver inlays.

CenterMark
P.O. Box 4066 Parnassus Station
New Kensington, PA 15068
Phone: 412-335-1319
Replica gun kits.

Chambers Flintlocks, Ltd., Jim
Route One Box 513-A
Candler, NC 28715
Phone: 704-667-8361
Siler lock kits.

Chopie Mfg., Inc.
700 Copeland Ave.
LaCrosse, WI 54603
Phone: 608-784-0926
Specialized wrenches.

CVA
5988 Peachtree Corners East
Norcross, GA 30071
Phone: 404-449-4687
FAX: 404-242-8546
Blackpowder firearms, kits and accessories.

DeHass Barrels
RR 3 Box 77
Ridgeway, MO 64481
Phone: 816-872-6308
Muzzleloader rifle barrels.

DGS, Inc.
1117 East 12th St.
Casper, WY 82601
Phone: 307-237-2414
Custom muzzleloader plans, peep sights and unfinished Storey Takedown Buggy Rifle

Dixie Gun Works
Hwy. 51 South
Union City, TN 38261
Phone: 901-885-0700
Order: 800-238-6785
FAX: 901-885-0440
Blackpowder gunmaking supplies and parts.

Eades' Muzzleloader Builders' Supply, Don
201-J Beasley Drive
Franklin, TN 37064
Phone: 615-791-1731
Muzzleloader supplies and parts.

Fort Hill Gunstocks
12807 Fort Hill Road
Hillsboro, OH 45133
Phone: 513-466-2763
Gunstocks.

Getz Barrel Co.
P.O. Box 88
Beavertown, PA 17813
Phone: 717-658-7263
Muzzleloader barrels.

Golden Age Arms Co.
115 E. High St.
Ashley, OH 43003
Phone: 614-747-2488
Gunmaking supplies, parts, kits and wood for stocks.

Grace Metal Products, Inc.
P.O. Box 67
Elk Rapids, MI 49629
Phone: 616-264-8133
Muzzleloader metal parts.

Green Mountain Rifle Barrel Co.
RFD #2, Box 8 Center
Conway, NH 03813
Phone: 603-356-2047
FAX: 603-356-2048
Muzzleloader barrels.

House of Muskets, Inc., The
P.O. Box 4640
Pagosa Springs, CO 81157
Phone: 303-731-2295
Gunmaking accessories and ramrod tips.

Jantz Supply
P.O. Box 584-BHG
Davis, OK 73030
Phone: 405-369-2316
FAX: 405-369-3082
Gunsmithing tools and supplies.

Jones Co., Dale
680 Hoffman Draw
Kila, MT 59920
Phone: 406-755-4684
Muzzleloader barrels.

Kennedy Firearms
10 North Market Street
Muncy, PA 17756
Phone: 717-546-6695
Pistol kits.

L&R Lock Co.
1137 Pocalla Road
Sumter, SC 29150
Phone: 803-775-6127
Locks and triggers.

Laurel Mountain Forge
P.O. Box 224
Romeo, MI 48065
Phone: 313-749-5742
Metal finishing products.

Log Cabin Sport Shop
8010 Lafayette Rd.
Lodi, OH 44254
Phone: 216-948-1082
Gunmaking parts and supplies.

Lyman Products Corp.
Rt. 147 West St.
Middlefield, CT 06455
Phone: 203-349-3421
FAX: 203-349-3586
Sights and muzzleloader kits

Michaels of Oregon (Uncle Mike's)
P.O. Box 13010
Portland, OR 97213
Phone: 503-255-6890
FAX: 503-255-0746
Sling swivels, ramrod guides and gun-making parts.

Mountain State Muzzleloading Supply
Box 154-1, Rt. 2
Williamstown, WV 26187
Phone: 304-375-7842
FAX: 304-375-3737
Muzzleloading parts, tools, supplies and kits.

MSC Industrial Supply Co.
151 Sunnyside Blvd.
Plainview, NY 11803-9915
Phone: 516-349-0330
Complete selection of shop tools.

Navy Arms Co.
689 Bergen Blvd.
Ridgefield, NJ 07657
Phone: 201-945-2500
FAX: 201-945-6859
Muzzleloader kits.

North Star West
P.O. Box 488
Glencoe, CA 95232
Phone: 209-293-7010
Phone: 510-432-1833
Muzzleloader kits and parts.

October Country
P.O. Box 969, Dept. BHG
Hayden Lake, ID 83835
Phone: 208-772-2068
Gunmaking information source.

Olde Pennsylvania
P.O. Box 912
New Kensington, PA 15068
Phone: 412-337-1552
Brass accessories.

Olson, Myron
989 West Kemp
Watertown, SD 57201
Phone: 605-886-9787
Jug choking shotguns.

Orion Rifle Barrel Co.
RR #2 137 Cobler Village
Kalispell, MT 59901
Phone: 406-257-5649
Muzzleloader barrels.

Pecatonica River Longrifle
Box 6285
Rockford, IL 61125
Phone: 815-968-1995
FAX: 815-968-1996
Muzzleloader stocks.

Pioneer Arms Co.
355 Lawrence Road
Broomall, PA 19008
Phone: 215-356-5203
Sidehammer locks.

R.E. Davis Co.
3450 Pleasantville NE
Pleasantville, OH 43148
Phone: 614-654-9990
Locks and gunmaking accessories.

Reinhart Fajen, Inc.
1000 Red Bud Drive, P.O. Box 338
Warsaw, MO 65355
Phone: 816-438-5111
FAX: 816-438-5175
Muzzleloader stocks.

Sharon Rifle Barrel Co.
14396-D Tuolumne Rd.
Sonora, CA 95370
Phone: 209-532-4139
Rifle barrels.

Starrett Co.
121 Crescent St.
Athol, MA 01331
Phone: 617-249-3551
Precision measuring instruments.

Talley, Dave
P.O. Box 821
Glenrock, WY 82637
Phone: 307-436-8724
Muzzleloader scope mounts.

Thompson/Center Arms
Farmington Rd., P.O. Box 5002
Rochester, NH 03867
Phone: 603-332-2394
Muzzleloader gun kits, flintlock and percussion.

Thunder Mountain Arms (TMA)
P.O. Box 593
Oak Harbor, WA 98277
Phone: 206-679-4657
FAX: 206-675-1114
Hawken locks.

Tiger-Hunt
RD #1 Box 464
Ebensburg, PA 15931
Phone: 814-472-5161
Gunstocks.

Tom's Gun Repair, Thomas G. Ivanoff
76-6 Route Southfork Rd.
Cody, WY 82414
Phone: 307-587-6949
Color case-hardening.

Track of the Wolf, Inc.
P.O. Box 6
Osseo, MN 55369-0006
Phone: 612-424-2500
FAX: 612-424-9860
Gunmaking supplies.

Traditions
P.O. Box 235
Deep River, CT 06417
Phone: 203-526-9555
FAX: 203-526-4564
Muzzleloader kits.

Warne Manufacturing Co.
9039 SE Jannsen Rd.
Clackamas, OR 97015
Phone: 503-657-5590
FAX: 503-657-5695
Muzzleloader scope mounts and peep sights.

Warren Muzzleloading Co., Inc.
Hwy. 21 North General Delivery
Ozone, AR 72854
Phone: 501-292-3268
Ramrod tips and brass accessories.

Williams Gun Sight Co.
7389 Lapeer Rd., Box 329
Davison, MI 48423
Phone: 313-653-2131; 800-530-9028
FAX: 313-658-2140
Muzzleloader sights.

Woodworker's Supply
1108 North Glenn Road
Casper, WY 82601
Phone: 307-237-5354
Woodworking supplies.